D1564951

Managing RISK with FINANCIAL FUTURES

Hedging, Pricing, and Arbitrage

Robert T. Daigler

PROBUS PUBLISHING COMPANY
Chicago, Illinois
Cambridge, England

Dedication

To my family and friends
Since it is the good times that make life worth living

In particular I dedicate this book to:

My wife Joyce,
a special person who also makes life's burdens less troublesome

My daughters Wendy and Shaina,
I could not ask for any better

My parents, Raymond and Josephine,
for without their encouragement and understanding
I would never have earned my Ph.D.

My loving and caring sister Carol

My special friends and family:
Amy, Bob, Cynthia, Don, Jerry, and Norma, among others

And to my colleague friends,
who make all those conventions more enjoyable

Table of Contents

Preface

Today's financial manager must be able to use all of the tools available to control a company's exposure to financial risk. Futures contracts are one type of risk management tool.

This book is written as a guide to the concepts and uses of financial futures markets. The organization of this book allows the chapters to be covered in a number of different sequences, or one may read selected chapters to fulfill a particular set of objectives. The goals of this book are:

- To provide a thorough, informative, and accurate guide to the concepts, empirical evidence and applications of financial futures markets.
- To show how futures markets are employed to adjust the risk and return characteristics of a portfolio.

This book is written for those who desire to understand the financial futures markets. But be warned, there is no "free lunch": this book does not promise to make you $1 million. The "Speculator's Guide to Riches" is found on the next shelf, next to the astrology books. Here we discuss the *techniques*, *strategies*, and *evidence* concerning futures markets, not the hopes and dreams of the gullible. The "no free lunch" motto also applies to the hedger: there are tradeoffs—to obtain the lower risk associated with hedging one must give up potential higher returns. Futures contracts are risk-management tools; they will not solve your profit and marketing problems.

The topics in this book examine the important aspects of the financial futures markets, especially hedging, pricing, and arbitrage. These topics comprise the important risk management concepts and evidence concerning the financial futures and debt markets. The orientation employed here is geared toward *understanding* how these markets work and how they can be used.

ORGANIZATION OF THE BOOK

To use the financial futures markets properly, one must comprehend many aspects of these markets, such as: their mechanics, the underlying cash markets, and the various relevant techniques and strategies. Consequently, the ability to use the markets requires mastering the topics and interrelationships presented in this book.

Part I provides an overview to the futures markets, shows the characteristics and quotation procedures for futures, and discusses the key concepts and terminology for these markets. Understanding these topics is essential for a participant in the futures markets.

Part II discusses the pricing of futures contracts, as well as arbitrage between futures and cash markets. After examining the basic issues relating to pricing and arbitrage in Chapter 4, specific determinants of the pricing of stock index and debt financial futures contracts are examined in individual chapters. Pricing issues are critical because the risk involved in various futures strategies is affected by the relationship between the futures contract characteristics and the cash instrument traded. Arbitrage exists when risk-free profits can be obtained. The concept of arbitrage, various arbitrage strategies, and the empirical evidence on the ability of traders to obtain risk-free profits on a consistent basis is examined for financial futures contracts.

Part III covers hedging concepts and techniques. Hedging techniques covered include naive procedures, the portfolio/regression method, and duration. These hedging techniques provide procedures to minimize risk with futures or by using "immunization" in the cash debt markets. Empirical evidence illustrates the ability of the various techniques to minimize risk. Hedging is the most widespread application of futures markets and provides a low-cost and effective means to reduce the risk of a position substantially.

Part IV illustrates applications of hedging to achieve risk management goals. Portfolio managers use various strategies involving futures markets, including duration and portfolio insurance, to reduce the risk of price declines. Financial institutions employ financial futures to manage the risk between assets and liabilities. Corporations and insurance companies use futures to manage various risk issues.

KEY FEATURES OF THIS BOOK

The important features of this book are:
- It provides an *up-to-date* and *thorough* coverage of the concepts, applications, and evidence concerning futures markets. The coverage includes both a breadth of topics and a depth of selected concepts typically not found in other books. In particular, this book emphasizes hedging techniques, hedging applications, and the pricing of futures contracts. Consequently, the reader will obtain sufficient knowledge concerning these markets in order to understand and implement risk management strategies.
- The organization of the material allows the reader to cover those topics and chapters which are relevant to his/her particular objectives, depending on the reader's goals.
- Examples help to illustrate the equations and concepts. These examples are easy to follow and help clarify important ideas.
- Focus sections and other illustrations highlight interesting and important aspects of how the markets work and the concepts associated with these markets.

Acknowledgements

M any individuals have helped improve the quality, readability, and completeness of this book. Reviewers of this book noted important areas for improvement and clarification. Officials at the Exchanges and financial institutions graciously provided information and ideas concerning the markets that helped to make this book more relevant to the users. Finally, my experiences at the Graduate School of Business at Stanford allowed me to clarify issues related to futures markets and how models are employed on Wall Street. The gracious hospitality provided by the faculty at Stanford is appreciated and will remain a fond memory. I thank all of the above individuals, but retain the responsibility for any mistakes that may be contained herein.

My contacts and the Exchanges and institutions who helped in many respects to find important information are Patrick Catania, Ted Doukas, Terry Pacelli, Juliet Reinert, and Joseph Sweeney, The Chicago Board of Trade; Ira Kawaller and Todd Petzel, The Chicago Mercantile Exchange; William Mullen, Loomis-Sayles, Inc.; and Mark Powers, Powers Research Inc. and *The Journal of Futures Markets.*

Much of my practical knowledge of how the markets work is due to the kind assistance of The Chicago Board of Trade, which over the years has provided many valuable sponsored research and educational programs. The Chicago Mercantile Exchange helps to sponsor the research program at The Center for the Study of Futures Markets, Columbia University. This Center has advanced the knowledge of futures research.

Those who read most or all of the manuscript and provided extremely helpful suggestions and ideas are: Robert E. Brooks, The University of Alabama; Andrew H. Chen, Southern Methodist University; Ted Doukas, The Chicago Board of Trade; David Emanuel, The University of Texas at Dallas; William Falloon, *Risk Magazine;* Timothy Gallagher, Colorado State University; Shantaram P. Hegde, The University of Connecticut; Avraham Kamara, The University of Washington; Daniel R. Pieptea, formerly of The University of Texas at Dallas and Illinois State University; and Thomas V. Schwarz, Southern Illinois University. Those who read individual and multiple chapters also helped me to clarify specific issues: Marcelle Arak, University of Colorado, Denver; Anthony F. Herbst, The University of Texas, El Paso; A.J. Senchack, The University of Texas, Austin; and Joseph Vu, Depaul University.

I owe a debt of gratitude and thanks to many individuals at Stanford and Berkeley. All of the faculty and staff were very kind to me during my stay at Stanford as a Visiting Scholar. In particular, I would like to thank Darrell Duffie, Allan Kleidon, Anne Peck, Paul Pfleiderer, and Kenneth Singleton at Stanford University; and Mark Rubinstein at The University of California, Berkeley.

My colleagues at Probus made sure the development of the book proceeded as planned, and produced it in record time. Last but certainly not least are those who helped me obtain information, prepare the manuscript, and make typing corrections. My colleague Simon Pak solved several perplexing problems for me. My very able student assistants were Jumiaty Nurawan and Luisa Chong, who worked long and hard for slave wages, while Carole Johnson helped with typing corrections with her usual smile. Finally, Edward Newman set up the quotations in Chapter 2.

Robert T. Daigler
Miami, Florida

Part I

Introduction and Concepts

Chapter 1

Financial Futures: Unique Markets

This chapter examines the concepts of forward and futures contracts. In particular, the ability of forwards and futures to adjust the risk and return of a portfolio provides benefits not obtained solely by dealing in the cash market. Here we discuss the differences between forward and futures transactions and examine the criteria used to determine the usefulness of a futures contract. The important criteria for futures are price discovery and **hedging** effectiveness. In addition, the discussion of the advantages and criticisms of futures markets serves as a preview to an examination of the uses of futures by traders and hedgers. Overall, this chapter provides a perspective on what futures are, and of ways they fit into the financial markets. This knowledge provides a foundation for the concepts examined in the remaining chapters of Part I and the rest of the book.

A VIEW OF FORWARD AND FUTURES MARKETS

Forward Contracts

A **forward** contract is a *private* transaction made now to purchase a specified amount of a cash asset at a specific price with the exchange of funds and asset taking place at an agreed-upon time in the future. Each forward contract typically has unique terms. Forward transactions are completed every day for agricultural commodities, Treasury securities, foreign currencies, and interest rate agreements made in London. For example, a farmer often makes a forward contract with an intermediary (called a "grain elevator") whereby the farmer agrees to sell grain to the elevator after harvesting. This contract specifies the number of bushels of grain, the price per bushel, and the delivery date of the grain. This forward contract allows the farmer to plan for the future with the certainty of a profit, at least if a natural weather disaster does not occur.

An example of a forward transaction for a Treasury bill is an agreement to purchase a cash T-bill in 90 days that will have a 60-day maturity at that time. Thus, the agreement sets the price *now*, with the T-bill and cash changing hands in 90 days and the buyer

1

receiving a T-bill maturing 60 days later. An example of a currency forward transaction is the agreement to receive 10 million yen in one month for a price of 140 yen per dollar ($.00714 per yen). In one month the buyer would receive 1 million yen by paying $71,420. The price of the transaction is set at the time of the original agreement, and is *not* affected by changes in the exchange rate over the subsequent month before the currencies are exchanged. It is interesting to realize that the institution that provides the forward contract often hedges its risk in the futures market.

Futures Contracts

Futures contracts standardize the agreement between a buyer and a seller, specifying a trade in an **underlying cash asset** for a given quantity at a specific time. The quality, size, pricing, and other terms of a futures contract are known as the **contract specifications or characteristics.** Two important advantages of a futures contract are its tradeability and its **liquidity** (i.e., one can trade large positions without affecting prices). In addition, one can profit with a futures contract without having to buy the cash asset. Futures exist because they provide risk and return characteristics that are not available solely by trading cash instruments such as stocks and bonds. Speculators can obtain very high rates of return with futures due to the **leverage** effect of magnifying gains (and losses) from a small cash down

---

FOCUS 1-1: What Is a Futures Contract?

An introduction to the meaning of a futures contract will help put the material in Part I into perspective. There is a distinct difference between owning a futures contract and owning the "underlying cash asset." Buying a futures contract obligates the purchaser to complete one of the following actions: (1) sell the futures before the futures stop trading, or (2) receive the underlying cash asset when the futures stop trading. Thus, buying a futures contract *only* creates an obligation to buy the cash asset described by the futures contract *if* the contract is held until the end of its trading life. (Some futures contracts transfer money rather than transfer the cash asset when the futures stop trading.) Before trading ceases, the buyer of the futures can sell the contract to avoid receiving the cash asset (the futures buyer pays or receives only the *change* in price in the futures for the time period the contract is held). In most circumstances the futures buyer does trade the futures contract rather than receive the cash asset.

The "underlying cash asset" simply refers to the asset that will be received by the futures buyer *if* the contract is delivered. The "underlying cash asset" is important because changes in the price of this asset *cause* changes in the price of the associated futures contract. Finally, since a futures contract does *not* require the *immediate* purchase or sale of the cash asset, the amount of down payment or "good faith deposit" required is only a fraction of the value of the underlying cash asset (typically 2 percent to 10 percent of the cash value).

payment; moreover, holders of cash securities can hedge with futures to eliminate most of the price change risk inherent in their portfolios.

Comparing Forwards and Futures

Examining the differences between forward and futures transactions is important so that one can determine which type of contract is superior for a particular situation. Forward contracts are useful for small transactions, wherein the forward contract is tailored to the individual transaction in terms of the size, expiration date, and type (quality) of the asset, since all terms of the forward contract are negotiable. A futures contract has standardized contract terms for size, date, and quality, which often do not meet the needs of the potential smaller user. Another advantage of forward contracts is the lack of cash deposit requirements; that is, cash does not change hands until the asset is delivered.

Futures contracts possess their own set of advantages in relation to forward commitments, and these advantages are often significant for larger market participants. Since each forward contract has its own unique terms, it is typically difficult to trade these instruments.[1] On the other hand, the standardized quantity and time to expiration characteristics of futures make futures contracts extremely liquid, a feature that promotes a very active trading environment. Since forward contracts cannot typically be traded, they *require* **delivery** of the cash asset, whereas a futures contract can either be delivered or traded.

Another important advantage of futures markets is their substantial safeguards against defaults, including the exchange clearinghouse guarantees, the default fund, and the daily cash adjustments to account balances as prices change. Forward transactions have the disadvantage that the intermediary who issues the contract might default. Although a default is infrequent for forwards, it is not uncommon. The typical result of such a default is bankruptcy for all concerned. In view of the possibility of default, the participants in forward transactions either must have a good credit standing or post a security deposit to cover the change in the price of the asset. Another important advantage of futures is their lower cost; such lower costs arise from lower commissions and the lack of the intermediary's profit and risk premiums. Moreover, forward contracts typically have unique terms that promote delivery, whereas futures contracts actively trade on any business day. Exhibit 1-1 summarizes the characteristics of futures and forward markets.

Overall, the use of a forward versus a futures contract depends on the availability of these instruments for a specific transaction *and* the relative importance of the factors discussed above for the market participant. The significant use of futures markets by a large number of participants shows that many people believe that the benefits of futures far outweigh the disadvantages. More specifically, large forward markets often exist if they were established before futures began to trade or if they provide advisory services not available with futures; in that case the participants are reluctant to deal with an unknown futures market. In general, traders prefer futures to forward contracts because of their tradeability and the virtual elimination of bankruptcy risk. However, the uses and concepts

---

1   Forward rate agreements on short-term interest rates made in London are an exception to this rule, because they have sufficient liquidity for trading.

EXHIBIT 1-1: Characteristics of Forward Versus Futures Contracts

Forward Contracts	*Futures Contracts*
• All terms negotiable; private transaction	• Standardized terms; traded on an exchange
• Default risk (thus participants must have good credit standing or post a deposit)	• No default risk
• No cash flow requirements	• Daily cash flows as prices change to guarantee performance of contract
• Creating contract often costly because of intermediary's profit	• Low cost
• Cannot trade before delivery	• Can trade contract on an exchange with liquidity
• No price variability or quality risk from negotiated contract	• Risk related to differences between standardized contract and security desired

---

of forward contracts are very similar to those of futures, and therefore some individuals treat the two instruments as indistinguishable.

Importance of Financial Futures Markets

There are several reasons why futures markets are important:
- The fluctuation in interest rates, currency values, and stock market prices causes severe problems for financial planning and forecasting; futures markets are a tool to help alleviate these problems.
- Financial executives and money managers employ financial futures as risk management tools to reduce significantly the potential losses of a cash position.
- Futures provide speculators a degree of leverage that typically is not available with other instruments and thus allow speculators to change their risk profiles.

During the late 1970s the financial community started to realize the potential of hedging with futures to control risk. Formal identification and evaluation of risk for securities transactions, capital budgeting projects, and other asset and liability decisions had been a major undertaking for the two decades preceding the introduction of financial futures. However, controlling risk for these situations was a difficult proposition. For example, using either betas or portfolio analysis only allows the investor limited flexibility in changing the amount of risk in the portfolio. Moreover, betas and portfolio risk measures change over time. Futures provide a more effective and flexible alternative to adjusting the return and risk characteristics of a cash position. The realization that hedging could revolutionize risk management caused an explosion of research efforts to measure hedging effectiveness, empirical studies on risk measurement, strategies to enhance risk control, and theoretical research on the relationship between hedging and the economy. The use of futures for hedging, financial planning, and speculation requires the acquisition of new knowledge concerning how these markets operate, the strategies one can employ, and techniques for using these markets optimally. Thus, knowledge of these markets aids the effective understanding and use of futures markets.

The Growth of Financial Markets

The explosive growth of the cash stock and debt markets illustrates the need for futures markets for hedging and other purposes. Figure 1-1 illustrates the size and growth of common stock activity by showing the total number of shares and the number of institutional shares traded on the NYSE over the past 20 years. The significant increase in trading by financial institutions shows the need for hedging instruments for these institutions to control the risk of stock ownership.

Figure 1-2 shows the growth in the issuance of *new* government debt, segregated by type of debt instrument. The size and growth of this new debt demonstrates the importance of the government sector of the market. In particular, the T-bill and T-note issuance is substantial, with more than $525 billion and $1,250 billion issued in 1990, respectively. The new dollar issuance of T-bonds is smaller than for T-bills or T-notes, but the cumulative

---

FIGURE 1-1: NYSE Common Stock Activity

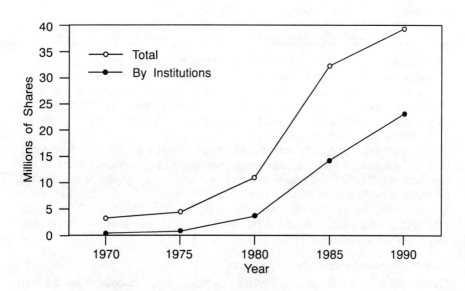

Source: Data from the *NYSE Fact Book,* New York: New York Stock Exchange, annual.

FIGURE 1-2: Newly Issued Government Debt

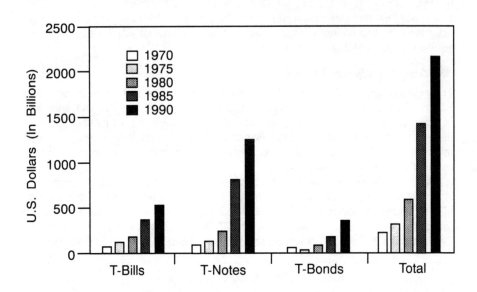

Source: Data from Treasury Bulletins, various years.

effect of the total value of the outstanding T-bonds is significant, given the typical 25- to 30-year maturity for T-bonds. Figure 1-3 shows the growth of total *outstanding* government debt; the significant growth of government debt since 1980 is obvious from this graph. Overall, the growth of these markets indicates the increasing importance of trading activity for government securities over the past decade. Unfortunately, no accurate data on the size of this trading activity are available.

The ability to adjust the risk and return characteristics of a position with futures contracts and the liquidity of futures have made these markets a tremendous success. In fact, the underlying dollar value of futures markets is as large as the corresponding cash markets for common stocks and debt instruments. Figure 1-4 illustrates the significant growth in futures volume that has occurred since 1980, especially for debt futures. The increasing debt structure of the U.S. government will likely create additional interest in futures markets for risk management purposes.

Risk Management with Futures Contracts

The discussion of the concepts of forward and futures contracts pointed out the most important reason why these instruments exist: to adjust risk. Pension funds, financial institutions, corporations, insurance companies, and any large organization with an invest-

FIGURE 1-3: Total Gross Public Debt Outstanding

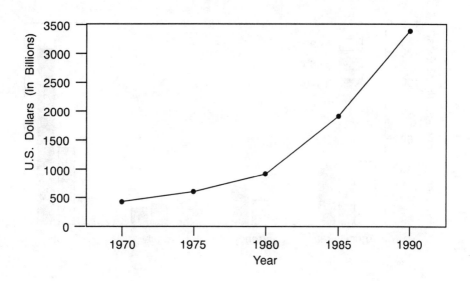

Source: Data from Treasury Bulletins, various years.

ment portfolio or exposure to interest rate fluctuations wants to avoid losses. Hedging with futures provides the tool to reduce the risk associated with potential losses, a method of eliminating most of the fluctuation in the value of the cash asset held by the hedger. For example, the owner of a portfolio of common stocks can *sell* stock index futures if he or she believes that the market is going to decline. If stock prices do decline, then the profits from **shorting** the futures contract offset most of the decline in the value of the common stock. Consequently, hedging with futures provides a means to *control* the risk of price changes.

Futures also provide the means for obtaining a temporary substitute for a cash position. Futures transactions are less costly and can be executed more quickly than dealing solely in the cash market. Numerous strategies involving common stocks use this substitutability characteristic of futures markets.

Speculators also use futures to adjust the risk characteristics of their position, as well as using them as a substitute for trading cash instruments. Speculation involves the purchase (**long**) or sale (**short**) of a futures contract to profit from a change in the price of the contract. Although some individuals consider trading in any asset (such as common stocks) as speculation, futures and similar types of contracts typically are called "speculative instru-

FIGURE 1-4: Total Futures Volume by Category

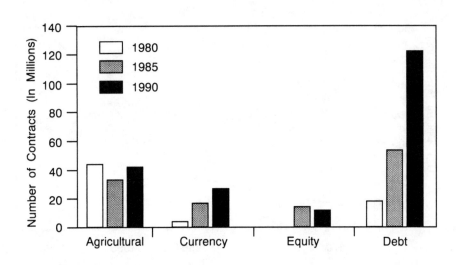

Source: Data from CBT and CMEX Annuals (various years).

ments" because of the significant degree of leverage inherent in them. Thus, changes in the price of the contract magnify the gains or losses to the speculator (and therefore the risk), since the speculator needs to deposit only a small percentage of the value of the underlying cash instrument.

This book examines the important aspects of the financial futures markets, especially hedging and speculation. Most of the topics discussed are relevant for both speculators and hedgers, since one must understand the motivations of each type of participant in the market to be a successful **trader**.

FUTURES MARKETS: CRITERIA, CRITICISMS, AND USES

CFTC Criteria

The two criteria employed by the Commodity Futures Trading Commission (CFTC), the regulatory agency for futures, to evaluate the potential usefulness of a new futures contract summarize the importance and usefulness of futures:

- Price discovery: the ability of futures to provide information on current and future cash prices based on known information.
- Hedging ability: the potential for the futures contracts to provide risk reduction capabilities for the cash position.

Some individuals include speculation as a necessary ingredient for futures markets. Although speculation provides liquidity to the markets, speculative interest is not needed for a futures contract to be approved for trading.

The price discovery criteria of a futures contract relates to both the current and future price of the cash asset. Whereas financial markets typically have active cash markets, agricultural and other commodity markets are often less active and/or are private markets where prices are not disseminated widely or constantly throughout the day. For these latter markets, futures provide a price discovery mechanism concerning the current value of the commodity. Even for financial markets, the futures markets provide a current price discovery role for **dealer** markets. For example, the Treasury bond, T-bill, and Eurodollar interest rate markets are dealer- and bank-dominated. Thus, computer screens provide up-to-the-minute quotes *only* for these dealers; in these markets futures show *nondealers* the status of the market.

Futures also provide information concerning the stock market; during volatile market periods, for example, the cash stock market index values lag the true value by 15 to 40 minutes because of the effect of the less frequent trading of smaller stocks and the greater liquidity of futures contracts.[2] Thus, stock index futures provide market participants with information on the true current level of the index. In addition, the Major Market Index (MMI) stock index futures opens 15 minutes before the New York Stock Exchange (NYSE), thereby providing important information concerning the behavior of stock prices *before* they start to trade.

The second part of the price discovery criteria relates to the ability of futures markets to provide a consensus estimate of the *future* value of the underlying cash asset. Such an estimate provides useful information for planning purposes. Whereas current and expected future interest rates play a key role in futures pricing, sufficient trading interest from the financial community generates a forecast of the future price based on both current information and the consensus *expectations* of the market participants. An interesting example of the ability of futures to reflect new information (and hence to provide price discovery) is the study by Richard Roll,[3] who has determined that orange juice futures are a *better* predictor of severe winter weather than forecasts from the National Weather Bureau.

Finally, financial economists agree that the most important criterion for a futures contract is its usefulness in reducing the risk of a position by employing hedging techniques. By hedging, the risk averter substantially reduces any adverse effect of price changes in the associated cash market position. Proper hedging can eliminate most of the potential loss in a cash position when interest rates increase or cash prices fall. Its use reduces the possibility of bankruptcy for a financial institution when short-term interest rates rise significantly, or eliminates much of the risk for a dealer who has cash assets to sell. Thus, hedgers shift risk to speculators, thereby "locking in" the price for the hedger. This practice permits better

2 Chapter 5 on pricing stock index futures examines the evidence on the lead of futures prices over stock indexes. Kawaller, Koch, and Koch conclude that futures lead stock indexes by up to 45 minutes. See Ira Kawaller, Paul Koch, and Timothy Koch, "The Temporal Relationship Between S&P Futures and the S&P 500 Index," *Journal of Finance*, Vol. 42, No. 5, December 1987, pp. 1309-1329.

3 Richard Roll, "Orange Juice and Weather," *American Economic Review*, Vol. 74, No. 5, December 1984, pp. 861-880.

planning and provides a more accurate estimate of costs for hedgers and, consequently, a more stable price for the product. For example, a construction company that hedges interest rate costs helps to guarantee a stable price for the finished house. Hedging also allows intermediaries to make a forward contract with a producer or user without an undue risk premium, since intermediaries can hedge the resultant risk with futures.

Criticisms of Futures Markets

The critics of futures markets claim that futures do not provide benefits to the economy and society. Moreover, politicians sometimes state that futures actually *cause* many of the economic evils of our society: higher interest rates, greater volatility of prices and rates, scarcity of resources, and a "legalized place to gamble." In the past, Congress has gone so far as to outlaw trading in onion futures because farmers claimed futures were the cause of the large volatility in cash onion prices. More recent examples of volatile markets where futures were blamed are the silver price roller coaster ride associated with the Hunt brothers, who attempted to corner the silver supply in order to create a monopoly, and the stock market crash of October 1987. These episodes brought new waves of criticism and a move to increase the regulation of the futures markets, including the major policy studies on the silver and stock market crashes authored by several federal agencies.

How valid are the criticisms of the futures markets? Undoubtedly, there exist unscrupulous brokers who take advantage of unsuspecting customers by churning accounts in the quest for large commissions. Moreover, powerful groups such as the Hunts attempt to manipulate markets. However, in general, futures markets only reflect the consensus opinions of the market: higher interest rates forecasted by a financial futures market only reflect economists' and business executives' expectations of the economy and government actions. Greater volatility for currencies, stock prices, and interest rates show the markets' concerns for international trade deficits, the economy, and the federal debt. Likewise, some of the other evils attributed to futures markets are unfounded in economic reasoning and evidence. Let us briefly look at the specific criticisms and the benefits of futures.

Rebuttals: Futures and the Economy

Francis[4] provides a response to the criticisms listed above. The most frequent criticism of futures is that these markets are simply a sophisticated form of gambling. However, gambling is the *artificial creation* of risk, in which something of value is gained or lost on a game of chance or uncertain event. Unlike gambling, the risks from futures markets are not artificially created; rather, they arise naturally from the price fluctuations of the underlying cash market. Hence, futures markets do not create new risk; they simply allow the hedger to shift the risk of price fluctuations to a speculator who is willing to assume the risk and who provides trading volume and liquidity. Other differences from gambling are that futures trading consists of a legal contract with specific conditions, and that government regulatory agencies constantly monitor the markets to prevent manipulation or unfair practices. Finally, speculation is by no means limited to the futures markets (or its cousins, the

---

4 Jack Clark Francis, "Speculative Markets: Valuable Institutions or Dens of Inequity?" *Federal Reserve Bank of Philadelphia Business Review*, July-August 1972.

stock and **option** markets) but is prevalent in many other areas, such as real estate. In fact, the purchasers of homes in California in the late 1970s were surprised to find out later that they owned one of the most speculative investments of the early 1980s.[5]

The second criticism of futures markets is that they do not provide a useful function to society. In addition to the important aspects of hedging and price discovery discussed above, the rebuttal to this criticism involves a number of factors that show the benefits of futures:

- Speculators' profit motives tend to reduce extreme price fluctuations, providing more stable prices for both the futures *and* cash markets. This result occurs because speculators enter the market when prices become undervalued or overvalued because of an imbalance in either supply or demand. The stability of prices in the futures market is then transmitted to the cash market via the association between the futures and cash markets.
- Futures markets allow a more efficient economy by providing a better flow of funds and goods between different segments of the economy. For example, futures help allocate agricultural supplies for the season of the year and for geographic usage, inasmuch as commodities are stored to receive a higher price, which is locked in via the futures market, rather than forcing producers to receive a low current cash price.[6]
- Users of commodities are able to guarantee the purchase of the commodities they need at a specific price without paying for the product now; this reduction in potential inventory reduces the cost of business and improves the firm's liquidity, benefits that can be passed on to the consumer.
- Futures markets equalize the bargaining power among the participants by putting the buyer and seller on equal terms; the result is a transaction at the market price rather than at a price dictated by the most powerful participant. Thus, differences in size, amount of cash, and aggressiveness have less effect in the futures market than in cash and forward market transactions.
- Futures allow the creation of new products, such as "**synthetic** fixed-rate loans" and guaranteed value insurance contracts. Futures provide this opportunity because they allow the institution offering the product to reduce its risk of losing money, and thus the product becomes more feasible to sell to its customers.

The most often challenged and criticized benefit listed above is the claim that futures markets actually help stabilize markets. Many critics believe these markets actually destabilize cash prices. Although the onion futures case mentioned previously is often stated by the uninitiated as an example of how futures increase the volatility of cash prices, the cessation of onion futures trading is a political rather than an economic statement. The evidence by

---

5 Adam Smith in *Paper Money* advances an interesting hypothesis that homeowners obtaining low fixed-rate mortgages during the 1960s and 1970s were speculating on higher interest rates. Consequently, the eventual reality of higher rates was the main motivating force in the large increases in the value of homes. See Adam Smith, *Paper Money*, New York: Summit Books, 1981.

6 The classic example of this benefit was the wheat harvests of the late 1800s. All of the farmers would bring their wheat into Chicago at the same time, and thus cash prices were forced down to 10 cents per bushel, thereby causing farmers to dump the grain in the street. Later in the year when wheat was not available, wheat prices rose to very high levels.

economists concerning the relationship between futures and cash prices is that futures help to *reduce* longer-term cash price fluctuations rather than increase them. Thus, although politicians often wish to blame futures markets for greater volatility in interest rates and cash market prices, the simple truth is that the changing status of the national and international economy is the cause for the variability; futures markets simply mirror the effects. In fact, the success of financial futures is a direct *result* of the greater volatility in cash interest rates, not the cause of the volatility.[7]

Advantages and Disadvantages of a Futures Market

Potential users of futures need to understand the advantages and disadvantages of these markets in comparison with the cash, forward, and options markets. Exhibit 1-2 summarizes and extends the previous discussions on the advantages and disadvantages of futures markets in relation to cash and forward markets. These advantages and disadvantages include macro- and microfactors. The macrofactors affect all participants in the market as well as the economy, whereas the microfactors primarily affect specific users of the futures markets.

Options provide an alternative type of hedging and speculative contract for a trader. More important, options have different characteristics from futures contracts. Call options provide the right, but not the obligation, to purchase a given quantity of the cash security at a specific "strike" price for a specific period of time. Put options give the buyer the right to *sell* these same securities. The security is traded at the strike price if the option is exercised. Options include a premium in their price that does not exist for a futures contract; however, options have a limited loss equal to the initial price of the option. Thus market participants must choose the specific market consistent with their goals and purposes.

A number of factors determine whether one should use a futures or an options market. The importance of specific factors for a particular futures strategy will become more apparent as we discuss various strategies throughout this book. Meanwhile, the following general uses and benefits of futures and options given by Jaffee[8] and Stoll and Whaley[9] in their review articles on stock index futures and options provide a perspective for our introductory overview. Futures are employed:

• To hedge the price risk of a cash asset at a minimum cost.

---

7   For example, Edwards shows that the introduction of futures contracts did not affect daily stock market and short-term interest rate volatility. However, the evidence for shorter-term volatility, such as within the day, is not conclusive. For example, futures-related program trades for stocks could actually increase volatility. The difficulty in examining intraday behavior is to determine whether an increase in volatility is due to fundamental factors, price pressure caused by large trade sizes, or the effect of futures markets. See Franklin Edwards, "Futures Trading and Cash Market Volatility: Stock Index and Interest Rate Futures," *The Journal of Futures Markets*, Vol. 8, No. 4, August 1988, pp. 421-439.

8   D. M. Jaffee, "The Impact of Financial Futures and Options on Capital Formation," *The Journal of Futures Markets*, Vol. 4, No. 3, Fall 1984, pp. 417-447.

9   Hans R. Stoll and Robert E. Whaley, "Futures and Options on Stock Indexes: Economic Purpose, Arbitrage, and Market Structure," *The Review of Futures Markets*, Vol. 7, No. 2, 1988, pp. 224-249.

EXHIBIT 1-2: Advantages and Disadvantages of Futures Markets

	Advantages	Reason
Macro Advantages	• Increased efficiency	• Centralized market brings together all segments of the market plus standardized contracts provide liquidity
	• Increased flow of information for planning	• Price, volume, expectations (cash market is too thin or information is not available)
Micro Advantages	• Less expensive hedging vehicle	• Commissions, bid-ask spreads, and short sale costs smaller than for cash transactions
	• More convenient forward price	• No calculations needed and intraday data available
	• Built in safeguards against credit risks	• Clearinghouse fund and daily cash settlement
	• Can create "synthetic securities"	• Cash and futures combinations that would be too expensive in cash market
	• Speculators can enter market	• Significant leverage exists; minimal capital needed

	Disadvantages	Effects
Macro Disadvantages	• Control of the market by a few individuals is possible (called a "squeeze")	• Prices rise above economic value, creating allocation problems in the economy
	• Futures accused of causing cash prices to be more volatile	• Would affect allocation process, but little evidence exists to support greater volatility claim
Macro Disadvantages	• Futures require cash deposit called "margin"	• Affects cash flow
	• Futures require payment of losses on a daily basis (called "marking-to-market")	• Affects cash flow and earnings on invested funds
	• Hedges are imperfect	• Complete loss might not be covered

- To "invest" new cash inflows temporarily until these funds are used to purchase the desired cash assets; that is, futures provide a temporary substitute to invest funds quickly and inexpensively.[10]
- To provide a method for specializing in stock selection by removing the risk of general market movements.
- To provide a means for changing allocations in stocks versus bonds quickly and inexpensively, without affecting the market in the individual assets.

Options markets are employed:
- To adjust the risk and return of a position at a minimum cost.
- To hedge both price and quantity risk; that is, options are preferable to futures when the quantity one wishes to hedge is uncertain.

Finally, as a summary of how futures are important, Stoll and Whaley[11] note the three most important benefits of futures to society:
- Futures provide a means of allocating risk.
- Futures summarize price information that is useful in allocating resources.
- Futures allow a more flexible risk-return structuring of the position at a *lower cost* than that available in the cash markets.

Education and Publications

Education is a significant factor that explains the eventual use and trading volume of futures markets, since potential hedgers must be comfortable with their applications of futures. Otherwise, potential hedgers might avoid these markets because the perceived risk of using a poorly understood tool often is larger than the perceived risk of not using the tool at all. For example, a few banks actually have used futures mistakenly to "unhedge" a well-structured balance sheet, creating more risk than originally existed.

The exchanges and various institutions have taken a significant role in educating users of futures by conducting seminars in major cities on how to use these markets. Explanatory and research articles increase our knowledge about futures markets by providing new ideas and applications, empirical evidence, and theoretical advances. They also suggest alternative strategies for a changing environment. Focus 1-2 provides information on sources involving futures markets.

SUMMARY AND LOOKING AHEAD

This chapter provided an overview to the financial futures markets. In particular, it examined the benefits, importance, and risk management aspects of futures markets. This information provides a general perspective for the rest of Part I and the remainder of the book.

---

10 Two examples of when futures would provide a benefit as a cash substitute are: When dealing with the asset itself would have high trading costs; or when it would be cumbersome to trade the cash asset. A "cumbersome cash asset" with high trading costs is a portfolio of all the stocks in the Standard & Poor's 500 Index (S&P 500). A futures trade in this portfolio is easy to make, whereas a trade in all 500 stocks is more costly and can be difficult to execute.

11 Hans R. Stoll and Robert E. Whaley, "Futures and Options on Stock Indexes: Economic Purpose, Arbitrage, and Market Structure," *The Review of Futures Markets*, Vol. 7, No. 2, 1988, pp. 224-249.

Chapter 2 shows how to interpret financial futures quotes for stock indexes, debt instruments, foreign exchange, and other futures markets. Chapter 3 provides a basic understanding of how these markets work by discussing terminology and concepts.

FOCUS 1-2: Publications on Futures

Futures Magazine publishes short concise reports on various aspects of futures and options markets of interest to speculators and certain professionals. The articles in *Futures* are nontechnical features on the market and specific products, with reports on hedging strategies and basic analytical tools. *Futures* has a significant amount of advertising from various aspects of the industry, especially ads catering to the speculator. Newsletters published by various brokerage houses, financial institutions, and the exchanges provide an important source for ideas and strategies on futures, plus information on new products and seminars.

The Journal of Futures Markets (JFM) is a premier professional publication involving futures markets and their applications; it began publication in 1981 and has quickly become a respected journal. *JFM* examines hedging applications to industry, empirical evidence involving futures markets, and important issues of interest to the industry. Professionals use *JFM* to keep up-to-date on the issues relating to futures markets. "Futures Bibliography" is a regular feature in *The Journal of Futures Markets* that lists the research and application articles from all publications by subtopic area.

The Review of Futures Markets publishes proceedings of The Chicago Board of Trade's research and industry conferences. Its research articles are similar to other academic journals in their rigor and use of statistical and quantitative tools. The industry proceedings and published commentaries on the research articles in the *Review* provide a rare look into the viewpoints of a cross section of floor traders, exchange staff, regulators, and academicians on a number of interesting questions related to the markets.

Advances in Futures and Options Research is an annual research journal published by Jai Press. It includes academic papers on both futures markets and options. Other academic journals in finance and economics also publish research articles relating to futures. The Center for the Study of Futures Markets at Columbia University sponsors research grants and conferences that examine specific problems in futures markets. These research efforts appear in a working paper series sponsored by the Center.

The following outline provides additional information.

Publication	Publisher	Audience
Futures Magazine	Oster Communications 219 Parkade Cedar Falls, IA 50613	Speculators and traders

Focus continues

FOCUS 1-2: Continued		
Publication	*Publisher*	*Audience*
Risk Magazine	53 West Jackson Suite 225 Chicago, IL 60604	Professionals and executives
Futures and Options World	Park House, Park Terrace Worcester Park Surrey KT47HY England	Speculators and traders
Newsletters	Exchanges and brokerage houses	Professionals and executives
The Journal of Futures Markets	John Wiley & Sons 605 Third Avenue New York, NY 10158	Professionals, executives, academicians
The Review of Futures Markets	Chicago Board of Trade LaSalle at Jackson Chicago, IL 60604	Financial economists, academicians
Advances in Futures and Options Research	Jai Press 55 Old Post Road #2 P.O. Box 1678 Greenwich, CT 06836	Academicians

Chapter 2

Quotations, Characteristics, and Concepts of Futures Markets

This chapter discusses the trading and quotation procedures for futures contracts. The quotations for each important U.S. stock index, interest rate, and currency futures contracts are discussed. Graphs of historical price behavior over time show both the need for hedging to reduce risk and the opportunities for speculators to profit by using futures contracts. This material provides the foundation needed to employ futures contracts for various strategies such as speculation, hedging, and **arbitrage**. Those who want to cover only one type of futures contract at a time can combine the relevant contract information in this chapter with the terminology and concepts found in Chapter 3.

BASIC INFORMATION FOR ALL TYPES OF FUTURES CONTRACTS

The newspaper quotations for all financial futures contracts follow the same general format. Stock index futures quotes are shown in Exhibit 2-1, and debt futures quotations are given

---

EXHIBIT 2-1: Stock Index Futures Quotations

S&P 500 INDEX (CME) 500 times index

	Open	High	Low	Settle	Chg	Lifetime High	Lifetime Low	Open Interest
Mar	416.40	422.50	415.65	421.65	+ 5.85	422.60	372.90	145,697
June	417.70	423.90	417.10	423.10	+ 5.95	423.90	374.50	4,010
Sept	419.40	425.40	418.45	424.50	+ 5.85	425.40	376.25	415

Est vol 55,272; vol Mon 45,848; open int 150,155, −235.
Index High 420.44; Low 414.32; Close 420.44 +6.10

NYSE COMPOSITE INDEX (NYFE) 500 times index

	Open	High	Low	Settle	Chg	Lifetime High	Lifetime Low	Open Interest
Mar	229.45	232.95	229.05	232.35	+ 3.20	232.95	205.70	4,766
June	230.00	233.50	229.70	232.85	+ 3.20	233.50	206.50	365
Sept	231.75	231.75	231.00	233.35	+ 3.20	232.35	212.55	133

Est vol 7,463; vol Mon 5,738; open int 5,264, −136.
Index High 231.60; Low 228.45; Close 231.57 +3.10

MAJOR MKT INDEX (CBT) 500 times index

	Open	High	Low	Settle	Chg	Lifetime High	Lifetime Low	Open Interest
Jan	347.50	351.70	345.70	351.00	+ 4.15	352.00	309.90	4,664
Feb	347.50	351.80	346.00	351.10	+ 4.20	351.90	311.50	854
Mar	347.00	352.00	346.50	351.30	+ 4.10	352.00	311.60	109

Est vol 2,500; vol Mon 1,177; open int 5,654, +45.
Index High 351.54; Low 345.23; Close 350.82 +4.38

Source: Data from Futures Exchanges, January 14, 1992.

later in this chapter. Here we discuss only the general format of the quotation process. The specifics of each futures contract will be covered later.

The months identified at the left of each futures contract represent the expiration months of the futures. The futures contract ceases to trade at some point during this month. During the expiration period the buyer of a deliverable futures contract receives the underlying **cash** security from the seller and the buyer pays the futures price. However, some futures, such as stock index futures contracts, are settled only with a net cash payment. This "cash settlement" is used for contracts for which delivery of the cash asset would be difficult or cumbersome. Cash settlement also minimizes the cost of settling the futures contract. The expiration months for all of the financial futures contracts except the Major Market stock index futures are March, June, September, and December; these expiration months are the financial cycle. The Major Market stock index futures also have expirations in the current and following two months as well as the financial cycle. The **nearby** expiration is the next futures to expire. The deferred contracts expire later.

The second through fifth columns of the futures quotations show the opening, high, low, and closing (settle) prices for the day, with the price change in the sixth column being the difference in price from the previous day's close.[1] The "lifetime high and low" columns reflect the highest and lowest price for that particular contract expiration since it started to trade.

The volume of trading per expiration month is not given in most publications, but the total volume for all expirations for any given day is given at the bottom of the quotations for each futures contract. The final column of the quotations shows the level of **open interest** in the futures contract. For each open interest contract there must be a buyer and a seller, since their combined transactions "create" a contract. Later, the buyer can reverse the position by selling, and vice versa with a seller, thereby eliminating one open interest position. For example, the following illustrates that in Period 1 an open interest contract is created when a buyer and seller trade. A contract in Period 2 still exists even though a trade occurs. In Period 3 the open interest contract disappears.

Period	Trader 1	Trader 2	Trader 3	Open Interest
0				0
1	Buys	Sells		1
2	Sells		Buys	1
3		Buys	Sells	0

For financial futures contracts the nearby expiration typically has the largest open interest, with the deferred expirations having smaller open interest positions. However, near the termination of trading the open interest for the nearby contract becomes a small number.

---

1 The official opening and closing prices are actually ranges of price transactions, with the midpoint of the range of the first and last minute of trading used for the printed opening and closing values. A committee officially determines the settle, but it is usually the midpoint of the closing range; however, for low-volume expiration months the committee can adjust the settle price to conform to the price structure of the other expiration months so as to obtain the appropriate differences in prices (spreads). When adjustments are necessary, they are typically required because different expiration months have their last trades at different times of the day.

Agricultural futures have large open interest values for the harvest month expirations. Figure 2-1 shows how the level of open interest changes over the life of the contract, with the September 1991 T-bond futures used as an example. Notice that the open interest builds slowly over time until June 1991 (the expiration month of the nearby futures contract), when the open interest for the September contract increases dramatically. The open interest remains high until the expiration month of September, when it falls dramatically as positions are covered and delivered.

STOCK INDEX FUTURES QUOTATIONS AND CHARACTERISTICS

The following sections present information on futures contracts, including the meaning of the quotes for each stock index futures contract and the relevant **contract characteristics** or **specifications** for each contract. Exhibit 2-1 illustrates stock index futures quotations.

These stock index futures contracts allow speculators and hedgers to trade in futures that mirror the movements of the associated cash market indexes. Thus, pension funds and other large investment portfolios of stocks can avoid large losses by selling stock index futures. These funds also employ stock index futures as a temporary substitute for eventual purchases or sales of stocks, since traders can execute futures transactions quickly and inexpensively. Finally, funds use futures for arbitrage, and therefore the institutions are able

FIGURE 2-1: Open Interest: Sept 91 T-bond Futures

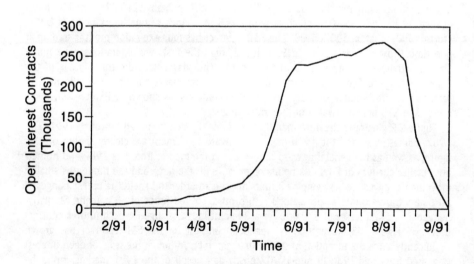

Source: Data from Tick Data, Inc.

to earn risk-free profits from mispriced combinations of stock and futures transactions. Speculators like stock index futures because they provide a means to buy or sell the entire market with a relatively small cash deposit, a feature that provides a significant degree of leverage. Focus 2-1 tells how trades of large baskets of stocks, called **program trades**, are executed and how they relate to futures trades by financial institutions. Exhibit 2-2 lists the characteristics of each of the stock index futures contracts in a convenient format. The following sections discuss the essential information from this exhibit.

Stock Index Futures

The S&P 500 and NYSE Index contracts began trading in 1982. The Major Market Index began in 1984. The open interest and volume values in Exhibit 2-2 show that the S&P contract is the most active of the stock index futures.

Cash settlement at expiration of the stock index futures works as follows: On the specified day of contract expiration the buyer and seller of the stock index futures settle any *differences* in value in their accounts in cash rather than by delivering or receiving actual stock. The reason for a cash settlement is obvious; for most stock index futures contracts it is impossible to deliver the number of stocks that make up the index or deliver the stocks in the proportions required by the index construction. Thus, since the contract is settled in cash, the important aspect of the future quotation is the *change* in the futures price from the time the futures contract was purchased or sold.

S&P 500 Index. The S&P 500 Index contract trades on the Chicago Mercantile Exchange (CMEX). The underlying cash "value" of the contract is determined by multiplying the Index by 500. For example, the value of the March expiration month in Exhibit 2-2 is found by multiplying the close (settle) of 421.65 by 500 to obtain $210,825. The minimum change in the Index is .05, which is worth $25. A change of one index point (1.00) is worth $500—that is, 500 X 1.00. The S&P contract has four expiration months trading at one time. However, as shown in Exhibit 2-2, only the first two expirations have much trading activity. The futures stop trading on the Thursday before the third Friday of the expiration month. The growth of the stock index futures markets has been significant. The total S&P futures volume of more than 50,000 contracts, as shown in Exhibit 2-2, totals more than $10 billion in value of the underlying stock.

Figure 2-2 illustrates the movement in the S&P 500 index from 1987 through 1991. The 1987 market crash and the 1990 major downward movement are clearly shown on this figure, as well as the general upward movement in the market from late 1987 and numerous smaller changes of 20 index points or more. Both the large and the numerous smaller movements suggest how to employ futures markets in order to benefit the user. Changes of 20 points translate into a speculator's return on deposited funds of 50 percent. Similarly, hedgers can avoid losses of $10,000 for a 20-point index change for each futures contract they use. Figure 2-3 illustrates how the open interest for the S&P contract has grown significantly since the inception of this futures contract. Although the level of open interest stagnated from mid-1986 to mid-1990, mostly as a result of the 1987 market crash, the growth in the S&P contract has recently resumed.

Major Market Index. The MMI trades on the Chicago Board of Trade (CBT). The Index includes 20 major companies, with 17 of these firms being part of the Dow Jones

FOCUS 2-1: Program Trading: Untouched by Human Hands?

The general perception of program trading is that computers control the entire transaction, from the identification of the arbitrage opportunity between stocks and futures to the execution of the trades. In fact, the *arbitrageur* makes the decision whether to execute the trades. Typically, the computer is programmed to identify when the futures price differs sufficiently from the fair price to prompt an examination of the situation. The computer also is programmed to *execute* the cash stock trades once the trader decides to enter the arbitrage. In other words, the computerized system at the NYSE allows the trader to program the computer to execute buy or sell orders on a given basket of stocks for a given predetermined number of shares for each stock by simply pressing a designated key on the computer keyboard. These orders are then electronically sent to each specialist's desk on the floor of the exchange and are executed immediately. However, the decision to execute the arbitrage transaction in the first place, and the appropriate size of the trade, are made by the arbitrageur.

Scott Hamilton* presents a history and discussion of program trading. His examination of this maligned technique shows its uses and advantages, both for futures-related trades and general portfolio management. In its original form, program trading was simply the orderly purchase or sale of an entire portfolio of securities. Specifically, in the mid-1970s, **stock index fund** managers needed a method to buy or sell a basket of securities at the closing price of the market, since their funds are priced to the public at the close. Since the purpose of an index fund is to track the cash index exactly, and since no security analysis or speculative trading is employed, trading at other times could create prices that would underperform the cash index closing value. Therefore, program trading was devised as a method to trade a basket of stocks at a guaranteed (closing) price. Overall, nonfutures-related program trades constitute more than half of all the program trades.

Program trading developed into a futures arbitrage strategy when liquidity developed in the futures market. Pension funds, corporations, and brokerage houses started to use arbitrage as a means of obtaining a risk-free return above the T-bill rate using short futures arbitrage, or to outperform the cash index for long futures arbitrage (by selling stocks currently owned and buying futures). Other uses for futures program trading are to move funds from one market to another (say, from stocks to bonds), or from one money manager to another, and to handle large cash inflows or outflows. Some claim these futures-related activities increase the volatility in the market because of the large volume generated by these trades. The issues of volatility and the relationship of program trades to the 1987 market crash are discussed in Chapter 5.

---

* Scott W. Hamilton, "Stock Portfolio Management with Program Trading and Futures," The First Boston Corporation, 1987, pamphlet.

EXHIBIT 2-2: Characteristics of Stock Index Futures Contracts

Futures Contract	Trading Unit	Deliverable Instrument	Price Quotation	Minimum Price Change		Last Trading Day	Last Delivery Day
				Units	Dollars		
S&P 500	500 X index	Cash	Index	.05	$25	(2)	(1)
MMI	500 X index	Cash	Index	.05	$25	3rd Fri. of month	(1)
NYSE	500 X index	Cash	Index	.05	$25	3rd Fri. of month	(1)

(1) No delivery is made since the contract is settled in cash. The cash settlement is made the day following the last trading day.

(2) Thursday before the third Friday of the expiration month.

Note: All stock index futures contracts trade on a March, June, September, and December expiration cycle, except for the Major Market Index. The MMI has expirations in the current month, the next two months, and the March, June, September, and December cycle.

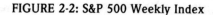

FIGURE 2-2: S&P 500 Weekly Index

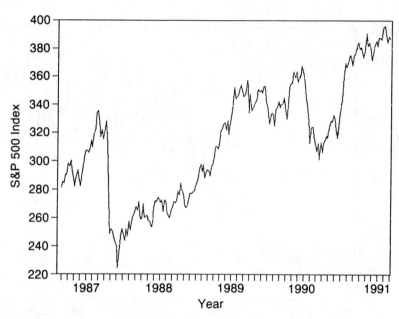

Year

Source: Data from Tick Data, Inc.

Industrial Index; hence, the MMI is comparable to the Dow Jones Industrial Index in terms of volatility. The cash MMI is determined by adding the prices of the 20 stocks and dividing by the appropriate divisor. The divisor as of late 1991 was 2.00822; the divisor changes with stock dividends and substitutions of stock in the index. The total underlying cash value of the MMI futures is then determined by multiplying the cash index by 500. The minimum change in the Index is .05, which is worth $25. One index point is worth $500. Expirations exist for the current and the next two calendar months, as well as for the financial cycle; however, typically only the first two contract expiration months are actively traded. The futures stop trading on the third Friday of the expiration month. Settlement is in cash.

NYSE Index. The NYSE Composite Futures Index trades on the New York Futures Exchange (NYFE). The Index is equivalent to the cash NYSE Index of all stocks traded on that exchange. The underlying cash value of the contract is 500 times the Index, the minimum change is .05, and the value of this change is $25. One index point is worth $500. Maturities follow on the financial cycle, with the first two expirations being most active. Settlement is in cash. The futures stop trading on the third Friday of the expiration month.

FIGURE 2-3: S&P 500 Futures Open Interest

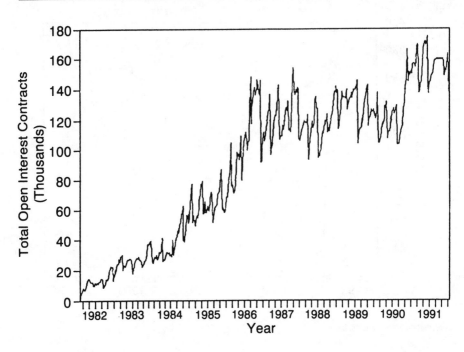

Source: Data from Tick Data, Inc.

Other Stock Index Futures Contracts. The Value Line contract is a low-volume futures, while over-the-counter futures are dormant. No industry or individual stock futures exist, since an agreement between the Commodity Futures Trading Commission (CFTC) and the Securities and Exchange Commission (SEC) allocates authority of all industry and stock products to the SEC. The SEC does not believe that industry futures are appropriate for trading at this time.

SHORT-TERM INTEREST RATE INSTRUMENTS

T-Bill Futures

Treasury Bill futures contracts started to trade in January 1976 on the International Monetary Market (IMM) of the Chicago Mercantile Exchange. They were the first short-term interest rate futures contracts to trade. Thus, T-bill futures are useful in protecting against changes in short-term interest rate changes, such as for loans where the interest rate is based on a short-term rate. Since the mid-1970s to 1982 proved to be a very volatile period for short-term rates, the T-bill futures contract became very popular during this time.

T-bill futures are based on a 90-day cash T-bill instrument with a face value of $1 million. If the futures contract is kept until expiration, then the owner (long position) of the futures receives cash T-bills with a 90-day maturity and a face value of $1 million.[2] The 360-day year conversion used for cash T-bills is also used for the futures. Each one **basis point** change (1/100 of 1 percent or .01 percent) in the T-bill futures price index causes a $25 change in the value of the contract. Hence, a 1 percent change in interest rates (a 100 basis point change) creates a $2,500 change in value.[3] Exhibit 2-3 illustrates the interest rate futures quotations. The examples used in this chapter are taken from these quotes.

The interest rates associated with T-bill futures are quoted in terms of the **bank discount interest rate**, or annualized rate of return on the *face value*, in order to be consistent with cash T-bill quotations. The T-bill futures "price" is actually an index value, with the index value equal to 100.00 minus the discount interest rate; that is, $I = 100 - D$. This index value system for T-bill futures reduces confusion. The logic of the T-bill futures quotation procedure is for long positions in the futures market to make money when the index increases and to lose money when the index declines. The reason is that interest *rates* change in the *opposite* direction to the price of fixed-rate instruments. Thus, as interest rates go *down* one basis point, the index value goes *up* one basis point, with long positions making money as the index value increases. The discount change in the next to last column of the table shows the difference in basis points from the previous day's close. Since each contract has a face value of $1 million, the total face value for all T-bill futures contracts traded on this day was in excess of $8.7 billion for this day, with the total open interest (the last column) being in excess of $55 billion. Example 2-1 describes the quotation procedure for the T-bill futures quotes shown in Exhibit 2-3.

T-bill futures expire according to the financial cycle of March, June, September, and December. Eight expirations (two years of contracts) trade at any one time; however, there is limited activity after the first three expiration months. Trading during the month of expiration ceases on the first day during the month when a 13-week T-bill is issued *and* an originally issued one-year T-bill has 13 weeks *remaining* until maturity. Although this procedure does cause the specific delivery day to change significantly from one expiration month to another since the delivery day must correspond to two separate cash T-bill maturities, it does increase the amount of cash T-bills available for delivery into the futures contract. Exhibit 2-4 summarizes the characteristics of T-bill futures and the other interest rate futures contracts examined below.

Figure 2-4 shows the extent of the fluctuation in T-bill interest rates since the inception of the T-bill futures contract in 1976. The figure shows the significant increase and volatility of short-term interest rates in the late 1970s and early 1980s, with each 1 percent change in interest rates creating a $2,500 gain or loss for each futures contract. In particular, the decline in rates from 15 percent to almost 6 percent in late 1979 and early 1980 translates to a profit or loss of almost $22,500 per contract (on a deposit of $1,500 per contract). In

---

2 Delivery is possible on any one of three days. Thus, the seller of the futures contract can substitute a 91- or 92-day cash T-bill for the 90-day contract maturity specified by the futures, with the appropriate interest payment (price) adjustment.

3 The $25 = 1 basis point is determined as followed: 1% of $1 million = $10,000; consequently, 1 basis point (1/100 of 1 percent) = $100; since the contract is for a 90-day T-bill, we have $100 X 90/360 = $25.

EXHIBIT 2-3: Interest Rate Futures Quotations

	Open	High	Low	Settle	Chg	Yield Settle	Chg	Open Interest
TREASURY BONDS (CBT) $100,000; pts. 32nds of 100%								
Mar	103-19	103-31	102-23	103-10	− 16	7.673	+ .048	304,584
June	102-17	102-29	101-23	102-09	− 16	7.773	+ .048	27,327
Sept	101-19	101-28	100-28	101-09	− 16	7.872	+ .050	7,644
Dec	100-22	100-30	100-01	100-12	− 15	7.962	+ .047	5,598
Mr93	100-05	100-05	99-07	99-18	− 14	8.044	+ .044	1,280
June	99-01	99-06	98-17	98-26	− 13	8.121	+ .042	188

Est vol 450,000; vol Mon 268,027; open int 346,756,-10,772.

	Open	High	Low	Settle	Chg	Yield Settle	Chg	Open Interest
TREASURY NOTES (CBT) $100,000; Pts. 32nds of 100%								
Mar	105-07	105-09	103-24	104-20	− 25	7.339	+ .108	117,817
June	104-06	104-08	102-25	103-19	− 25	7.483	+ .109	2,502

Est vol 60,000; vol Mon 41,221; open int 120,343, +7,168.

	Open	High	Low	Settle	Chg	Yield Settle	Chg	Open Interest
5 YR TREAS NOTES (CBT) $100,000; pts. 32nds of 100%								
Mar	05-245	105-26	104-27	105-13	- 16	6.709	+ .115	118,967
June	104-19	104-27	103-30	04-165	- 14	6.917	+ .102	2,531

Est vol 81,031; vol Mon 26,868; open int 121,498, +6,302.

	Open	High	Low	Settle	Chg	Yield Settle	Chg	Open Interest
2 YR TREAS NOTES (CBT) $200,000, pts. 32nds of 100%								
Mar	104-22	104-24	104-13	04-205	− 6	5.517	+ .097	17,124

Est vol 1,200; vol Mon 709; open int 17,124, +57.

	Open	High	Low	Settle	Chg	Yield Settle	Chg	Open Interest
30-DAY INTEREST RATE (CBT) S5 million; pts. of 100%								
Jan	95.97	95.97	95.96	95.96	− .01	4.04	+ .01	1,697
Feb	96.04	96.04	96.01	96.03	− .01	3.97	+ .01	2,044
Mar	96.05	96.05	96.02	96.04	− .02	3.96	+ .02	1,564
Apr	96.06	96.06	96.03	96.04	− .02	3.96	+ .02	772
May	96.05	96.06	96.02	96.04	− .02	3.96	+ .02	400
June	96.00	96.02	95.99	96.00	− .05	4.00	+ .05	968

Est vol 1,422; vol Mon 5563; open int 7,612, +73.

	Open	High	Low	Settle	Chg	Discount Settle	Chg	Open Interest
TREASURY BILLS (IMM) $1 mil.; pts. of 100%								
Mar	96.17	96.25	96.15	96.21	− .03	3.79	+ .03	38,404
June	96.07	96.12	95.97	96.08	− .04	3.92	+ .04	14,324
Sept	95.78	95.85	95.63	95.76	− .10	4.24	+ .10	2,453
Dec	95.30	95.30	95.20	95.27	− .12	4.73	+ .12	446

Est vol 8,771; vol Mon 6,227; open int 55,669, +1,162.

	Open	High	Low	Settle	Chg	Settle	Chg	Open Interest
LIBOR-1 MO. (IMM) $3,000,000; pts. of 100%								
Feb	95.88	95.91	95.78	95.85	− .07	4.15	+ .07	6,841
Mar	95.88	95.90	95.77	95.84	− .06	4.16	+ .06	3,438
Apr	95.89	95.91	95.79	95.87	− .06	4.13	+ .06	2,202
May	95.88	95.90	95.78	95.85	− .08	4.15	+ .08	1,047
June	95.75	95.75	95.66	95.71	− .08	4.29	+ .08	104

Est vol 2,441; vol Mon 3,597; open int 22,196, +1,548.

	Open	High	Low	Settle	Chg	Lifetime High	Low	Open Interest
MUNI BOND INDEX (CBT) $1,000; times Bond Buyer MBI								
Mar	96-18	96-27	96-06	96-12	− 9	97-20	88-00	20,893
June	96-03	96-03	95-17	95-25	− 7	97-02	93-04	145

Est vol 3,000; vol Mon 1,683; open int 21,038, -207.
The index: Close 96-22; Yield 6.68.

Exhibit continues

```
┌────────────────────────────────────────────────────────────────────────────┐
│                        EXHIBIT 2-3: Continued                                │
│                                                                              │
│ EURODOLLAR (IMM) $1 million; pts of 100%                                     │
│                                                      Yield          Open     │
│         Open    High    Low    Settle   Chg    Settle   Chg      Interest    │
│ Mar    95.83   95.89   95.75   95.83   - .06    4.17   + .06      289,724     │
│ June   95.62   95.67   95.49   95.62   - .07    4.38   + .07      209,926     │
│ Sept   95.32   95.38   95.11   95.24   - .15    4.76   + .15      160,764     │
│ Dec    94.70   94.80   94.51   94.65   - .19    5.35   + .19      108,419     │
│ Mr93   94.46   94.55   94.27   94.38   - .21    5.62   + .21       92,765     │
│ June   94.02   94.11   93.85   93.95   - .21    6.05   + .21       64,700     │
│ Sept   93.66   93.72   93.45   93.56   - .21    6.44   + .21       46,292     │
│ Dec    93.17   93.21   92.94   93.06   - .22    6.94   + .22       38,190     │
│ Mr94   93.11   93.17   92.89   92.98   - .23    7.02   + .23       34,788     │
│ June   92.88   92.94   92.66   92.74   - .24    7.26   + .24       24,251     │
│ Sept   92.67   92.72   92.41   92.52   - .25    7.48   + .25       17,123     │
│ Dec    92.30   92.35   92.14   92.15   - .25    7.85   + .25       13,229     │
│ Mr95   92.38   92.40   92.14   92.17   - .25    7.83   + .25       12,791     │
│ June   92.24   92.26   92.00   92.03   - .25    7.97   + .25        9,739     │
│ Sept   92.10   92.12   91.87   91.89   - .25    8.11   + .25        8,260     │
│ Dec    91.91   91.93   91.69   91.70   - .25    8.30   + .25        7,680     │
│ Est vol 442,374; vol Mon 323,817; open int 1,138,641, -11,757.               │
│                                                                              │
│ EURODOLLAR (LIFFE) $1 million; pts of 100%                                   │
│                                                    Lifetime         Open     │
│         Open    High    Low    Settle  Change   High    Low      Interest    │
│ Mar    95.83   95.87   95.80   95.86    ....   95.97   90.60       17,471     │
│ June   95.60   95.66   95.58   95.62   - .02   95.86   90.97        8,172     │
│ Sept   95.30   95.36   95.28   95.31   - .01   95.67   90.97        5,818     │
│ Dec    94.75   94.78   94.68   94.72   - .07   95.20   91.54        2,057     │
│ Mr93   94.45   94.46   94.45   94.46   - .11   94.93   91.55        1,069     │
│ June    ....    ....            94.04   - .11   94.13   92.60          839     │
│ Sept    ....    ....            93.64   - .11   94.08   92.82          276     │
│ Est vol 5,758; vol Mon 3,153; open int 35,712, -280.                         │
│                                                                              │
│ Source: Data from Futures Exchanges, January 14, 1992.                       │
└────────────────────────────────────────────────────────────────────────────┘
```

early 1992 short-term T-bill rates dropped below 4 percent, the lowest level since T-bill futures started to trade.

Eurodollar Futures

The Chicago Mercantile Exchange added **Eurodollar** time deposit contracts to its futures list in December 1981. Eurodollar futures are similar to T-bill contracts in concept, since both are based on short-term $1 million contracts and use the financial cycle months for expirations. Eurodollar futures initiated trading and became popular because of the importance of the U.S. dollar in international trade and the activity of the dollar deposits in the London financial market. This popularity soon made the Eurodollar futures more active than T-bill futures. Eurodollar futures are used to hedge loans based on LIBOR and for other floating-rate obligations such as interest rate swap agreements.

The quoting procedure for Eurodollar futures is similar to the T-bill futures contracts, except that the interest rate is based on a money market yield (with a 360-day year) rather than a bank discount rate in order to correspond with the cash Eurodollar time deposit market. Also note that T-bill futures are based on a specific tradable security, whereas Eurodollar time deposits are not a security and hence are not actively traded. Since Euro-

---

EXAMPLE 2-1: Interpreting T-Bill Futures Quotations

Treasury bill futures: $1 mil; points of 100 percent

			Discount	
	Settle	Chg	Settle	Chg
Mar	96.21	−.03	3.79	+.03

	Close	*Change*
Index Settle	96.21	−.03
Discount Settle	3.79	+.03
	100.00	.00

The T-bill index closing value and the discount rate close always add up to 100. Thus, 100 minus discount = index, and vice versa. The quote above is for a closing index value of 96.21, and therefore the discount interest rate for the futures contract must be 3.79%.

The change in the index value from the previous day is −.03 or a decline in value of −.03 × $25 = −$75 for those holding a long position in futures. Since the index and discount values add to 100, the change for the discount value from the previous day must be +.03. Thus, the "changes" for the index and discount values are the same, but they have opposite signs.

Note that the close of 96.21 for the index typically differs from the next day's open. There is no requirement that the close and the next day's open be the same value, since new information overnight as well as supply and demand factors can change the price traders are willing to pay for the futures contract.

dollar time deposits are not a security, Eurodollar futures settle in cash rather than through the delivery of a financial instrument.

Originally six expiration months traded at one time; now 16 expirations (four years) trade concurrently. Several years ago Eurodollar futures surpassed T-bill futures as the most active short-term interest rate contract. Eurodollar futures have a much larger volume than the S&P Stock Index futures and are the only futures contracts to have more than one million contracts of open interest.

One-Month LIBOR Futures

In 1990 the CMEX started to trade 30-day LIBOR Time Deposit futures contracts. The 30-day LIBOR futures are based on a $3-million, 30-day time deposit. Expiration months are the next seven consecutive months, with four to five months being active. Each basis point

EXHIBIT 2-4: Characteristics of Interest Rate Futures Contracts

Futures Contract	Trading Unit	Deliverable Instrument	Price Quotation	Minimum Price Change		Last Trading Day	Last Delivery Day
				Units	Dollars		
T-bills	$1,000,000	90 day T-bill	Index	.01	$25	(1)	(1)
Eurodollar	$1,000,000	Cash	Index	.01	$25	(2)	(3)
1-month LIBOR	$3,000,000	Cash	Index	.01	$25	(2)	(3)
T-bonds	$ 100,000	(4)	% of par: points and 32nds	1/32	$31.25	(5)	Last day of month
T-notes:							
10-year	$ 100,000	(6)	Same as T-bonds	1/32	$31.25	(5)	Last day of month
5-year	$ 100,000	(7)	(8)	1/64	$15.625	(5)	Last day of month
Municipals	$1,000 X Index	Cash	Same as T-bonds	1/32	$31.25	(5)	(3)

(1) Trading for T-bill futures ceases on the first day during the month when a 13-week T-bill is issued *and* a one-year T-bill has 13 weeks remaining until delivery. The following day is the delivery day.

(2) Second London business day before third Wednesday of the expiration month.

(3) No delivery since contract is settled in cash.

(4) Any cash T-bond that is noncallable and has at least 15 years to maturity on the first day of the delivery month is deliverable; callable bonds with at least 15 years to the first call date are deliverable.

(5) The eighth to last business day of the delivery month.

(6) Any cash T-note maturing in at least 6 1/2 years, but not more than 10 years, from the first day of the delivery month.

(7) Any cash T-note maturing in at least 4 1/4 years, but not more than 5 1/4 years, from the first day of the delivery month.

(8) Same as T-bonds and 10-year T-notes, except that the 5-year notes are quoted in one-half of 1/32 of a point.

Note: All interest rate futures contracts trade on a March, June, September, and December expiration cycle.

Source: Exchange pamphlets.

FIGURE 2-4: T-bill Futures Interest Rate

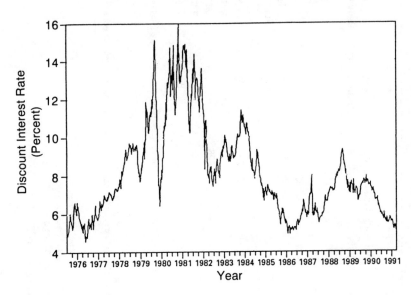

Source: Data from Tick Data, Inc.

---

is worth $25, and the contract settles in cash. This type of futures is most useful for strategies involving overnight to one-month interest rates.[4]

LONG-TERM INTEREST RATE INSTRUMENTS

Treasury Bond Futures

The Chicago Board of Trade introduced Treasury Bond futures in August 1977. The T-bond contract is used by speculators and hedgers of long-term interest rates. The huge government bond market could no longer function effectively without T-bond and T-note futures contracts. For example, when the government sells new T-bonds and T-notes, all of the dealers hedge their positions in the long-term interest rate futures to reduce their risk of price changes for the billions of dollars of bonds and notes that dealers buy. In addition, the initiation of a night trading session from Sunday through Thursday now allows Japanese traders access to the T-bond futures contracts. Since Japanese investors hold significant

---

4 In late 1988 the CBT started to trade futures based on a weighted average of the Federal Reserve (Fed) funds interest rate to date and an N-day term interest rate. These futures contracts expire on a monthly cycle. The CBT contract is based on $5 million of Fed funds and is quoted by taking 100 minus the interest rate. The size of each 1 basis point is $41.67, and the contract settles on the last day of the expiration month. The CBT contract has a volume of less than 1,000 contracts per day.

quantities of U.S. T-bonds, this session becomes useful to Far Eastern traders. Night volume averages 15,000 to 20,000 contracts but can rise to more than 40,000 contracts on active evenings. The total daily open interest and volume values for the T-bond contracts in Exhibit 2-3 show the tremendous success that this contract enjoys. In particular, nearby open interest and total volume values make T-bond futures the most active of all futures contracts.

The yield to maturity in *The Wall Street Journal* for T-bond futures is based on a hypothetical T-bond with an 8% coupon, 20 years to maturity, and a $100,000 face value. In fact, the *WSJ* calculates the *semiannual* **bond equivalent yield** for the hypothetical 20-year, 8% bond and then simply *doubles* that yield, rather than considering the effect of compounding. However, *any* T-bond with at least 15 years to maturity (or 15 years to the first call date, if it is a **callable bond**) can be used for delivery.[5] The benefit of allowing a number of bonds to be delivered is that it increases the liquidity for delivery purposes. A conversion process exists to adjust delivery prices for different bond coupons and maturities, as explained in a later chapter. The pricing of this futures contract is based on the futures market's perception of the appropriate future long-term interest rate.

T-bond futures quotes are equivalent to cash T-bond quotes in that they trade in 32nds of a point, with the price shown being a percentage of the face value. Hence, the price of 103–10 for the March maturity in Exhibit 2-3 means $103^{10}/_{32}$ as a percent of the $100,000 face value of the contract. Each $1/_{32}$ of a point changes the value of the contract by $31.25, with $^{32}/_{32}$ creating a change of $1,000. When interest rates rise above 8%, the prices of the T-bond futures contracts fall below the par value of 100, and vice versa.

Twelve separate futures expirations for the T-bond futures typically are traded at one time; that is, T-bond contracts are traded for the next three years. During the expiration month of the futures, the seller of the T-bond futures decides which day to deliver the cash T-bonds. *Any day* the exchange is open within the expiration month of the futures can be used for delivery. This feature provides some interesting alternatives for the seller, as discussed in Part II.

Figure 2-5 provides a graphical history of weekly T-bond futures prices. The figure shows that at the peak of long-term interest rates in 1981, T-bond futures prices were as low as 56–0. More important, each 5-point change in price translates to a profit/loss of $5,000 per $100,000 par futures contract. The figure shows numerous times when the T-bond futures changed by five points or more.

Treasury Note Futures

Ten-Year Notes. The CBT introduced 10-year Treasury Note futures in May 1982. These T-note futures are based on a hypothetical T-note with a $100,000 face value, an 8% coupon, and 10 years to maturity. Prices are a percentage of par, and each $1/_{32}$ of a point

---

5   Current callable cash Treasury bond issues have a five-year call provision. Hence, these bonds would need at least 20 years to maturity to be deliverable into the T-bond futures contract. The maturity requirement for the cash bonds is measured from the first day of expiration of the futures contract. Note that if there were a number of *different* Treasury bond futures contracts that employed special cash bonds with different coupons and/or years to maturity as the underlying cash instrument, then a significant dilution in the liquidity and pricing stability of the futures contracts would occur.

FIGURE 2-5: T-Bond Futures Prices

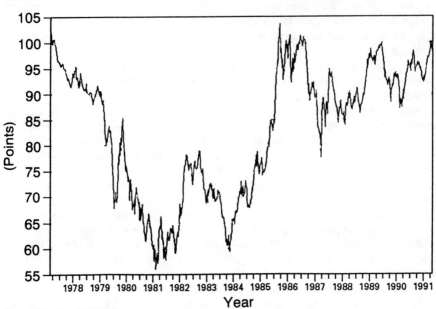

Source: Prices from Tick Data Inc.

change is worth $31.25. T-notes (*not* T-bonds) with maturities of 6½ to 10 years are employed for delivery. These contracts help to fill the gap in maturities between the long-term T-bond futures and the short-term T-bill futures. The shorter maturity of the T-note does cause its price to be less volatile than T-bond futures as interest rates change and thus causes T-note futures to be a better hedging device for those debt portfolios with a shorter maturity. The open interest and volume values for the "Treasury Note" futures in Exhibit 2-3 show that this contract has been successful, at least in terms of the nearby contract. Ten-year T-note futures currently trade six expiration months at one time, although only the first three are active.

Five-Year Notes. The introduction of $100,000, 8% coupon, five-year T-note futures in 1988 allows more precise hedging of intermediate-term debt securities by filling in the term structure below the 10-year T-note futures. Cash T-notes with maturities between 4¼ and 5¼ years are used for delivery purposes, as long as the original maturity was no more than 5¼ years. Thus, only five-year T-notes issued over the life of the futures contract are deliverable. Consequently, the futures price the *recently issued* five-year T-notes. The pricing scheme is similar to the 10-year T-note futures, although the five-year T-note is less volatile in nature. The five-year T-note futures are quoted as a percentage of par, with units of *one-half* of ⅟32 of a point. Thus, the June expiration price of 104–165 equals 104 and 16.5/32 as a percentage of par, which is equivalent to 104³³⁄64. Each one-half of ⅟32 is worth

$15.625. To date, the nearby contract is most liquid, but the first deferred contract also is tradable. Previous attempts to introduce shorter-term T-note futures were not successful; specifically, a four- to six-year T-note futures in June 1979 and a two-year T-note contract in January 1983 did not survive. A 1990 reintroduction of two-year T-note futures has achieved limited volume but reasonable open interest.

Two-Year Notes. The CBT trades two-year T-note futures with a $200,000 face value and an 8% coupon. T-notes with an original maturity between one year nine months and five years six months are used for delivery, as long as their maturity at delivery is between one year nine months and two years one month. Thus, this delivery range allows "trickle-downs" of longer-term T-notes to be delivered into the two-year contract. The price is quoted as a percentage of par, with units of *one-quarter* of $\frac{1}{32}$ of a point. These T-note futures started to trade in 1990 and currently have a volume of only several hundred contracts per day. The Board of Trade also tried a cash settled two-year T-note contract, but it failed because of lack of interest.

Swap Futures

In 1991, three-year and five-year interest rate swap futures started trading on the CBT. These contracts were instituted with the cash swap market in mind, where institutions trade ("swap") fixed-rate for variable-rate commitments. To date, five-year swap futures volume is low. Three-year swap futures are inactive. Currently, many swap dealers use the Eurodollar futures contracts to hedge their swap positions, especially for shorter-term swaps. Some dealers also use five-year T-note futures to hedge their swaps.

Municipal Bond Futures

The CBT has traded the Municipal Bond Index futures contract since 1985. Municipal Bond futures are useful for dealers and hedgers in the municipal bond market, since the interest rates on municipal debt can act differently than T-bond interest rates. The Municipal Bond Index, which substitutes for the underlying cash security, includes 40 actively traded, high-quality general obligation or revenue municipal bonds. As noted in Goodman,[6] bonds must have the following qualifications to be included in the Municipal Bond Index:
- Be rated A or better by Standard & Poor's or A or better by Moody's.
- Be at least $50 million in size ($75 million for housing issues).
- Have a remaining maturity of at least 19 years.
- Be callable prior to maturity, with the first call date being between 7 and 16 years from the inclusion in the bond index.
- Must have been reoffered at a price ranging from 95 to 105.
- Have a fixed, semiannual coupon.

The value of the futures contract is determined by multiplying the Bond Buyer Municipal Bond Index by $1,000. Five municipal bond dealers price the index daily, with the middle three quotes being used to form the index. Each bond is then divided by a conver-

---

6   Laurie S. Goodman, "The Municipal Futures Contract," paper presented at the American Banker/Bond Buyer Conference on Futures and Options, New York, September 10-11, 1987.

sion factor that simulates the price for a yield of 8%. The conversion factor makes each of the bonds approximately comparable in price movements. The 40 bonds are then averaged and multiplied by a coefficient that helps to maintain the continuity of the index when bonds in the index are changed (which can occur twice monthly). Some traders have criticized the calculation of the index, since the coefficient declines over time as a result of the price decline inherent in callable bonds. From 1983 to the end of 1990 the index declined from 1.0 to .8807, creating a declining volatility in the index. Hence, hedgers need to compensate for the lower index when using futures to reduce risk.

The contract expirations use the quarterly financial cycle, with the first two contracts being most active. As with other bond futures contracts, the Municipal Bond futures trade in 32nds, with $1/32 = \$31.25$. The eighth to last business day of the expiration month is the last day of trading. The contract settles in cash.

CURRENCY FUTURES

The International Monetary Market (IMM) of the Chicago Mercantile Exchange (CMEX) and the Financial Instruments Exchange of the New York Cotton Exchange (CTN) trade currency futures. Currency futures trading began on the IMM in 1972. Thus, currency futures have the distinction of being the first financial futures contracts.

IMM Contracts

The IMM of the CMEX actively trades currency futures contracts on the British pound, Canadian dollar, Japanese yen, Swiss franc, and German mark. The Australian dollar currently has minimal volume on the IMM, while the French franc and Mexican peso contracts are inactive. Each currency contract trades a specified number of units of the foreign currency. For example, the futures quotations in Exhibit 2-5 show that the British pound contract is based on 62,500 pounds, whereas the Japanese yen futures contracts are for 12.5 million yen. The number of units of the other foreign currencies used as the basis of the futures contract is listed with the futures quotations. When the seller of these futures delivers the foreign exchange, then the buyer of the futures contract receives the number of units of the foreign currency at the futures exchange rate existing at that time.

The quotes for the foreign currency futures contracts are all in dollars per foreign currency. For example, the March expiration of the Japanese yen contract has a settle price of .007867 dollars per yen, as shown in Exhibit 2-5. Multiplying by 12.5 million yen for one contract results in a value of $108,375. Similarly, one can determine that a change of .000001 in the value of the contract is worth $12.50. The currency futures typically trade the next four expirations in the quarterly financial cycle, although the nearby expiration month is most active.

Figures 2-6 and 2-7 show the historical Japanese yen per dollar and German DM per dollar exchange rates from the mid-1970s to the early 1990s. The value of the dollar has declined from 295 yen to the dollar in January 1977 to 133 yen in late 1991. More dramatically, there was a significant drop in the yen/dollar exchange rate from 295 to 180 in 1977 and 1978, and then a decline from 260 to 120 from March 1985 to December 1987. The German mark shows an even greater tendency for trends, declining from 2.60 DM/$ in 1976 to 1.70 DM/$ in 1979, then rising to 3.40 DM/$ in February 1985, before

EXHIBIT 2-5: Currency Futures Quotations

	Open	High	Low	Settle	Change	Lifetime High	Lifetime Low	Open Interest
JAPANESE YEN (IMM) 12.5 million yen; $ per yen (.00)								
Mar	.7905	.7926	.7856	.7867	+.0013	.8114	.7000	53,749
June	.7889	.7912	.7844	.7853	+.0016	.8097	.7015	4,125
Sept	....	....		.7846	+.0019	.8055	.7265	1,649
Dec	....	....		.7848	+.0019	.8005	.7512	1,623
Mar93		....	....	.7860	+.0028	.8005	.7960	1,112
Est vol 25,243; vol Mon 16,588; open int 62,258, +685.								
DEUTSCHEMARK (IMM) 125,000 marks; $ per mark								
Mar	.6310	.6329	.6200	.6211	−.0068	.6575	.5353	54,832
June	.6227	.6244	.6120	.6134	−.0064	.6490	.5322	2,540
Sept	.6155	.6162	.6060	.6069	−.0060	.6400	.5685	454
Est vol 63,440; vol Mon 39,923; open int 57,886, -340.								
CANADIAN DOLLAR (IMM) 100,000 dlrs.; $ per Can $								
Mar	.8668	.8682	.8636	.8646	−.0007	.8857	.8253	15,719
June	.8626	.8626	.8584	.8591	−.0007	.8820	.8330	1,864
Sept			....	.8540	−.0007	.8774	.8348	120
Est vol 5,437; vol Mon 3,766; open int 17,797, −599.								
BRITISH POUND (IMM) 62,500 Pds.; $ per pound								
Mar	1.7876	1.7930	1.7600	1.7620	−.0158	1.8646	1.5560	19,885
June	1.7580	1.7650	1.7320	1.7358	−.0146	1.8346	1.6410	1,095
Est vol 18,116; vol Mon 11,293; open int 21,078, -85.								
SWISS FRANC (IMM) 125,000 francs; $ per franc								
Mar	.7119	.7137	.7006	.7022	−.0049	.7398	.6225	23,626
June	.7065	.7075	.6945	.6963	−.0045	.7328	.6546	689
Est vol 24,438: vol Mon 17,152; open int 24,354, -2,607.								
AUSTRALIAN DOLLAR (IMM) 100,00 dlrs.; $ per A.$								
Mar	.7428	.7432	.7373	.7374	+.0011	.7880	.7307	1,390
Est vol 386; vol Mon 434; open int 1,398, +16.								
U.S. DOLLAR INDEX (FINEX) 500 times USDX								
Mar	86.76	88.08	86.55	87.96	+ .70	98.90	83.87	5,956
June	88.00	89.25	87.98	89.14	+ .54	100.15	85.45	192
Est vol 3,619; vol Mon 2,583; open int 6,154, +555.								
The index: High 86.87; Low 85.55; Close 86.81 +.63								

Source: Bank Currency Dealers and Futures Exchanges, January 14, 1992.

plunging to 1.60 DM/$ in December 1987. These extreme price moves provide opportunities for speculators in foreign exchange and currency futures, as well as illustrating periods where hedging is crucial for those dealing in foreign exchange markets.

U.S. Dollar Index

The Financial Exchange (FINEX) of the Cotton Exchange trades the U.S. Dollar Index. The purpose of this contract is to provide trading in an instrument based on the Federal Reserve's trade-weighted dollar index. The benefit of using the Index instead of a specific currency future is that a position is taken in the dollar, rather than taking a position solely in one other currency. The Index includes 10 foreign currencies and trades as 500 times

FIGURE 2-6: Yen/$ Exchange Rate

Source: Rates from Tick Data, Inc.

the geometric average of these currencies. The weights used in the Index for the individual currencies are based on the associated countries' world trade values. The use of the geometric average shows the *percentage* change in the value of the dollar over time. Thus, a value of 87.96 for the March expiration indicates that the dollar has declined in value by 12.04% since the base period of March 1973. Each .01 of 1% change in value is worth $5. The exchange calculates a cash price of the Index each 30 seconds, based on bank trades of the dollar with the 10 relevant currencies. The Reuter's Monitor network disseminates those values. Typically two expiration months have some activity. Exhibit 2-6 provides a listing of the characteristics of the currency futures.

Cross-Rate Futures

The CMEX initiated futures in several popular cross-rates in 1991. For example, the mark-yen cross-rate represents the exchange rate ratio between the German mark and the Japanese yen. However, the cross-rate futures failed because of lack of volume. One reason for this failure had to do with the practice of settlement in dollars, which created a risk that the dollar would change in value before the appropriate currency exchange could be made. For this reason, the CMEX plans to resurrect the mark-yen cross-rate futures with settlement in yen. However, it is still uncertain whether a cross-rate futures can build sufficient volume when transactions in mark futures, yen futures, and the dollar create the equivalent position by using more liquid contracts. In addition, there is an active market in cash cross-rates by the money center banks.

FIGURE 2-7: DM/$ Exchange Rate

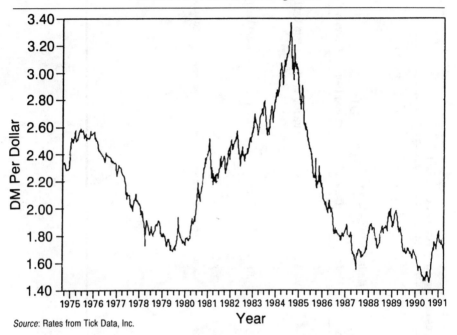

Source: Rates from Tick Data, Inc.

INTERNATIONAL FUTURES MARKETS

The success of futures contracts in the United States has generated an explosion of futures markets around the world. The most important international futures markets are in London, Tokyo, and France. In fact, the Chicago Exchanges recognize that international markets are important to consider; thus, the CMEX trades the Japanese Nikkei 225 stock average and dually lists contracts with the Singapore Exchange to promote Far Eastern activity.[7] The *Wall Street Journal* reports some of the more important and active international futures contracts and lists them with the U.S. interest rate futures, namely the German Government Bond (on LIFFE: the London International Financial Futures Exchange), Sterling (British short-term interest rates on LIFFE), and the Long Gilt (British bonds on LIFFE); see Exhibits 2-7 and 2-8. In addition, the *WSJ* lists T-bond futures and Eurodollar futures traded on LIFFE.

---

7   The CMEX Nikkei futures contracts employ a price-weighted average of 225 large and actively traded Japanese stocks. Those who trade Japanese stocks can use the Nikkei futures to speculate or hedge their positions, without having to consider changes in the currency exchange rate. The Nikkei futures are valued as $5 times the index, with a minimum price change of $25. They are settled in cash. The CBT listed a TOPIX Japanese stock index futures and a Japanese government bond futures; however, both failed to achieve the needed liquidity.

EXHIBIT 2-6: Characteristics of Currency Futures Contracts

Futures Contract	Trading Unit	Deliverable Instrument	Price Quotation	Minimum Price Change		Last Trading Day	Delivery Day
				Units	Dollars		
Currencies	(1)	Foreign currency	$/FC	Varies	Varies	2 trading days before 3rd Wed	3rd Wed.
U.S. dollar	500 X index	Cash	Index	.01	$5	3rd Wed	3rd Wed.

(1)   The number of units of the foreign currency (FC) for each specific futures contract is stated in the *WSJ*.

Note: All currency futures contracts trade on the March, June, September, and December expiration cycle (plus other months that are not active). Currencies trade from 7:20 A.M. to 2:00 P.M. central time.

Source: Exchange pamphlets.

EXHIBIT 2-7: International Futures Quotations

	Open	High	Low	Settle	Chg	Lifetime High	Lifetime Low	Open Interest
NIKKEI 225 Stock Average (CME) $5 times NSA								
Mar	22140.	22425.	22135.	22350.	+540.0	26725.	21780.	15,914

Est vol 1,233; vol Mon 865; open int 15,942, +85.
Index High 22019.94; Low 21662.99; Close 21775.13 + 78.27

	Open	High	Low	Settle	Chg	Lifetime High	Lifetime Low	Open Interest
GERMAN GOV'T. BOND (LIFFE) 250,000 marks; $ per mark (.01)								
Mar	n.a.	n.a.	n.a.	n.a.	n.a.	87.28	85.39	112,817
June	88.53	88.67	88.53	88.74	+ .24	88.75	87.25	1,049

Est vol 65,618; vol Mon 46,888; open int 113,866, -3,139.

	Open	High	Low	Settle	Chg	Lifetime High	Lifetime Low	Open Interest
STERLING (LIFFE) £500,000; pts of 100 percent								
Mar	89.48	89.62	89.42	89.60	+ .14	90.49	86.68	73,804
June	89.81	89.93	89.77	89.90	+ .11	90.46	87.45	59,604
Sept	90.07	90.19	90.03	90.17	+ .11	90.41	87.46	12,938
Dec	90.27	90.29	90.23	90.29	+ .06	90.43	87.55	10,122
Mr93	90.37	90.41	90.33	90.40	+ .02	90.52	87.50	7,355
June	90.39	90.43	90.35	90.41	+ .01	90.59	87.58	4,528
Sept	90.33	90.35	90.31	90.35	+ .03	90.50	87.20	4,234
Dec	90.31	90.31	90.26	90.28	- .03	90.39	88.95	3,774
Mr94	90.16	90.16	90.15	90.16	- .03	90.16	90.15	130

Est vol 67,395, vol Mon 40,669, open int 176,489, +3,920.

	Open	High	Low	Settle	Chg	Lifetime High	Lifetime Low	Open Interest
LONG GILT (LIFFE) £50,000; 32nds of 100 percent								
Mar	96-14	97-00	96-07	96-28	+ 0-16	97-28	93-28	53,286
June	96-19	96-24	96-19	97-03	+ 0-16	97-22	96-19	179

Est vol 32,429; vol Mon 23,047; open int 53,465. +5,515.

Source: Data from Futures Exchanges, January 14, 1992.

Active futures contracts traded on international exchanges, and not available on U.S. exchanges, include the German Bond futures, the *Financial Times* Stock Exchange Index futures (the British blue-chip index traded), and Eurosterling futures on LIFFE, the French Government Bond futures on the Marché à Terme International de France (Matif: Paris) Exchange, Japanese Bond futures on the Tokyo Stock Exchange, Euroyen contracts on TIFFE (the Tokyo International Financial Futures Exchange), and Australian debt and stock index futures. The French Government Bond futures traded more than 20 million contracts in 1991, and LIFFE's German Bond futures traded 10 million contracts. The Euroyen futures traded 25 million contracts, and Japanese Bond futures traded more than 20 million contracts. Europe's share of the world's futures and options volume was 20 percent in 1991 (McAuley),[8] while the United States kept the lead at 60 percent (down from 67 percent in 1990). However, LIFFE and Matif grew by 11 percent and 15 percent, respectively, in 1991. Other European exchanges include the Deutsche Terminborse in Germany and the planned 1992 initiation of Telematico, the computer-based system in Italy to trade bonds and futures. The Japanese bond contract principally attracts domestic hedgers and traders. Contracts traded on international exchanges are quoted in the home country currency. The

---

8 Tony McAuley, "Europe's Futures Markets Hotly Pursue U.S. Leaders," *The Wall Street Journal,* December 27, 1991, pp. C1, C10.

EXHIBIT 2-8: Characteristics of International Futures Contracts

Futures Contract	Trading Unit	Deliverable Instrument	Price Quotation	Minimum Price Change Units	Minimum Price Change Dollars	Last Trading Day	Last Delivery Day
Nikkei 225	$5 X index	Cash	Index	5	$25	(1)	(1)
Long Gilt	£50,000	(2)	Points and 32nds	1/32	£15.625	(3)	(3)
German government Bond	DM250,000	(4)	Points of 100	.01	DM 25	(5)	(5)
Three-month Sterling deposit	£500,000	Cash	Index	.01	£12.50	(6)	Cash

(1) First business day preceding the determination of the final settlement price, usually the business day preceding the second Friday of the contract month. The contract is settled in cash.

(2) A hypothetical 9% coupon gilt bond maturing in 2003.

(3) Last trading day is the third-to-last business day of the contract month (the financial cycle). The delivery day is any business day in the contract month at the seller's choice.

(4) A hypothetical German government bond with an 8 to 10½-year remaining life and 6% coupon.

(5) The last trading day is three Frankfurt business days before delivery. The delivery date is the tenth calendar day of the contract month or the following Frankfurt business day.

(6) The last trading day is the third Wednesday of the delivery month.

Source: Exchange pamphlets.

value of all such contracts is calculated in the same manner as equivalent futures contracts traded in the U.S.

Risk Management Magazine annually publishes the *Mitsubishi Finance Risk Directory*,[9] which lists the characteristics of the futures and options contracts currently trading on international exchanges.[10] Although *Futures Magazine* annually includes *all* of the futures contracts listed worldwide with their contract characteristics and trading hours for each futures, it does not distinguish between highly active and marginally active contracts, and contracts that do not trade. Currently 22 countries have futures exchanges.

OTHER FUTURES CONTRACTS

The Commodity Research Bureau (CRB) contract tracks a basket of 21 other futures contracts in the agricultural, financial, and metal markets. Thus, it provides an implicit contract representing inflation. With an open interest of more than 1,000 contracts, the CRB contract provides one means of hedging basic commodity prices. Other vehicles also exist to hedge inflation; for example, Goldman Sachs sold $200 million of inflation-adjusted three-year notes in 1991. The return on these notes is based on the return linked to 18 commodities tracked by the Goldman Sachs Commodity Index.

New financial futures contracts are constantly proposed and approved. Most do not survive. Some of the more interesting low-volume and dormant interest rate futures contracts are the 30-day Interest Rate futures, the Mortgage-Backed futures, and the differential interest rate futures between countries ("DIFFs"). At one time the exchanges proposed several macroeconomic futures contracts. For example, a Consumer Price Index (inflation) contract traded for almost a year before volume disappeared. A prime interest rate contract was discussed for a number of years, but never traded. Wholesale price indexes, housing starts, and other similar contracts never were approved by the CFTC.

Futures contracts recently introduced, or planned for introduction in 1992, include various versions of fertilizer futures (such as diammonium phosphate), insurance futures, Clean Air futures (often dubbed acid rain or "pollution" futures), electricity futures, and S&P Midcap 400 Stock Index futures (see Taylor[11]). One fertilizer contract has started trading and possesses reasonable support in the market. Health and property insurance futures have regulatory difficulties and skepticism from the insurance industry to overcome. The Clean Air futures will allow hedging of the pollution credits received by electricity producers. The S&P Midcap 400 futures will provide hedging opportunities for those holding midsize companies in their portfolios.

SUMMARY AND LOOKING AHEAD

This chapter covered the basic characteristics and quoting procedures for futures contracts for common stock indexes, and short-term and long-term debt instruments. An understand-

---

9 *Mitsubishi Finance Risk Directory 1990-91*, Chicago: *Risk Management Magazine*, 1991.

10 This annual also lists and describes software for institutional risk management, as available from vendors, and also lists financial consultants.

11 Jeffrey Taylor, "A Boom Year for Newfangled Trading Vehicles," *The Wall Street Journal*, December 26, 1991, pp. C1, C10.

ing of these characteristics and quoting procedures are important in order to comprehend the applications and techniques involved with futures contracts. The next chapter discusses futures terminology and concepts.

Chapter 3

Terminology and Concepts for Futures Markets

This chapter covers the terminology and concepts related to how futures markets operate. This information provides a foundation for discussions of pricing, hedging, and
speculation issues in later chapters. Important terminology and concepts include margins,
price limits, convergence, the importance of the clearinghouse, and delivery of certain
futures contracts. This chapter also includes evidence on the return and risk of trading
futures contracts, the relative importance of hedgers and speculators to the futures markets,
whether futures are unbiased predictors of subsequent cash prices, and the accuracy of
futures as a predictor of prices.

FUTURES TERMINOLOGY AND CONCEPTS

Margins

Initial Margin. The **initial margin** is the amount of funds placed in the account of the
trader or **hedger** as a *good faith* deposit against adverse price changes that create losses for
the account. This margin is used to make sure that a trader does not default when losses
occur. Thus, margins reduce **default risk**. Since futures margins are not used to buy the
asset (as is the case with stock margins), no additional funds need to be borrowed from the
brokerage house to trade futures. Since futures margins are a good faith deposit, the margin
amount is a relatively small percentage of the underlying value of the contract.

Margins are stated as *dollar* amounts for each futures contract. These amounts change
over time. The size of the good faith futures margin varies from a low of about 2 percent of
the underlying cash value for some agricultural futures to 10 percent or more of the
underlying cash value for stock index futures. The size of the margin relates to such factors
as the recent volatility of the relevant futures market and the desire by the futures regulatory agency to keep unsophisticated individuals out of stock index futures. The initial
margin for futures contracts can be made with cash Treasury bills, with the customer
retaining the implicit interest on the T-bills. Consequently, using cash instead of T-bills for
margin creates an **opportunity loss**, since interest is not received on any cash deposit.
Whereas hedgers consistently use T-bills or letters of credit for the initial margin, small- to
medium-size speculators often post cash for margin because of their smaller accounts, or out
of ignorance. Most brokerage houses also allow traders to use 80 percent of their stock
value as margin.

Marking-to-Market and Maintenance Margin. As futures prices fluctuate over time,
the customer's profits or losses in the futures account also change. These price movements

necessitate **marking-to-market** rules and **maintenance margin**. Marking-to-market is the adjustment in a customer's account balance to reflect the change in value of the futures contract on a daily basis. Maintenance margin is the smallest margin balance allowed before additional funds are required in the account. Thus if the *value* of the futures position declines (i.e., the position loses money), the customer's good faith margin account balance also declines. When the margin account balance becomes less than the required mainte-nance margin, the customer receives a margin call requiring the customer to put up additional margin funds to return the balance of the account to the initial margin level. If this is not accomplished by the beginning of trading on the next trading day, then the brokerage house is authorized to close out the futures position at the current market price. The maintenance margin and marking-to-market rules protect the brokerage house from sustaining losses on individual accounts. Losses will occur if the change in value exceeds the initial margin *and* the customer does not pay the brokerage house for the additional losses. Additional margin funds can be deposited in cash, Treasury bills, or letters of credit (despite the common misconception that additional margin can be made only in cash).

If the futures account generates profits from price changes, then the customer can withdraw any excess funds above the initial margin amount on a daily basis. These funds then can be deposited elsewhere to draw interest. Margins vary depending on the type of trading strategy employed. A hedging strategy involves less risk and therefore requires a smaller initial margin. **Spreading** also is a low-risk strategy whereby a trader buys one (say stock index) futures and sells another, or buys one expiration month and sells a different month. Spreading margins are extremely small, and thus significant leverage effects are created.

Margin amounts change as the volatility of the futures contracts change; that is, margins increase when the price volatility increases significantly. Hence the exchange margins provided in Tables 3-1 and 3-2 for speculative, hedging, and spreading positions are for guidance only. The margin/volatility relationship is based on the Standard Portfolio Analysis of Risk (SPAN) margining system. The SPAN system directly associates margins with the volatility of each market, attempting to determine an "optimal" margin amount.[1] Also be aware that many brokerage houses request larger margins than the exchange-listed mini-mums given here, especially for smaller customers. Example 3-1 shows the essential aspects of the operation of the margin process and marking-to-market.

The marking-to-market and maintenance margin rules make it imperative for the cus-tomer to stay in touch with the brokerage house concerning the status of the customer's account. A futures trader who takes a secluded vacation in the mountains often finds out later that the vacation had a disastrous effect on the trader's futures account! A major movement in the stock market for even *one* day could wipe out the trader's margin

---

1 An explanation of how the SPAN system calculates margin is available from The Chicago Board of Trade by requesting their current margin document. Note that the size of the initial margin can be related to the maximum allowable daily price change; see the next section and footnote 2. SPAN also considers the risk of an entire portfolio, including the characteristics of both futures and options. SPAN allows traders to use excess margin from one contract *or* exchange to cover deficiencies in other contracts. Alternatively, a trader who does not have excess margin to withdraw can make an additional cash deposit to decrease the possibility of a margin call.

TABLE 3-1: Margins and Price Limits for Stock Index Futures

Contract	Speculative Margins		Hedging Margins	Spread Margins[a]	Price Limit[b]	Trading Hours[c]
	Initial	Maintenance				
S&P 500	$22,000	$9,000	9,000	490	(1)	8:30 AM – 3:15 PM
MMI	18,000	7,400	7,400	0	(2)	8:15 AM – 3:15 PM
NYSE	9,000	4,000	4,000	200	(3)	9:30 AM – 4:15 PM

[a] Across expirations. Intercommodity spreads vary according to the instruments used in the spread.

[b] The stock index futures contracts have a series of "circuit breakers" or price limits that are activated when a given large move in the futures price occurs (in addition, see Focus 3-1 for information on trading halts).

(1) For the S&P 500 contract: if the futures *drop* by 12 points then that price limit stays in effect for 30 minutes. After 30 minutes, a 20-point limit becomes effective. In addition, there is a 5-point up or down opening limit; that is, the open price can vary from the previous day's close by a maximum of 5 points.

(2) For the MMI contract: if the futures either fall or increase by 15 points then the price limit stays in effect for 30 minutes. There also is a 10-point up or down opening limit.

(3) For the NYSE contract: if the futures *fall* by 7 points then this price limit is in effect for 30 minutes. If the futures then fall by a total of 12 points, this limit exists for one hour. A drop of 18 points creates a price limit that exists for the rest of the day. An opening limit of 3 points (up or down) also exists. A price limit of 18 points exists on the up side, which stays in effect for the entire day.

[c] All times are local times.

Note: Margins change on a regular basis.

Sources: Adapted from Chicago Board of Trade, "Margins," photocopied, 1991; and Chicago Mercantile Exchange, "Minimum Performance Bond/Margin Requirements and Contract Specifications," photocopied, 1991.

TABLE 3-2: Interest Rate Futures Margins and Price Limits

Contract	Speculative Margins		Hedging Margins	Spread Margins[a]	Price Limit	Trading Hours[b]
	Initial	Maintenance				
T-bills	540	400	400	200	none	7:20 AM – 2:00 PM
Eurodollar	540	400	400	200	none	7:20 AM – 2:00 PM
One-month LIBOR	540	400	400	270	none	7:20 AM – 2:00 PM
T-bonds	2,700	2,000	2,000	200	96/32	8:00 AM – 2:00 PM
T-notes:						
10-year	1,300	1,000	1,000	200	96/32	8:00 AM – 2:00 PM
5-year	675	500	500	0	96/32	8:00 AM – 2:00 PM
Municipals	1,350	1,000	1,000	0	96/32	8:00 AM – 2:00 PM

a Across expirations. Intercommodity spreads vary according to instruments employed.

b All times are local times. Evening hours also exist from 5:00-8:30 P.M. Central Standard Time or 6:00-9:30 P.M. Central Daylight Saving Time, Sunday through Thursday for T-bonds and 10-year T-notes. Half-size contracts trade on the Mid-America Exchange; this exchange trades until 3:15 P.M.

Note: Margins change on a regular basis.

Sources: Adapted from Chicago Board of Trade, "Margins," photocopied, 1991; and Chicago Mercantile Exchange, "Minimum Performance Bond/Margin Requirements and Contract Specifications," photocopied, 1991.

EXAMPLE 3-1: Margins and Marking-to-Market

The following examples illustrate how initial margins, maintenance margins, and marking-to-market interact to affect the cash flows from a futures transaction. Here we provide examples for a speculator who purchases a futures contract on stock index futures and sells a Eurodollar futures contract. A similar table is applicable for hedgers or spreaders, since margins and marking-to-market affect all transactions by those who are not at the exchange, regardless of the type of trader. Traders on the exchanges do not need to post initial margins, since their positions are marked-to-market each day. Margins listed in Tables 3-1 and 3-2 are employed in these examples. Margin balances that fall below the maintenance margin are identified within the table. In these cases a margin call occurs and the trader must restore the margin account to the initial margin level.

Long S&P 500 Stock Index Futures

Date	Settle Price	Underlying Value of the Contract	Mark-to-Market Amount (Change in Value)	Margin Account Balance
8/9	385.65	$192,825		$22,000
8/16	376.25	188,125	$-4,700	17,300
8/23	366.35	183,175	-4,950	12,350
8/30	351.45	175,725	-7,450	4,900[a]
9/6	340.20	170,100	-5,625	16,375
9/13	336.80	168,400	-1,700	14,675

[a] The margin balance falls below the maintenance margin of $9,000, and therefore additional funds must be deposited to bring the balance back up to $22,000.

Short Eurodollar Futures

Date	Settle Index	Mark-to-Market Amount (Change in Value)	Margin Account Balance
8/16	93.99		$540
8/23	93.87	$ 300	840
8/30	93.98	-275	565
9/6	94.09	-275	290[a]
9/13	94.20	-275	265[a]
9/20	94.17	75	615
9/27	94.34	-425	190[a]

[a] The margin balance falls below the maintenance margin of $400, and therefore additional funds must be deposited to bring the balance back up to $540.

balance, with the customer being liable for any losses in excess of the margin amount placed with the brokerage house.

Price Limits

The Concept of Price Limits. *Price limits* reflect the maximum amount a futures price can change in one day. No trading can occur outside the daily price limit, although trading can continue within the allowed daily price range. The argument for supporting price limits is that they allow time for the market to assimilate and evaluate major events without causing large swings as the result of speculative panic. In addition, the existence of price limits allows the brokerage houses time to collect additional margin money from customers to cover losses from the large market moves. Without price limits, the brokerage houses might liquidate customers' positions during the day to reduce losses, which would put additional pressure on prices. Thus, some market regulators argue that without price limits the combination of large speculative price fluctuations and high leverage would cause many market participants to be forced out of the market with huge losses, only to find that the price move had been exaggerated, with prices subsequently moving back to a more appropriate price level.

Ma, Rao, and Sears[2] examine the price adjustments of futures contracts after they hit a limit. They find no significant difference between the price level before hitting the limit versus the price in the following market period of trading. Thus, Ma, Rao, and Sears conclude that *excess* demand/supply does *not* delay additional trading in the futures. This suggests that the volatility that activates price limits is related to traders *overreaction* to price movements. Consequently, they conclude that price limits are not detrimental to the pricing function of futures markets.[3]

Limit Effects and Variable Price Limits. Even though price limit moves are relatively rare, sometimes they have been more of a difficulty for futures markets than a benefit. For example, during the severe winter freeze of 1980-81, the damage to the orange groves in Florida caused orange juice concentrate futures to increase by 70 cents per pound over a seven-day period. Although growers assessed the damage within two days, the 10-cent daily

---

2 Christopher K. Ma, Ramesh P. Rao, and R. Stephen Sears, "Limit Moves and Price Resolution: The Case of the Treasury Bond Futures Market," *The Journal of Futures Markets*, Vol. 9, No. 4, August 1989, pp. 321-336. Christopher K. Ma, Ramesh P. Rao, and R. Stephen Sears, "Volatility, Price Resolution, and the Effectiveness of Price Limits," *Journal of Financial Services Research*, Vol. 3, No. 2/3, December 1989, pp. 165-200.

3 Brennan develops a theory of the existence of price limits. First, he argues that neither prevention of excessive price changes nor daily resettlement of margins is an adequate reason for the existence of price limits. He argues that closing a market to reduce panic and large price changes creates other problems. Moreover, the existence of price limits for most futures markets does not explain why other futures markets and other speculative markets do not have limits, or why an entire day has to pass before the limits are revised. (In fact, stock index futures now have price limits that change *within* the day.) Brennan also argues that the daily settlement procedure does not completely explain the existence of limits, since not all futures have price limits (it would explain, though, why certain futures have price limits but other markets do not). Brennan's theory of price limits is that they exist as a partial substitute for margin requirements; that is, the initial margin deposit can be reduced when price limits provide daily resettlement before default is contemplated by traders. Thus, such limits reduce the information to traders concerning the total potential losses, thereby reducing the likelihood of default. (See Michael J. Brennan, "A Theory of Price Limits in Futures Markets," *The Journal of Financial Economics*, Vol. 16, No. 2, June 1986, pp. 213-233.)

FOCUS 3-1: Circuit Breakers for Stock Index Futures

Price limits existed for stock index futures when these futures started trading in 1982. However, these limits were removed soon after these contracts started to trade. Even though stock index futures operated continuously and reasonably effectively throughout the October 1987 crash, unlike other markets, the events of the crash caused the reintroduction of a type of price limit for these contracts. These new price limits are called "circuit breakers." Circuit breakers take two forms. The first involves price limits that restrict the size of the opening price change (either up or down) as well as limiting trading beyond the price limit if the market *falls* a designated amount. If the price limits are hit after the open, then prices cannot change more than the limit for a specified period of time (e.g., 30 minutes, one hour, or two hours). For example, the S&P 500 contract has a series of circuit breakers, including a 12-point circuit breaker that stays in effect for 30 minutes. Table 3-1 lists the circuit breaker price limits.

The second part of the circuit breaker system is related to NYSE rules concerning trading halts for stocks and restrictions on program trading. If stocks stop trading, futures trading also is halted. The restrictions and halts are as follows:

- If the Dow increases or decreases by 50 points, then all program trades executed (index arbitrage trades) must help to *stabilize* prices (e.g. if stock prices are falling, then orders must be purchase orders). This rule is in effect for the rest of the day, unless the Dow retracts by 25 points.
- If the S&P 500 futures decline by 12 points, then a "sidecar" becomes effective: *any* program trading order entered via the computer system is held up for five minutes. In addition, there is a prohibition on new "stop" orders from institutions or "stop" orders from individuals for more than 2,000 shares.
- If the Dow declines by 250 points, then trading is halted in stocks and futures for one hour.
- If the Dow declines 400 points, then the markets close for two hours.

These rules, though complicated, were put into place to reduce potential adverse effects of computer-based program trading and to reduce panic selling. Although the effectiveness of such circuit breakers has not been proved, they are one result of the market crash that traders must accommodate.

---

price limit on orange juice futures ($1,500 per contract) kept the futures price from rising to the level where trading would resume until seven trading days had passed. Since no one would sell orange juice futures during this upward price adjustment period, no trading took place, forcing short traders to place increasing amounts of funds into their margin accounts to cover their losing positions.

During the period when price limits are affecting the futures markets, the hedging and pricing activities associated with these markets also are inoperative, negating these important benefits of futures. Consequently, variable price limits reduce the delay effect of sequential daily limits on futures price adjustments. Variable price limits cause the size of the daily limit to increase once the futures contract has experienced a normal price limit move for a given number of days. Although the variable limit rule differs from one exchange to another, a general rule is that after a futures contract has hit a limit move for one or two days, then the limit is expanded to 150 percent of the initial price limit and then to 200 percent of the initial limit.[4] In addition, many futures contracts do not have daily price limits during the month of **delivery**. Hence these futures expirations immediately react to major factors affecting the cash markets.[5]

Basis, Basis Risk, and Convergence

Basis is the difference between the price of a cash investment and the price of the relevant futures contract (i.e., $P_C - P_F$). **Basis risk** is the price *variability* between the cash price and the futures price; that is, it represents the extent to which the basis changes. The extent of this basis risk shows how effective a hedge is between the cash security and the futures contract. For example, extensive basis risk (a poor hedge) can occur when an over-the-counter stock portfolio is hedged with the S&P 500 futures contract. Thus, if the relationship between the values for these two types of portfolios change (i.e., the basis changes), then the risk reduction obtained from hedging the over-the-counter stock position is limited.

Convergence is the movement in the price of the underlying cash security toward the futures price as the delivery or expiration date of the futures contract approaches. Until delivery, the time value of money causes the futures and cash price to differ.[6] As convergence occurs, the basis between the cost price and futures price becomes smaller. The futures and cash prices *must* converge at delivery, otherwise an **arbitrageur** could buy the lower-priced instrument (e.g., the cash security) and sell the higher-priced instrument (e.g., the futures contract), using the delivery process to obtain risk-free profits. Similarly, before expiration the cash and futures prices differ only by the time value of money plus an amount attributable to unique factors of the futures contract. Figure 3-1 shows how the convergence of the basis occurs over time between the S&P 500 futures and the associated cash index. Since the futures price is above the cash index, the basis $(P_C - P_F)$ is negative. Notice that the convergence is not smooth over time.

---

4   Although actual price limit rules change occasionally, the current rules are as follows: (1) Chicago Board of Trade: if a financial futures contract hits a limit price for one day, then 150 percent of the original price limit applies for each of the three subsequent consecutive days; this rule becomes effective only if the futures prices hit a limit for each of three of the contract months of the current calendar year (or two expiration months if only two are being traded). (2) Chicago Mercantile Exchange: if a futures contract hits a limit price for two days in a row, then 150 percent of the original limit price applies for the third day *if* any expiration month hits a limit price on the second day, with 200 percent of the original limit price applying for the fourth day if any expiration hits a limit price on the third day; the 200 percent limit applies until no expiration month hits a limit.

5   When limits are in force, then traders often move to other markets. For example, on October 19, 1987, the T-bond futures contract hit its limit. Traders then switched to options on T-bond futures.

6   The time value of money—equivalently, the cost of carrying the cash security until the futures expire—includes the interest cost of the funds used to purchase the cash security plus the storage cost for nonfinancial assets. Part II covers cost of carry pricing.

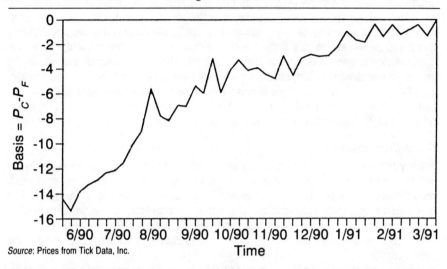

FIGURE 3-1: Convergence of the Basis: S&P Futures

Source: Prices from Tick Data, Inc.

Exact convergence to zero when trading ceases for "cash delivery" futures exists by design. Some futures contracts such as the stock index futures, Eurodollar futures, and the municipal bond futures contracts are settled in *cash*; that is, the price of the futures contract is set equal to the cash asset price at the end of the last day of trading. An arbitrageur who holds the equivalent of the cash index therefore would experience the desired convergence to zero of the difference between the cash and futures prices. There are two benefits to cash delivery. First, it avoids problems in obtaining the exact cash asset needed to correspond to the futures contract. For example, to deliver the S&P 500 basket one would need all 500 stocks in the index *and* hold them in the exact weights these stocks appear in the index. Second, cash delivery reduces unusual supply and demand pressures on the cash assets near the expiration period of the futures contract. In general, cash positions having characteristics that differ from the futures contract encounter significant basis risk.

Making Trades and the Clearinghouse

Futures transactions are completed at specific physical locations known as futures exchanges. The major financial futures exchanges are the Chicago Board of Trade (CBT), The Chicago Mercantile Exchange (CMEX), The New York Futures Exchange (NYFE), The Commodity Exchange (COMEX) in New York, and The London Futures Exchange (LIFFE).[7] A completed futures transaction is legally a transaction between the market participant and the exchange **clearinghouse**. This association is made for two reasons. First, if one side of the trade defaults, then the other market participant is not adversely

---

7 The Mid-America Exchange (Chicago) deals in smaller futures contracts that mimic the contracts traded on the other exchanges. These minicontracts typically are half the size of the normal contracts.

affected; since the transaction is legally with the exchange clearinghouse, the clearinghouse absorbs the loss on the trade, keeping intact the reputation of the exchange and eliminating the default risk for the nondefaulting market participant. Second, if one side of the open interest contract desires to close its position, then the "closing trade" is accomplished easily in the futures pit (e.g., selling if the trader originally purchased futures, and vice versa). Thus, the closing trade does *not* have to be made with the same individual with whom the position was originally created; rather, it is executed with anyone willing to take a position. Such flexibility with futures trades is possible because the name associated with the con-tract is simply changed on the clearinghouse's books when the trade is accomplished. Consequently, the clearinghouse procedure solves several potentially troublesome problems.

The Delivery Procedure

Delivery is the procedure that forces the price of the futures contract to converge to the cash price when a cash settlement system is not relevant. Cash settlement exists for stock index futures, Eurodollar futures, and municipal bond futures contracts. The specifics of asset delivery are important to arbitrageurs and to those who carry futures positions into the delivery period. Delivery refers to the physical delivery of the underlying cash commodity or security from the seller to the buyer of the futures contract during the expiration of the futures contract.

Physical delivery of agricultural commodities to a specified location involves transporta-tion costs (including insurance and spoilage). Therefore, many agricultural hedgers use the futures markets to hedge the *price* of a commodity, but then cover the futures contract (repurchase the futures) and actually sell their physical commodity in the local cash market. In other words, the purpose of futures markets for commodities is to enhance the transfer-ence of risk, *not* to deliver the commodity. However, some delivery mechanism (or cash settlement procedure) must exist so that the futures contract prices the appropriate cash instrument precisely. Since futures do not promote delivery, most traders believe that less than 2 percent of the open interest of agricultural commodity futures are actually delivered to fulfill these futures contracts. Recent research by Peck and Williams[8] contradicts this belief. They show that sellers deliver 8 percent to 19 percent of the *maximum* open interest for wheat, corn, and soybeans, and 25 percent to 65 percent of the open interest existing on the first day of the futures expiration month for these contracts.

Delivery for interest rate futures involves an inexpensive wire transfer of securities and funds, a much simpler mechanism than for commodity positions. Moreover, interest rate futures are more homogeneous in quality, especially cash T-bills that must have a maturity of either 90, 91, or 92 days. On the other hand, the user (buyer) of an agricultural futures contract may need a specific quality of that commodity for a specific purpose, which does not correspond to the quality priced by the futures contract. Finally, interest rate futures are much easier to arbitrage, with the delivery process being the culmination of the arbitrage transaction. Consequently, delivery for interest rate futures often can be 20 percent or more of the open interest.

---

8 Anne E. Peck and Jeffrey C. Williams, "Deliveries on CBT Wheat, Corn, and Soybean Futures Contracts: 1964-65 to 1988-89," *Food Research Studies*, Vol. 22, No. 2, 1991, pp. 129-225. Anne E. Peck and Jeffrey C. Williams, "Deliveries on Commodities Futures Contracts," *Economic Record*, forthcoming, 1992.

Delivery occurs only during a specified period of time, which varies from one type of futures contract to another. For T-bill futures, the delivery period is three specified days in the month of expiration of the contract. For Treasury bond futures, delivery can occur any day during the expiration month of the contract, at the option of the seller of the futures. Consequently, a speculator with a long futures position must be wary of holding a contract during the delivery period unless he either wants to obtain the underlying cash instrument or is confident that his position is sufficiently down the delivery list where delivery will not immediately take place. Since the long position chosen for delivery is based on the oldest long in existence, those who hold long positions for a lengthy time possess a high probability of having the cash asset delivered into the futures contract. Exhibit 3-1 shows the delivery procedure for buyers and sellers of T-bond futures when the short executes delivery. Delivery can occur on any day in the expiration month.

SPECULATION, HEDGING, AND SPREADING IN FUTURES MARKETS

Open Interest in Futures Markets

Table 3-3 and Figure 3-2 illustrate the speculative, hedging, and spreading activity for a number of financial futures contracts by showing the breakdown of open interest positions within the hedging and speculative categories. The hedging and speculative open interest figures in the table and figure show positions for large reporting traders.

Table 3-3 and Figure 3-2 show which markets have active hedging programs, whether the hedging positions are short or long, and the relative size of the hedging, speculative, and spreading positions. For the larger markets, hedging activity represents the major portion of the open interest. In fact, the long and short hedging activities are approximately balanced for most futures listed in Table 3-3. Figure 3-3 shows that the large hedging (commercial) positions in the S&P futures have grown from 50 percent of the 200 percent of the total positions in 1983 to 140 percent by 1988. Meanwhile, the large speculative (noncommercial) positions have dropped substantially. Smaller (nonreporting) positions also have become less important. In general, the reporting speculative positions do not represent a large proportion of the open interest; that is, relatively few large speculators are active in these markets in relation to the total size of the open interest. Alternatively, a large percentage of the activity can be associated with the nonreporting positions—that is, with speculators, spreaders, hedgers, and arbitrageurs that have positions smaller than the reporting requirements.

Risk, Return, and Diversification with Futures

Bodie and Rosansky[9] compute the historical annual return and risk (standard deviation) for a number of commodity futures contracts based on a deposit of the *entire* value of the futures contract for margin purposes. Table 3-4 shows the average annual return and volatility of these contracts. The two most striking features of these results are:

- The highest and lowest returns for each commodity futures would provide substantial returns and losses, especially if the actual required margins are used.

---

9   Zvi Bodie and Victor Rosansky, "Risk and Return in Commodity Futures," *Financial Analysts Journal*, Vol. 36, No. 3, May-June 1980, pp. 27-39.

EXHIBIT 3-1: T-Bond Futures Delivery Procedure

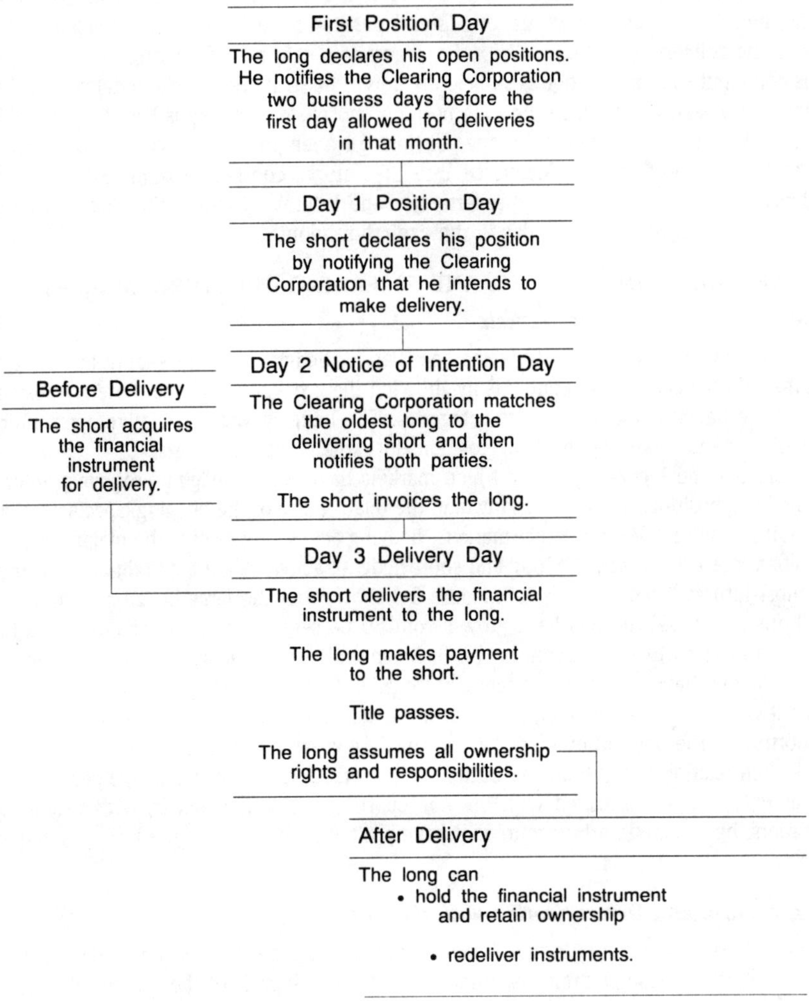

First Position Day

The long declares his open positions.
He notifies the Clearing Corporation
two business days before the
first day allowed for deliveries
in that month.

Day 1 Position Day

The short declares his position
by notifying the Clearing
Corporation that he intends to
make delivery.

Before Delivery

The short acquires
the financial
instrument
for delivery.

Day 2 Notice of Intention Day

The Clearing Corporation matches
the oldest long to the
delivering short and then
notifies both parties.

The short invoices the long.

Day 3 Delivery Day

The short delivers the financial
instrument to the long.

The long makes payment
to the short.

Title passes.

The long assumes all ownership
rights and responsibilities.

After Delivery

The long can
- hold the financial instrument
  and retain ownership

- redeliver instruments.

Source: "Understanding the Delivery Process in Financial Futures," Chicago Board of Trade, p.5.

TABLE 3-3: Reported Speculative, Hedging, and Spreading Futures Activity

Type of Contract	Total Open Interest	Percentage of Open Interest[a]				
		Hedging		Speculative		
		Long	Short	Long	Short	Spread
Stock indexes:						
S&P 500	159,403	69.6	52.7	4.7	22.1	0.3
NYSE	5,012	23.8	14.7	26.2	22.3	1.0
Major Market	8,740	84.6	75.0	6.3	11.6	0.3
Long-term debt:						
T-bond	277,383	50.3	59.1	9.3	4.1	5.4
10-year Note	84,992	44.5	66.0	12.5	1.6	5.9
Muni Bonds	9,075	58.5	59.6	22.3	29.0	0.0
Short-term debt:						
Eurodollar	724,558	54.9	63.6	8.4	1.4	1.9
T-bills	49,757	54.8	73.1	21.5	10.1	0.0

[a] Hedging plus speculative long or short percentages do not total 100 percent because of nonreportable positions.

Source: Adapted from Commodity Futures Trading Commission, "Reportable Positions," November 1991.

FIGURE 3-2: Reported Futures Open Interest

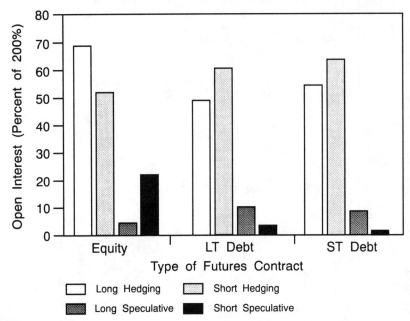

Source: Developed from Table 3-3.

- The large standard deviations (risk) shows the inconsistency of the returns over time.

The Bodie and Rosansky results also show that an equally weighted commodity futures portfolio is comparable to a portfolio of common stocks. This result illustrates the diversification potential of futures contracts; that is, the low or negative correlations between futures eliminates most of the risk inherent in the individual contracts. In fact, a portfolio of 60% stock and 40% commodity futures has a return equivalent to a stock portfolio, but only two-thirds of the risk of the stock portfolio.[10]

---

10 Irwin and Brorsen find that portfolios of public futures funds, common stocks, and T-bills reduced portfolio risk by .6% to 3.7% compared to a stock and T-bill portfolio for the same return. Herbst and McCormack determined that including futures in a portfolio improves only low and moderate return/risk portfolios because of the benefits of low to negative correlations, thereby suggesting that futures are beneficial for risk-adverse investors. See S. H. Irwin and B. W. Brorsen, "Public Futures Funds," *The Journal of Futures Markets*, Vol. 5, No. 3, Fall 1985, pp. 463-485; and Anthony F. Herbst and Joseph P. McCormack, "An Examination of the Risk/Return Characteristics of Portfolios Combining Commodity Futures Contracts with Common Stocks," *The Review of Futures Markets*, Vol. 6, No. 3, 1987, pp. 416-425.

FIGURE 3-3: S&P Proportions of Open Interest

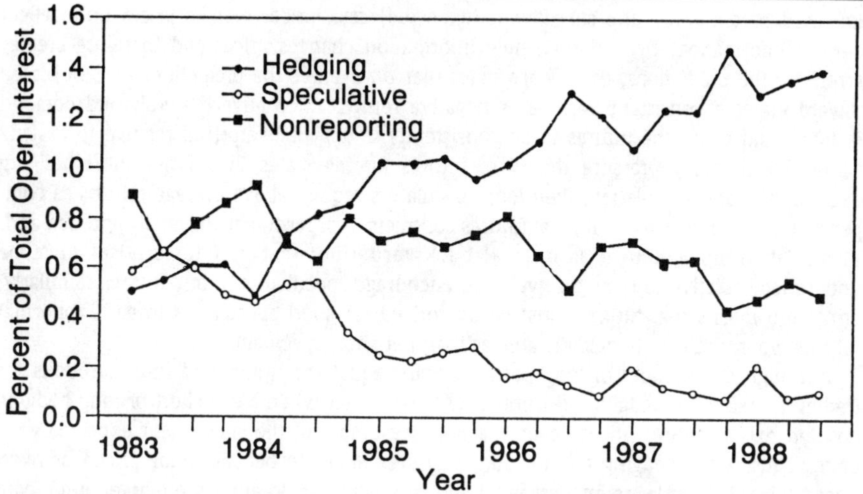

Source: Robert Daigler, "The S&P Index Futures: A Hedging Contract," *CME Financial Strategy Paper*, Chicago Mercantile Exchange, 1990.

TABLE 3-4: Historical Commodity Futures Returns and Risks

Commodity Futures	Mean Return[a]	Standard Deviation	Highest Annual Return	Lowest Annual Return
Wheat	3.18	30.75	113.0	−40.0
Corn	2.13	26.31	101.6	−26.1
Soybeans	13.57	32.32	131.6	−40.5
Potatoes	6.91	42.11	125.0	−73.3
Cotton	8.94	36.24	163.2	−41.2
Orange juice	2.51	31.77	74.5	−32.3
Cocoa	15.71	54.63	197.5	−37.5
Propane	68.26	202.09	559.2	−48.2
Copper	19.79	47.20	130.1	−32.2
Sugar	25.40	116.22	492.0	−71.8

[a] Annual returns (percent per year), 1950-76.

Source: Zvi Bodie and Victor Rosansky, "Risk and Return in Commodity Futures," *Financial Analysts Journal*, Vol. 36, No. 3, May-June 1980, p. 35.

Futures as Unbiased (or Biased) Predictors of Cash Prices

One view of futures prices as a forecast of subsequent cash prices is that futures provide an unbiased prediction of the subsequent (expected) cash price; that is, prices only reflect current information. Even though new information changes prices and therefore creates errors for the predictions, this theory states that *on average* the predictions are not biased toward either a consistent positive or negative return. Alternatively, supply and demand factors could cause the futures to be consistently under- or overpriced relative to its true value. The hedging pressure theory of futures pricing states that if net short hedging exceeds net long speculation, then long speculators require above average returns as compensation for purchasing additional futures contracts in order to equate supply and demand. This relationship is known as **normal backwardation**; that is, futures prices must be underpriced relative to their true value to encourage speculators to buy futures. Similarly, **contango** means that futures must be overpriced for short speculators to earn abnormal returns when net long hedging is greater than net short speculation.

Although the number of long positions *must* equal the number of short positions for trading to exist, the hedging pressure theory states that when a *net* short or long hedging position exists, futures prices become a biased estimate of the subsequent expected cash price. Thus, a net hedging position forces futures prices to become underpriced or overpriced (biased) in order to encourage additional speculators to enter the market and create the needed activity to offset the hedgers' activity in the market. Figure 3-4 illustrates the effect of a supply/demand imbalance of open interest on futures prices. When net **short hedgers** predominate (points A and B on Figure 3-4), then net long speculators are needed to balance open interest. In this case of normal backwardation the current futures price is below the expected future cash price. Conversely, when net long hedging predominates (points C and D) then net short speculation is needed and the current futures price lies above the expected future cash price.

Keynes[11] and Hicks[12] developed the normal backwardation and contango concepts. They stated that futures typically have net short speculators; in other words, futures prices typically create excess returns for long speculators due to the normal backwardation of futures markets. The issue of excess returns for speculators, or equivalently whether futures provide *on average* an unbiased or biased prediction of subsequent cash prices, has received substantial interest in the literature.

Two early and well-known studies of whether futures are an unbiased or biased predictor of subsequent cash prices are by Houthakker[13] and Rockwell.[14] Although they employed similar methodologies, Houthakker concluded normal backwardation existed, whereas

---

11 John Maynard Keynes, *Treatise on Money*, 2nd ed. London: Macmillan, 1930, pp. 142-144.

12 J. R. Hicks, *Value and Capital*, 2d ed. Oxford: Oxford University Press, 1946, Chap. 10.

13 H. S. Houthakker, "Can Speculators Forecast Prices?" *The Review of Economics and Statistics*, Vol. 39, No. 1, 1957, pp. 143-151.

14 C. Rockwell, "Normal Backwardation, Forecasting and Returns to Commodity Futures Traders," *Food Research Institute Studies*, Vol. 7 Supplement, 1967, pp. 107-130.

FIGURE 3-4: The Effect of Net Open Interest on Futures Prices

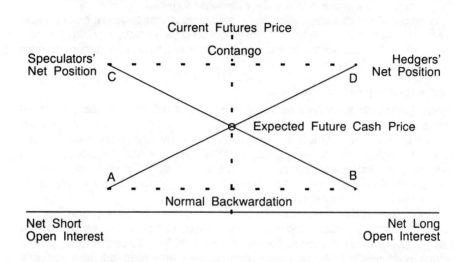

Rockwell's study of a larger set of data states the opposite conclusion. Fama and French[15] find weak support for normal backwardation. One of the most complete studies on normal backwardation is by Murphy and Hilliard,[16] who conclude that normal backwardation does *not* exist after 1974. Kolb[17] uses nearly one million daily futures prices to determine that only 7 of 29 futures show evidence of normal backwardation or contango, with currencies and debt futures providing unbiased estimates of the subsequent cash prices (stock index futures are not examined). Although Bodie and Rosansky[18] support normal backwardation by finding positive returns for 22 of 23 commodities, only three of these turned out to be statistically significant. Hartzmark[19] finds that speculators lose money overall, which is inconsistent with normal backwardation and contango. Phillips and Weiner[20] use intraday

15 Eugene F. Fama and Kenneth French, "Commodity Futures Prices: Some Evidence on Forecast Power, Premiums, and the Theory of Storage," *Journal of Business*, Vol. 60, No. 1, January 1987, pp. 55-73.

16 Austin Murphy and Jimmy E. Hilliard, "An Investigation into the Equilibrium Structure of the Commodity Futures Market Anomaly," *The Financial Review*, Vol. 24, No. 1, February 1989, pp. 1-18.

17 Robert W. Kolb, "Is Normal Backwardation Normal?" *The Journal of Futures Markets*, Vol. 12, No. 1, February 1992, pp. 75-91.

18 Zvi Bodie and Victor Rosansky, "Risk and Return in Commodity Futures," *Financial Analysts Journal*, Vol. 36, No. 3, May-June 1980, pp. 27-39.

19 Michael L. Hartzmark, "Returns to Individual Traders of Futures: Aggregate Results," *Journal of Political Economy*, Vol. 95, No. 6, December 1987, pp. 1292-1306.

20 Gordon M. Phillips and Robert J. Weiner, "Trading Performance in Forward Markets: A Microdata Test of Normal Backwardation," Center for the Study of Futures Markets Working Paper No. 217, Columbia University, July 1991.

trades in the petroleum forward markets to determine that no identifiable group of traders make significant profits using daily prices. However, using within-the-day transactions data, the Japanese trading houses with superior *information* do profit.

In general, the studies noted above and other studies relating to normal backwardation are not consistent in their conclusions. However, most of the evidence, especially the more recent evidence, rejects normal backwardation in favor of futures as an unbiased estimate of the subsequent cash price.[21]

The Accuracy of Futures Prediction

Futures can provide an unbiased prediction of subsequent cash prices *on average*, but still can cause large errors in the prediction process. In fact, even if the futures and cash markets include all current information, market participants are not able to anticipate all future economic developments accurately. Thus, the actual cash price when the futures contract expires differs from the estimated price provided by the futures contract during its trading life because of the availability of new information. The question is: how *variable* is the futures forecast of subsequent cash prices?

MacDonald and Hein,[22] Hegde and McDonald,[23] and Howard,[24] among others, examine the relative ability of futures interest rates to predict accurately the subsequent cash interest rates at futures expiration. Figure 3-5 shows the results from Howard, which compares futures, no-change, and "best time series" forecasts of the subsequent cash interest rates for various weeks before futures expirations.[25] The mean absolute percentage error (MAPE) between the futures interest rate and the actual interest rate is 8.24% for a time horizon of four weeks and increases rapidly to 15.41% for 12 weeks. Obviously, the forecasting ability of futures is limited, especially as the time to expiration of the futures contract lengthens. However, for periods of eight weeks or longer, the futures forecasts are superior to both the no-change forecast and to the "best time series" estimate, with the superiority of the futures forecasts increasing as the time horizon increases. These results differ from earlier studies

---

21 In addition, Table 3-4 and Figures 3-6 and 3-7 illustrate that the reportable long and short hedging positions for financial futures contracts often have net hedging positions that are near zero. This fact negates the key assumption of the normal backwardation/contango concepts for financial futures. However, no in-depth study of the net reportable hedging positions has been undertaken for financial futures contracts.

22 S. Scott MacDonald and Scott Hein, "Future Rates and Forward Rates as Predictors of Near-Term Treasury Bill Rates," *The Journal of Futures Markets*, Vol. 9, No. 3, June 1989, pp. 249-262.

23 Shantaram P. Hegde and Bill McDonald, "On the Informational Role of Treasury Bill Futures," *The Journal of Futures Markets*, Vol. 6, No. 4, Winter 1986, pp. 629-644.

24 Charles T. Howard, "Are T-bill Futures Good Forecasters of Interest Rates?" *The Journal of Futures Markets*, Vol. 2, No. 4, Winter 1982, pp. 305-315.

25 The "best time series" values are obtained by using the Box-Jenkins procedure, which finds the best-fit equation by employing both an autoregressive (time series regression) and a moving average simultaneously. Forward forecasts provide almost identical, but inferior, forecasts of the cash rate; therefore, the forward forecasts are omitted from the graph. Calculating forward rates is discussed in Chapter 4. MacDonald and Hein (see footnote 22) show that the futures provides superior information to the forward rate for forecasting purposes. The Howard study is emphasized here because of its inclusion of alternative procedures of forecasting the cash interest rate.

by Fama[26] and by Hamburger and Platt,[27] who concluded that a no-change model is superior to a forward contract forecast. However, the Fama and Hamburger and Platt studies employed data from a much less volatile interest rate period: namely, the 1950s and 1960s.[28] Logically, a no-change model would be a less accurate procedure during the volatile period of the late 1970s and early 1980s, the time period employed in the aforementioned study by Howard.

SUMMARY AND LOOKING AHEAD

This chapter has covered the key terminology of futures and the basic strategies used by traders. An understanding of the terminology is needed to comprehend how the markets operate, and the strategies are important to provide an overview of the rest of the book. The reader now has an idea of how the cash and futures markets work and why they are useful. This knowledge now can be employed in studying pricing, arbitrage, and hedging. Part II covers pricing and arbitrage for futures markets, Part III examines hedging, and Part IV applies hedging concepts to specific types of companies.

FIGURE 3-5: T-Bill Futures Forecasting Ability

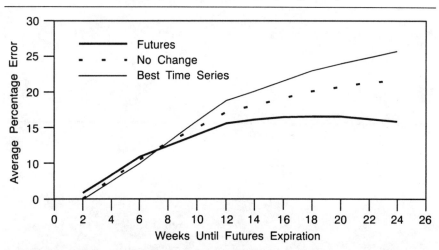

Source: Abstracted from results in Charles T. Howard, "Are T-bill Futures Good Forecasters of Interest Rates?" *The Journal of Futures Markets*, Vol. 2, No. 4, Winter 1982, pp. 305–315.

26 Eugene Fama, "Forward Rates as Predictors of Future Spot Rates," *Journal of Financial Economics*, Vol. 3, No. 4, 1976, pp. 361-372.

27 Michael J. Hamburger and Elliott Platt, "The Expectation Hypothesis and the Efficiency of the Treasury Bill Market," *Review of Economics and Statistics*, Vol. 57, No. 2, 1975, pp. 190-199.

28 The Fama and the Hamburger and Platt studies referenced in footnotes 26 and 27 use forward rates rather than futures. Hedge and McDonald (see footnote 23) show that the R^2 values of regressions between the futures errors and the no-change errors is relatively high for the four weeks before futures expiration, but then drops below 15%. In other words, there is a significant amount of variability around the MAPE value.

Part II

Pricing and Arbitrage

Chapter 4

The Basics of Futures Pricing and Arbitrage

Determining the fair (forward) price of financial futures is important for speculators, hedgers, spreaders, and arbitrageurs. If the actual futures price differs significantly from the fair price, then speculators and hedgers need to alter their trading strategies. Pricing differences are even more important for spreaders and arbitrageurs, since these traders focus on pricing discrepancies to obtain profits.

The pricing and arbitrage processes associated with the cost of carry model link the cash and futures markets via the net financing cost (the financing cost less the cash inflow). For example, the cost of carry model for stock index futures shows that the cash and futures prices should deviate only by the financing cost and the effect of dividends. If the futures are priced correctly (linked to the cash market), then speculators and hedgers can be confident that strategies based on correct cash market analysis will be successful. If futures prices deviate substantially from their fair prices, then arbitrage profits are possible.

Here we discuss the terminology, concepts, and issues involving financial futures pricing and arbitrage, including calculating forward rates and implied financing rates. Subsequent chapters in Part II delve into the specifics of how one prices various financial futures contracts and implements arbitrage strategies.

PRICING AND ARBITRAGE BASICS

Pricing and Arbitrage Building Blocks

The pricing of futures contracts and arbitrage between futures and cash are closely related concepts. The fair price of a futures contract is determined by a pricing model that incorporates the value of the underlying cash asset, the time to expiration of the futures contract, the cost of financing the cash position, the cash inflows of the asset, and any special characteristics of the futures contract at expiration.[1] In perfect markets—that is, when transactions costs and tax effects are not relevant—the actual futures price equals the fair price.

---

1 Costs for physical assets include storage and transportation costs and insurance.

Arbitrage exists when the actual futures price deviates from the fair price by more than transactions costs. When sufficiently large profits above the risk-free return exist, arbitrageurs step in and buy the lower-priced security (e.g., the cash asset) and sell the higher priced security (e.g., the futures contract). Such actions force the futures price back toward the fair price. Without arbitrage, the futures price could deviate significantly from the fair price, causing hedgers to avoid using futures markets because of poor hedging results and the uncertainty of the pricing process.

An illustration of arbitrage will help to clarify the process. Let us use gold futures, since gold is a basic cash asset that does not have cash flows. Assume that on the futures expiration day gold futures are priced at $350 an ounce and cash gold is trading for $345. If trading costs are minimal, an arbitrageur could buy gold in the cash market for $5 less than it is trading in the futures market. The arbitrageur eliminates any chance that the price difference will change between the two markets by having two telephones and talking to both the cash and futures traders of gold at the same time. The arbitrageur then can immediately use the cash gold to fulfill the delivery requirement of the futures contract, making a risk-free and immediate profit. Actions by many arbitrageurs to obtain these risk-free profits would cause the cash and futures prices to converge, since the demand for cash gold forces that price up and the selling of futures forces the futures price down. These actions eliminate the arbitrage profits and cause the futures and cash prices to be equivalent. When a period of time exists before the expiration and delivery period of the futures, then the comparison of prices becomes more complicated. In this case the arbitrageur must consider the cost of financing the position via the cost of carry model described below.

The pricing of futures is based on one key concept: *significant deviations from the fair price should not be possible if the futures and cash markets are effectively linked together.* Arbitrage strategies provide the mechanism that **integrates the cash and futures markets**. The cost of carry model determines the fair futures price in terms of the variables that influence this price.

The Cost of Carry Model

The cost of carry model explains the relationship between the cash asset price and futures price. Simply stated, this model shows the relationship created between these markets when an arbitrageur buys the cash asset now, holds and finances the asset with borrowed funds for the life of the futures contract, and then delivers the cash asset into the futures contract when the futures expire. Under these circumstances Equation (4-1) determines the fair futures price:

$$P_{FAIR} = P_C (1 + i)^t \qquad (4\text{-}1)$$

where P_{FAIR} = the fair price for the futures

P_C = current price of the cash asset

i = the financing rate (interest rate)

t = the proportion of the year until the futures expire

In a perfect market P_{FAIR} should equal the current futures price.

Using gold provides a good example of how the cost of carry relationship works. For example, an arbitrageur purchases gold (with borrowed funds) and sells gold futures. The gold is held until the futures expire, at which time the gold is delivered into the futures contract. An example of the cash flows for this relationship is given in Exhibit 4-1. This procedure of buying the cash asset and holding it until futures expiration causes the futures price to be a function of the cash price, the time until futures expiration, and the financing cost. This price relationship exists because the arbitrageur buys the lower-priced gold and sells the higher-priced futures contract so that futures prices do not deviate significantly from the fair futures price. (One also could sell gold and buy the futures.) Similarly, the cost of carry model explains pricing for agricultural futures markets. Thus, a grain merchant sells the futures contract, buys wheat with the use of borrowed money, stores the wheat until the futures expire, and then delivers the wheat into the futures contract.[2]

The cost of carry model for financial futures works in a similar manner. For example, a money manager purchases a portfolio of common stocks that is equivalent to the S&P 500 index, sells the corresponding futures contract, and then holds the position until the futures expire. The important difference in contrast to the gold and agricultural examples is that stock index futures are settled in cash; that is, the futures index is set equal to the cash index at the end of the last trading day for the futures. Thus, one must sell the cash common stocks when the futures expire rather than deliver them into the futures contract. The pricing of interest rate futures contracts is more complicated due to their delivery procedure. The remaining chapters in Part II examine these issues.

EXHIBIT 4-1: Cash Flows for the Cost of Carry Model

To illustrate how cash flows explain the cost of carry equation let us use the following prices and interest rates:

Price of gold	$350
Futures price of gold (expiration and delivery in one year)	$385
Interest rate for financing	10%

Transaction	Cash Flow at Time = 0	Cash Flow at Time = 1 Year
Borrow $350 for one year at 10%	$+350	$-385
Buy one ounce of gold at cash price	-350	
Sell futures contract at t = 0 (P = 385) for delivery of gold at t = 1	0	+385
Total cash flow	$ 0	$ 0

This exhibit illustrates that the cost of carry equation $P_{FAIR} = P_C (1 + i)^t$ equates the cash flows from the futures and the cash transactions.

---

2 For wheat futures, the financing cost includes both the cost of borrowed funds *and* the cost of storing the wheat. If merchants who store the wheat use their own funds to finance the cash asset, then the financing cost measures the opportunity cost of funds for the merchant rather than the interest rate on borrowed funds.

FOCUS 4-1: Impediments to Pricing Futures: Squeezes and Large Trades

The cost of carry model shows that futures prices are linked to the underlying cash value, the financing rate, any cash inflows, and the time to futures expiration. However, when traders attempt to squeeze the market by obtaining a large portion of the cash asset, unusual pricing and volatility can result. Similarly, large volume also creates havoc in the markets. Several famous attempted squeezes and large volume situations are described below.

• **The Russian Wheat Deal.** In the early 1970s the Soviets purchased massive quantities of U.S. wheat and corn by separate secret deals with U.S. grain dealers. These dealers hedged their sales in the futures market. The resulting wheat shortage in the U.S. caused prices to increase significantly. Farmers who had hedged their crop with forwards and futures were locked in to the agreed-upon price. Since the futures market price increased before harvest time, futures were blamed for the higher wheat prices. A similar situation occurred in the late 1980s when drought in the Midwest caused prices to rise on the futures exchanges before harvest, which encouraged stores to increase the price of wheat products *before* the harvest. These actions by the stores created yet another charge that futures traders *caused* higher prices for food.

• **The Potato Default.** Potato futures require the delivery of Maine potatoes. However, the majority of potatoes are grown in Idaho and surrounding states. In 1976 two major Idaho potato producers, J. R. Simplot and the Taggares family, sold futures contracts to deliver 50 million potatoes. They assumed that the large supply of Idaho potatoes would cause prices to fall. However, those who purchased the futures bought up most of the *Maine* potatoes, creating a short squeeze. Simplot and the Taggares chose to default rather than pay off the long futures positions. After long court battles, no one emerged as a winner.

• **Silver and the Hunts.** The Hunt Brothers purchased millions of ounces of silver and silver futures contracts, causing the price to increase substantially. Although a large amount of silver existed, only a small portion met the standards needed for delivery into a futures contract. The Hunts made millions of dollars by selling contracts and taking delivery. Feeling successful, they attempted to play the game again in 1979 and 1980. Prices rose from $8 an ounce to $50 an ounce. As prices increased, the Hunts used the profits from these positions to purchase additional contracts. This time the CFTC and the exchanges stepped in, ordering high margins and a liquidation of the Hunts' position. The selling of the cash and futures holdings in silver caused prices to fall to $5 an ounce.

• **Soybeans and the Hunts.** The Hunts began purchasing soybeans when their advisors predicted a shortage of protein, of which soybeans are a major source. The Hunts purchased a total of 24 million bushels of soybeans. The CFTC argued the Hunts acted as one group and therefore were subject to the position limits discussed in Chapter 3—namely three million bushels. While court cases ensued, the Hunts were told merely not to collaborate again. Meanwhile, Cook Industries (a large commodities firm in Memphis) analyzed that soybeans were overpriced. While their analysis was eventually correct, Cook went bankrupt holding onto short futures positions as soybean prices rose.

Arbitrage Concepts

Arbitrage, the existence of risk-free profits, is illustrated by the cash flow relationships presented in Exhibit 4-2. This example shows the "cash and carry" relationship given in the cost of carry model; here the cash gold is purchased, "carried" in storage, then delivered into the short futures position. The difference between Exhibits 4-2 and 4-1 is the arbitrage profit obtained in Exhibit 4-2 resulting from $P_F > P_C (1 + i)^t$; that is, $P_F > P_{FAIR}$.

Similarly, Exhibit 4-3 shows how to profit when $P_F < P_C (1 + i)^t$, that is, $P_F < P_{FAIR}$. In this case, the arbitrageur sells gold short, and the cash proceeds from the short sale are lent out to receive interest; when the long futures position expires, the gold received is used to fulfill the short sale.

The above examples are often described as "perfect arbitrage," since perfect markets without transactions costs are assumed to exist. The examples above and the cost of carry Equation (4-1) can be extended to include transactions costs. Thus, with transactions costs, arbitrage exists if a profit can be made by satisfying the following equation:

$$P_C(1 + i)^t + T < P_F < P_C(1 + i)^t - T \qquad (4\text{-}2)$$

where P_F = the futures price as determined by the market

  T = transactions costs per unit of the cash asset

Note that if $P_C(1 + i)^t + T < P_F$ then the arbitrageur purchases the less expensive cash asset and sells short the more expensive futures. If $P_F < P_C(1 + i)^t - T$, then the less expensive futures contract is purchased and the cash asset is sold. If neither case exists (i.e., P_F lies within the inequality bounds), then no arbitrage is possible.

An arbitrageur can hold a position until the expiration of the futures contract, when either physical delivery is implemented or the cash settlement procedure forces the arbitrageur to cover the futures position. However, the arbitrageur does not have to wait until the

---

EXHIBIT 4-2: Cash and Carry Arbitrage

Price of gold		$350
Futures price of gold (expiration and delivery in one year)		$387
Interest rate for financing		10%

Transaction	Cash Flow at Time = 0	Cash Flow at Time = 1 Year
Borrow $350 for one year at 10%	$+350	$−385
Buy one ounce of gold at cash price	−350	
Sell futures contract at t = 0 (P = 387) for delivery of gold at t = 1	0	+387
Total cash flow	$ 0	$ 2

This exhibit shows how risk-free profits are obtained when the futures price is above the fair futures price.

EXHIBIT 4-3: Reverse Cash and Carry Arbitrage

Price of gold		$350
Futures price of gold (expiration and delivery in one year)		$382
Interest rate for financing		10%

Transaction	Cash Flow at Time = 0	Cash Flow at Time = 1 Year
Sell short one ounce of gold	$+350	
Lend proceeds from the short sale for one year at 10%	−350	$+385
Buy futures contract at t = 0 (P = 382) and receive delivery of gold at t = 1	0	−382
Use gold received at t = 1 to cover short sale		0
Total cash flow	$ 0	$ 3

This exhibit shows how risk-free profits are made when the futures price is below the fair futures price.

---

expiration of the futures contract in order to liquidate the arbitrage transaction. If the difference between the futures price and the cost of carry forward price narrows significantly before the futures expire, then it often is beneficial to reverse the futures and cash positions and take the profits on the position. Although these profits may be less than would be the case if the arbitrageur waited until the expiration of the futures, these funds will be available for executing other arbitrage trades. Such "temporary" arbitrage positions are often taken in the stock index futures market, where the differences between the futures and forward prices often change significantly, even within the day. In general, profitable arbitrage positions exist for only a short time before disappearing. Such transactions also require large amounts of funds and exchange floor contacts to achieve effective execution of the trade.

Pure and Quasi-Arbitrage

Pure Arbitrage. **Pure arbitrage** exists when funds are borrowed to complete the arbitrage transaction. For pure arbitrage the transaction must consider the cost of borrowed funds, transactions costs, and the size of the difference between the futures and cash prices. This type of arbitrage is employed frequently for interest rate and currency futures markets.

The interest rate associated with the cost of financing T-bond and T-bill arbitrage is often the **repurchase (repo) rate**. The repo rate is the interest rate on short-term funds, where the funds are backed by government securities. The borrower of funds for the repo agreement provides the government securities as collateral, with the borrower promising to "repurchase" these securities at a later date and pay interest on the funds. An arbitrage transaction is profitable when the return on the pure arbitrage transaction before considering the financing costs is greater than the repo rate associated with the financing.

Quasi-Arbitrage. **Quasi-arbitrage** exists when internal funds are employed to execute the arbitrage transaction. Quasi-arbitrage is a viable transaction when the futures-cash arbitrage provides higher returns than an equivalent cash security investment. For example, quasi-arbitrage exists when a manager obtains a higher return with a T-bill futures quasi-arbitrage than with an equivalent maturity cash T-bill investment. This strategy is also known as an alternative return strategy.

Another example of an alternative return or quasi-arbitrage strategy using futures is to buy stocks that are equivalent to the S&P 500 index and sell futures. If this strategy provides a return above a T-bill or similar risk-free rate, then the arbitrage position obtains a higher alternative return.

Trading costs and the size of the difference between the futures and cash prices are the important factors that determine whether a quasi-arbitrage transaction is preferable to a cash-only position. In reality, the implementation of quasi-arbitrage transactions is less frequent than pure arbitrage transactions when interest rate securities are involved. Quasi-arbitrage is less frequent because the portfolio manager must decide whether quasi-arbitrage is a preferable portfolio strategy to simply selling the cash instrument. The lack of familiarity with futures markets by most financial institutions and some money managers is the main reason for a lack of quasi-arbitrage activity for debt instruments. The reluctance to execute quasi-arbitrage strategies, in conjunction with the widespread use of pure arbitrage, typically results in profits for those who do engage in quasi-arbitrage strategies.

On the other hand, quasi-arbitrage is the dominant strategy for stock index futures strategies. Pension funds and other large pools of funds employ stock futures arbitrage to earn returns above the risk-free return. Brokerage houses often do not operate pure arbitrage programs because of the availability of higher-yielding alternative uses for these funds and because of pressure to avoid arbitrage transactions.

Restrictions on Arbitrage Profits

The Factors. The previous discussion on arbitrage identifies transactions costs as an impediment to profitable transactions. Let us identify the components of transactions costs and other restrictions to profitable arbitrage transactions. Such restrictions are:

- Transactions costs: commissions to brokers, fees to the exchange, and bid-ask spreads. The bid-ask spread is the cost of buying from a dealer at the higher ask price and selling at the bid price.
- Short selling restrictions: when the cash asset is sold short for reverse cash and carry transactions, then our example assumes that all of the proceeds are available to invest in an interest-bearing security. Often, only part (or none) of the funds are available to the short seller. In addition, short sellers of stock must wait for an "uptick" in the stock price to execute a short sale.
- Borrowing funds: the cash and carry transactions assume that the entire cost of the asset can be borrowed. Arbitrageurs using repurchase transactions for debt futures typically

obtain 90 percent to 100 percent of the asset's value. However, only 50 percent of stock purchases can be financed.

- Equal borrowing and lending rates: Equations (4-1) and (4-2) assume that the cost of borrowing funds for a cash and carry transaction equals the interest received on depositing funds for a reverse cash and carry transaction. This often is not the case.
- Interest received or paid on marking-to-market: Equations (4-1) and (4-2) treat futures as a forward contract; that is, no intermediate cash flows occur. The next paragraph describes the effects of marking-to-market.

Marking-to-Market and Variable Interest Rates. Cash transactions are not marked-to-market. However, futures prices are marked-to-market on a daily basis for all traders; that is, an additional deposit equal to any loss must be made, and profits can be withdrawn, both on a daily basis. If additional funds to cover losses are made in cash, then the trader must finance these funds. This financing typically is calculated at the current short-term interest rate. Similarly, profits can be withdrawn and invested at the short-term interest rate. If the *daily* interest rate is used for financing and investment purposes, then the unpredictable variability of interest rates affects the overall profitability of the futures arbitrage transaction. However, if the arbitrage uses Treasury securities to cover the margin calls, then the effect of **variable interest rates** is mitigated.

STOCK INDEX FUTURES PRICING AND ARBITRAGE

The basic cost of carry model given in Equation (4-1) can be amended for stock index futures to consider the dividends received from holding the stocks in the index:

$$P_{FAIR} = P_C (1 + i)^t - D \tag{4-3}$$

where P_{FAIR} = the fair futures price for a stock index

P_C = the current value of the underlying cash stock index

i = the financing rate of interest or equivalent investment return desired

D = the dollar dividend amount in index points received on the stocks in the index from now until the expiration of the futures contract[3]

t = number of days until expiration of the futures divided by 365

For example, if $P_C = 400.00$, $i = 5\%$, $t = \frac{1}{4}$ year, and $D = 3.0$ index points over the next three months, then

$$P_{FAIR} = 400 (1 + .05)^{.25} - 3 = 401.91$$

Equation (4-3) illustrates both the relationship between the futures and current cash values and the net difference between the financing (or opportunity) costs and the income received. In particular, the larger the difference between interest cost and dividends, the larger the price difference between P_{FAIR} and P_C. In addition, the larger the value of t, the larger the price difference between the futures and cash prices.

Figure 4-1 illustrates the difference between the S&P 500 futures price and the fair price for five-minute intervals during February 1988. Equation (4-3) is used to calculate the fair

---

3   Theoretically, the futures value of these dividends until contract expiration is appropriate here. However, the difficulty of calculating the dividends and the uncertainty of the dividends makes the present value calculation less useful in reality. Chapter 5 presents an alternative dividend yield model that considers continuously compounded values.

price, with the S&P cash index being employed for P_C. The figure shows that many of the futures prices are within .5 index points of the fair price, with very few observations being more than 1.0 index points from the fair value. However, there is a tendency late in the month for the futures price to be above the fair price; that is, the points in the figure are above 0. Chapter 5 discusses stock index pricing and arbitrage issues, and helps to explain why differences from the fair price exist and whether arbitrage is possible. The chapter includes examples on stock index pricing and arbitrage.

FORWARD AND IMPLIED REPO RATES: THE FOUNDATION OF DEBT ARBITRAGE

The pricing and arbitrage of interest rate futures contracts is based on the calculation of **forward rates** and the comparison of these rates with the futures interest rates. If the difference between the forward and futures rates is large enough to cover transactions costs, then arbitrage is possible. Short-term interest rate futures rely on the forward rate and similar calculations to determine the pricing accuracy of the futures and whether arbitrage exists. Long-term interest rate futures start with forward rate calculations and then consider factors unique to these futures contracts. This section illustrates how to calculate and use

FIGURE 4-1: S&P Futures – Fair Price: February 1988

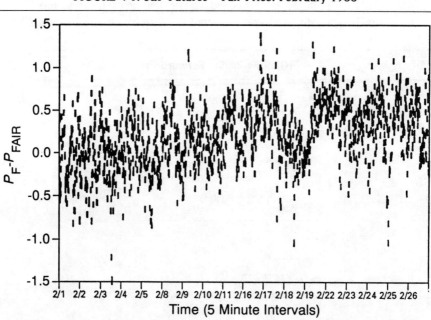

Source: Data from Robert T. Daigler, "Stock Index Arbitrage with Intraday Data," working paper, Florida International University, 1991, and from Tick Data, Inc.

forward rates for pricing and arbitrage. Subsequent sections discuss specifics of short-term and long-term interest rate futures arbitrage.

Calculating Forward Rates

Forward rates are important for debt futures, especially for short-term interest rate contracts. Figure 4-2 illustrates the concept of a forward rate as the resulting interest rate obtained from owning a longer-term debt instrument and selling short a shorter-term debt instrument. Conceptually, a forward rate is the compounded "difference" between the longer-term and shorter-term rates. Thus, forward interest rates are calculated by using two cash interest rates from debt instruments with different maturities. First, the calculation of forward rates are described in terms of periods, often thought of as years. Hence, one determines a one-year forward interest rate starting one year from now by calculating the specific interest rate, when compounded with an initial one-year cash rate, which is equivalent to a two-year cash rate. Typically all interest rates are annualized regardless of the time periods employed. Equation (4-4) specifies how to find a one-period forward rate starting one period from now; that is,

$$r[1,2] = \frac{(1 + R[0,2])^2}{(1 + R[0,1])} - 1 \qquad (4\text{-}4)$$

where $r[1,2]$ = the one-period (annualized) forward rate from time 1 to time 2 (the one-period forward rate starting at time period 1)

$R[0,1]$ = the current one-period interest rate from time 0 (now) to time 1

$R[0,2]$ = the current two-period interest rate from time 0 (now) to time 2

FIGURE 4-2: The Forward Rate

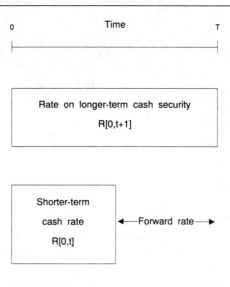

Note that R stands for the current cash rate, whereas r represents a forward rate. Thus, the one-period forward rate r[1,2] starting at time 1 is determined from the current two-period cash rate R[0,2] and the current one period cash rate R[0,1].

One can generalize the one-period forward rate in Equation (4-4) to determine a one-period forward rate starting at any time period; that is,

$$r[t,t+1] = \frac{(1 + R[0,t+1])^{t+1}}{(1 + R[0,t])^t} - 1 \tag{4-5}$$

where   r[t,t+1] = the one-period forward rate from time t to time t + 1

R[0,t] = the current t period interest rate from time 0 to time t

The first number in the brackets is the starting time period for the interest rate, and the second number is the ending time period. The difference between the two numbers states the number of periods employed to calculate the rate. A multiperiod forward rate is determined by further generalizing the above equations:

$$r[a,b] = \left[\frac{(1 + R[0,b])^b}{(1 + R[0,a])^a}\right]^{1/(b-a)} - 1 \tag{4-6}$$

where   r[a,b] = the (b − a) period forward rate from time a to time b (the forward rate for b − a periods starting at time period a)

Thus, for example, r[1,3] is the two-period forward rate from time 1 to time 3 (the two-period forward rate starting at time period 1). Example 4-1 shows how to determine a one-year forward rate starting one year and four years from today, and a two-year forward rate starting two years from today.

The Forward Transaction for Short-Term Debt Instruments

Figure 4-3 shows the diagram of a forward contract transaction for T-bills: a commitment entered into today to purchase a 90-day cash T-bill at time t = 90. The figure shows that a forward transaction can be created by buying a 180-day cash T-bill and selling short a 90-day cash T-bill, thereby leaving the net transaction for the last 90 days of the 180-day period as a long forward position. A similar transaction can be completed for Eurodollar time deposits. A dealer, say a bank, who sells a forward contract creates this instrument by instituting these long and short cash market transactions. The interest rate associated with this forward transaction is the relevant forward interest rate.

Forward Versus Futures Rates: Identifying Arbitrage Possibilities

The forward rate is employed to determine whether a **short** or a **long arbitrage** is appropriate and whether an arbitrage is profitable. A short arbitrage is when futures are sold; a long arbitrage occurs when futures are purchased. The equation to determine the forward rate when the periods are less than one year is simply an application of Equation (4-6) with a and b equaling the maturities of the shorter- and longer-term cash rates. Thus, the equation when the shorter-term cash has 90 days to maturity and the longer-term cash has 180 days to maturity, creating a 90-day forward rate starting 90 days from now, using fractions of the year, is:

EXAMPLE 4-1: Calculating Forward Rates

Equation (4-5) shows how to find a one period forward rate; that is,

$$r[t,t+1] = \frac{(1 + R[0,t+1])^{t+1}}{(1 + R[0,t])^t} - 1 \tag{4-5}$$

The following calculations determine the one-period forward rates starting one year from now ($r[1,2]$) and four years from now ($r[4,5]$).

Years to Maturity	Actual N-Year Rate
1	.06
2	.065
3	.07
4	.077
5	.084

$$r[1,2] = \frac{(1.065)^2}{(1.06)} - 1 = .0700$$

$$r[4,5] = \frac{(1.084)^5}{(1.077)^4} - 1 = .1125$$

We can also calculate a two-year forward rate starting two years from today:

$$r[a,b] = \left[\frac{(1 + R[0,b])^b}{(1 + R[0,a])^a}\right]^{1/(b-a)} - 1 \tag{4-6}$$

$$r[2,4] = \left[\frac{(1.077)^4}{(1.065)^2}\right]^{1/2} - 1 = .0891$$

$$r[.25,.5] = \left[\frac{(1 + R[0,.5])^{.5}}{(1 + R[0,.25])^{.25}}\right]^{1/(.5-.25)} - 1 \tag{4-7}$$

Exhibit 4-4 shows the relationship between the forward rate and the futures rate, as well as the type of arbitrage implied by this relationship.[4] Example 4-2 illustrates how to calculate a short-term forward rate for T-bills and compares it to the futures rate. One calculates Eurodollar time deposit forward rates in the same manner as for T-bills, except the Eurodollar money market rates do *not* have to be converted from bank discount rates to yields as is done for T-bills.

---

4 Marking the futures to market and the type of financing employed affects the final decision of whether an arbitrage is possible. Marking-to-market is a minor factor and typically is ignored. Chapter 8 discusses financing as well as other qualifications of the forward/futures comparison.

FIGURE 4-3: Diagram of a Forward Transaction

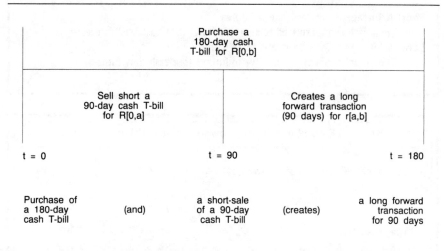

The Implied Repo Rate

The **implied repo rate** (or, more generally, the implied financing rate) is another straightforward method for deciding whether a short or long arbitrage position is appropriate. The implied financing rate represents the short-term interest rate for the near-term period when a longer-term cash security is purchased and a futures contract is sold, or vice versa. Figure 4-4 shows the implied financing rate relationship in diagram form; that is, the implied repo rate is determined by finding the rate that, when compounded with the futures rate, equals the long-term cash rate. Equation (4-8) shows how to calculate this rate.

$$IFR = [(1 + R[0,b])^b / (1 + r^*[a,b])^{(b-a)}]^{1/a} - 1 \qquad (4-8)$$

where   IFR = the implied financing rate

            r^* = the futures rate

An implied financing rate resulting from a 180-day cash T-bill and a T-bill futures contract expiring in 90 days can be determined by applying Equation (4-8) to generate the following after converting to fractions of a year:

$$IFR = [(1 + R[0,.5])^{.5} / (1 + r^*[.25,.5])^{(.5-.25)}]^{1/.25} - 1 \qquad (4-9)$$

Once calculated, the implied financing rate is compared with the actual short-term financing rate in order to determine whether a short or long arbitrage strategy provides arbitrage profits. Note that this approach typically ignores transactions costs; however, such costs need to be considered before an arbitrage is attempted. Exhibit 4-5 presents the decision rules and associated strategies using the implied financing rate. An example of calculating the implied financing rate and its comparison with the actual financing rate is given in Example 4-3.

EXHIBIT 4-4: Arbitrage Rules for Comparing Futures and Forward Rates

---

Short Arbitrage: If forward rate > futures rate,
  • Then cash is underpriced relative to futures (buy cash, sell futures)
Long Arbitrage: If forward rate < futures rate,
  • Then cash is overpriced relative to futures (sell cash, buy futures)

EXAMPLE 4-2: Short-Term Forward Rates and Futures Rates

On September 20, 1982, the following rates were in effect*:

	Bank Discount Rate	Yield
90-day cash T-bill	7.74%	7.99%
180-day cash T-bill	9.38%	9.97%
Dec. 82 T-bill futures index	89.62	
T-bill futures interest rate	10.38%	10.66%

Using Equation (4-7) we can determine the forward rate from the current cash yields as follows:

$$r[.25,.5] = \left[\frac{(1 + R[0,.5])^{.5}}{(1 + R[0,.25])^{.25}}\right]^{1/(.5-.25)} - 1 \qquad (4\text{-}7)$$

$$= [(1.0997)^{.5}/(1.0799)^{.25}]^4 - 1$$

$$= [1.048666/1.019403]^4 - 1$$

$$= 1.1199 - 1$$

Hence the forward rate = 12.00%
  Comparing the forward rate to the futures rate:
            forward rate > futures rate
            12.00% > 10.66%

From Exhibit 4-4 this result shows that short arbitrage is appropriate.

---

*   The actual interest rates depicted here reflect an unusual and very volatile environment, as shown by the 71 basis point range for the T-bill futures on this day (the highest futures interest rate for the day is used in the example). Typically such large differences between the 90-day and 180-day cash rates or between the forward rate and the futures rate do not exist. The purpose of this example is to show that arbitrage is possible during volatile time periods. Also note that the T-bill rates chosen here are for the December 16 and March 17 maturities, which differ from the simplified example of using 90- and 180-day maturities. These maturity differences have only a minor effect on the calculated results.

FIGURE 4-4: The Implied Financing Rate

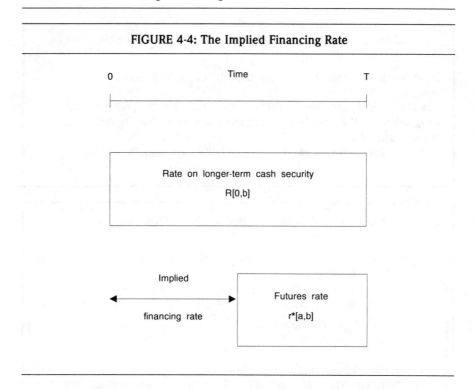

EXECUTING SHORT-TERM INTEREST RATE ARBITRAGE

Eurodollar and T-bill futures arbitrage are similar in concept but differ in the specifics of how they are executed. Here we list the basic transactions involved in short-term interest rate futures arbitrage. Chapter 8 discusses Eurodollar and T-bill pricing and arbitrage in detail. Examples 4-2 and 4-3, given earlier in the Chapter, show how to make the calculations and comparisons necessary for determining the possibility that arbitrage exists and the potential profits obtainable from such a transaction.

Exhibit 4-6 illustrates the transactions necessary for the execution of short and long Eurodollar and T-bill futures arbitrage. Note that transactions costs need to be considered in the analysis. Exhibit 4-6 shows that for a short arbitrage the arbitrageur borrows funds via a loan. These funds are then invested for (say) six months in a Eurodollar time deposit or cash T-bill. At the same time, the futures are sold. Since the forward rate > futures rate + transactions costs for a short arbitrage, the above set of transactions guarantees a profit. In other words, selling the futures contract locks in an interest rate on the cash instrument starting in three months.

Three months later (at T + 3) the initial loan is rolled-over to a new three-month loan, with the latter rate being previously locked in with the futures transaction. (The interest on the initial three-month loan must be paid.) At the end of six months the arbitrage profits have been earned, since the cost of the loans are less than the earnings from the time deposit.

EXHIBIT = 4-5: Arbitrage Rules Using the Implied Financing Rate

---

Short Arbitrage: If the implied financing rate > short-term financing rate = If forward rate > futures rate,
- Then cash is underpriced relative to the futures (buy cash, sell futures)

Long Arbitrage: If the implied financing rate < short-term financing rate = If forward rate < futures rate,
- Then cash is overpriced relative to the futures (sell cash, buy futures)

EXAMPLE 4-3: Determining the Implied Financing Rate

Using the data from Example 4-2, we can determine the implied financing rate from Equation (4-8) as follows:

$$IFR = [(1 + R[0,b])^b / (1 + r*[a,b])^{(b-a)}]^{1/a} - 1 \qquad (4\text{-}8)$$
$$IFR = [(1.0997)^{.5}/(1.1066)^{.25}]^4 - 1$$
$$= [1.048666/1.025646]^4 - 1$$
$$= 1.0928 - 1$$

Hence the implied financing rate is 9.28%.

Comparing the implied financing rate to the actual overnight short-term financing rate of 8.31%, we have:

Implied financing rate > financing rate*
9.28% > 8.31%

From Exhibit 4-5 this result indicates that a short arbitrage is appropriate.

---

* Most arbitrageurs employ the overnight financing rate rather than a three-month financing rate. This practice adds an element of risk that the financing rate will change. Chapter 8 discusses the use of the overnight versus three month financing rate.

A similar (but opposite) strategy is relevant for long arbitrage. These strategies, numerical examples, and the associated empirical results are covered in Chapter 8.

FACTORS AFFECTING T-BOND PRICING AND ARBITRAGE

The basic cost of carry model is relevant for T-bond futures pricing and arbitrage. For short arbitrage a cash bond is purchased, financed by a loan or other funding method, such as a repo, the bond is carried until the futures delivery month, and then the cash instrument is

---

EXHIBIT 4-6: Transactions for Executing Short-term Interest Rate Futures Arbitrage

---

Short Arbitrage: If the implied financing rate > short-term financing rate = If forward rate > futures rate, then
- Obtain funds from borrowing
- Invest in the six-month interest-bearing instrument
- Sell the futures contract

Long Arbitrage: If the implied financing rate < short-term financing rate = If forward rate < futures rate, then
- Obtain funds from borrowing
- Invest in a three-month interest-bearing instrument
- Buy the futures contract

---

delivered into the short futures position.[5] The implied repo method is employed to examine the profitability of this opportunity. However, those who do T-bond futures pricing, such as arbitrageurs and hedgers, also need to consider other factors that affect the process:
- The size of the coupon of the relevant deliverable bond in *comparison* to the financing rate is an important factor affecting the pricing and arbitrage of long-term debt futures contracts.
- The **conversion factor method** (CFM) is employed to allow delivery of *any* T-bond with at least 15 years to maturity or 15 years to the call date (if callable). This procedure significantly affects both the pricing and arbitrage of debt futures. The system was developed to calculate the delivery price for T-bonds with varying coupons and maturities. However, the CFM creates biases that affect the relative delivery pricing of bonds in comparison with their value, causing one **"cheapest-to-deliver"** bond to exist. This lowest-cost bond maximizes the arbitrageur's profits and therefore is the bond that directly controls the futures price.[6]
- **Delivery options** allow the seller of the debt futures contract several alternatives concerning which bonds to deliver and when to deliver them. These options complicate the pricing of the futures contracts just before and during the delivery month.

---

5 Municipal bond futures contracts are settled in cash.

6 In general, quality differences affect which cash asset is cheapest to deliver. For example, grains have different qualities. Although lower-quality grains can be delivered only at a discount to the futures price, it still may be more profitable to deliver the lower-quality grain if the cash price difference is larger than the prespecified futures discount. For financials, lower-quality (higher-risk) bank CDs dominated the pricing of CD futures contracts, since the lower the quality, the cheaper the CD that could be delivered. In general, the cheapest-to-deliver concept is modified by one caveat: there must be sufficient liquidity in the specific cheapest-to-deliver cash instrument to allow for sufficient purchases of that instrument without adversely affecting the cash price.

The complications and uncertainties created by these three major factors create pricing difficulties for T-bond futures and provide opportunities for arbitrageurs to increase their profits. These factors are discussed in Chapter 7 in an effort to examine their effects on the pricing process. These factors overshadow the pure versus quasi-arbitrage issue, although T-bond arbitrage is typically a pure arbitrage transaction executed by government bond dealers who finance their positions. Other long-term debt futures have similar pricing and arbitrage considerations as do T-bond futures.

A SUMMARY OF PRICING FUTURES CONTRACTS ACROSS MARKETS

In addition to the financing costs associated with the cost of carry model, other factors affect the pricing of financial futures contracts. The following list summarizes the effect of differing cash flow characteristics for different types of financial futures contracts, and shows that futures specifications and market characteristics affect cash flows and, hence, the pricing of the contracts. These characteristics are discussed in detail in Chapters 5, 7, and 8.

- Stock index futures prices are lowered by the size of the expected dividends on the stocks in the index. The uneven payments of dividends creates difficulties in pricing stock index futures.
- The futures price tracks the *cheapest-to-deliver* cash instrument that fulfills the specifications of the futures contract.
  - The effects of differing coupons and maturities for different cash T-bonds and T-notes are minimized by the conversion factor method. However, the conversion factors do create errors for pricing and in turn create a cheapest-to-deliver bond.
  - Actual or perceived risk differences can exist for different deliverable cash instruments. This situation presented a major difficulty for both the bank certificate of deposit and commercial paper futures contracts (neither of which trade now), where the various deliverable cash CDs and commercial paper issues had varying risks and thus created a cheapest instrument for the riskiest asset.
- The T-bond and T-note contracts possess delivery options that provide choices to the seller concerning when and what to deliver. These options affect the pricing of the futures contract.
- Differences between when the cash security last traded and when the futures contract traded can *imply* that arbitrage opportunities exist, when in reality such pricing differences are due to using an "old" cash price that is no longer relevant. This problem is especially relevant for stock index futures contracts.
- Cost differences between the cash and futures markets, such as commissions, margin costs, and bid-ask spread differences, affect the size of the no-arbitrage bands. As these costs change, the pricing of futures contracts in terms of the cash prices change.
- Tax and accounting treatments affect the futures and cash markets in different ways. For example, before the 1981 Tax Act, T-bill futures with expirations greater than six months were priced differently than the T-bill futures with less than six months to delivery. This difference was due to differing tax treatments between the cash and deferred futures expirations.

SUMMARY AND LOOKING AHEAD

The Capital Asset Pricing Model links the return on a futures contract to its systematic risk. The hedging pressure theory states that an imbalance of net hedging causes futures prices to be biased so as to cause additional speculators to enter the market. The cost of carry model shows that futures prices are linked to the underlying cash price via the financing costs to arbitrageurs.

We showed that futures prices are best described by the cost of carry model. This model then is adjusted for the cash flow of the asset and any delivery options. Arbitrage exists when risk-free profits are possible, which occurs when the futures and forward prices deviate by more than transactions costs. Pure arbitrage involves borrowed funds whereas quasi-arbitrage employs assets owned by the arbitrageur. Interest rate futures pricing and arbitrage can be examined by calculating forward rates and implied repo rates. Rules are available that determine whether futures are overvalued or undervalued.

Chapter 5 discusses pricing and arbitrage of stock index futures, including various issues related to program trading and the difficulties in implementing successful trades. Chapter 6 covers the basics of the cash debt markets and bond portfolio management. Chapter 7 discusses pricing and arbitrage of T-bond futures, including issues concerning the conversion factor method and the delivery options. Chapter 8 examines short-term interest rate futures pricing, especially techniques for implementing strategies involving arbitrage with these contracts.

Appendix 4A
Spreads and Strips

PRICING SPREADS

A spread occurs when a trader buys one futures expiration month and sells another expiration month (a calendar spread), or buys one type of contract and sells a different type of futures contract (a cross spread). The principal factor affecting the pricing (size) of a spread between futures expirations for financial futures is the financing rate. Let us illustrate this point by using a pure commodity, gold. A trader or arbitrageur purchases a January gold futures contract and sells a March gold futures contract. Assume that the arbitrageur takes possession of the gold in January when the futures contract expires and holds the gold for delivery into the March futures contract. Then the only important factor affecting the difference in price between the January and March futures contracts is the cost of financing the gold purchase for the two months that the gold is held. For other futures contracts, in particular T-bond futures, the delivery options also affect pricing. Exhibit 4A-1 shows the cash flow for a spread transaction in gold, and Table 4A-1 illustrates the pricing relationships for a spread.

The price structure between expiration months for any type of financial future is either an increasing price as one examines the more distant expirations (a **carrying charge market**) or a decreasing price for the more distant expirations (an **inverted market**). For a carrying charge market the net cost of financing a position determines the size of the price difference between futures expirations. Specifically, arbitrage keeps the size of the price spread from increasing much beyond the effect of the net financing cost when a carrying charge market exists since a larger price spread would create risk-free profits. The arbitrageur would create profits if a larger price spread existed by taking delivery of the asset from the nearer-term long futures position, holding the cash asset until the short futures contract neared expiration, and then delivering the asset into the short futures contract. The profits from this strategy would be larger than the net financing cost. Of course, trades by arbitrageurs would help to reduce the excessive price spread. Consequently, any risk to an arbitrageur associated with a full carrying charge market is limited to changes in the financing rate. For example, if the short-term financing rate increases, then the size of the spread typically increases.

Inverted markets are more difficult to price. For inverted markets the size of the spread may not be limited by arbitrage. Since the near-term futures contract is priced higher than the deferred futures, buying the near-term and selling the deferred creates a loss. However, the financing cost is actually less than the income when the yield curve is upward sloping— that is, when the price structure is inverted. Overall, the loss on the price side may or may not be offset by the net income effect. On the other hand, by *shorting* the near-term contract and going long the deferred contract it is possible to create a maximum price

EXHIBIT 4A-1: Cash Flow for a Spread

Price of gold	$350
Futures price of gold (expiration and delivery in 1 year)	$385
Futures price of gold (expiration and delivery in 2 years)	$423.50
Interest rate for financing	10%

Transaction	Cash Flow at Time = 0	Cash Flow at Time = 1 year	Cash Flow at Time = 2 years
Buy futures contract at t = 0 with expiration at t = 1 (P = 385)	$0	$−385*	
Sell futures contract at t = 0 with expiration at t = 2 (P = 423.50)	0		$423.50*
Borrow $385 at t = 1 for 1 year at 10%		+385	−423.50
		$ 0	$ 0

* Gold is purchased by receiving delivery from the futures. The gold is then held until it is sold by executing the short futures contract at t = 2.

TABLE 4A-1: Pricing a Gold Spread

(1) Futures Spread	(2) Futures Price Difference	(3) Financing Cost[a]	(4) Difference: (2) − (3)
February-April	$2.10	$2.16	$−.06
February-June	$4.20	$4.36	$−.16
June-December	$6.60	$6.63	$−.03

[a] The financing rate times the cost of the cash asset (i.e., the nearby futures price), adjusted for the time interval of the spread. Here the financing rate is 3.7%, the February futures price is $355.20, and the June futures price is $359.40.

spread. However, the complications and costs relating to providing delivery on the nearby short position make such an arbitrage less likely, unless the price differences are large. Consequently, for an inverted market arbitrage typically guarantees a *minimum* price spread but *not* a maximum spread.

INITIATING SPREAD TRANSACTIONS

Factors Affecting Spreads

In order to profit from a spread transaction, the trader attempts to determine whether the size of the *difference* between the prices of the two contracts will increase or decrease. A spread earns a profit if the correct direction of the price difference is forecasted *and* the appropriate spread transaction is set up in conjunction with the changing price structure of the futures contract. Exhibit 4A-2 states the appropriate spread positions to implement to obtain a profit when the spread is forecasted to widen or narrow in conjunction with an increasing (carrying charge market) or decreasing (inverted market) price structure.

While the net financing tends to dominate the price movements of spreads, other factors complicate the decision whether and when to set up a spread position. Specifically, many financial futures spreads that seem to present opportunities are often affected by other characteristics that mitigate this opportunity. For example, some contracts such as stock indices and currencies have significantly less liquidity in deferred months. This lack of liquidity affects both the actual pricing of the deferred contract by the traders and the apparent pricing of the contract in terms of *when* the last trade took place for the deferred contract. If the last trade does not occur at the same time for both the nearby and deferred contracts, then this timing difference may make it appear that a profitable spread opportunity exists, when in fact it does not. For example, assume that the nearby stock index futures changes from 315.0 to 317.0 near the end of the day, but that the deferred futures contract does not trade at that time. Then the (reported) spread between the first two contracts appears large, when in fact the difference is due to the timing difference of the

---

EXHIBIT 4A-2: Profitable Spread Opportunities

	Increasing Price Structure: Carrying Charge Market	Decreasing Price Structure: Inverted Market
Spread widens	Buy deferred and sell near term	Buy near term and sell deferred
Spread narrows	Buy near term and sell deferred	Buy deferred and sell near term

last trades of the two contracts. No trader could exploit this apparent price difference in the spread because no trade has or would take place at this unrealistic spread value.[1]

Risk and Return for Spreads

In recognition of the reduced risk for spreads, margins on calendar spread positions are much less than the margins on pure long or short positions, hence the leverage for spreads is increased. Risk is reduced since both sides of the spread usually move in the same direction, even though their prices can change by different amounts.

Whereas the futures expiration months for a calendar spread almost always move in the same direction, the risk for a cross spread between different types of futures contracts depends on the extent the contracts are influenced by the same underlying factors. Hence, the risk for a T-bill futures to Eurodollar futures spread is determined by changes in the credit risk relationship; on the other hand, a spread between T-bill futures and T-bond futures is even more risky because one can lose on both sides of the transaction if the relationship between short- and long-term interest rates changes. A spread between two unrelated contracts (e.g., gold and soybeans) often is more risky than one speculative position.

Figures 4A-1 and 4A-2 illustrate how the changing relationships between different futures contracts can create profitable spreading opportunities. The T-bill–Eurodollar spread (called the TED spread) has varied significantly since the Eurodollar futures inception. For each 20 basis point change (.20 in the figure), the spread position profits or loses $500. Since the TED spread margin is $270 per contract, the percentage profit or loss on the initial margin deposit per 20 basis points is almost 200 percent per contract.[2] Figure 4A-2 shows the municipal bond futures versus T-bond futures spread, or the MOB spread. The behavior of this spread over time not only shows the potential profits/losses available (with every 2 points equaling $2,000 and the spread margin being $550), but also illustrates the importance of having *different* futures contracts available to hedge differing types of risk.

Example 4A-1 provides an example of a spread in which the trader expects the price difference to narrow. The subsequent actual narrowing of the spread allows the trader to make a profit of $1,750 per spread, or a return of 875 percent on margin. Of course, if the spread had widened (the difference between the prices increased over time), the speculator would have lost money.

---

1   Spreaders previously benefitted from the tax advantages of tax straddles. Tax straddles exist when taxable income can be postponed by taking the losses on one side of a spread but rolling over the gains from the spread into future years. However, the 1981 tax law eliminated this tax benefit for floor spreaders as well as for off-the-floor straddlers by taxing gains and losses on *all* positions at the end of each year, whether or not the positions had been terminated. The result of this tax law change has been to reduce significantly the liquidity of deferred contracts since one of the economic benefits to the spreader was eliminated.

2   The Eurodollar rate is always larger than the T-bill rate in Figure 4A-1, creating a positive spread for Eurodollar futures. Two factors cause this relationship. First, Eurodollar rates are money market rates, whereas T-bill rates are quoted on a discount basis. Second, Eurodollar rates include a credit risk differential, whereas T-bills are considered to be default-free.

FIGURE 4A-1: Eurodollar less T-bill Rates

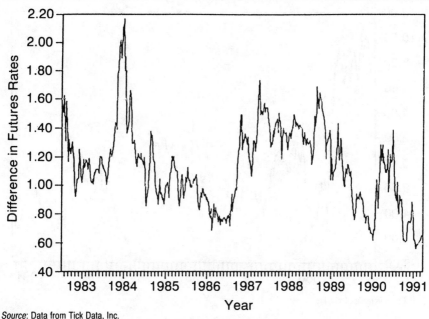

Source: Data from Tick Data, Inc.

STRIPS: THE PRICING AND ARBITRAGE OF
DEFERRED FUTURES CONTRACTS

One method used to price deferred futures contracts, as well as considering the potential alternative return benefits of futures over a pure cash investment, is to employ a **strip** of futures. A strip of futures is simply a series of futures purchased with sequential expirations. Here we use Eurodollar futures strips as an example because of the popularity of these contracts.

As shown in Example 4A-2, one can compare a cash alternative with a futures strip; that is, the following are equivalent strategies:

- Invest in a long-term cash Eurodollar time deposit for the entire holding period.
- Alternatively, buy a sequence of futures, plus invest in a short-term Eurodollar time deposit now, such that the cash time deposit matures exactly when the nearby futures contract expires. When the first cash time deposit matures, the funds are placed in another 90-day Eurodollar time deposit; the rate on this second (and subsequent) time deposit is locked-in via the original purchase of the futures contracts. In this way the strip of Eurodollar futures purchases guarantees the exact cost and yield of this investment at the time of the original purchase of the strip.

FIGURE 4A-2: Munis Less T-bond Futures Prices

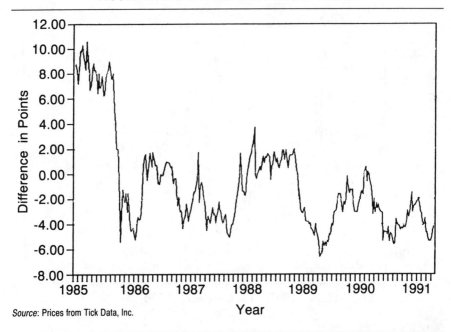

Source: Prices from Tick Data, Inc.

If the futures and cash markets are equivalently priced, then the ending dollar value for the futures strip strategy will equal the ending dollar value for the long-term cash Eurodollar time deposit that has the same maturity as the strip of futures. Alternatively, if a particular strategy produces a higher yield than the other, then one can undertake a quasi-arbitrage transaction (alternative return strategy) and choose the alternative with the highest ending dollar value.

Table 4A-2 compares the pricing of time deposits to Eurodollar futures by comparing yields on the cash and futures instruments for different time frames. The table shows the quoted interest rates, annual yields, and differences between futures over cash for strips of Eurodollar futures in comparison with the associated cash time deposits. When differences between the futures strips and the cash only rates are small, then one concludes that the futures and cash markets are integrated and that the futures contracts are priced in accordance with the cash market. If many institutions and traders compare these alternatives, then their subsequent actions cause the pricing of the deferred futures contracts to be comparable to their associated cash forward rates.

EXAMPLE 4A-1: A Spread Transaction

Before the market crash in 1987 a speculator expected the spread between the December and March S&P 500 futures to become smaller (less negative). To profit from this possibility the trader purchased the lower-priced futures and sold the higher-priced futures. Profits occured when the spread narrowed two weeks later.

	Nearby Futures	Deferred Futures	Spread
October 14, 1987	Buy the lower priced December S&P 500 futures at 304.8	Sell the higher priced March S&P 500 futures at 308.8	−4.0
October 28, 1987	Sell (cover) the December futures at 232.0	Buy back (cover) the March futures at 232.5	−0.5
Change in value:	Loss of $36,400	Gain of $38,150	Narrowing of 3.5
	(i.e., −72.8 × $500)	(i.e., 76.3 × $500)	

Net gain: $1,750
Margin deposit (for 10/87): $200
Return on margin deposit: 875%

TABLE 4A-2: Pricing Eurodollar Futures by Using a Strip of Futures

Futures Contract	Maturity of Cash	Futures Interest Rate	Futures Average Yield[a]	Cash Yield[b]	Futures to Cash Difference[c]
September	December	5.57		5.50	+.07
December	March	5.79	5.72	5.67	+.05
March	June	5.81	5.80	5.75	+.05
June	September	6.10	5.95	5.87	+.08

a   Running average annualized compounded yield of the futures rates. When time deposits are rolled over into a new time deposit, they create a compounded return for the length of the combined time period (e.g., 6 months). This return then is annualized to obtain a simple annual return to compare with the cash yield which is quoted as a simple annual return.

b   Eurodollar time *deposit* rates—that is, London Interbank *bid* rates (typically bid rates are 1/8 lower than offer rates).

c   Part of the difference relates to the 1/8 -point intervals for quotations used for the cash quotes.

Note: In this example the September futures will expire within a few days, therefore, current cash funds are not placed in a time deposit until the September futures expire. In general, the first transaction is to place funds in a time deposit that matures when the nearby futures expire; at that time the funds are placed in a new three-month time deposit.

EXAMPLE 4A-2: Alternative Returns: Comparing a Cash Eurodollar Rate to a Strip of Futures

---

Alternative 1: On September 20 place $1 million in a one-year cash Eurodollar time deposit at a money market rate of 5.87 percent and keep the time deposit until it matures in one year.

Alternative 2: Before September 20 buy one contract of Eurodollar futures expiring September 20, December 20, March 20, and June 20. (*Note*: Assume funds are not available for a time deposit until September 20. Also, actual futures expirations vary by several days from one expiration month to another.) Futures rates locked-in at the time of purchase are 5.57%, 5.79%, 5.81%, and 6.10%. For this alternative, the original cash amount of $1 million is invested in a three-month Eurodollar time deposit on September 20, with the rate on this time deposit being locked-in with the purchase of the September futures contract. This procedure is repeated in December, March, and June. Since all futures contracts are purchased at the same time, the exact cost is known on that date.

The portfolio manager would choose the alternative with the higher return:

Alternative 1: One-year Eurodollar deposit

$$\$1,000,000\ (1+.0587) = \$1,058,700$$

Alternative 2: Strip of futures

$$\$1,000,000\ (1+.0557/4) = \$1,013,925$$
$$\$1,013,925\ (1+.0579/4) = \$1,028,602$$
$$\$1,028,602\ (1+.0581/4) = \$1,043,542$$
$$\$1,043,542\ (1+.0610/4) = \$1,059,456$$

The strip of futures provides the highest total interest.

Appendix 4B

The Pricing of Currency
Futures Contracts

Pricing a gold, stock index, or debt futures contract is based on the (net) financing cost of holding the cash asset (the cost of carry model). Currency futures and forwards represent the *relative* exchange rate between two currencies, starting at a specific time in the future. Thus, currency futures pricing reflects the *relative* interest rate/financing costs for the two currencies.

As with other futures contracts, the fair pricing of currency futures is based on a "no-arbitrage" relationship—that is, the price at which risk-free profits are not available. **Interest rate parity** is the formal name of the no-arbitrage relationship for currency futures and forward pricing. If the interest rate in the U.S. is greater than the interest rate for foreign currency funds (i.e., if $i_{U.S.} > i_{foreign}$), then the futures exchange rate > cash exchange rate.[1]

The following discussion develops the futures pricing equation. The notation used is as follows:

- $S(t)$ is the domestic (U.S.) currency price of cash foreign exchange at time t in terms of dollars per unit of foreign currency (American terms).
- $F[t,t+T]$ is the domestic (U.S.) currency price of a futures or forward contract in foreign exchange at time t for settlement at time t + T (the time of the futures expiration).
- i is the annual interest rate on Eurocurrency deposits for the domestic (U.S.) currency.
- i* is the annual interest rate on Eurocurrency loans for the foreign currency.
- i and i* are money market interest rates that are quoted using a 360-day year (the British pound rates use 365 days); money market rates are *not* compounded.

The following discussion shows the transactions that create a no-arbitrage situation—that is, a fair futures price. Note that the first three steps are initiated *at the same time*, and that none of the arbitrageur's funds are employed in the transaction.

Step 1: Borrow 1 unit of the domestic currency ($1) at i at time t. Repay the loan plus interest at time t + T, with the loan being held for the time period T: thus, repay

$$1 + i\,(T/360) \qquad (4B\text{-}1)$$

Step 2: Convert the 1 unit of the domestic currency ($1) into $1/S(t)$ units of the foreign currency. Deposit this amount at the money market interest rate i*. At the end of time t + T receive the principal plus interest:

---

[1] The relationships and examples in this appendix assume the currency futures contract is based in the United States and is quoted in dollars. For futures or forwards based in other countries one substitutes "domestic" for "U.S." Also note that the relationship of the futures rate > cash exchange rate when $i_{U.S.} > i_{foreign}$ holds because futures are quoted in American terms—that is, the number of dollars per one unit of the foreign currency.

$$[1/S(t)] \ [1 + i^*(T/360)] \tag{4B-2}$$

Step 3: In order to ensure that changing currency values do not create a loss, the trader locks-in the domestic value by executing a futures (or forward) contract: sell the futures in the foreign exchange for expiration at time t + T; that is, create F[t,t+T]. The total domestic (U.S.) value of the futures transaction at time t + T is

$$[1/S(t)] \ [1 + i^*(T/360)] \ F[t,t+T] \tag{4B-3}$$

Step 4: At time t + T,
- Receive the deposit of the foreign currency, including interest (step 2).
- Use the foreign currency to fulfill the forward contract—that is, exchange the foreign currency for the domestic currency (U.S. dollars) by executing the forward contract at the exchange rate determined at time t (step 3).
- Repay the domestic (U.S.) loan (step 1).

Since none of the arbitrageur's funds are used, the "no-arbitrage" rule states that no profits should exist. Consequently, the cost from the domestic loan should exactly offset the interest received from the deposit of the foreign currency:

$$1 + i(T/360) = [1/S(t)] \ [1 + i^*(T/360)] \ F[t,t+T] \tag{4B-5}$$

Solving for the futures/forward rate F[t,t+T] we obtain the fair futures price for foreign exchange, as determined by the interest rate parity theorem:

$$F[t,t+T] = \frac{S(t) \ [1 + i(T/360)]}{1 + i^*(T/360)} \tag{4B-6}$$

This equation shows that the fair futures price for currencies is a function of the cash exchange rate, the domestic interest rate, and the foreign interest rate. In turn, the interest rates are affected by the business conditions, money supplies, and inflation rates in the two countries. Example 4B-1 illustrates the calculations.

EXAMPLE 4B-1: Calculating a Fair Currency Futures Price

The fair currency futures price is calculated for a contract expiring in 90 days, given the following: cash yen exchange rate = 145 yen/$ (i.e., $.0068966/yen), i_{dollar} = 8%, and i^*_{yen} = 5%.

$$F[t,t+T] = \frac{S(t) \ [1 + i(T/360)]}{1 + i^*(T/360)} \tag{4B-6}$$

$$F[0,90] = \frac{\$.0068966/yen \ [1 + .08 \ (90/360)]}{1 + .05 \ (90/360)}$$

$$= \$.0068966/yen \ [(1.02)/(1.0125)]$$

$$= \$.0069477/yen$$

Chapter 5

Stock Index Futures Pricing and Arbitrage

The cost of carry model for stock index futures shows that the cash and futures prices should deviate only by the financing cost and dividends. However, the nonconstant dividend effect and the lead-lag effect arising from stocks that do not trade frequently complicate the pricing process.

Stock index arbitrage is often called program trading, although program trading is a more general term (see Focus 2-1). Program trading involves trading a basket of stocks in order to mimic the behavior of an entire cash index. Critics claim that program trading creates greater market volatility, as well as being one cause of the October 1987 crash; this chapter examines these allegations.

The factors affecting arbitrage transactions are the financing cost, transactions costs, the liquidity in the cash market, restrictions on selling short cash stocks for long arbitrage, the nonconstant payment of dividends over time, and the difficulty of creating a perfect arbitrage situation for some index contracts. Empirical evidence shows that apparent profitable arbitrage exists when end-of-the-day prices are employed, but most of these profitable opportunities disappear quickly when intraday data is tested. Therefore, arbitrageurs often must take on risk or monitor the market carefully to obtain profits. However, futures occasionally do become mispriced; thus hedgers, speculators, and arbitrageurs must be able to recognize when such mispricings occur and be able to adjust for factors that affect pricing. This chapter shows how to price stock index futures and illustrates arbitrage trades for stock index contracts. In addition, it discusses the relationship between program trading, market volatility, and the market crash.

PRICING STOCK INDEX FUTURES

The price of a futures contract depends on the underlying cash value. Stock indexes are a portfolio of stocks, weighted by size or other factors. Stock index futures quotations are covered in Chapter 2.

Institutional investors employ stock indexes as benchmarks for comparison purposes. In addition, a number of mutual funds attempt to match exactly the performance of the S&P 500 index. Moreover, the existence of stock index futures markets has caused many other funds to institute investment strategies based on a portfolio that mimics the S&P index.

Applying the Cost of Carry Model to Stock Index Futures

The fair futures price calculated by the cost of carry model for stock index futures must consider the dividends received from holding the stocks in the index; that is,

$$P_{FAIR} = P_C (1 + i)^t - D \tag{5-1}$$

where P_{FAIR} =   the fair futures price for a stock index

            P_C =   the current value of the underlying cash index

            i =   the financing rate of interest or equivalent investment return desired, in percentage terms

            D =   the dollar dividend amount in index points received on the stocks in the index from now until the expiration of the futures contract[1]

            t =   number of days until expiration of the futures, divided by 365

The dollar dividend, D, must be recalculated whenever a stock in the index pays its quarterly dividend or a firm alters its dividend. The model shows that the effect of receiving dividends over the life of the futures contract is to *lower* the futures price. This relationship occurs because (1) the dividends received reduce the net funds needed to finance the cash position and (2) a purchase of the futures contract is an alternative to holding the cash stocks, but a long position in futures does *not* provide any income from dividend payments.[2]

The continuous time equivalent to the above cost of carry equation is used frequently, since only the dividend yield rather than the frequently changing total dollar dividends are needed for its calculation:

$$P_{FAIR} = P_C \, e^{(i-d)t} \tag{5-2}$$

where d = the dividend yield on the stock index

If one has only the dividend yield, then an alternative to using Equation (5-2) is to convert the yield to dollar dividends, as shown in Equation (5-3):

$$D = d \, P_C \, t \tag{5-3}$$

Note that Equation (5-1) provides the most accurate calculation of the effects of dividends and therefore is employed in many of the arbitrage computer models.

Equations (5-1) and (5-2) and Example 5-1 illustrate both the relationship between the futures and current cash index values and the net difference between the financing costs and the dividend income received. In particular, the larger the difference between i and d, the larger the price difference between P_{FAIR} and P_C. In addition, the larger the value of t, the larger the price difference between the futures and cash index values. Figure 5-1 shows

---

1   The future value of the dividends at contract expiration could be calculated. However, the difficulty of the process and the uncertainty of future dividends makes this approach undesirable in practice, especially given the small effect on P_{FAIR}. For example, if expected dividends during the two months before futures expiration are 1.90 index points and the interest rate is 8%, then the future value effect adds .014 index points to the calculation. This is equivalent to $7 per futures contract. Note that the dividend yield model given in Equation (5-2) does consider future values.

2   The stock index futures pricing equation is developed in two ways. One approach is to set the returns from the arbitrage transaction equal to the risk-free interest rate. Thus one would buy stock, sell futures, and receive dividends, which would be equivalent to owning a T-bill (transactions costs are ignored in the pricing equation). The second approach is to compare the returns from holding a stock portfolio to those from a futures position plus buying T-bills. This approach is equivalent to comparing two alternative strategies that have the same amount of risk. The only difference is that the stock position receives dividends whereas the futures position does not. The equivalent equation is derived if futures are purchased and stocks are sold short, since dividends must be paid in this circumstance. Later the cash flows for short and long stock index futures are presented.

EXAMPLE 5-1: Determining the Fair Value of a Stock Index Futures Contract

---

The following values represent actual stock market values:

S&P 500 Index	319.72
T-bill yield	6.59%
Dividend yield on the Index stocks	3.02%
Days until expiration of the futures	84

Using these data, the fair price is calculated as follows:

$$P_{FAIR} = P_C \, e^{(i-d)t} \tag{5-2}$$
$$P_{FAIR} = 319.72 \, e^{(.0659-.0302)(84/365)}$$
$$= 319.72 \, e^{.0082159}$$
$$= 319.72(1.0082497)$$
$$= 322.36$$

One also can use Equation (5-1) to calculate the fair price if the dividend yield first is converted to total dollar dividends (or if the total dollar dividends expected over the life of the futures contract are added up separately for the individual stocks). Equation (5-3) is employed to convert dividend yields to dollar dividends:

$$D = d \, P_C \, t \tag{5-3}$$
$$D = (.0302)(319.72)(84/365) = 2.222$$

Then one is able to calculate the fair price as follows:

$$P_{FAIR} = P_C \, (1+i)^t - D \tag{5-1}$$
$$P_{FAIR} = 319.72(1+.0659)^{84/365} - 2.222$$
$$= 319.72(1.01479) - 2.222$$
$$= 322.23$$

Notice that the two calculated values for the fair futures price differ slightly. There are two reasons for this. Most important, Equation (5-1) calculates the dividend value in index points, whereas Equation (5-2) uses the dividend yield. [Compare the results for Equation (5-1) to the results when $P_{FAIR} = P_C(1 + i - d)^t$ is calculated.] Moreover, the first formulation uses discrete compounding, whereas the second employs continuous compounding.

---

the net financing and time to expiration effects on the size of the cash/futures difference when the current cash index value is 400.

Example 5-1 also illustrates that Equations (5-1) and (5-2) for determining the fair futures price can provide slightly different values for P_{FAIR}. Which equation the trader employs depends on the trader's beliefs concerning which equation best describes the cash flow process *and* which method is used by other traders in the market. Considerations concerning the uneven payments of dividends are covered shortly. These considerations imply that

FIGURE 5-1: Time and Net Financing Effects

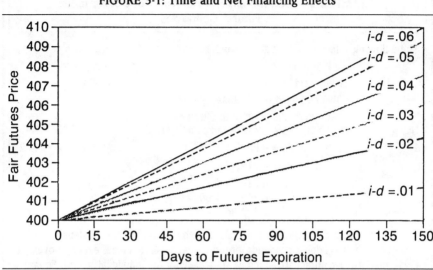

Equation (5-1) would be more useful in practice if *actual* dividends are calculated over the life of the futures contract.

Dividend Payments and the Pricing Process

Although the pricing equations for stock index futures given above, especially Equation (5-2), are employed on the basis of the assumption that total dividends are received *evenly* throughout the period, dividends are actually paid out quarterly by corporations. Moreover, many of the corporations pay dividends at approximately the same time in the quarter. For example, about 70 percent of the dividends for the MMI contract are paid in the second month of each quarter, whereas 75 percent of the dividends for the S&P 500 index are paid during the last seven weeks of the quarter. Figure 5-2 shows the changing relationship between financing costs and dividends over time for the MMI contract. Notice that dividends are *greater* than financing costs for the latter part of the quarter. The financing cost and the dividend income decline over time since they measure the total cost from the date in question *until the futures expires.*

As the time until expiration decreases, the financing cost and dividends received decreases. Figure 5-3 relates the net financing cost (financing less dividends) to the actual futures-cash basis for the MMI futures contract to show when the futures are over- and underpriced. When $P_F - P_C$ > net financing cost, then futures are overpriced, and vice versa (where P_F designates the current futures price). Figure 5-3 shows that futures can become mispriced by more than one index point when using end-of-day prices, with the mispricing fluctuating from overpricing to underpricing. If such mispricings occur within the day, then arbitrage profits are possible.

Because of the dividend effect, it is possible for stock index futures to sell at a *discount* to the cash index because of this so-called "seasonality" effect of the time at which divi-

FIGURE 5-2: MMI Futures: Financing Costs Versus Dividends

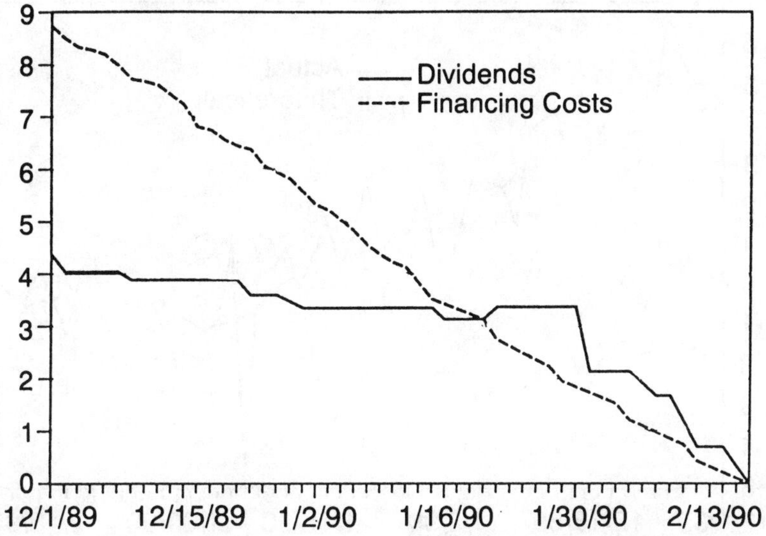

Source: Chicago Board of Trade, "Dividend Payouts and the MMI," *Financial Futures Professional,* Vol. 14, No. 4, April 1990, The Chicago Board of Trade, p. 4.

dends are paid. Futures sell at a discount when the dividend yield until the expiration of the futures contract exceeds the risk-free rate. Figure 5-3 shows this discount effect during the latter part of the quarter. The MMI contract is particularly affected by dividend season-ality, since the stocks composing the MMI index have high dividend yields. Thus, the dividend effects are greater for the MMI in comparison with other stock index futures for spreads over calendar months, or spreads with other futures contracts. For example, a constant relationship over time does not exist between various MMI calendar spreads.

Another dividend factor affecting futures pricing is that dividends are only owed by the corporation once they are approved by the Board of Directors. Dividends are increased or cut, depending on the needs of the firm.[3] This situation creates uncertainty that does not exist for other futures contracts. Although some researchers believe the dividend effects discussed here are relatively minor in most circumstances (for example, see Saunders and Mahajan[4]), many arbitrageurs calculate total expected dividend payments on a daily basis to determine the most accurate forward price possible.

---

3   An unexpected dividend increase creates larger profits for a short futures arbitrage and smaller profits for a long futures arbitrage.

4   Edward M. Saunders, Jr., and Arvind Mahajan, "An Empirical Examination of Composite Stock Index Futures Pricing," *The Journal of Futures Markets,* Vol. 8, No. 2, April 1988, pp. 211-228.

FIGURE 5-3: MMI Futures: Actual Basis Versus Net Financing Costs

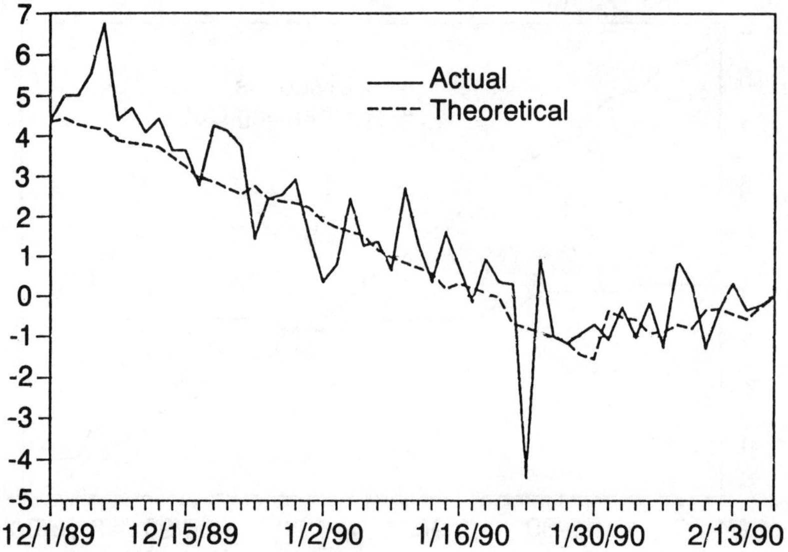

Source: Chicago Board of Trade, "Dividend Payouts and the MMI," *Financial Futures Professional*, Vol. 14, No. 4, April 1990, The Chicago Board of Trade, p. 4.

Evidence on Pricing Stock Index Futures

Employing the cost of carry model, early studies using the end of day stock index futures prices typically conclude that mispricings are relatively large for the time periods studied. Cornell and French[5] found mispricings for the S&P and NYFE contracts for the initial futures expirations, attributing the mispricings to a tax timing option related to obtaining capital gains for the cash stocks. However, Cornell[6] shows empirically that tax timing did not affect the results and that the mispricings began to disappear as the contract gained volume.[7] Saunders and Mahajan[8] adjust for several assumptions made in other studies by considering mark-to-market effects and providing a partial adjustment for nonconstant dividend payments. Employing a regression analysis on daily data for the S&P and NYFE contracts from

5   B. Cornell and K. French, "The Pricing of Stock Index Futures," *The Journal of Futures Markets*, Vol. 3, No. 1, Spring 1983, pp. 1-14. Also, B. Cornell and K. French, "Taxes and the Pricing of Stock Index Futures," *Journal of Finance*, Vol. 38, No. 2, June 1983, pp. 675-694.

6   B. Cornell, "Taxes and the Pricing of Stock Index Futures: Empirical Results," *The Journal of Futures Markets*, Vol. 5, No. 1, Spring 1985, pp. 89-101.

7   Critics of stock index futures program trades claim that futures cause an increase in cash market volatility. These critics have called for an increase in futures margins to reduce the importance of stock index futures.

8   Edward M. Saunders, Jr., and Arvind Mahajan, "An Empirical Examination of Composite Stock Index Futures Pricing," *The Journal of Futures Markets*, Vol. 8, No. 2, April 1988, pp. 211-228.

late 1982 to 1984 they conclude that the pricing process of stock index futures improved over time. However, all daily pricing studies are affected adversely by the 15-minute timing difference that exists between the futures and cash market closing times. More meaningful analysis requires intraday data.

MacKinlay and Ramaswamy[9] perform the only cost of carry pricing study on stock index futures that involves intraday data. Using the S&P 500 contract from June 1983 to June 1987, they examine the mispricing of futures contracts from their fair value for every 15-minute interval. MacKinlay and Ramaswamy determine that a positive or negative *persistence* in mispricing exists, and that these mispricings are a function of the number of days until expiration, with larger mispricings occurring farther from expiration.

Timing Differences Between the Index Futures and Cash Prices

A factor affecting *apparent* mispricings of stock index futures is timing differences between cash index values and futures prices. These timing differences cause futures price changes to lead cash index changes. The conventional wisdom is that stock index futures prices lead the cash index by 20 to 30 minutes. This timing effect is an example of the "price discovery" criteria for futures discussed in Chapter 1. Several reasons exist to explain this timing difference:

- Infrequent trading of smaller stocks
- Higher cost in the cash market
- Lower futures margins

Let us briefly explain each of these factors.

Infrequent trading for smaller stocks in the S&P and NYSE cash indexes cause these indexes to be "old." Since the cash indexes reflect only the *last* trade for each stock, the futures contract is a better indicator of the current status of the overall market, whereas the cash index reflects *past* price information on the individual stocks.

Higher commissions, bid-ask spreads, and liquidity costs in the cash market make trades on a portfolio of individual stocks very costly, especially in comparison with equivalent trades in a futures index. Overall, cash trades are 10 times more costly than equivalent futures transactions. Thus, market participants wishing to implement a "market basket" trade immediately can do so quicker, more effectively, and with less cost in the futures market.

Market participants with relevant information or differing expectations from the market price prefer the futures markets to the cash markets because of the lower margin requirements for futures. The lower margins provide greater leverage for speculators and a reduced cost for arbitrageurs.[10]

Evidence of the Lead-Lag Effect

Research on the lead-lag and price discovery issues for stock index futures examine whether there is a timing difference between the futures and cash prices changes. Kawaller, Koch,

---

9   C. MacKinlay and K. Ramaswamy, "Index-Futures Arbitrage and the Behavior of Stock Index Futures Prices," *Review of Financial Studies*, Vol. 1, No. 2, Summer 1988, pp. 137-158.

10 Moreover, the Cornell and French studies assume investors can use the entire proceeds of the short sale of stocks in order to earn interest. These funds typically are available only to dealers.

and Koch[11] examine minute-by-minute S&P 500 futures and cash data for 42 days in 1984 and 1985. They determine that the futures contract leads the cash index for as long as 20 to 45 minutes, even though equivalent price changes often occur simultaneously. Laatsch and Schwarz[12] find simultaneous pricing for minute-by-minute data for the Major Market Index (MMI) contract. However, Finnerty and Park[13] conclude that a significant lead-lag relationship between the futures and cash price changes exists. Herbst, McCormack, and West[14] determine that futures lead the cash index for the S&P 500 and Value Line futures contracts, with the lead time varying from zero to 16 minutes.

Stoll and Whaley[15] employ correlation coefficients to examine five-minute intervals for the S&P and MMI contracts. They determine that futures provide a price discovery function with a lead time of five minutes on average and up to 10 minutes or more occasionally *after the cash index is adjusted for nontrading and bid-ask effects*. Swinnerton, Curcio, and Bennett[16] determine that a lead time of five minutes is the best predictor of the cash index, although the futures provide some predictive ability for up to 30 minutes. In summary, the research on the lead-lag effect provides consistent conclusions that futures do lead cash prices during most time periods, although equivalent price changes between the futures and cash markets often occur. This result shows that pricing and arbitrage models need to consider this timing difference.

STOCK INDEX FUTURES ARBITRAGE: PROGRAM TRADING

Observations on Program Trading

Institutional funds and brokerage houses with millions of dollars invested in the market practice stock index arbitrage. Consequently, arbitrage did not interest the general public until program trading of baskets of stocks and stock index futures was blamed for creating wild swings in the stock market. Soon program trading became synonymous with stock index arbitrage. The popular press interest in program trading peaked after the stock market crash in October 1987 and the minicrash of 190 points in the last 90 minutes of trading in October 1989. Program trading was labeled as one of the culprits of these crashes.[17]

---

11 Ira Kawaller, Paul Koch, and Timothy Koch, "The Temporal Relationship Between S&P Futures and the S&P 500 Index," *Journal of Finance*, Vol. 42, No. 5, December 1987, pp. 1309-1329.

12 Francis E. Laatsch and Thomas V. Schwarz, "Price Discovery and Risk Transfer in Stock Index Cash and Futures Markets," *The Review of Futures Markets*, Vol. 7, No. 2, 1988, pp. 272-289.

13 J. E. Finnerty and H. Y. Park, "Stock Index Futures: Does the Tail Wag the Dog?" *Financial Analysts Journal*, Vol. 43, No. 2, March-April 1987, pp. 57-61.

14 A. F. Herbst, J. P. McCormack, and E. N. West, "Investigation of a Lead-Lag Relationship Between Spot Stock Indices and Their Futures Contracts," *The Journal of Futures Markets*, Vol. 7, No. 4, August 1987, pp. 373-381.

15 Hans Stoll and Robert Whaley, "The Dynamics of Stock Index and Stock Index Futures Returns," *Journal of Financial and Quantitative Analysis*, Vol. 25, No. 4, December 1990, pp. 441-468.

16 Eugene A. Swinnerton, Richard J. Curcio, and Richard E. Bennett, "Index Arbitrage Program Trading and the Prediction of Intraday Stock Price Change," *The Review of Futures Markets*, Vol. 7, No. 2, 1988, pp. 300-323.

17 After the market crash of 1987 many of the brokerage houses eliminated program trading *for their own accounts* for public relations purposes. Thus, the critics of program trades created an adverse public clamor, and brokerage houses did not want to alienate their individual customers. However, most houses continued to execute program trades for their institutional customers. Grossman compares 10 months of daily program

Although such accusations were challenged by many, including the various government and exchange studies on the crash, the outcry for controls on program trading caused the NYSE to place limitations on the intraday movement of the cash indexes and futures prices. These limitations are called circuit breakers. One aspect of circuit breakers is to trigger adjustments to how traders execute program trades through the **Designated Order Turn-around** or DOT system after a market move of at least 50 Dow Jones points. The benefit of the DOT system is that it provides major traders with a computer-linked system to the floor of the exchange; such a system speeds up the execution of a stock index futures arbitrage transaction significantly. Additional circuit breakers place price limits on price changes and stop trading in the cash and futures markets for 30 minutes or more, depending on the size of the price change. Chapter 3 provides details on circuit breakers.

Initiating Stock Index Futures Arbitrage

When the actual stock index futures price differs from the cost of carry forward price by more than transactions costs, arbitrage profits are possible. We can restate Equation (5-1) as

---

FOCUS 5-1: Stock Market Volatility and Futures Markets

Two issues of concern to market professionals are a possible increase in stock market volatility in the 1980s and the critics' claims of a relationship between the market's volatility and futures markets. Concern over the increase in market volatility in the past decade stems mostly from large daily moves in the Dow Jones Industrials during this time period. However, with the Dow ranging from 1000 to 2800 during most of the 1980s, the percentage changes in prices generally have been consistent with time periods when the Dow was below 1000.

Even though overall price volatility in the 1980s seems to be consistent with past time periods, there have been specific days and time periods where prices have changed dramatically. *Business Week* (see Laderman*) chronicles these changes through early 1986 and associates them with program trading. More dramatically, on September 11, 1986, and January 23, 1987, the markets gyrated more than 100 points on an intraday basis; on January 23, 1987, more than 300 million shares were traded, the largest daily volume to date, and a 115-point drop in the Dow occurred in only 71 minutes. On October 13, 1989, the Dow dropped 190 points in the last 90 minutes of trading. And then there was the market crash in October 1987, as discussed in Focus 5-2. On a more consistent basis, there was significant market volatility at the quarterly expiration of the futures and options contracts, which became known as the "triple witching hour." On these expiration dates, the Dow Jones Index sometimes moved 100 points within the last hour of trading.

Focus continues

---

trading activity with market volatility, determining that program trading is not associated with volatility. See Sanford J. Grossman, "Program Trading and Market Volatility," *Financial Analysts Journal*, Vol. 44, No. 4, July-August 1988, pp. 18-28.

FOCUS 5-1:   Continued

The large intraday price moves and the volatility during the triple witching hours were blamed on baskets of trading with stocks, called program trading. However, data for the S&P 500 futures contract show that the volume of program trading was not large during the declines in September 1986 and January 1987 (see Brodsky**). In fact, in January and October 1987, the market moved too fast for the program traders to execute their trades.

On the other hand, the price swings associated with the last hour of trading before the expiration of the futures and options contracts logically could be related to arbitrageurs' closing their positions. Recall that the stock index futures contracts are settled in cash at expiration by setting the futures price equal to the closing cash index value. Consequently, for arbitrageurs to avoid price risk, both futures and cash trades typically have to be closed at the end of trading on the expiration day. This activity often creates market imbalances for the individual stocks. In fact, the stock arbitrage positions are closed with a "market on close" order, where the brokerage house trades the stock during the last minute of trading. This concentrated activity can create conditions for wildly chaotic markets. For example, during the expiration of the December 1986 futures contract, 86 million shares were traded on the NYSE in the last *minute* of trading, using market on close orders.

Stoll and Whaley*** examine the relationship between expiration days and market volatility. They find that futures and option expirations contribute to both volume and price effects. In particular, volume is about twice the normal level in the last hour before futures and options expire. Moreover, S&P 500 stocks decline significantly during the last hour when futures expire. However, the price effects during this time period seem to be consistent with the effects of block trading by institutions during other time periods.

In order to reduce the effects of the triple witching hour on market volatility, the exchanges decided to stagger the expirations of the stock index futures, options on futures, and options on individual stocks. In particular, the S&P futures would stop trading at the third Thursday's close but would be valued at the next day's open. These changes in the closing procedures, starting with the June 1987 contract, have reduced volatility on expiration day.

---

*Jeffrey M. Laderman, "Those Big Swings on Wall Street," *Business Week*, April 7, 1986, pp. 32-36.

**William J. Brodsky, "Demystifying Stock Index Products," *Market Perspectives*, Vol. 5, No. 7, September 1987, pp. 1-5.

*** Hans Stoll and Robert Whaley, "Expiration Day Effects of Index Options and Futures," Series in Finance and Economics, Monograph 1986-3, Solomon Brothers Center for the Study of Financial Institutions, 1986. Also, Hans Stoll and Robert Whaley, "Program Trading and Expiration-Day Effects," *Financial Analysts Journal*, Vol. 43, No. 2, March/April 1987, pp. 16-23.

follows to consider transactions costs to define the arbitrage opportunities for stock index futures:

$$P_C(1 + i)^t - D + T < P_F < P_C(1 + i)^t - D - T \qquad (5-4)$$

or more compactly as

$$P_{FAIR} + T < P_F < P_{FAIR} - T \qquad (5-5)$$

with T being the total transactions costs.

There are two possible arbitrage strategies: short and long futures arbitrage. Which strategy is relevant depends on whether $P_{FAIR} \pm$ T is less than or greater than P_F, as given in Equation (5-5). If the relationship in Equation (5-5) is not met, then no potential arbitrage exists. Short futures arbitrage (selling futures) occurs when the cost of carry forward price $P_{FAIR} + T < P_F$. In this case the arbitrageur purchases stocks that are the equivalent of the cash index and the futures contract is sold. The arbitrageur then typically holds the position until the futures expiration, or unwinds it before expiration if it is more profitable to do so. If the position is held until futures expiration, then the arbitrageur simply arranges to sell the cash stocks at *exactly* the same time the futures stop trading by placing a "market on close" or "market on open" order, whichever is relevant. The market on close/open is effective in eliminating price risk since the futures contract price is set equal to the cash index at the end of trading for the futures contract, that is, the contract is settled in cash. This procedure guarantees a profit equal to $P_F - P_{FAIR} - T$, as long as no other factors affect the results. Of course, the arbitrageur also could close both sides of the trade before the futures expiration if it is profitable to do so. Exhibit 5-1 shows the cash flows for cash-and-carry stock index futures arbitrage. Examples 5-2 and 5-3 provide numerical illustrations of short futures arbitrage opportunities for the S&P 500 and MMI futures contracts.

Long futures arbitrage (buying futures) occurs when $P_{FAIR} - T > P_F$. One way to initiate a long arbitrage transaction is to purchase the futures and sell short the equivalent of the cash index. Alternatively, if the cash stocks are already in the arbitrageur's portfolio, the arbitrageur sells the stocks and invests the resultant funds in T-bills or other short-term instruments. This technique creates a position equivalent to the original stock position (less dividends) plus an excess return resulting from the arbitrage. This position is then held until the futures expire, at which time the stocks are repurchased. Exhibit 5-2 shows the cash flows for this reverse cash-and-carry arbitrage. Example 5-4 describes a case of long futures arbitrage.[18]

The typical *short* arbitrage strategy involves the use of only the arbitrageur's funds to purchase stocks, although borrowing 50 percent of the funds is a strategy also employed. The typical *long* arbitrage is employed by pension funds and other institutions that sell stocks currently in the portfolio and buy the equivalent futures. This strategy is called stock replacement. Factors that affect the profitability or risk of these strategies are transactions costs, short selling risks, dividends and margin effects, tracking risk, cash index lag effects, and stock price movements. These factors are explained in detail in the next section.

18 An arbitrageur can calculate a type of implied financing rate for stock index arbitrage; namely,
Implied financing rate = basis yield + dividend yield
where basis yield = $(P_F - P_C)/P_C$.
Thus, both the basis yield and dividend yield are in percentage terms. The implied financing rate then can be compared to either the financing rate or the equivalent yield one would receive on T-bills if funds were invested in that risk-free instrument. If the implied repo rate is higher than these other rates, then short futures arbitrage can provide enhanced returns, and vice versa. Of course, transactions costs need to be considered.

EXHIBIT 5-1: Cash and Carry Arbitrage for Stock Index Futures

Transaction	At Initiation of Arbitrage (Time t)	From Initiation to Futures Expiration	At Futures Expiration (Time T)
Buy stocks at time t to mimic stock index (sell stocks at time T)*	$- P_C(t)$	$+ D$	$+ P_C(T)$
Borrow funds or use own funds**	$+ P_C(t)$		$- P_C(1 + i)^t$
Sell stock index futures at time t***	0		$P_F(t) - P_C(T)$
Total	0	D	$P_F(t) - P_C(1 + i)^t$

The cash flow is $P_F(t) - P_C(1 + i)^t - D$.

If the futures price at time t equals the fair price, then $P_F(t) = P_{FAIR}(t) = P_C(1 + i)^t - D$. Alternatively, if $P_F(t) > P_C(1 + i)^t - D$, then arbitrage is possible if transactions costs are covered.

* Dividends should be reinvested; however, the difference in total return is marginal.

** Only 50 percent of the purchase price of stocks can be borrowed. The cost of borrowed funds is the financing rate, whereas the cost of the institution's own money is the opportunity cost of funds. The average cost is labeled i for this situation.

*** At time T (the futures expiration) the stock index futures price is set equal to the cash index.

Considerations for Stock Index Arbitrage

Implementing risk-free stock index arbitrage transactions is not as straightforward as the previous section may have implied. Several complications and risks must be taken into account, including the dividend and lag effects discussed earlier in relation to pricing stock index futures. The following discussion describes these considerations.

Transactions Costs. Commissions and bid-ask spread costs must be included in the profit analysis before implementing the arbitrage. Commissions for large transactions are relatively small, $.03 to $.06 per share each way for the stocks and $12 to $15 round-trip for each futures contract.[19] The bid-ask spread on stock trades is important because, everything else considered, the arbitrageur buys stocks at the specialist's ask price and sells at the

---

19 Funds intending to sell a market basket of stocks *independently* of the possibility of arbitrage can profit when $P_F > P_{FAIR}$ (when short futures arbitrage exists), since their *marginal* transactions costs involve only a futures commission. However, few funds use this type of arbitrage strategy.

EXAMPLE 5-2: Short Arbitrage and the S&P 500 Index

Using the data and results from Example 5-1 we find that the fair price for the S&P 500 contract is 322.23. The actual futures price on the same day is 323.95. Since the actual futures price of 323.95 is greater than the fair price of 322.23, one is able to profit by selling the higher-priced futures contract and purchasing the equivalent of the lower-priced index. Each of the relevant factors affecting the potential arbitrage is considered here:

Sell futures at	323.95
Buy the stocks in the S&P Index at	319.72
Futures premium	4.23
Plus dividends received	+2.22
Gross profit	6.45
Less opportunity ("financing") costs (see below)	−4.85
Less transactions costs (see below)	−1.09
Projected net profit	.51

or .51 (500) = $255 net profit per contract

Annualized return above T-bill rate = [.51/319.72] [365/84] = .0069; that is, the return is 69 basis points higher than the yield on T-bills.

Opportunity ("Financing") Costs per One Futures Contract:

The cost of holding the position is based on the arbitrageur's opportunity cost of funds and/or the borrowing rate, whichever is relevant. Here the arbitrageur is using internal funds and therefore is simply attempting to earn a return in excess of the T-bill rate. The opportunity cost is determined as follows:

Cost in index points = (T–bill yield) (index value) (no. days/365)
= (.0659) (319.72) $(84/365)$ = 4.85

Transaction Costs per Futures Contract:

			Index Points
Stock: $.08 per share round trip × 2,895 shares	= $231.60	=	.46
Futures: $15 per contract round trip × 1 contract	= $ 15	=	.03
Market impact (bid-ask) effects		=	.60
			1.09

EXAMPLE 5-3: An MMI Arbitrage Example

The following summarizes an arbitrage using the MMI futures contract:

February 26, 1986
Sell 35 MMI March 1986 futures contracts at 313.55.
Purchase 2,000 shares each of the 20 stocks in the MMI at a total cost of $2,749,000.
Borrow 50% of the needed funds at 8.5% and obtain the other 50% of the funds needed from the arbitrageur's own account.

March 21, 1986
Buy back 35 MMI March 1986 futures at 328.07.
Sell all of the stocks purchased on February 26 for $2,893,000.
Pay interest of $8,438 on borrowed funds.
Consider opportunity cost of own funds at 8.5 percent, totaling $8,438.
Pay transaction costs of $1,100.
Dividends on stocks received $6,820.

Net Cash Flows

Futures loss [(313.55 × 35) − (328.07 × 35)] =	$−127,050
Cash market gain ($2,893,000 − $2,749,000) =	144,000
Transaction costs	− 1,100
Dividends	+ 6,820
Interest on loan	− 8,438
Opportunity cost on invested funds	− 8,438
Arbitrage profit	$ 5,794

Source: Jeffrey M. Laderman, "Those Big Swings on Wall Street," *Business Week,* April 7, 1986, pp. 32-36.

bid. Often only half the bid-ask spread is relevant in arbitrage calculations, since the closing stock trades are executed at a "market on open" or "market on close" order so as to link the stock prices to the expiring futures contract price.[20] Although current bid and ask values for stocks and total bids/asks for portfolios of stocks are shown on many computer screens, bids and asks are often old values that change with new trades.

---

20 If an arbitrageur believes that most stocks will sell at the ask price when a short futures arbitrage is unwound, perhaps because of significant arbitrage activity, then a full bid-ask spread cost would be justified.

EXHIBIT 5-2: Reverse Cash and Carry Arbitrage for Stock Index Futures

Transaction	At Arbitrage Initiation (Time t)	From Initiation to Futures Expiration	At Futures Expiration (Time T)
Sell stocks currently in portfolio at time t; buy back stocks at time T*	$+ P_C(t)$		$- P_C(T)$
Receive funds from sale of stocks and invest in T-bills (or equivalent)**	$- P_C(t)$		$+ P_C(1 + i)^t - D$
Buy stock index futures at time t***	0		$P_C(T) - P_F(t)$
Total	0		$P_C(1 + i)^t - D - P_F(t)$

The cash flow is $P_C(1 + i)^t - D - P_F(t)$.

If the futures price at time t equals the fair price, then $P_F(t) = P_{FAIR}(t) = P_C(1 + i)^t - D$. Alternatively, if $P_F(t) < P_C(1 + i)^t - D$, then arbitrage is possible if transactions costs are covered.

* An alternative is to sell stocks short. In this case the short seller must *pay* out dividends when they are paid by the corporation.

** Dividends are subtracted from $P_C(1 + i)^t$ at time T because stock prices are adjusted *downward* when dividends are paid.

*** At time T (the futures expiration) the stock index futures price is set equal to the cash index.

Short Selling Considerations for Long Futures Arbitrage. Brokerage houses have access to the funds generated when they sell stocks short.[21] However, since other arbitrageurs often do not have access to these funds, higher financing costs are created for such transactions. Higher costs arise because needed funds must be borrowed or because the arbitrageur has an opportunity cost from lost interest on the arbitrageur's funds. Moreover, short sellers of stock are hampered by the "uptick" rule; that is, stocks can be sold short only if the most recent *change* in price was positive. This rule attempts to reduce the

21 Brokerage houses act as the principal pure arbitrageurs for stock index futures activity, since their financing costs are lower than those of other potential pure arbitrageurs and their marginal commissions are zero for their cash trades. However, Stoll and Whaley state two reasons why brokerage house arbitrage activity is limited in this market (exclusive of the potential adverse publicity): (1) the availability of capital to institute such trades is constrained by net capital requirements; and (2) they may have more profitable uses for their borrowed funds. See Hans Stoll and Robert Whaley, "Program Trading and Expiration-Day Effects," *Financial Analysts Journal*, Vol. 43, No. 2, March/April 1987, pp. 16-23.

EXAMPLE 5-4: Long Futures Arbitrage

Profits from long futures arbitrage may exist when the actual futures price is less than the forward price. In this case an arbitrageur would buy futures and sell stocks, as long as the profits are greater than the costs. Let us use the values and costs derived in Example 5-2:

Investment interest in index points	4.85*
Transactions costs	1.09
Dividends paid or given up on stocks, in index points	2.22**

The futures price is 323.95 and the forward price now is 325.40. A pension fund holds the equivalent of the S&P 500 index, which it is willing to sell now and replace with a futures contract (the stocks are repurchased later). The objective is to hold the *equivalent* of the S&P 500 with the futures contract *as well as* earning a risk-free rate of return via the arbitrage. The calculations to determine whether a profit is possible are:

Sell S&P equivalent stocks in portfolio at	322.74
Buy futures at	323.95
Futures discount	−1.21
Plus investment yield in T-bills	+4.85
Less dividends forgone	−2.22
Gross profit	+1.42
Less transactions costs	−1.09
Projected net profit	.33

Annualized return above T-bill rate = [.33/322.74] [365/84] = .0058 or 58 basis points above the T-bill yield.

* For short arbitrage this amount is a cost of funds or opportunity cost, while here it represents the interest received from taking the funds received and investing in a T-bill or equivalent instrument.

** Stocks are sold (or sold short); therefore, dividends are given up (or they must be paid out on a short sale).

---

downward pressure on stock prices when prices are falling. When the futures price is below the cash index value and prices are falling, a pure arbitrageur would like to buy the futures contract and short the stocks; however, short sales may not be possible for all stocks because of the "uptick" rule. Because of these problems, most long futures arbitrage is conducted by institutions that *already own* the relevant stocks. To implement a long futures arbitrage they buy the futures and sell the stocks already in the portfolio, creating the net effect desired. The funds obtained from the stock sale are invested in T-bill or equivalent short-term instruments. Such a quasi-arbitrage transaction is often called a stock replacement strategy. Example 5-4 earlier in the chapter illustrates this strategy.

Cash Flow Effects. Dividends are *not* a constantly decreasing function of time; that is, dividend payments occur in spikes during each quarter, as discussed in relation to the pricing process and shown earlier in Figures 5-1 and 5-2. Moreover, companies can change their dividend payout before the futures contract expires. The mark-to-market effect of the futures contract often creates a cash flow during the life of the arbitrage transaction, creating an uncertain amount of interest received or paid on these funds (at least if cash funds are employed for margin calls). Although these factors do not cause a major bias in the arbitrage model, many investment houses include these effects in their computer models.

Tracking Risk. The S&P index is composed of 500 stocks, with each stock's weight in the index being determined by its market value in proportion to the market value of the total index; the NYSE index is made up of 1,800 stocks, also proportionally weighted. Generating a cash portfolio that exactly matches the relevant cash index is costly, since the arbitrageur must include all 500 or 1,800 stocks in the transaction *and* the weights in the portfolio must be matched to the weights in the index. Therefore, many arbitrageurs have used a portfolio of 50 to 200 stocks that closely track the activity of the S&P 500 index in order to execute a "near" arbitrage transaction. However, this procedure creates tracking errors (basis risk) between the 50- to 200-stock portfolio and the index, creating imperfect arbitrage. Such a strategy has created large losses in certain circumstances in the past. Now, most S&P 500 arbitrage trades are completed by matching the cash index exactly, a practice that necessitates a minimum of $25 million.[22] Of course, the NYSE index *cannot* be effectively matched with a reasonable amount of funds. The MMI futures require only $3 million to avoid tracking risk. Although arbitrageurs would like to trade large positions in the MMI, liquidity often does not exist. For the NYFE contract, the arbitrageur compensates for the tracking error by requiring a greater difference between the futures and cash index prices before the arbitrage is undertaken. The NYSE contract also has limited liquidity for large trades.

The Lag Effect. The lag of cash prices to futures prices examined in the pricing section also has an effect on the arbitrage process. If futures lead cash index prices by 5 to 20 minutes (or more), then using simultaneous data to calculate the potential arbitrage profits provides erroneous results. In addition, the use of end-of-day prices to infer potential arbitrage situations is hazardous, inasmuch as the futures contracts stop trading 15 minutes *after* the common stocks end trading. Evidence given below elaborates on this factor.[23]

Potential Stock Price Movements. Since trades are executed by the DOT system within two minutes, individual stock prices typically do not change significantly (if at all) before execution. More importantly, stock prices that increase are offset by those that decrease, unless a major market move is underway. Also, the arbitrageur does not usually move the market since each individual stock in the arbitrage trade only constitutes a few

---

22 When the DOT system is employed, the trader can execute any odd size order in excess of 100 shares. Thus, the smallest stock must trade 100 shares but other stocks can trade 101, 102, etc. shares. Thus the arbitrageur can mimic the S&P 500 index with $25 million by buying all 500 stocks in the S&P 500 index in the exact same proportions as found in the index.

23 Although composite bid-and-ask prices for the portfolio of stocks making up the cash index do appear on traders' screens, these bid-and-ask values also are old, since specialists update the quotes only as time permits.

hundred shares or less. Brokerage houses that institute arbitrage trades for funds provide at least two options for clients. One is a "guaranteed price" for the portfolio; another is a "best efforts price" for the portfolio. The commission costs for the first alternative is higher than for the second.

Evidence Concerning Stock Index Arbitrage

Modest and Sundaresan[24] completed an early study of stock index futures arbitrage by applying the cost of carry model to daily data. They calculated no-arbitrage bands based on their assumed transactions costs, finding that the daily futures versus cash relationships fell within the bands if the proceeds from short sales were not available; arbitrage *was* possible when short sale proceeds were available for reinvestment. However, the transactions costs used by Modest and Sundaresan are much higher than institutions pay. Moreover, their assumption that long futures arbitrage is unduly costly (because of the uptick short sale rule) does not conform to the industry practice by pension funds of initiating long futures arbitrage by selling stocks already in their portfolios.

MacKinlay and Ramaswamy[25] provide limited arbitrage results in conjunction with their pricing results examined earlier. They employ intraday data, but their choice of the size of the transactions bands seems to be arbitrary at .6% of the value of the cash index, and they do not provide information on average arbitrage profits. However, MacKinlay and Ramaswamy do find that the average time that futures prices are above the upper transaction bound is two hours and the average time they are below the lower bound is 36 minutes (using 15-minute interval data). The large number of upper plus lower bound violations averages 234 intervals per three-month contract; the number of boundary crossings averages 41 per period. Further analysis of the arbitrage violations leads MacKinlay and Ramaswamy to conclude that the arbitrage violations are path dependent, that is, once an arbitrage boundary is crossed it is less likely for the mispriced value to cross the opposite arbitrage boundary.

Merrick[26] examines early unwindings and rollovers of arbitrage positions before futures expiration to determine whether such dynamic strategies affect the profits of arbitrage transactions. Although Merrick only employs daily S&P data, he finds that the *effective* total transactions cost is only 73% of the original anticipated transactions cost when unwindings and rollovers are employed as part of a complete arbitrage strategy.

Daigler[27] uses five-minute intervals to calculate arbitrage profits for the three major stock index futures contracts: the S&P 500, the Major Market Index, and the NYFE Index. Daigler employs an exact cost structure for the arbitrage transactions, examines the effect

24 David M. Modest and Mahadevan Sundaresan, "The Relationship Between Spot and Futures Prices in Stock Index Futures Markets: Some Preliminary Evidence," *The Journal of Futures Markets*, Vol. 3, No. 1, Spring 1983, pp. 15-41.

25 C. MacKinlay and K. Ramaswamy, "Index-Futures Arbitrage and the Behavior of Stock Index Futures Prices," *Review of Financial Studies*, Vol. 1, No. 2, Summer 1988, pp. 137-158.

26 John J. Merrick, Jr., "Early Unwindings and Rollovers of Stock Index Futures Arbitrage Programs: Analysis and Implications for Predicting Expiration Day Effects," *The Journal of Futures Markets*, Vol. 9, No. 2, April 1989, pp. 101-112.

27 Robert T. Daigler, "Stock Index Arbitrage with Intraday Data," working paper, Florida International University, 1991.

of timing lags between the futures and cash indexes on the reported arbitrage profits, and provides implicit evidence of the tracking risk on arbitrage results. Table 5-1 shows the average arbitrage profits for a $25 million portfolio when only the end-of-the-day and early morning arbitrage results are determined. The end-of-the-day results compare futures prices that close 15 minutes later than the stock market and are shown in column 2. The early morning results in column 3 show the results for simultaneous prices (no lags in the cash index). Columns 4 and 5, respectively, show the effect of a 5- and 15-minute cash index lag. The lagged values are useful for observing the effect of stocks that take at least 10 minutes to open.

Table 5-1 shows that the use of end-of-day prices apparently generates large arbitrage profits after transactions costs. Early-morning results with no cash lags show even larger apparent profits. However, the early-morning profits decline quickly to near zero or negative when 5- and 15-minute cash lags are considered; that is, once most of the stocks in the index trade and their new prices are recorded in the index, then the apparent arbitrage profits shown in the early morning disappear. Correspondingly, the large end-of-day profits are likely caused by the 15-minute difference in closing between the futures and cash markets.

The importance of the timing effects becomes even clearer when one compares the intraday results from Table 5-2 and Figure 5-4. This table and figure show the size of the arbitrage profits when *intraday* cash and futures prices are employed. The profits for the simultaneous intraday cash and futures prices in column 2 of Table 5-2 are significantly smaller than the simultaneous profits found in Table 5-1, especially when the October-December 1987 period is eliminated from the results. In addition, even the profits shown in column 2 essentially disappear for the S&P and MMI contracts when cash prices are employed with a five-minute lag, as given in column 3. (December 1987 is the exception.) Moreover, the arbitrage profits are eliminated for the NYFE contract when a 15-minute lag is employed (exclusive of December 1987). Thus, the lag effect due to "old" prices in the cash index explains average arbitrage profits, except for unusual periods such as October to December 1987, although the NYFE contract takes a longer time (15 minutes) for the lag effect to manifest itself. Although it is not shown here, all three contracts have a large number of *apparent* arbitrage possibilities per three-month period; that is, prices *temporarily* deviate outside the transactions bounds, but these deviations are due to the lag effect of the cash index. Figure 5-4 dramatically illustrates the effect of lags on the average results (the December 1989 quarter is excluded).

Chung[28] calculates the value of the cash index by using actual subsequent *trades* on each of the stocks making up the MMI index *after* the arbitrage opportunity appears. Using data from 1984 to 1986, Chung finds that the size and the frequency of arbitrage profits are significantly smaller than the *daily* studies referenced above, especially for transactions costs of .75% and 1%. In fact, only the .5% transactions costs are consistently profitable when actual trades are employed. He also finds that the existence of arbitrage profits has declined over time.

---

28 Y. Peter Chung, "A Transactions Data Test of Stock Index Futures Market Efficiency and Index Arbitrage Profitability," *Journal of Finance*, Vol. 46, No. 5, December 1991, pp. 1791-1809.

TABLE 5-1: Average Arbitrage Profits per $25 Million Portfolio:
End-of-the-Day and Early-Morning Results
(Profits in Thousands)

Expiration (1)	End of Day Profits (2)	Early Morning Profits		
		No Lag (3)	5-Min Lag (4)	15-Min Lag (5)
A. S&P 500				
Mar 87	36.4	36.1	− 7.0	−32.6
Jun 87	52.0	98.4	33.4	0.4
Sep 87	42.6	29.2	−16.8	−28.1
Dec 87	98.5	333.3	235.0	178.8
Mar 88	74.9	91.9	12.8	−20.1
Jun 88	57.0	56.2	10.8	−11.7
B. MMI				
Mar 87	30.8	40.7	− 4.6	−20.6
Jun 87	36.5	74.2	12.6	− 3.2
Sep 87	22.6	29.1	− 2.1	− 8.4
Dec 87	159.5	363.2	266.7	182.2
Mar 88	52.6	87.9	16.6	−14.5
Jun 88	25.5	53.9	2.3	−19.4
C. NYFE				
Mar 87	69.2	50.1	.3	−27.4
Jun 87	82.4	110.7	53.1	10.5
Sep 87	42.5	37.0	−10.8	−39.0
Dec 87	85.6	329.7	233.7	124.6
Mar 88	96.1	119.9	37.2	−21.2
Jun 88	54.4	59.6	13.9	−13.5
D. Averages				
S&P 500				
with Dec 87	60.2	107.5	44.7	14.4
w/o Dec 87	52.6	62.4	6.6	−18.4
MMI				
with Dec 87	54.6	108.2	48.6	19.4
w/o Dec 87	33.6	57.2	5.0	−13.2
NYFE				
with Dec 87	71.7	117.8	54.6	5.7
w/o Dec 87	68.9	75.5	18.7	−18.1

Source: Robert T. Daigler, "Stock Index Arbitrage with Intraday Data," working paper, Florida International University, 1991.

TABLE 5-2: Average Arbitrage Profits per $25 Million Portfolio:
Intraday Results
(Profits in Thousands)

Expiration (1)	No Lag (2)	Intraday Results 5-Min Lag (3)	15-Min Lag (4)
A. S&P 500			
Mar 87	21.3	− 2.5	−10.7
Jun 87	24.8	6.9	− 2.3
Sep 87	11.5	− 7.3	−16.1
Dec 87	194.0	167.6	146.5
Mar 88	24.1	− 1.8	−13.8
Jun 88	26.4	13.0	.9
B. MMI			
Mar 87	18.8	3.3	− 6.4
Jun 87	17.7	− 1.3	−11.0
Sep 87	18.9	8.8	1.2
Dec 87	250.2	225.8	205.0
Mar 88	24.8	5.8	− 4.0
Jun 88	17.2	.5	− 8.8
C. NYFE			
Mar 87	35.1	6.1	− 3.7
Jun 87	38.0	21.3	7.5
Sep 87	13.1	−12.7	−23.9
Dec 87	138.3	116.7	94.6
Mar 88	42.2	22.5	8.2
Jun 88	31.0	19.2	7.6
D. Averages			
S&P 500			
with Dec 87	50.4	29.3	17.8
w/o Dec 87	21.6	1.7	− 7.9
MMI			
with Dec 87	57.9	40.5	31.5
w/o Dec 87	19.5	3.4	− 3.2
NYFE			
with Dec 87	49.6	28.9	15.7
w/o Dec 87	31.9	11.3	− .1

Source: Robert T. Daigler, "Stock Index Arbitrage with Intraday Data," working paper, Florida International University, 1991.

FIGURE 5-4: The Effect of Lags on Arbitrage Profits

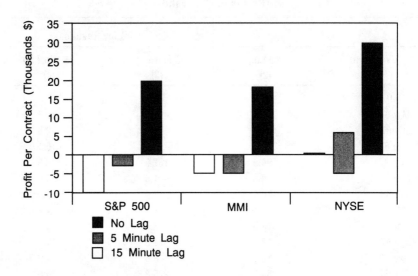

Source: Adapted from Robert T. Daigler, "Stock Index Arbitrage with Intraday Data," working paper, Florida International University, 1991. Data from Tick Data, Inc..

Several important conclusions are derived from these studies on stock index arbitrage. First, the use of closing or early-morning prices to examine the pricing and arbitrage aspects of stock index futures markets causes difficulties in determining the actual potential for arbitrage as a result of the nonsimultaneous nature of end-of-the-day prices and the cash index lag effects. Second, assumptions concerning the cost structure for the marginal arbitrageur are critical in determining the existence of arbitrage profits. Third, apparent intraday arbitrage profits are mostly illusionary because of the lag effect of the cash index prices. Finally, the cost of carry model apparently does a good job of describing stock index futures prices once the factors noted above are considered, although additional evidence is needed concerning the relationship between these factors and futures pricing.

FUTURES AND THE MARKET CRASH

Although many critics blame stock index futures for the stock market crash of 1987, financial economists explain that futures reflected market sentiment during that time. Why should we care about this historical event? First, the behavior of futures prices calls into question the pricing mechanism of futures markets. Second, we want to know whether it is important to find ways of protecting stock portfolios from another potential crash. Third, the crash actually did result in regulatory changes for the market. In particular, exchanges placed circuit breakers (price limits) on stock index futures to reduce volatility during market panics and to avoid criticism concerning the crash.

What did happen on "Black Monday" and how was the market behavior affected by futures? Here we examine the explanations and criticisms as related to futures markets. Figure 5-5 shows the extent of the crash on an intraday basis and the resultant volatility on the next day. This figure shows the almost straight decline in the S&P 500 futures on the 19th. The index then opened up higher on the 20th before retreating again until the market closed in midday. Focus 5-2 provides a background for our discussion by explaining the events of the crash.

Program Trading and the Crash

Although futures markets and program trading did not serve their typical market adjustment and arbitrage roles on October 19 (because of the breakdown of the system, as described in Focus 5-2), neither did they *cause* the market decline. In fact, stock index arbitrage was very difficult to execute on Monday: bid-ask spreads for futures were 1 point and for stocks (when the latter were trading) were 1% or more of the price of the stock. Moreover, traders were not confident about the execution price of their orders once the orders came to the floor of the exchange. In addition, most of the pension funds and institutions that typically executed program trades were at their trading limit, since they had initiated trades the

---

FIGURE 5-5: Stock Index Futures: October 19 and 20, 1987

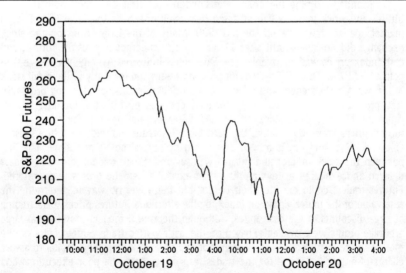

Source: Prices from Tick Data, Inc.

FOCUS 5-2: The Market Crash and Program Trading

On "Black Monday" (October 19, 1987) the Dow Jones Industrial Index fell 508 points or 22.6%, in comparison with the 12.8% one-day drop in 1929. Panic reigned on Wall Street and in other financial capitals. How did program trading relate to this devastating market crash? How did the market function on that day? What can we learn from this catastrophic event?

A number of commentaries on the market crash were written. In fact, several government agencies conducted hearings and issued special reports on the events of the crash. Two of the more interesting commentaries are by Joanne Hill* and Scott Hamilton**; these commentaries were written soon after the crash and form the basis of the following discussion.

Early warnings of a problem in the stock market began on October 6 when the Dow Jones Industrials declined 91 points in one day. During the following week the market declined more than 90 points each day on Wednesday and Friday, October 14 and 16, and 57 points on Thursday the 15th. The market was down a total of 10% on these three days and 15% over the two-week period. Volatilities in the stock, futures, and options markets were up 25% to 30% before the crash. The merchandise trade deficit news was discouraging, and interest rates were increasing. On the weekend before Black Monday, news programs focused on the market's problems, on Treasury Secretary Baker's remarks concerning prospects for further declines in the dollar, on technical indicators turning bearish, and on the problems in the Mideast.

On Monday morning the Tokyo and London markets fell sharply. Both the U.S. futures and stock markets had amassed heavy sell orders by the open. The futures market opened down 7% on the S&P 500. Many of the large issues on the stock exchange did not open until after 11 A.M., and thus comparison of the futures and cash index prices was impossible. The Dow Jones Industrial Average was down 190 points by 11 A.M. The DOT system for program trades and for many of the retail stock orders was overburdened, and most program trading desks stopped taking orders. In fact, program trading never really effectively operated on Monday, October 19, because most of the major stocks in the S&P 500 were not open in the morning, the futures prices were too volatile, the cash bid-ask spreads too wide to assure reasonable execution, and prices moved downward by several points at a time. The link between the stock market and futures was severed. Stock traders saw their orders delayed and executed at lower prices than existed when the orders were entered. Futures traders could execute their orders, but there was no way to determine the true value of the underlying cash index; by the afternoon, futures prices were trading at large discounts to the cash index. Although theoretical models showed that large arbitrage profits were available, based on the last reported trade values of stocks, the markets were in turmoil. Brokers were not willing to risk their own capital to assure clients of a specified price for the trades, especially given the poor executions and unfilled orders that existed.

Focus continues

FOCUS 5-2: Continued

Trading in the S&P futures was 162,000 contracts, which represented 1.5 times the previous week's daily average. Cash stocks traded 604 million shares, three times the previous week's average. Futures volume declined as the week progressed, representing only one-third of its typical ratio to cash market activity. For the week the S&P index was down 12.2%, the Dow Industrials 13.2%, and the OTC market 19.2%, including the partial recovery from Monday's decline. Stock indexes were down 26% to 30% from their highs at the end of August. Markets around the world fell significantly.

---

* Joanne Hill, "Massive Selling Strains Worldwide Equity and Index Derivative Markets," *Stock Index Weekly Report*, Kidder, Peabody and Co., October 23, 1987.

** Scott W. Hamilton, "Did Program Trading Cause the Crash?" Equity Research Report SF2873, The First Boston Corporation, October 23, 1987.

---

previous week and did not have funds for additional trades. Statistics reveal that only 9 percent of the volume on the 19th and 2 percent on the 20th was index arbitrage.

Portfolio Insurance as a Factor

The effect of **portfolio insurance** on the market decline is harder to measure. Portfolio insurance is a technique that allows participants to benefit from market advances by increasing the exposure to stocks during up-markets and providing insurance from market declines by selling stocks during down-markets. The declines occurring before October 19 should have triggered portfolio insurance sell programs, but futures open interest figures suggest that such selling was only about 15 percent of total stock market volume on the 19th and 20 percent on the 20th; however, it does account for nearly 40 percent of the *sales* of futures contracts. Moreover, portfolio insurers often use futures only to execute trades quickly and at low cost; eventually, they cover the futures positions and sell the stocks. Hence, at worst, futures were used only for convenience by the portfolio insurers; in fact, the discounts on the futures were so large that many portfolio insurers simply traded solely in the cash market and/or waited until later in the week to trade. Of course, the *potential* for portfolio insurers selling on Monday may have panicked other money managers into selling at the open on October 19. In fact, Jacklin, Kleidon, and Pfleiderer[29] developed a model that associates uncertain portfolio insurance positions with the potential for a market crash. Overall, the technique of portfolio insurance did not work well in the market collapse.

The Cash-Futures Basis During the Crash

Figure 5-6 shows the basis between the S&P 500 cash index and the S&P 500 futures during the crash period. The substantial futures discount and the widening of the basis from

---

29 Charles J. Jacklin, Allan W. Kleidon, and Paul Pfleiderer, "Underestimation of Portfolio Insurance and the Crash of October 1987," *Review of Financial Studies*, Vol. 5, No. 1, Spring 1992, pp. 35-64.

midday on the 19th through the 20th shows the lack of arbitrage activity in the market.[30] However, this widening of the basis also creates a mystery: *why* did the futures fall *faster* than the cash index? Was it solely due to a lack of index arbitrage? Three explanations help to clear up this mystery.

- Harris[31] shows the cash index fell slower than futures before 11 A.M. on the 19th because many of the major stocks did not open until 10:30 to 11 A.M. Thus, the cash index was "old" because it reflected the *last* price of each stock in the index, which in this case was Friday's close on the 16th for stocks that had not yet opened on Monday, as well as old prices for smaller stocks in the index that do not trade often.

- Blume, MacKinlay, and Terker[32] found that the S&P 500 stocks fell 7 percentage points more than non-S&P stocks on the 19th. By the morning of the 20th the difference had disappeared. They also found the decline in the S&P stocks was related to order imbalances. Thus, Blume, MacKinlay, and Terker suggest that activity related to the S&P futures affected the market.

- Kleidon[33] determines that on the afternoon of the 19th and on the 20th the cash-futures basis did not close because of mechanical reasons on the NYSE. In particular, buy-limit orders arrived on the exchange floor up to 45 minutes after traders placed them because of printer delays and breakdowns. These buy-limit orders kept cash prices at a higher level than dictated by supply and demand forces; that is, the limit orders created "stale" prices. Since the crash, the NYSE has upgraded its order-taking system.

Conclusions on the Crash and Futures Markets

Program trading and futures were blamed for the market catastrophe. The above argument maintains that this blame was generally misplaced. Moreover, other world stock markets did not have significant program trading or portfolio insurance programs, and their decline was comparable to the fall in the U.S. markets. The studies of "Black Monday" also stated that futures markets were not the culprit in the market crash. Scott Hamilton[34] described the situation best when he commented on those placing the blame: "Monday's market was somewhat analogous to a group of individuals finding themselves in a smoke-filled room. Those with foresight and preplanning used futures and options to find the exit quickly. Others, without the benefit of these instruments, were left to slower and less efficient means of departure. It's not unusual for those who find themselves at the back of the line to complain that those in front had an 'unfair' advantage."

---

30 Notice the behavior of the MMI futures contract during midday on the 20th. Manipulation of the MMI contract was suspected during this period, but no proof was forthcoming from the investigations of the crash period.

31 Lawrence Harris, "The October 1987 S&P 500 Stock-Futures Basis," *Journal of Finance*, Vol. 44, No. 1, March 1989, pp. 77-99.

32 M. Blume, A. MacKinlay, and B. Terker, "Order Imbalances and Stock Price Movements on October 19 and 20, 1987," *Journal of Finance*, Vol. 44, No. 4, September 1989, pp. 827-848.

33 Allan W. Kleidon, "Arbitrage, Nontrading, and Stale Prices: October 1987," *Journal of Business*, Vol. 65, No. 4, October 1992, pp. 483–508.

34 Scott W. Hamilton, "Did Program Trading Cause the Crash?" Equity Research Report SF2873, The First Boston Corporation, October 23, 1987.

FIGURE 5-6: The Cash–Futures Basis During the Crash

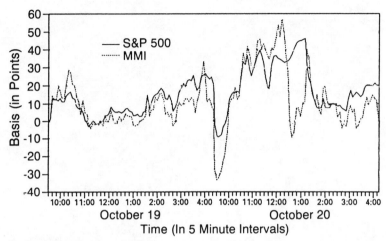

Source: Prices from Tick Data, Inc.

SUMMARY AND LOOKING AHEAD

This chapter examined the concepts and applications of pricing and arbitrage for stock index futures. Understanding stock index futures pricing and arbitrage concepts is important not only to those who execute program trades but to anyone who deals with futures markets, since pricing is a key component in the appropriate implementation of most trading and hedging strategies. This chapter showed that a number of factors affect futures pricing and whether a stock index arbitrage is profitable. Consequently, such a trade is not the straightforward undertaking implied by the mass media. In particular, the lag effect created by stale cash index prices creates a particular problem for evaluating pricing models and arbitrage trades. The next chapter covers basic cash bond pricing issues and related information needed for debt futures and bond portfolio management. Chapters 7 and 8 examine pricing and arbitrage for bond futures and short-term interest rate futures, respectively.

Chapter 6

Debt Instruments, Yield Curves, and Bond Portfolio Management

A concrete foundation of knowledge concerning debt instruments, yield curves, and bond portfolio management is necessary for bond portfolio managers to perform successfully. This knowledge also is needed to comprehend debt futures pricing and related strategies for hedging and speculating. Yield curves depicting the maturity-bond yield relationship are emphasized here, including a discussion of the different historical shapes of the yield curve and an examination of why specific issues do not fall on the smoothed yield curve. Bond portfolio management is examined both by determining which factors influence bond prices the most and by explaining bond portfolio models.

A FEW BASIC CONCEPTS

Accrued Interest

Interest on T-bonds, T-notes, and most corporate bonds are paid semiannually; the total price for a bond or note between interest payments is the quoted transactions price *plus* the unpaid **accrued interest**. Accrued interest is the amount of interest earned, but not yet paid, since the last interest date. Equation (6-1) calculates the amount of accrued interest. Note that the calculation of accrued interest uses the actual number of days from the last interest payment to the sale of the bond. Example 6-1 shows how to calculate accrued interest.

$$\text{Accrued interest} = \frac{(CP)\,(NL)}{NB} \qquad (6\text{-}1)$$

where   CP = coupon payment amount
   NL = the number of days since the last coupon payment
   NB = the number of days between coupon payments

Yield to Maturity Versus Realized Compound Yield to Maturity

The yield to maturity (YTM) is the interest rate that equates the current bond price with the present value of the bond's cash flows. Although this yield to maturity calculation does consider the original coupon yield and the expected change in the bond price as it moves toward par value, it also assumes that coupons will be reinvested *at the YTM*. Thus, the YTM sometimes is referred to as the promised yield, since the reinvestment rate on the coupons is uncertain and the true reinvestment rate changes as interest rates change over time. Consequently, the true rate of return that a portfolio manager earns on a bond

121

FOCUS 6-1: The History of Real Interest Rates

The **real rate of interest** is the nominal interest rate less the *actual* ex-post inflation rate for the period in question. Since the actual inflation rate typically differs from the expected inflation rate, the real rate of interest is either positive or negative, and it fluctuates significantly over time. During much of the inflationary period from the early 1970s until the early 1980s, investors' after-tax real rate of return from debt instruments was negative. However, the Fed's policies to control inflation in conjunction with the capital market influences of the deficit financing by the government caused large positive real rates starting in 1982. In other words, actual inflation fears declined while expected inflation fears and capital market supply and demand factors kept **nominal interest rates** high. This situation in turn created an unusually strong U.S. dollar until 1985, as foreign investors purchased dollars to obtain interest rates in T-bills and T-bonds that were significantly above the actual U.S. inflation rate. From 1982 until early 1990, the U.S. economy remained strong, inflation low, and real rates of return positive. By 1991 the United States was in a recession. By 1992 short-term interest rates declined below 4%, and inflation remained low. Figure 6-1 shows the history of short-term and long-term interest rates and their difference. Rates were high in the early and mid-1980s and low in the early 1990s. In the late 1970s and early 1980s, short-term interest rates were extremely volatile and often were higher than long-term rates. Since 1982, long-term rates have been above short-term rates. Thus, forecasts of the size and movement of nominal interest rates must consider the major economic, inflationary, and capital market factors that affect the level of interest rates.

FIGURE 6-1: The History of Interest Rates

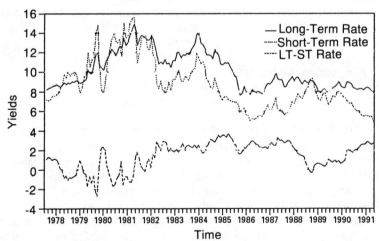

Source: Data from Tick Data, Inc.

EXAMPLE 6-1: Calculation of Accrued Interest

One determines the accrued interest for a bond by using Equation (6-1):
   Annual coupon interest rate: 12%
   Coupon date: August 15
   Bond face value: $1,000
   Current date: June 9
   Number of days since the last coupon: 114
   Number of days between coupon payments: 181

The number of days since the last coupon is calculated as follows (note that interest typically is paid on the 15th of the month for most bonds):

February	13
March	31
April	30
May	31
June	9
	114

$$\text{Accrued interest} = (CP)\ (NL)/NB$$
$$= (\$60)\ (114)/181$$
$$= \$37.79$$

FOCUS 6-2: Information Technology and Bond Management

MarketMaster, more commonly known as the Bloomberg bond system, is the computer system most desired by bond traders and bond portfolio managers. In addition to real time government and mortgage bond prices and other bond information, the system provides historical graphs and evaluates bond positions. Durations, yield analysis when the bond manager exchanges bonds, and hedge positions are examples of the type of analysis performed on the Bloomberg system.

Portfolio managers can obtain a complete bond inventory on the system within 15 seconds, whereas traders can tell clients the effects of exchanging zero-coupon bonds for Treasuries. The key aspect of the system is the integration of real time data, graphs, a menu system to operate the system, and extensive analytical programs to evaluate bonds.

The key to this merger of information technology and financial products is how such a system speeds and improves decision-making by bond managers. As such systems proliferate, managers can worry less about calculations and concentrate on ways to meet the objectives of the bond portfolio.

portfolio depends on the *reinvestment rate* obtained on the coupons received and reinvested, as well as the original coupon yield and the change in bond price. Hence, another measure is needed to take into account the changing reinvestment rate on intermediate cash flows. The **realized compound yield to maturity** (RCYTM) measures the *total* annual average compound return after all cash flows are reinvested. RCYTM is useful as a more realistic overall rate of return measure *after* the fact, whereas YTM provides a value of the *expected* return.

The RCYTM is determined as follows:

$$RCYTM = (TV/IV)^{1/N} - 1 \qquad (6\text{-}2)$$

where   TV = total final dollar value of the bond portfolio, including coupons and returns from reinvesting coupons

   IV = initial dollar value of the portfolio

   N = number of periods until the bond or bond portfolio matures[1]

TV/IV often is referred to as the terminal value ratio. Note that if the reinvestment rate equals the yield to maturity for all coupons then the RCYTM equals the YTM. If the reinvestment rate is greater than the YTM, then RCYTM > YTM, and vice versa. The concepts of reinvestment rates and RCYTM need to be considered when large amounts of fixed-income funds are being managed.

Zero-Coupon Bonds

A zero-coupon bond is a bond that only pays an ending principal payment (it has no coupons). Since a zero-coupon bond has no intermediate cash flows to reinvest, its RCYTM equals the original YTM. Hence, a zero-coupon bond avoids the uncertainty concerning reinvestment rates that is present for coupon-paying bonds. Zero-coupon bonds exist for Treasury securities and corporate bonds.

YIELD CURVES

The Bond Yield-Maturity Relationship

The average time until maturity for a fixed-rate portfolio is one of the few factors that can be managed effectively in the bond investment process. Since the maturity effect is directly related to the size and volatility of bond price changes, the maturity of a bond is an important consideration for investment decisions. Consequently, a discussion of **yield curves** (the bond yield versus maturity relationship) is needed before one examines specific strategies concerning bonds.

The yield curve shows the relationship between the maturity of a fixed-rate instrument and its yield to maturity. The yield curve typically is developed from Treasury securities in order to remove the default risk effect of corporate and municipal bonds. More sophisticated Wall Street models examine the **term structure** curve. The term structure ignores the effects of coupons on the yield and concentrates on the forward rate.

Shapes of The Yield Curve

Figure 6-2 shows the four shapes of the yield curves for Treasury securities. Note that the Y-axis is the yield on government bonds, whereas the X-axis indicates the year of the

---

1   Note that if N is measured in semiannual periods, then RCYTM represents a six-month yield.

FIGURE 6-2: The Four Types of Yield Curves

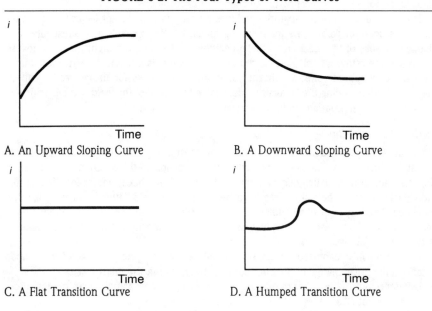

A. An Upward Sloping Curve

B. A Downward Sloping Curve

C. A Flat Transition Curve

D. A Humped Transition Curve

maturity of the given instrument. The upward sloping yield curve depicted in Figure 6-2A was the prevalent shape during the economic expansion of the 1950s and 1960s and much of the 1980s after 1982; hence it is known as the "normal" curve. The upward sloping yield curve generally occurs during periods of low inflation and relatively low interest rates.

The downward sloping yield curve or "inverted curve" depicted in Figure 6-2B often occurs during periods of relatively high inflation and relatively high interest rates. In fact, from the early 1970s to the early 1980s the downward sloping curve was the prevalent shape of the yield curve. The year 1981 was the last time that a downward sloping curve existed. The downward sloping curve usually is described as indicating a near-term decline in inflation since the higher short-term rates reflect high short-term inflation forecasts, whereas lower longer-term rates are forecasting a decline in inflation by the intermediate term.[2]

Figures 6-2C and 6-2D show transition yield curves—that is, situations where the shape of the yield curve changes from an upward sloping to a downward sloping curve or vice versa. Humped curves often occur when the level of interest rates is high and the rates are about to decline. In fact, the humped curve shows that the transition from higher to lower

2 On the other hand, if the general consensus of the markets is that a high, long-term inflation rate is likely to continue (such as in a number of South American countries—e.g., Brazil), then the yield curve could be upward sloping, but at a very high interest rate that would reflect both a high inflation rate and the expectation that inflation would exist for the longer term.

rates (or vice versa) has already started to occur in the short-term range, with the intermediate range not yet fully reacting to the change in expectations.[3]

The relationship between maturity and interest rates is a significant factor in the money
manager's decision parameters for investing funds. Changing levels of interest rates and
changing shapes of the yield curve make decisions concerning the maturity of the investments and the reinvestment rates for short-term investments difficult. In particular, changing yield curve shapes offer significant opportunities *and* risks for the aggressive money
manager. Understanding the factors that determine the shape of the yield curve is critical in
determining the appropriate maturity strategy.

Fitting the Yield Curve

Yield curves are constructed by determining the "best-fitting" smooth curve through individual Treasury issues. The best-fit procedure used depends on the accuracy and sophistication desired; conceptually, one can think of fitting a nonlinear regression line to the
individual points. A best-fit approach to determine the yield curve is needed because
individual Treasury issues have different characteristics that cause minor deviations from a
smooth curve. The reasons individual issues would deviate from the overall yield curve
pattern are as follows:

• Differences in coupon rates cause slightly different yields, since the size of the coupon
  affects the price change of the bond for a given change in the interest rate.
• Differences in the liquidity of off-the-run bonds affects their actual versus quoted prices
  for a large lot size.
• Differences in the timing of the last transaction for specific bond issues cause a discrepancy between the reported last trade price and the true current bid-ask price for that
  bond; that is, when a given bond does not trade after a change in interest rates occurs,
  then the last reported price of a bond is an inaccurate measure of its true value.
• Supply and demand influences, i.e., specific T-bill or T-note issues that are uniquely used
  to fulfill futures contracts, can cause yields to differ from the smoothed curve.

Econometric term structure curve-fitting techniques are employed by Wall Street firms
for situations requiring a precise relationship between interest rates. However, for most
fixed-income portfolio decisions, the shape of the yield curve and forecasts concerning
changes in this shape are sufficient considerations. For these situations an approximation of
the best curve is obtained by a computer-drawn curve that minimizes the differences of the
individual securities from the curve (a regression model). Often those who are active in the
market develop yield curves based solely on recently issued securities in order to avoid the
coupon and liquidity factors.

ANALYZING BOND PORTFOLIO RETURNS

The preceding discussion has examined factors affecting bond prices and the construction
and interpretation of yield curves. These concepts now are integrated into a foundation for
decision making for fixed-income securities. In particular, the purpose of the following

---

3 The humped curve can provide profitable arbitrage trading strategies, since one can purchase the lower-priced
   and sell the higher-priced securities; profits occur when the curve becomes flat and the positions are reversed.

FOCUS 6-3: The Importance of Fitting Yield Curves

The procedure described in the text implies that the fitting of a yield curve is relatively arbitrary, with no precise rationale for determining the "average yield curve" from the individual bonds. However, on Wall Street, the investment houses need very precise measurements of the Treasury rate for various maturities in order to price numerous over-the-counter products sold by these houses, and to determine accurate hedging models. For example, many of the option products created by the investment houses rely on an accurate estimate of the true Treasury default-free interest rate. In addition, mortgage models also employ the Treasury rate.

Fitting the yield curve is difficult because of the uncertain behavior of interest rates, including the relationship between short- and long-term interest rates, and the need for pure discount interest rates. Thus, on Wall Street they do not fit the yield curve as presented here; rather, they fit the pure discount interest rates for various maturities. Pure discount rates consider *only* payments on the maturity date, rather than the series of coupons and the principal payment available for typical Treasury issues. The difficulties in solving these problems is one example of why Wall Street firms hire "rocket scientists." These financial economists develop and implement mathematical models that price various financial products, including pricing the pure discount rate curve.

Cox, Ingersoll, and Ross* developed an important model used on Wall Street that explains the relationship between the short- and long-term rates. This complicated mathematical model precisely associates the movement in long-term interest rates with short-term rates. Consequently, to model the movement in the pure discount rate term structure, one only needs a forecast of the short-term rate. Similarly, if one desires a measure of the risk associated with an interest rate of a particular maturity, all one needs is the variability of the short-term rate plus the equations developed by Cox, Ingersoll, and Ross. Abken** provides a lucid, nonmathematical explanation of the Cox, Ingersoll, and Ross model.

Current methods for estimating the pure discount rate curve include numerical methods called "splines," which fit separate straight-line segments of the yield curve. An accurate fitting of the curve eliminates possible arbitrage opportunities. The key difficulty in this exercise is to have the various segments of the splines fit together without gaps. Although Treasury strips would serve a function similar to these complicated models, the strips are not liquid, and therefore the pricing is not accurate. The resultant pure discount interest rate curve from the models then is employed as the risk-free rate for any model based on interest rates.

---

* John C. Cox, Jonathan E. Ingersoll, Jr., and Stephen A. Ross, " A Re-Examination of Traditional Hypotheses about the Term Structures of Interest Rates," *Journal of Finance*, Vol. 36, No. 4, September 1981, pp. 769-799.

** Peter A. Abken, "Innovations in Modeling the Term Structure of Interest Rates," *Federal Reserve Bank of Atlanta Economic Review*, Vol. 75, No. 4, July/August 1990, pp. 2-27.

discussion is to examine the factors that determine the total price change of a bond and to illustrate the relative importance of these factors historically. Such concepts are important for implementing bond management and futures hedging programs.

A number of factors affect the overall bond portfolio return, with the level of and changes in interest rates being the overriding criteria. Although bond managers cannot control the interest rate in the economy, the portfolio manager can structure the portfolio to benefit from changes in the level of interest rates and/or relationships between yields of different maturity bonds.

Price Change Factors

We can identify the factors affecting bond price change as follows, separating them into expected and unexpected changes.

Expected price changes (those affected by the level of interest rates) are:

1. "Changes due to time": the **amortization of the price discount or premium**—that is, the effect of the passage of time on the bond price due to the movement toward the bond's par value as a result of the difference between the coupon rate and the current interest rate.
2. "Changes due to maturity": the return from **"riding the yield curve,"**—that is, the return obtained from a reduction in maturity of the bond in conjunction with an upward sloping yield curve (the lower interest rate for a shorter maturity causes higher bond prices).

Unexpected price changes (those affected by changes in interest rates) are:

1. "Changes due to shifts in the yield curve": changes in the location or shape of the yield curve—that is, macrochanges in interest rate levels.
2. "Changes due to unique factors": changes in price caused by the characteristics of the specific security and changes in the corporate-government spread.

Historical Results

McEnally[4] examines historical data on bonds to determine the importance of the four factors described above. He concludes that:

- Built-in appreciation from the "time effect" is a reliable source of price change gains for short- and intermediate-term bond maturities, although the total dollar value of such changes is relatively small in view of the short maturities of these securities.
- Obtaining returns from the "maturity shift" or "riding the yield curve" is not a promising method because of changing short-term yields.
- The changing location and shape of the yield curve is significantly more important for intermediate- and longer-term maturities than the expected price change generated from the time and maturity shift factors.
- Risk increases significantly as the maturity increases, due to shifts in the yield curve and the increased importance of the unique factor.
- The importance of diversification for bonds is significant: for long-term bonds it can eliminate up to 50 percent of the risk of the portfolio!

---

4 Richard McEnally, "What Causes Bond Prices to Change?" *Journal of Portfolio Management*, Vol. 7, No. 3, Spring 1981, pp. 5–12.

- Since risk increases with maturity because of the unexpected factors, the relative return-risk trade-off is unfavorable for long-term maturities unless unexpected changes in the long-term rates are forecasted and/or the unique factors diversified away.

FIXED-INCOME PORTFOLIO MANAGEMENT

This section discusses fixed-income portfolio management concepts. These techniques employ the term structure of interest rates as the key ingredient for analyzing bond portfolio performance. Static and dynamic models of bond portfolios allow the user to evaluate the performance of bond managers and to determine appropriate changes in bond structure for specific forecasts of the factors affecting the bond portfolio.

Bond Management Models

The Objective. Bond portfolio models are employed: (1) to evaluate the portfolio manager's contribution to the portfolio return, and (2) to determine the important factors affecting returns for a given portfolio so that the manager can make the appropriate changes in response to forecasts of these factors. Consequently, the critical aspect of bond portfolio analysis becomes the appropriate measurement of returns for each of the various components of the portfolio. The components of the portfolio return described in this chapter are changes due to: time, maturity, shifts in the yield curve, and the unique factors. Measuring returns due to time and maturity are straightforward, while the returns from shifts in the yield curve (term structure) and the unique factors need elaboration.

The Concept and the Return Components. The historical analysis of bond returns discussed in the chapter provides some interesting results and conclusions; however, this analysis is limited to past trends, as well as excluding corporate and municipal bond behavior. In order to structure a bond portfolio that provides optimal control and evaluation, one must employ an active bond management program. Dietz, Fogler, and Hardy[5] and Fong, Pearson, and Vasicek[6] provide active bond portfolio models. Although both models are similar, the Dietz, Fogler, and Hardy (DFH) approach is a **static model,** while the Fong, Pearson and Vasicek (FPV) model is **dynamic** in nature. A static model does not allow additions to or changes in portfolio composition during the evaluation period, while a dynamic model does. Thus, the former is easier to use, but the latter model gives more accurate results.

These two active bond portfolio management models employ similar price factors as those examined earlier in the chapter. Specifically, the components of bond returns used by the models (with previously given descriptions shown in parentheses) are:
- Known or anticipated factors based on the yield to maturity and income factors:
  (a) coupon payments
  (b) amortization of the price from par value ("changes due to time")
  (c) the maturity effect occurring from the slope of the term structure ("changes due to maturity").

5 Peter Dietz, H. Russell Fogler, and Donald Hardy, "The Challenge of Analyzing Bond Portfolio Returns," *The Journal of Portfolio Management,* Vol. 6, No. 3, Spring 1980, pp. 53–58.

6 Gifford Fong, Charles Pearson, and Oldrich Vasicek, "Bond Performance: Analyzing Sources of Return," *The Journal of Portfolio Management,* Vol. 9, No. 3, Spring 1983, pp. 46-50.

- Unknown or unanticipated factors affecting price changes:
  - (a) changes in the interest rate due to changes in the location or shape of the term structure ("changes due to shifts in the yield curve")
  - (b) changes in the sector spreads between different industries or quality spreads occurring between bond ratings as economic factors change ("changes due to unique factors")
  - (c) individual security factors ("changes due to unique factors").

The Model. Figures 6-3 and 6-4 illustrate the effects due to changes in the interest rate in relationship to the term structure. This process is accomplished by implementing the following steps:

1. The coupon effect is found simply by using the coupon payment for each bond.
2. Fit the Treasury yield curve at the beginning of the period (often a quarter) by an appropriate best-fit procedure (labeled as curve "1993" in Figure 6-3).
3. The amortization effect or the "change due to time" is calculated by determining the difference between the present values of each bond for the time periods M (for exam-

---

FIGURE 6-3: Bond Pricing Effects of Term Structure Changes: Yield Curve For 1993

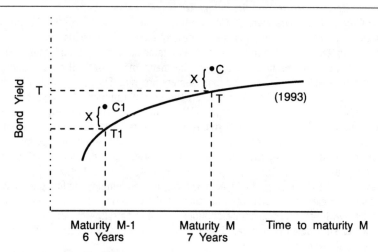

| | Maturity M-1 | Maturity M | Time to maturity M |
| | 6 Years | 7 Years | |

T   is the yield for a default-free Treasury bond on yield curve 1993 with maturity M (7 years)

T1   is the yield for a Treasury bond with maturity M-1 (6 years)

C   is a corporate bond's yield at time 1993 with bond maturity M (7 years)

C1   is the corporate bond's projected yield at time 1993 if it has maturity M-1 (6 years) and no other differences existed

X   is the difference between the yields for corporate bond C and Treasury bond T

T–T1 (the vertical distance) gives the maturity effect or "changes due to maturity"

C–T   is the yield difference between the specific bond and the Treasury bond at time 1990 for maturity M (7 years)

ple, 7 years) and M-1 (6 years), using the discount interest rate at time M. This effect cannot be shown on the figure.

4. The maturity effect is based on the vertical difference on the Y-axis between T and T1 as shown by curve "1993" in Figure 6-3 (or equivalently by the difference between C and C1 which represents a corporate bond); this difference is converted to prices by using the present value equation.

5. Find the yield for each bond in the portfolio versus the yield for the same maturity on the Treasury curve (for example, one corporate bond is labeled "C" in Figure 6-3, with the Treasury equivalent bond labeled "T"; the difference between the yields is labeled "X").

6. Fit the Treasury yield curve at the end of the period (labeled curve "1994" in Figure 6-4).

7. Find the appropriate Treasury equivalent yield on the new yield curve "1994" for each bond in the portfolio for its new maturity (for our example, in Figure 6-4 the Treasury yield on curve "1994" is labeled T2).

**FIGURE 6-4: Bond Pricing Effects of Term Structure Changes:
Yield Curves for 1993 and 1994**

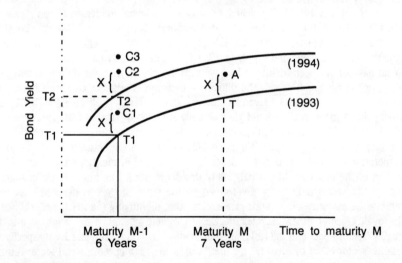

T2   is the yield for a Treasury bond on the yield curve 1994 with maturity M–1 (6 years)

T2 – T1 or C2 – C1 is the change in yield from "changes due to shifts in the yield curve"

C2   is the corporate bond's projected yield for yield curve 1994 with maturity M–1 (6 years) if no unique factors cause changes in the yield relationship

C3   is the corporate bond's yield at time 1994 with maturity M–1 (6 years)

C3 – C2 is the change in yield due to "unique factors" (sector/quality and security factors)

8. The difference in the Treasury yields for the two yield curves (1993) and (1994) for the same maturity M–1 (6 years) provides the difference due to changes in the term structure, which is illustrated by the difference between T1 and T2 in Figure 6-4 or, equivalently, by the difference between corporate bonds C1 and C2 in Figure 6-4.

9. Determine the sector/quality and residual effects by finding the difference in yields of the bonds after the other effects are eliminated. (The "changes due to unique factors" is shown in Figure 6-4 as the difference between C3 and C2.)

10. Convert the yields in the above steps to prices to determine the precise dollar effect of each factor.

Let us examine the above process and the accompanying figures.

• First, the coupon and amortization effects are determined. These effects are not shown on the figures since they do not affect bond yields; these known factors are easily calculated by using the coupon rate and the present value equation for bonds.

• Next the maturity effect, the effect of term structure changes, and other factors are segregated and quantified. The maturity effect is separated from the other factors by finding the expected change in yield as the maturity of the bond changes from M to M–1, as illustrated by the difference between T and T1 on curve "1993."

• The difference between the corporate bond (labeled C) and the equivalent Treasury bond (labeled T) on Figure 6-3 is designated as X; this difference is due to the sector/quality and individual security factors. X then is used to define the difference on the yield curve at maturity M–1 (6 years), which also is relevant to identify C1 on Figure 6-3 and C2 on Figure 6-4. Thus, the estimated corporate bond yield in 1994 after considering the shift in the term structure is A2. Consequently, the effect due to the term structure changes is defined simply as T2 – T1 or equivalently C2 – C1.

• What has not yet been identified is the return associated with the unique factors. The effect of the unique factors is the difference between where the corporate bond yield should be on curve "1993," given its maturity and interest rate effects (labeled C2), and where the *actual* corporate bond yield actually is in 1994 (labeled C3). This remaining effect (C3 – C2) is separated into sector/quality effects and security effects. Indices often are employed to define the yield/price behavior for various quality bond ratings for corporate and municipal bonds (AA versus A versus BBB, etc.) as well as for various sectors of the economy (industrial, utility, transportation). The interest rate changes of the quality/sector indices are determined by the same process as described above to remove the maturity and interest rate effects. After identifying the specific effects due to the quality/sector index change, the C3 – C2 yield change is decomposed into the quality/sector effect and the residual security effect. Dietz, Fogler, and Hardy specify the quality/sector effect by identifying a matrix of quality/rating returns and sector returns, creating cells that combine these two effects into weighted returns for each combination of quality/ratings and sectors. They also provide an example of this breakdown using historical data.

A Dynamic Model. The analysis of bond returns discussed above is extended by Fong, Pearson, and Vasicek (FPV) to consider the dynamic effects of changes in the portfolio over the evaluation period in question. This approach is undoubtedly more representative of actual returns, especially those due to timing effects, but it also is more complicated and costly. The FPV approach also extends the previous model by considering the maturity composition of the quality/sector factor, which is ignored if only indices are used for these areas. Fong, Pearson, and Vasicek present a substantial amount of detail on the correct procedure to measure this quality/sector effect, including more complete sector indices and information on how to measure the dynamic aspects of the other components. Perhaps most important, FPV emphasizes a **maturity management** factor that considers the relative effect of changes in the maturity structure of the portfolio on its returns.

Analyzing Bond Returns

Analyzing bond portfolios determines which factors affect the returns of a given bond manager or a specific portfolio. Performance then may be judged in its appropriate context, including determining if the bond manager has specific forecasting abilities. Alternatively, knowing the structure of a given portfolio allows appropriate changes to be made when reliable forecasts of interest rate changes or quality spread changes are obtained. Specifically, the following forecasted changes in the unanticipated factors can increase the returns of a portfolio if the composition of the portfolio is changed in an appropriate manner:

- Forecasts of changes in the interest rate level or shape of the term structure: maturity management of the bond portfolio affects returns since prices of longer-maturity bonds change more than prices of shorter ones.
- Forecasts of changes in the spreads for various quality ratings or sectors: changing the sectors or maturities increases returns based on the forecasted change.
- Security factor forecasts: avoid companies with financial problems or issues with liquidity problems.
- Timing: price effects due to correct timing are a part of each of the above factors, with the dynamic nature of some portfolios being an important part of their return.

Comparisons of the DFH and the FPV models would be relevant for those who need to determine the best bond management model for their purposes. A summary of the relative advantages of each model not only provides information on these specific bond models, but also indicates the important factors to consider when evaluating any bond model employed for analysis.

The relative advantages of the Dietz, Fogler, and Hardy model are:

- Its relative simplicity (such as fewer variables and data requirements) minimizes the cost of implementation and usage.
- The use of the familiar yield-to-maturity approach is similar to the traditional bond analysis approach, which is well-known by bond managers.
- The model is appropriate as a periodic control technique, given the limitations of a static model.

The Fong, Pearson, Vasicek model's advantages are:

- The model's assumptions and makeup are more realistic, consequently the results should be more accurate.
- Transaction costs and cash flows during the period, such as contributions and trading activity, are considered in the analysis: the model is dynamic rather than static.
- The timing effects of trading decisions, such as changing the maturity structure of the portfolio, are considered.

The choice of a particular model is based on its relative advantages and costs. Similarly, the use of any model depends on the usefulness of that information to the market participant. The complicated factors affecting bond returns suggest that any large bond portfolio manager would want some type of bond analysis to determine the effectiveness of the bond management, to analyze the quality of the component forecasts, and to employ information on the makeup of the portfolio to aid future portfolio decisions.

INTEREST RATE SWAPS

An **interest rate swap** is a financial agreement to exchange interest payments of a fixed-rate loan with a variable-rate loan. The *net* difference in interest payments exchanges hands for each payment period. Principal amounts are *not* swapped. Swaps often are arranged between financial institutions in the United States and Europe, since U.S. institutions prefer fixed-rate loans, but the demand is for variable-rate loans; however, the opposite situation exists in Europe. The purpose of these swaps is to change the interest rate risk of the institution. For example, a savings and loan often is forced to issue fixed-rate mortgages, especially during low interest rate environments, because of the demand of consumers. In order to control its interest rate risk, the savings and loan converts the fixed-rate mortgage to a variable-rate loan via a swap. The size of this over-the-counter swap market has grown from zero in 1981 to more than $700 billion in the latter 1980s.

An interest rate swap also can create interest savings compared to alternative agreements. To create such a benefit both parties must be creditworthy, since the net interest payments are transferred only when the interest is due. Example 6-2 shows how an exchange of payments can benefit the two parties in a swap when a relative credit risk premium exists between the two parties in the swap.

Swaps directly relate to futures markets, since it can be shown that swaps are equivalent to a portfolio of forward contracts. Thus, swaps are essentially equivalent to futures. The liquidity of these markets and the usefulness of changing the risk factors of a loan show its importance to firms and financial institutions. In fact, market-makers that take on one side of a swap temporarily until they find the other side of the swap will hedge their positions with futures, typically with the Eurodollar futures market.

SUMMARY AND LOOKING AHEAD

This chapter covered the basic concepts relating to interest rate instruments and bond portfolio management. It began with basic bond concepts, and continued with an analysis of yield curves and fixed-income portfolio management. Pricing and arbitrage for T-bond, Eurodollar, and T-bill futures are covered in the next two chapters.

EXAMPLE 6-2: An Interest Rate Swap

	Firm A	Firm B	Differential
Fixed-rate loans	8.5 percent	9.1 percent	60 bp
Variable-rate loans	LIBOR + 15 bp	LIBOR + 35 bp	20 bp
Net differential			40 bp

where bp stands for basis points.

Firm A has a better credit rating than Firm B, therefore its cost of funds is lower for both fixed- and variable-rate loans. However, the differential between firms A and B for the fixed-rate loan is 60 basis points, whereas it is only 20 basis points for a variable-rate loan. The initiation of a swap can generate total savings of 40 basis points for the two firms and any broker who acts as an intermediary. Thus, let us assume that the following loans are initiated, including an agreement between the two firms on how to split the benefits:

	Firm A	Firm B
Fixed-rate loans	Obtains loan at 8.5%	Pays swap rate of: 8.9% fixed to Firm A
Variable-rate loans	Pays swap rate of LIBOR + 30 bp to Firm B	Obtains loan at LIBOR + 35 bp
Net payment	LIBOR + 30 bp + (8.5 − 8.9) = LIBOR − 10 bp	8.9 + [LIBOR + 35 bp − (LIBOR + 30 bp)] = 8.95
Savings	LIBOR + 15 bp − (LIBOR −10 bp) = 25 bp	9.1 − 8.950 = 15 bp

The swap saves Firm A 25 basis points as compared with a variable-rate loan taken directly by the Firm A, and it saves Firm B 15 basis points on a fixed-rate loan. If a broker is involved, then a fee of 5 to 10 basis points is paid to the broker.

Chapter 7
T-Bond Futures Pricing and Arbitrage

T-bond futures are a very active and important contract. Moreover, the complexities of the pricing of the T-bond futures contract create numerous opportunities for profit for short arbitrageurs *and* short hedgers, as well as difficulties in determining the fair price of the contract. Because of the pricing difficulties, unsophisticated traders can lose without even realizing why a loss has occurred. Short hedgers holding a position into the delivery month should take advantage of the opportunities available with the delivery process in order to benefit fully from a short position in futures.

T-bond futures pricing and arbitrage are affected by the net financing cost (financing cost less interest received), the conversion factor method, and the delivery options associated with the futures contract. The conversion factor determines the cheapest-to-deliver cash instrument priced by the futures contract; proper consideration of this factor increases profits from an arbitrage. The four delivery options are the quality option (which is related to the conversion factor), the timing option of when during the expiration month to deliver, the wild card option, and the end-of-the-month option.

One method to determine whether arbitrage exists is to calculate the implied repo (financing) rate; this chapter examines the factors that affect the calculation of this rate, then shows how to use the delivery options and examine evidence concerning the value of these options. In fact, whether T-bond arbitrage transactions are profitable often is directly associated with the price and proper use of these delivery options.

T-BOND FUTURES PRICING: THE COST OF CARRY FACTOR

The contract specifications, price history, and importance of the T-bond futures contract are presented in Chapter 2. This material is necessary for a complete understanding of the material on pricing T-bond futures. Although this chapter concentrates on T-bond pricing and arbitrage, the same factors affect T-note pricing and arbitrage.

The Cost of Carry Model for Debt Futures

The basic cost of carry model presented in Chapter 4 is amended for the income received from the coupons of the bond as follows:

$$P_{FAIR} = P_C (1 + i - r)^t \tag{7-1}$$

or equivalently for continuously compounded rates,

$$P_{FAIR} = P_C e^{(i-r)t} \tag{7-2}$$

where P_{FAIR} = the fair futures price determined by the cost of carry model
P_C = the adjusted cash bond price

137

i = the annual financing rate

r = the annual rate of income received on the cash bond

t = the number of days until the futures expiration divided by 365

For the cash bond price to be comparable to the futures price one of these two prices must be adjusted to consider maturity and coupon between the instruments. The conversion factor method, discussed shortly, makes this adjustment. For Equations (7-1) and (7-2), it is sufficient to realize that the cash price used, P_C, has already been adjusted to be comparable to the futures price.[1]

Unlike other futures contracts, T-bond and T-note futures prices are affected by factors other than the basic cost of carry variables; that is, the conversion factor method and the delivery options also are important factors. However, the cost of carry model represents a reasonable first approximation to the fair futures price.

The Financing Versus Income Relationship

The Relationship. The financing versus income (or *net* cost of carry) relationship is the most important factor affecting the pricing of T-bond futures contracts. Thus, let us use the cost of carry model to compare the theoretical price difference between the futures and cash markets to the actual price difference between these markets.[2]

The net cost of carry model in Equations (7-1) and (7-2) shows that the greater the income received on the bond, the lower the futures price. This relationship occurs for two reasons: (1) the larger the income, the smaller the *net* cost of financing the position, and (2) the purchase of the futures contract is an alternative to holding the cash bond, and a long position in futures does *not* receive coupon payments. The timing of the coupon income received also affects the futures price, since cash income received earlier in the period creates greater reinvestment returns. Thus, the payment schedule of one T-bond versus another affects the net financing cost.

The net cost of carry relationship from Equation (7-1) is altered and rearranged slightly to show the relevance of the income versus financing relationship in comparison to the futures versus cash price:

$$\frac{P_F - P_C}{P_C} = (i - r)\,t \tag{7-3}$$

where P_F = the futures price. Note that the left side of Equation (7-3) is simply the percentage difference between the futures and cash prices, while the right side of the equation is the time-adjusted percentage difference between the financing rate and the income rate. Using time simply adjusts for the effect of convergence as the time until futures expiration shortens.

Equation (7-3) shows that when the financing rate is *less* than the income received (that is, when the yield curve is upward sloping for cash T-bonds), then the futures price must

---

1   Technically, the cash bond used must be the "cheapest" cash bond, as shown below.

2   This approach and example ignores the complications for pricing caused by the conversion factor method. In reality, one should determine the cheapest-to-deliver bond by employing the conversion factor method, and then employ *that* bond for the price spread analysis between the futures and cash markets shown in this section. This example arbitrarily picks one bond. Also, the financing rate for the arbitrageur, usually the overnight repo rate, is more appropriate than the T-bill rate employed here. Later in this chapter a more detailed analysis of the cheapest-to-deliver bond is provided.

be less than the cash price and the deferred futures prices must be less than the nearby futures price. Conversely, when the financing cost is above the income received on the bond, the futures price must be greater than the cash price and the deferred futures price must be greater than the nearby futures price. This relationship exists for T-bond futures when there is a downward sloping yield curve for cash T-bonds. Exhibit 7-1 shows examples of these price structures.

One can justify the relationship between the cash and futures prices in Equation (7-3), as well as the structure of futures prices in Exhibit 7-1, by determining the net cash flow to an arbitrageur who buys the cash bond and sells the futures contract. For an upward sloping yield curve (the left set of numbers in Exhibit 7-1), the arbitrageur earns more money from holding the cash bond than is paid out due to the financing cost. Thus, the arbitrageur is willing to accept a *loss* from buying cash at a price above the sales price of the futures [thus $P_C > P_F$ on the left side of Equation (7-3)], as long as this loss is equal to or smaller than the difference between the income received from the bond and the financing cost [as given on the right side of Equation (7-3)]. Similarly, for a downward sloping yield curve (the right set of numbers in Exhibit 7-1), the arbitrageur loses money from the net cash flow because the financing cost is greater than the income received from owning the asset. Consequently, the arbitrageur wants a larger difference $P_F - P_C$ [on the left side of Equation (7-3)] as the time until futures expiration increases in order to offset the loss from the net financing cost [on the right side of Equation (7-3)].

An Example. To examine the pricing relationship for T-bond futures let us assume that i = 8 percent, r = 7 percent (an inverted curve relationship), and there are six months until the expiration of the futures contract. Equation (7-3) provides the appropriate financing/income relationship:

$$(i - r)t = (8\% - 7\%)\ 182/365 = \tfrac{1}{2}\%$$

EXHIBIT 7-1: The Effect of the Net Financing Rate on T-Bond Futures Prices

i − r < 0 or r > i *Upward Sloping Yield Curve* *(Normal Curve)*		*i − r > 0 or i > r* *Downward Sloping Yield Curve* *(Inverted Curve)*	
March 1992	103-10	March 1982	62-04
June	102-09	June	62-14
September	101-09	September	62-28
December	100-12	December	63-04
March 1993	99-18	March 1983	63-15

where: i = the financing rate
            r = the rate of income on the T-bond

Note: The year 1982 was the last time there was an inverted curve.

Thus, the financing cost is greater than the income received. Consequently, the actual percentage price difference $(P_F - P_C)/P_C$ from the left side of Equation (7-3) also should be approximately $\frac{1}{2}$ percent. For a bond priced near 100, if $P_F - P_C > {}^{16}\!/_{32}$, then the profit from delivering the bond would be *greater* than the extra financing cost from the bond's financing rate being above the coupon yield.[3] Conversely, a price difference $P_F - P_C$ that is *less* than ${}^{16}\!/_{32}$ would create an overall loss for the arbitrageur, since the loss generated from the financing rate being greater than the coupon yield would be greater than the gain obtained from the $P_F - P_C$ price spread.

Table 7-1 provides an example of the cost of carry and actual price differences (on one specific day) for a positively sloped yield curve environment—that is, a declining price structure for the futures prices. The most important result shown in this table is that the actual price differences (column 6) are almost identical to the theoretical cost of carry differences (column 5) for all futures expirations. Thus, the prices for the T-bond futures are justifiable, and the futures and cash markets are linked together. This effect is shown clearly in Figure 7-1.

T-BOND FUTURES PRICING: CONVERSION FACTORS AND DELIVERY OPTIONS

The Conversion Factor Method

The Chicago Board of Trade developed the conversion factor method (CFM) so that traders, hedgers, and arbitrageurs could deliver a wide range of cash T-bonds into the T-bond futures contract. Although previous promotional literature from the exchange stated that the T-bond contract "prices" a hypothetical long-term cash T-bond with an 8% coupon, no such cash bond exists. Therefore, the CBT allows *any* T-bond with at least 15 years left to maturity (or 15 years to the first call date, if the bond is callable) to be used as a deliverable bond. Since each cash bond possesses different coupon and maturity characteristics, and therefore different prices, a method is needed to adjust the futures price for the delivery of different cash bonds. The conversion factor is a factor multiple that adjusts the futures price in order to obtain a fair cash bond price for delivery purposes.

The advantage of the conversion factor method is that it allows futures shorts to deliver a wide range of T-bonds, thereby guaranteeing a sufficient number of cash bonds to avoid a squeeze or other delivery problems. The disadvantage of the CFM is that it creates several biases that determine the "best" bond to deliver and thus affect the pricing of the futures contract. Because of these biases, the CFM creates *one* and *only* one cheapest-to-deliver bond at any given time. Consequently, the futures market uses this cheapest-to-deliver instrument to price the T-bond and T-note futures contracts.

The delivery price and conversion factor for T-bonds is specified as follows: the **invoice amount** (the delivery price the buyer pays the seller) when a T-bond is used for delivery is

$$IA = (SP)\ (\$100{,}000 \text{ face amount})\ (CF) + AI \qquad (7\text{-}4)$$

where   IA = the invoice amount (i.e., the value the buyer pays the seller)

---

3   The profit arising from $P_F - P_C$ occurs since the arbitrageur buys the cash bond at P_C, while *receiving* a price of P_F from the sale of the futures contract. This price difference becomes a profit when the cash bond is delivered into the futures contract.

TABLE 7-1: Bond Cost of Carry versus Actual Cash/Futures Differences

(1)	(2)	(3)	(4)	(5)	(6)	(7)
					Percentage Difference	
Contract Expiration	Months to Expiration	Futures Price	Financing Rate[a]	Cost of Carry Difference[b]	Actual Difference[c]	Error (5)−(6)
March	2	97-14	6.87	− .22	− .19	−.03
June	5	97-03	6.87	− .55	− .55	0
September	8	96-28	7.18	− .68	− .77	+.09
December	11	96-24	7.25	− .87	− .90	+.03
March	14	96-20	7.30	−1.05	−1.03	−.02
June	17	96-15	7.35	−1.20	−1.19	−.01

a   The financing rate is obtained from the Treasury yield curve based on the relevant number of months until maturity.

b   The cost of carry difference is based on the right side of Equation (7-3) in the text, using a coupon yield of 8.2% for the cash bond.

c   The actual price difference is calculated by taking the percentage difference between the futures price and the cash bond price—that is, the left side of Equation (7-3). The cash bond price is 97-20 in January for the hypothetical 8% coupon bond due in 17 years. Using an 8% coupon simplifies the calculation by avoiding an adjustment for the conversion factor.

FIGURE 7-1: Bond Cost of Carry and Actual Differences

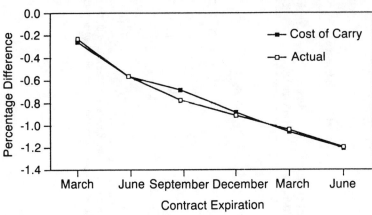

Source: Table 7-1.

SP = the futures settlement price as a percentage of par, based on the closing price of the futures contract on the day that the delivery notice is given

CF = the conversion factor, which is the multiple given to the particular T-bond being delivered and is based on the maturity and coupon of the bond

AI = accrued interest on the cash bond being delivered

The conversion factor is determined as follows:

1. One must find the time until maturity (or to the call date) for the appropriate bond, as measured in *complete* three-month quarters of a year. Parts of a quarter are ignored in the maturity calculation; that is, the maturity calculation is rounded *down* to the nearest quarter. The first day of the delivery month for the futures contract is employed to begin the calculation for the time to maturity of the bond.

2. The bond's term to maturity and coupon rate are used in conjunction with Equation (7-5) to determine the conversion factor. Tables also are available.

The following equation calculates the conversion factor for an even number of quarters:

$$CF_E = \sum_{t=1}^{n} [(C_t/2) / (1 + .08/2)^t]/100,000 \qquad (7\text{-}5)$$

where CF_E = the conversion factor for a bond with an even number of quarters before maturity or call date

t = the time period, measured semiannually[4]

n = the number of semiannual periods

---

4 The time variable, t, is measured in semiannual periods for compounding purposes when coupons are paid semiannually. Thus, the 8% discount rate is divided by two in order to equate the compounding periods to one-half of the year.

C_t = the cash flows for the bond in question—that is, the coupon and principal amounts received during time t. The annual coupon is divided by two, since coupons are paid semiannually. This equation uses a face value of $100,000, although one can use any par value as long as the denominator is adjusted accordingly.

If the number of quarters is odd, then the following adjustment is made to determine the conversion factor:

$$CF_O = (CF_E + [C_t/2]/100,000)/(1 + .08/2)^{.5} - C_t/4]/100,000 \qquad (7\text{-}6)$$

The CF procedure given in Equations (7-5) and (7-6) uses the hypothetical 8% coupon of the futures contract as the discount rate, and divides by 100,000 in order to obtain a conversion factor per $1 of the face value of the bond. In other words, the conversion factor represents the price of the bond *if the yield was 8%*, divided by the par value of the bond. For example, a $100,000 par value bond with a maturity of $17\frac{1}{2}$ years and a coupon of 10% would have a price of $118,660 if the yield was 8%; thus, the conversion factor for this bond would be 118,660/100,000 or 1.1866. Example 7-1 shows how to find the conversion factor and invoice amount for a T-bond.

One basic use of the conversion factor is to compare the cash bond and futures prices. Equation (7-7) shows how to obtain the adjusted cash price used earlier in Equations (7-1) and (7-2):

$$\text{Adjusted } P_C = \text{actual } P_C/CF \qquad (7\text{-}7)$$

Similarly, the futures price is converted into an adjusted futures price to compare to the cash price; that is,

$$\text{Adjusted } P_F = P_F (CF) \qquad (7\text{-}8)$$

These comparisons are important when one wants to find the cash bond priced by the futures contract.

Table 7-2 provides conversion factors for various futures expiration dates for those T-bonds eligible for delivery. Note that bonds with coupons below 8% have conversion factors below one, and bonds with coupons above 8% have conversion factors above one. Also, after adjusting for coupon effects, longer-term bonds have higher conversion factors than shorter-term bonds. The conversion factor tables are available quarterly from the Chicago Board of Trade.

Biases Caused by the Conversion Factor Method and the Cash Market

The Issues. The CF uses only whole quarters when it is calculated. The rounding down of the time to maturity of the bond to the nearest quarter, in conjunction with the use of the 8% hypothetical yield as the discount rate, causes biases in calculating the exact value of the bond for delivery purposes. In addition, biases relating to how the cash market values certain bonds causes such bonds to be preferred for delivery at certain times. These two effects create what is known as the "cheapest-to-deliver" cash T-bond. An approximation method to determine the cheapest bond based on the CFM is the one with the *lowest* cash price/conversion factor ratio, or more accurately the lowest (cash price + accrued interest)/conversion factor ratio. In symbolic terms we have

$$CTD = MIN_B \, [(P_0 + AI)/CF] \qquad (7\text{-}9)$$

EXAMPLE 7-1: Example of Calculating Conversion Factors and Invoice Amounts

Bond Characteristics

February 15, 2015, bond with a coupon of 7⅝%
Delivery for June 11, 1993
Futures settlement price on position day of 83-16, or 83.50 as a percent of par

Conversion Factor (Even Number of Quarters)

As of June 1, 1993, the bond in question is callable in 21 years, 8 months, and 14 days; rounding down to the nearest quarter we obtain 21 years and 2 quarters (43 semiannual periods). Using Equation (7-5) we calculate a conversion factor value stated in terms of a per dollar of par value figure (the conversion factor is determined as a ratio of the par value). Present value calculations are used to obtain 20.37079 (the present value of an annuity for 43 periods and 4%) and .18517 (the present value of a single amount for 43 periods and 4%).

$$CF = \sum_{t=1}^{n} [(C_t/2)/(1 + .08/2)^t]/100,000 \qquad (7\text{-}5)$$

$$CF = \sum_{t=1}^{43} [(7,625/2)/(1.04)^t + 100,000/(1.04)^{43}]/100,000$$

$$CF = [3,812.5\,(20.37079) + 100,000\,(.18517)]/100,000$$
$$= (77,663.66 + +18,516.82/100,000 = .96180$$

Invoice Amount

Accrued interest is determined based on the number of days since the last coupon payment, which was February 15. Thus, interest accrues from February 15, but is not paid until August 15. There are 116 days from (but not including) February 15 to and including June 11. The semiannual coupon is $3,812.50 for a $100,000 face bond (i.e., 7⅝% × $100,000/2). To determine the amount of accrued interest we multiply the daily interest amount by the number of days of accrued interest, as follows:

Daily interest = $\dfrac{\text{semiannual coupon amount}}{\text{number of days between coupons}}$

Daily interest = $3,812.50/181 = $21.06354
Accrued interest = $20.9478022 × 116 days = $2,443.37

Thus, the invoice amount is:

Invoice amount = futures settlement price × $100,000 × conversion factor + accrued interest   (7-4)
Invoice amount = (.835 × $100,000) × .9618 + $2,443.37 = $82,753.67

Calculation of Conversion Factors for an Odd Number of Quarters

To illustrate how Equation (7-6) is implemented to determine the conversion factor for an odd number of quarters, let us use the above results, with the one exception of having the bond mature in 21 years and 3 quarters. Employing Equation (7-6) we find:

$$CF_O = (CF_E + [C_t/2]/100,000)/(1 + .08/2)^{.5} - [C_t/4]/100,000 \qquad (7\text{-}6)$$
$$CF_O = (.96180 + [7,625/2]/100,000)/(1 + .08/2)^{.5} - [7,625/4]/100,000$$
$$= [(.96181 + .038125)/(1.04)^{.5}] - .0190625$$
$$= .999925/1.01980 - .0190625$$
$$= .961445$$

where   CTD = cheapest-to-deliver
         MIN_B = the minimum ratio for all deliverable bonds
         P_0 = the current price

Conversion Factor Biases. The objective of the conversion factor method is to adjust the futures price in order to conform to the maturity and coupon differences of the individual cash bonds available for delivery. The CF is the price of the bond *if* the yield is 8%, divided by its par value. Theoretically, this conversion is intended to *equate* the relative value of all bonds by finding the value of the cash bond *relative* to the futures benchmark 8% bond, such that the *invoice amount per dollar of investment is the same for all deliverable bonds*. Unfortunately, the CF adjustment creates biases in the relative conversion factors among the bonds available for delivery such that there is a difference between the calculated conversion factors and the fair conversion values of the bond. The next two sections detail the causes and effects of these conversion factor biases as well as the cash market biases created by the preferences of market participants for certain bonds.

The most important of these biases often occurs when rates are above 8%, since the use of an 8% discount rate overvalues distant cash flows. Since low coupon bonds have much of their cash inflow in the principal repayment, these bonds possess conversion factors that are larger than warranted. Similarly, long maturity bonds tend to be overvalued by the conversion factor method. Consequently, the long position would pay more for these low coupon bonds than they are worth, since the conversion factor method sets the payment price for delivery purposes.

Causes of the Conversion Factor Biases

The method for calculating conversion factors creates biases in the relative bond conversion factors, causing differences between the calculated conversion factors and the fair values of the bonds. In addition, preferences for certain bonds by market participants creates bond prices that differ from fair bond values. These latter preferences are called cash market biases.

The conversion factor method creates biases when the yield differs from 8%. These biases are caused by the following factors:[5]

- Using a discount yield of 8% to value a bond when the actual yield differs from 8% creates a bias away from the fair value of the bond. In particular, using an 8% discount yield when the actual yield is above 8% causes low-coupon bonds with long maturities

5 These biases and their effects are discussed in additional detail in Arak, Goodman, and Ross; Arak and Goodman; and Meisner and Labuszewski. Killcollin analyzes the two distinct conversion factor methods employed by the CBT and NYFE. The discussion here deals only with the CBT method since the NYFE contract no longer trades. Marcelle Arak, Laurie S. Goodman, and Susan Ross, "The Cheapest to Deliver Bond on the Treasury Bond Futures Contract," *Advances in Futures and Options Research*, Vol. 1, Part B, 1986, pp. 49-74. Marcelle Arak and Laurie S. Goodman, "How to Calculate Better T-Bond Hedge Ratios," *Futures*, February 1986. James F. Meisner and John W. Labuszewski, "Treasury Bond Futures Delivery Bias," *The Journal of Futures Markets*, Vol. 4, No. 4, Winter 1984, pp. 569-577. Thomas Eric Killcollin, "Difference Systems in Financial Futures Markets," *Journal of Finance*, Vol. 37, No. 5, October 1982, pp. 1183-1197.

TABLE 7-2: T-Bond Conversion Factors for Specific Bonds

T-Bonds, Eligible for Delivery July 1, 1991

	Coupon	Maturity	Amount[a]	Sep 91	Dec 91	Mar 92	Jun 92	Sep 92	Dec 92	Mar 93	Jun 93
1.	7¼	May 15, 2016	18.82	0.9200	0.9201	0.9205	0.9206	0.9211	0.9212	0.9217	0.9218
2.	7½	Nov 15, 2016	18.86	0.9463	0.9463	0.9466	0.9466	0.9470	0.9470	0.9474	0.9474
3.	7⅞	Feb 15, 2021	11.01	0.9858	0.9860	0.9858	.9860	0.9859	0.9861	0.9860	0.9862
4.	8⅛[b]	May 15, 2021	11.75	1.0141	1.0139	1.0140	1.0138	1.0140	1.0437	1.0139	1.0137
5.	8⅛	Aug 15, 2019	20.01	1.0137	1.0138	1.0136	1.0137	1.0135	1.0137	1.0134	1.0136
6.	8½	Feb 15, 2020	10.06	1.0555	1.0555	1.0552	1.0553	1.0549	1.0550	1.0546	1.0547
7.	8¾	May 15, 2017	18.19	1.0811	1.0806	1.0806	1.0801	1.0800	1.0795	1.0795	1.0790
8.	8¾	May 15, 2020	10.01	1.0837	1.0833	1.0833	1.0829	1.0829	1.0825	1.0825	1.0820
9.	8¾	Aug 15, 2020	21.01	1.0837	1.0837	1.0833	1.0833	1.0829	1.0829	1.0825	1.0825
10.	8⅞	Aug 15, 2017	14.02	1.0946	1.0946	1.0941	1.0940	1.0935	'1.0934	1.0928	1.0927
11.	8⅞	Feb 15, 2019	19.25	1.0963	1.0962	1.0957	1.0957	1.0952	1.0951	1.0946	1.0946
12.	9	Nov 15, 2018	9.03	1.1100	1.1094	1.1094	1.1088	1.1087	1.1082	1.1081	1.1075
13.	9⅛	May 15, 2018	8.71	1.1230	1.1225	1.1223	1.1217	1.1216	1.1210	1.1208	1.1202
14.	9¼	Feb 15, 2016	7.27	1.1327	1.1325	1.1318	1.1315	1.1308	1.1305	1.1298	1.1295
15.	9⅞	Nov 15, 2015	6.90	1.1987	1.1978	1.1973	1.1963	1.1958	1.1948	1.1943	1.1932
16.	10⅜	Nov 15, 2007–12	11.03	1.2122	1.2103	1.2089	1.2069	1.2053	—	—	—
17.	10⅝	Aug 15, 2015	7.15	1.2769	1.2762	1.2749	1.2741	1.2728	1.2720	1.2706	—
18.	11¼	Feb 15, 2015	12.67	1.3404	1.3394	1.3378	1.3367	1.3350	1.3339	1.3322	—
19.	11¾	Nov 15, 2009–14	6.01	1.3545	1.3520	1.3500	1.3473	1.3452	1.3425	1.3403	1.3374
20.	12	Aug 15, 2008–13	14.76	1.3653	1.3630	1.3599	1.3575	1.3544	1.3518	1.3458	1.3458
21.	12½	Aug 15, 2009–14	5.13	1.4224	1.4200	1.4168	1.4143	1.4110	1.4083	1.4050	1.4022
22.	13¼	May 15, 2009–14	5.01	1.4899	1.4863	1.4833	1.4795	1.4763	1.4725	1.4692	1.4652
23.	14	Nov 15, 2006–11	4.90	1.5188	—	—	—	—	—	—	—

Table continues

TABLE 7-2: Continued

T-Bonds, Eligible for Delivery July 1, 1991

Coupon	Maturity	Amount[a]	Sep 91	Dec 91	Mar 92	Jun 92	Sep 92	Dec 92	Mar 93	Jun 93
1. 7¾	Feb 15, 2001	11.01	0.9837	0.9842	0.9843	0.9848	0.9849	0.9854	0.9856	0.9861
2. 7⅞	Apr 15, 1998	8.53	0.9938	—	—	—	—	—	—	—
3. 7⅞	Nov 15, 1999	10.07	0.9927	0.9927	0.9931	0.9930	0.9934	0.9934	0.9938	—
4. 8	Aug 15, 1999	9.76	0.9998	1.0000	0.9998	1.0000	1.9998	1.0000	—	—
5. 8[b]	May 15, 2001	11.96	1.0000	0.0008	1.0000	0.9998	1.0000	0.9998	1.0000	0.9998
6. 8¼[c]	Jul 15, 1998	9.00	1.0126	1.0125	—	—	—	—	—	—
7. 8½	Feb 15, 2000	10.01	1.0296	1.0291	1.0283	1.0278	1.0269	1.0264	1.0255	1.0250
8. 8½	Nov 15, 2000	11.07	1.0316	1.0308	1.0304	1.0296	1.0291	1.0283	1.0278	1.0269
9. 8¾	Aug 15, 2000	10.50	1.0463	1.0456	1.0445	1.0437	1.0425	1.0417	1.0404	1.0396
10. 8⅞	Nov 15, 1998	9.90	1.0462	1.0447	1.0437	1.0437	—	—	—	—
11. 8⅞	Feb 15, 1999	9.50	1.0472	1.0462	1.0447	—	—	—	—	—
12. 8⅞	May 15, 2000	10.03	1.0532	1.0519	1.0510	1.0496	1.0486	1.0472	1.0462	1.0447
13. 9⅛	May 15, 1998	9.17	1.0499	—	—	—	—	—	—	—
14. 9	Aug 15, 1998	11.34	1.0640	1.0624	—	—	—	—	—	—
15. 9⅛	May 15, 1999	9.53	1.0625	1.060	1.0594	1.0576	1.0562	—	—	—

Total eligible for delivery: $151.38 billion.

a In billions of dollars.

b Most recently auctioned 10-year T-Note eligible for delivery.

c Most recently auctioned seven-year T-Note eligible for delivery.

Source: CBOT Financial Instruments Guide.

to be more profitable to deliver than high-coupon, short-maturity bonds. The larger the difference between the 8% discount yield and the actual yield, the greater the bias.[6]

- Conversion factors for callable bonds that trade *below par* should be calculated on a yield to maturity basis rather than by calculating the yield to call date, since these bonds would not be called at current interest rates. This bias also favors low coupon bonds.

- The procedure to round down to the nearest quarter to calculate the conversion factor ignores any interest receivable after the beginning of the final quarter. Thus, bonds maturing toward the end of the quarter are worth more than those maturing near the beginning of the quarter.

- An upward sloping yield curve causes lower coupon bonds to be more attractive to deliver, whereas a downward sloping yield curve makes high coupon bonds more attractive.[7]

The most important of these biases often is the first one: when rates are above 8%, the use of an 8% discount rate overvalues distant cash flows. Since low coupon bonds have much of their cash inflow in the principal repayment, these bonds possess conversion factors larger than warranted since the CFM uses the 8% discount rate. Similarly, long maturity bonds often are overvalued by the conversion factor method. Consequently, the long position would pay more for these low coupon bonds than they are worth, since the conversion factor method sets the payment price for delivery purposes.

Figure 7-2 shows the effect of the conversion factor biases on hypothetical 30-year bonds with various coupons. The figure plots the conversion factor ratios measuring the theoretical CF without any biases divided by the actual CF. At an 8% market yield no bias exists. For other yields the CF ratio moves away from the no-bias ratio of 1.0. Also, the figure shows that bonds with different coupons are affected by the CF bias in different degrees, with higher coupons having the greatest bias. Although maturity also affects the bias slightly, coupons are the dominant factor affecting the CF bias.

Cash Market Biases

Cash market preferences for certain types of bonds also create biases:

- Different bonds have different price changes for a given change in interest rates, with the size of the price change depending on the bond's coupon and maturity. Bond portfolio managers want to minimize reported losses and maximize reported gains. Thus, there is a preference by bond portfolio managers to deliver low coupon bonds when a loss on the cash bond portfolio exists, since the dollar change on low coupon bonds is less than the dollar change on high coupon bonds.[8] Similarly, high coupon bonds are delivered when

---

6 For a proof and discussion of this point, see Arak, Goodman, and Ross, "Cheapest to Deliver Bond," pp. 49–94.

7 This bias occurs because the relationship between the dollar bond price and a change in the discount interest rate is nonlinear. The greater the difference between the 8% discount yield and the actual yield, the larger the error. See the discussion of convexity in Chapters 11 and 12 for a further discussion of this point.

8 One of the bond theorems presented in Chapter 6 states that low coupon bonds change more in *percentage terms* than high coupon bonds for the same change in yield. Hence, for an equal dollar *investment* in both types of coupon bonds, the lower coupon bond creates a larger dollar change in value. However, here the seller delivers $100,000 *face* value, in which case the low coupon bond changes less in dollar terms.

FIGURE 7-2: Theoretical/Actual Conversion Factors

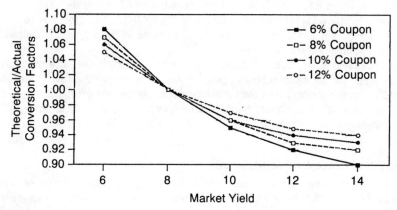

Source: Adapted from data in Alex Kane and Alan J. Marcus, "The Quality Option in the Treasury Bond Futures Market: An Empirical Assessment," *The Journal of Futures Markets*, Vol. 6 No. 2, Summer 1986, pp. 231-248.

there is a gain in the cash portfolio. Of course, shorter maturities are delivered when a loss occurs since it causes a smaller loss, and longer maturities are delivered when a gain exists. The size of the dollar investment also is important for financing considerations; that is, the total value of the bond position affects the cost of carrying the bond. Low coupon bonds create a smaller investment and therefore a lower financing cost.

- Premium bonds (those selling above par) often possess higher yields than discount and par value bonds, causing the prices for premium bonds to be underpriced. This relationship occurs because institutional investors do not buy premium bonds since institutions do not want a loss when the bond matures at par value. This benefit favors using high coupon bonds for delivery, which at times can offset the conversion factor biases.
- Historically, discount bonds sometimes had lower yields than par bonds due to favorable capital gains treatment; however, the 1986 Tax Act eliminated most of these benefits.

These cash market biases have sometimes caused deliveries of bonds other than what would be expected when only the conversion factor biases are considered. The effect of all of the biases outlined on the actual deliveries into the T-bond futures contract is examined shortly.

Cheapest-to-Deliver Bond

The biases created by the conversion factor method and the cash market preferences, plus the effect of differing ratios of financing costs to coupon returns for different bonds, cause some bonds to provide a higher rate of return for arbitrage positions than other bonds. In fact, typically there is only *one* bond that is best for an arbitrageur for a given market yield. This bond is called the cheapest-to-deliver bond and is used by the futures market for pricing purposes.[9] Thus, in order to maximize profits, arbitrageurs choose this cheapest-to-deliver bond (if it has sufficient liquidity) when exercising their arbitrage strategy. As previously shown in Equation (7-9), an approximation method to find the cheapest-to-deliver bond is to determine the bond with the lowest $(P_O + AI)/CF$. This procedure considers all of the biases, but it does not consider the importance of the size of the coupon in relation to the financing cost.

The cheapest-to-deliver bond often changes as interest rates change since the relative arbitrage profits for the different bonds change. These profits change because (1) the ratios and rankings of the prices of the bonds to the conversion factors are affected as the rate of interest changes, due to the biases discussed previously, and (2) the ratio of the financing rate to the coupon rate affects the net profit of the arbitrage position over the term of the holding period.

Delivery Experience for T-Bond Futures

In general, the deliveries into the T-bond futures contract correspond to the biases associated with the conversion factor method and the cash market biases. Figure 7-3 shows that coupons were delivered into T-bond futures from 1980 to 1985 (for an upward sloping yield curve). Low coupon bonds predominate as the delivery mechanism when high yields exist, while high coupons predominate for lower yield levels. The high coupon deliveries correspond to declining interest rates—that is, when a gain in the cash portfolio exists and these bonds are selling below fair value.

Figure 7-4 illustrates the delivery experience when a downward sloping yield curve exists. The hypothesis that high coupon bonds would be delivered to offset the high financing costs is shown to be incorrect. Thus, the factors such as the bias for low coupon bonds dominate the downward sloping yield curve effect.

Delivery Options

The delivery options[10] for the T-bond and T-note futures contracts affect the pricing of these contracts and the size of the arbitrage profits for these futures, especially during the month of delivery. These options provide choices to the seller of the futures concerning when and what to deliver. For T-bond and T-note futures, the seller can deliver on *any* day during the delivery month that the exchange is open. The delivery options are a benefit to the futures seller who is instituting arbitrage, since these options increase profits on the transaction. If arbitrageurs fully employ these options, then the corresponding futures contracts should sell at a lower price than would be the case if no such options existed. The end of this chapter examines the value of these delivery options using historical data.

The delivery options for T-bond and T-note futures are as follows:

---

9   Often the "best bond for delivery" is described as the only bond providing a *positive* return for a given market yield. In fact, because of the delivery options described below, even the best bond typically does not have a positive return before consideration of the value of the delivery options.

10 Gay and Manaster examine the concepts covered in this section in detail. Gerald Gay and Steven Manaster, "The Quality Option Implicit in Futures Contracts," *Journal of Financial Economics*, Vol. 13, No. 3, September 1984, pp. 353-370. Gerald Gay and Steven Manaster, "Implicit Delivery Options and Optimal Delivery Strategies for Financial Futures Contracts," *Journal of Financial Economics*, Vol. 16, No. 1, May 1986, pp. 41-72.

FIGURE 7-3: T-Bond Deliveries for Different Yield Levels

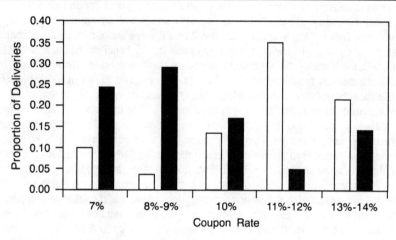

Source: Chicago Board of Trade (1980 to 1990), "Delivery Statistics."

FIGURE 7-4: T-Bond Deliveries for a Downward Sloping Yield Curve

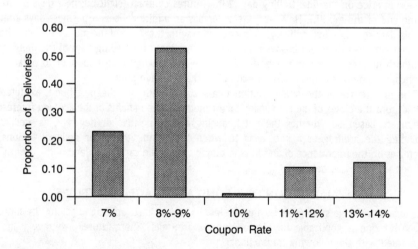

Source: Chicago Board of Trade (1980 to 1990), "Delivery Statistics."

- The **quality option**: the futures seller is given the option to deliver *any* of the cash T-bonds that meet the specifications of the contract—that is, any T-bonds having at least 15 years to delivery or 15 years to the first call date. The quality option makes it difficult to undertake "long arbitrage" (i.e., selling cash bonds and buying futures), since the arbitrageur does not know which T-bond will be delivered into the long futures contract that is being held.[11] However, the quality option is very beneficial to the short arbitrageur because it allows the arbitrageur to choose the "cheapest-to-deliver" T-bond that fulfills the delivery specifications of the futures contract. The quality option is the result of the conversion factor and cash market biases discussed previously.
- The **accrued interest** (or "timing") **option**: the seller has the option of choosing *when* to deliver the cash bond during the futures expiration month. If the costs of financing exceed the current income from the coupon (the accrued interest), then this option provides an incentive to deliver early in the month. Similarly, if the financing costs are less than the accrued interest, then it is profitable (all other timing options being ignored) to deliver toward the end of the delivery month. This accrued interest option typically is used in conjunction with the other delivery options to provide the seller with opportunities during the delivery month to execute the quality and "wild card" options.
- The **wild card option**: the seller can announce delivery up to 8 P.M. Central time on any trading day during the delivery month. If delivery is undertaken, then the 2 P.M. futures closing price is employed to calculate the invoice price. If the cash price drops significantly after the futures close, the arbitrageur can (a) use the cash market to obtain any needed cash bonds at a lower price in order to complete the arbitrage position, or (b) substitute the new cheapest-to-deliver bond for the bond currently being held by the arbitrageur.
- The **end-of-the-month option**: the final invoice price for delivery is set based on the closing price on the final trading day of the futures contract (eight business days before the end of the month). However, the seller has an additional seven business days after this date to announce delivery. Consequently, with the "end-of-the-month option" the seller can wait to determine what happens in the final cash trading days of the delivery month in order to obtain the best price to buy any needed cash bonds, or to obtain a cheaper-to-deliver bond in order to complete the arbitrage position.

The importance of the quality option is associated with the cheapest bond, as determined from the biases of the conversion factor method. The benefits of the accrued interest option are based on whether the net financing cost is positive or negative, as well as providing the arbitrageur a choice as to when to execute the other delivery options. Strategies on the importance of and how to employ the "wild card" and "end-of-the-month" options are discussed below.

IMPLEMENTATION OF T-BOND ARBITRAGE STRATEGIES

The logical arbitrage strategy of buying the less expensive instrument and selling the more expensive one is applicable for T-bond futures arbitrage. Short futures arbitrage is implemented with the following transactions:

11 A long arbitrage spread strategy may be profitable. Thus, the arbitrageur would buy the nearby futures and sell the deferred futures. After receiving delivery of the bond from the nearby futures, the arbitrageur would hold the bond for three months and then deliver it into the deferred contract.

- The cheapest long-term cash T-bond is purchased.
- The T-bond futures contract is sold.
- Funds are borrowed to finance the holding of the cash bond until the delivery date.
- At the optimum time during the delivery month the cash bond is delivered into the futures contract.

For optimum arbitrage results, the cheapest-to-deliver bond must be determined by considering the biases created by the conversion factor method and the delivery options must be used wisely to maximize the profits from the arbitrage transaction. The cash flows of this cash and carry trade results in Equation (7-1) and is equivalent to the examples given in Chapters 4 and 5, with the exception of the bond coupons representing the cash inflows during the arbitrage.

Pure Arbitrage Transactions

Government bond dealers are the primary pure arbitrageurs in the T-bond futures market. Bond dealers keep a significant amount of cash T-bonds in inventory, are not affected by cash transactions costs, and finance 99 percent of their inventory. In fact, a large percentage of the open interest in T-bond futures is attributable to the activity of these dealers in arbitraging *and* hedging their inventory. These arbitrage positions are financed via the repo market, as discussed below.

In general, a major arbitrageur takes a cash position in the most recent T-bond issue, which is also the most liquid. They then switch to the cheapest bond at a later date; one reason for initially buying the **bellwether** bond is that less liquid bond prices are affected if an institution decides to take a large position in a particular bond. While certain cash T-bonds are sometimes in short supply near futures expiration, which would adversely affect the liquidity of the bond if it was the cheapest-to-deliver, *dealers* typically do not have a significant problem obtaining any particular bond.[12]

Long pure arbitrage involves difficulties not present in short T-bond arbitrage. Namely, the short side of the futures transaction determines *which* T-bond is delivered via the quality delivery option. Someone transacting a long arbitrage situation (i.e., buying the futures and shorting the cash security) does not know which cash bond will be delivered. Thus, the arbitrage transaction would not be perfect. The only alternatives for the long arbitrageur are: (1) to sell the T-bond delivered and purchase the appropriate bond to cover the original short sale, an expensive and risky undertaking; (2) to forecast which T-bond will be delivered in order to determine the correct bond and number to sell so as to equate the futures and cash dollar price changes, also a risky undertaking; (3) buy the nearby futures and sell a deferred futures, thereby allowing redelivery of the bond originally received, although the potential profits of such a strategy are uncertain. These costs and

---

12 See Nancy Johnson's discussion of the paper by Resnick and Hennigar for comments on how institutional factors affect arbitrage trades. Bruce G. Resnick and Elizabeth Hennigar, "The Relationship Between Futures and Cash Prices for U.S. Treasury Bonds," *The Review of Research in Futures Markets*, Vol. 2, No. 3, 1983, pp. 282-299. "Discussion," pp. 300-313.

FOCUS 7-1: When Arbitrage is Risky: The Salomon Squeeze

In May 1991, Salomon Brothers, in conjunction with several large hedge funds, controlled more than 90 percent of the $12.26 billion two-year T-note auction, even though Treasury rules stipulate a single dealer can hold only 35 percent of any particular issue via the auction. Salomon benefited from cornering this issue by squeezing the other players in the market. The following events are based on reports by Mitchell.* A particular issue starts trading in the "when-issued" or preissue market one week before the issue is sold by the Treasury. Historically, new two-year issues start increasing in price before the auction as the result of demand, and then fall after the issue is sold. Many players on Wall Street arbitrage this predictable price change in the cash market by selling short the two-year new issue before the auction and buying another equivalent cash position, or buying futures contracts. For this auction traders had shorted $5 billion of the two-year issue. However, in May of 1991 Salomon owned such a large part of the T-notes that those who shorted the issue had to either buy it back or borrow the issue from Salomon at an expensive price. In fact, one week after the auction the T-notes sold at $100^5/_{32}$, which was an increase from the auction price of $99^{29}/_{32}$. The $^8/_{32}$ price difference caused a price appreciation of $30.6 million on the original issue. The unusually high price persisted for more than a month after the auction. Salomon subsequently paid a fine and payments of $290 million. Salomon also slipped from No. 5 in the underwritings to No. 10.

This squeeze created losses of more than $100 million for many large and small bond players across the U.S. In fact, since the squeeze, many bond traders have lost their jobs and funds playing the new issue game, gone bankrupt, exited the market, or scaled down operations. Continental Bank even gave up its role as a primary dealer after losing money in the May auction. This perception of a lack of fairness in the markets concerns regulators because investors could decide to avoid the U.S. bond market, causing interest rates on government debt to increase. When new Salomon officers and the government investigated this squeeze, they found other situations where Salomon and other investment houses attempted to control government bond and note issues. Moreover, dealers have shared information about their bids on Treasury issues for the past decade. This cooperation prompted the Treasury to change the auction rules to allow a wider group of players into the auction process.

---

* Constance Mitchell, "Critical Issue: Did Salomon Seek to Control 2-Year Sale?", *The Wall Street Journal*, August 19, 1991, p. A4. Constance Mitchell, "Salomon's 'Squeeze' in May Auction Left Many Players Reeling," *The Wall Street Journal*, October 31, 1991, p. A1, A6.

---

uncertainty reduce the attractiveness of generating a long pure arbitrage with T-bond futures.[13]

---

13 Nancy Johnson (see the discussion to Resnick and Hennigar, ibid.), who is a trader in the T-bond pit, states that "when a contract expires—there is this heavy trading going on during the last 60 seconds because the long wants it to close one way and the short wants it to close another to give the advantage to their arbitrage."

Financing via Repo Transactions

The method employed by dealers to finance a T-bond arbitrage is to use a repurchase (repo) transaction. A repo agreement allows the arbitrageur to sell *temporarily* a cash T-bond to receive funds, with the agreement that the T-bond will be repurchased after a stipulated time period. Thus, the interest rate associated with borrowing the funds received from the repo (with the T-bond acting as collateral) is the appropriate financing rate. However, the arbitrageur still receives the coupon income from the bond.

A term repo is a repurchase agreement for a specific period of time—for example, the length of the arbitrage. In view of the illiquidity of the term repo market and the inflexibility associated with longer-term financing, most dealers use the overnight repo market for financing. The overnight repo market is extremely liquid. The rates on overnight repo transactions are slightly less than the federal funds rate. Consequently, a series of overnight repos are employed to obtain funds for the arbitrage. Since overnight repo rates can change daily, this financing procedure creates uncertainty concerning the total financing cost.

Using the Conversion Factor Biases

The existence of the biases from the conversion factor method and cash market preferences, resulting in a cheapest-to-deliver T-bond, create opportunities for the T-bond futures arbitrageur. For example, on January 23, 1985, the 10⅜ of 2012 was the cheapest-to-deliver bond for the June futures contract. If this bond had continued as the cheapest bond, then the appropriate futures price would have been 72.1595 on May 9, 1985. However, the 7⅝ became the cheapest bond, causing the actual futures price to be 71.4063, a price difference of 24/32.[14] Obviously, changes in the cheapest cash bond can have an important effect on the price of the futures contract and the potential arbitrage profits.

A simple approximation method to determine the cheapest bond, as noted previously in Equation (7-9), is to calculate $[P_C + AI]/CF$, where AI is the accrued interest on the bond until delivery.[15] The cash T-bond with the *lowest* $(P_C + AI)/CF$ ratio is the cheapest bond; in other words, the arbitrageur wishes to deliver the bond with the *largest* invoice price relative to the cash market value in order to maximize profits. However, the quality option created by the conversion factor biases approaches a zero value as the yield in the market approaches 8%. This option has greater value as the yield differs substantially from 8%.

Determining the Cheapest Bond

A more accurate approach to determine the cheapest-to-deliver T-bond than Equation (7-9) is to determine the implied repo rate or the annualized rate of return on the arbitrage position. Specifically, one calculates the implied repo rate for *each* deliverable bond; the bond with the *highest* implied repo rate is the cheapest. The implied repo rate is preferable to the approximation methods noted above since arbitrageurs desire accurate values for

---

14 See Arak, Goodman, and Ross, "Cheapest to Deliver Bond," pp. 49–74.

15 For an additional discussion on using the P_C/CF or $(P_C + AI)/CF$ ratios, see Meisner and Labuszewski, "Treasury Bond Futures, pp. 569–577.

transactions involving tens of millions of dollars. The calculations to determine the implied repo rates consider the following factors:[16]

- The cost to purchase the cash instrument.
- The amount received when the cash T-bond is delivered into the T-bond futures contract.
- The net cost of carry; that is, the cost of financing the cash position held less the value of the accrued interest and reinvestment income from coupons received.

Table 7-3 shows the important variables needed to determine an implied repo rate and an annualized return. These calculations determine the cheapest bond for delivery and for arbitrage transactions. The bond with the highest annualized rate of return (column 8) or, equivalently, the highest implied repo rate (column 10), is the cheapest-to-deliver bond. Note that no bond in column 8 of Table 7-3 has an implied repo rate above the financing rate (alternatively, no bond has a positive annual rate of return) based solely on the cost of carry formulation. Thus, column 8 shows that the delivery options have value that are not captured by the cost of carry model. Hence, the delivery options affect the pricing of the futures contract.

The basic idea of the process shown in Table 7-3 is to compare the invoice price for futures delivery with the cash market price of the bond (adjusted for the net financing cost); the cash T-bond with the most advantageous difference is the cheapest-to-deliver bond. Each of the relevant variables affecting the arbitrage returns are expressly considered in Table 7-3, with the relevant equations listed below the column titles.[17] Note the significant differences in net returns in column 8 for bonds with different coupons and maturity dates. Thus, the conversion factor and cash market biases have major effects on the potential arbitrage returns for the deliverable Treasury issues.

As interest rates change, the relative rates of return for the bonds in Table 7-3 also change, since:

- The prices of the cash bonds are affected in different degrees as the rate of interest changes.
- The conversion factor biases affect the deliverable bonds differently as interest rates change.
- The ratio of the financing rate to the coupon rate affects the net profit of the arbitrage position over the holding period.

Consequently, the cheapest-to-deliver bond often *changes* as interest rates change. A computer program can determine at what point another bond becomes the new cheapest-to-deliver. This change in the cheapest bond can have significant affects on the arbitrageur's profits; hence, arbitrageurs often sell a bond if it is no longer the cheapest-to-deliver and buy the new cheapest bond. Such transactions must consider the effect of transactions costs. Moreover, arbitrageurs use the delivery options to maximize their profits when interest rates change and a new cheapest-to-deliver bond comes into existence.

---

16 For two equations and their associated procedures to determine the implied repo rate for T-bond arbitrage situations, see Arak, Goodman, and Ross, "Cheapest to Deliver Bond," pp. 49–74.

17 The effect of some of the delivery options are considered shortly.

TABLE 7-3: Bond Implied Repo Rates

(1) Coupon	(2) Maturity	(3) Cash Price	(4) Conversion Factor	(5) Adjusted Futures Price[a] $P_F \times (4) = P_F^*$	(6) $P_F^* - P_C$ $(5)-(3)$	(7) Net Cost of Carry[b] $(3) \times [i-(1/3)] \times t$	(8) Annualized Rate of Return[c] $\{[(6)-(7)]/(3)\} \times \{1/t\}$	(9) Coupon (points) $(1) \times t$	(10) Implied Repo Rate $\{[(6)+(9)]/(3)\} \times \{1/t\}$
7.25	2016	81.7188	0.9171	81.4786	-0.2401	-0.0274	-0.0211	0.8938	0.0649
7.5	2016	84.2188	0.9444	83.9040	-0.3147	-0.0317	-0.0273	0.9247	0.0587
9.25	2016	101.6875	1.1375	101.0598	-0.6277	-0.0622	-0.0451	1.1404	0.0409
8.75	2017	96.9063	1.0833	96.2444	-0.6618	-0.0513	-0.0511	1.0788	0.0349
9.875	2015	107.8750	1.2054	107.0923	-0.7827	-0.0737	-0.0533	1.2175	0.0327
8.875	2017	98.2188	1.0977	97.5238	-0.6950	-0.0528	-0.0530	1.0942	0.0330
10.625	2015	115.4063	1.2871	114.3508	-1.0555	-0.0863	-0.0681	1.3099	0.0179
10.375	2012	110.2500	1.2284	109.1357	-1.1143	-0.1102	-0.0739	1.2791	0.0121
9.125	2018	101.0938	1.1262	100.0558	-1.0379	-0.0531	-0.0790	1.1250	0.0070
12.5	2014	130.2500	1.4498	128.8057	-1.4443	-0.1601	-0.0800	1.5411	0.0060
11.25	2015	121.5938	1.3534	120.2411	-1.3526	-0.0978	-0.0837	1.3870	0.0023
12	2013	125.1250	1.3917	123.6438	-1.4812	-0.1528	-0.0861	1.4795	-0.0001
11.75	2014	124.3438	1.3764	122.2845	-2.0592	-0.1302	-0.1258	1.4486	-0.0398

Numbers in parentheses refer to the relevant columns.

[a] The futures price P_F is 88–27.

[b] A negative value indicates that the coupon income is greater than the financing cost; i is the financing rate = 8.60% annually; t is the proportion of the year the position is held, where $t = 45/365$ in this example. One could employ compounded rates such as in Equations (7–1) and (7–2) instead of simple rates of return.

[c] An arbitrageur considers the cost of financing the accrued interest paid when the bond is purchased and the reinvestment returns from coupons received during the holding period. However, these technicalities only complicate the example and do not significantly change the results. See Schneeweis, Hill, and Philipp for consideration of these variables. Thomas R. Schneeweis, Joanne M. Hill, and Michael B. Philipp, "Hedge Ratio Determination Based on Bond Yield Forecasts," *Review of Research in Futures Markets*, Vol. 2, No. 3, 1983, pp. 338–349.

Using the Delivery Options

The "wild card" and "end-of-the-month" delivery options increase the profits of the arbitrageur by providing an opportunity to obtain deliverable bonds at prices below the futures invoice price. These options allow the futures short to announce delivery of cash bonds either hours or days *after* the futures delivery price is set. Consequently, any advantageous changes in the cash bond prices after the futures price is set are used by an arbitrageur to increase profits. These two delivery options create an option for the seller concerning *when* the cash bond can be delivered; this option is called an **implied put option,** and is illustrated graphically in Figure 7-5. These delivery options can be separated into the "tail" of the arbitrage and changes in the cheapest bond.

The "Tail" of the Arbitrage. The wild card and end-of-the month options are beneficial to arbitrageurs since they purchase only $100,000/CF par value of the current cheapest cash bond per one short futures contract. This ratio equates the dollar change in the cash position with the dollar change in the futures position, since the futures price follows the cheapest cash price. However, $100,000 par value of cash must be delivered into the futures contract; the arbitrageur still needs $100,000(1 − 1/CF) par value of a deliverable bond (if the conversion factor is greater than one). This remaining $100,000(1 − 1/CF) par value per futures contract is called the "tail" of the arbitrage; that is,

$$\text{Tail} = 100,000 \ (1 - 1/CF) \tag{7-10}$$

The wild card and end-of-the-month options are used to determine *when* the remaining tail of the cash bonds for the arbitrage is purchased to maximize profits. If cash prices decline after the 2 P.M. futures market closing time (or after trading ceases) during the delivery month, then the arbitrageur can purchase the deliverable cash bonds at a cheaper price

---

FIGURE 7-5: The Implied Put Option

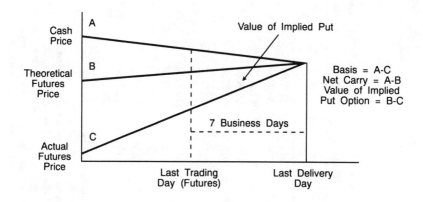

than the invoice price calculated from the future price, increasing the profits of the arbitrage.[18] However, if the cheapest bond has a conversion factor near one, then the tail of the arbitrage is negligible and this portion of the wild card and end-of-the-month options are near zero. Example 7-2 illustrates this use of the tail of the arbitrage.

Changes in the Cheapest Bond. Another application of both the wild card and end-of-the-month options is to react to a change in interest rates that *changes* the *cheapest* bond after the futures market closes by selling the entire amount of the cash bond currently being held and buying the new cheapest bond to be purchased. The wild card option then is used to deliver cash bonds that have an invoice amount above their cost; similarly, the end-of-the-month option is used for the same purpose during the last seven days of the month when futures no longer trade.[19] Although transactions costs do have to be considered before implementing such a switch, such substitutions are often made by arbitrageurs, as shown by Arak, Goodman, and Ross.[20] Finally, it is important to note that the potential profit associated with changes in the cheapest bond, wild card, and end-of-the-month delivery options is greatest for bonds with the largest conversion factors; that is, the value of these options is an increasing function of the conversion factor. The end of this chapter discusses the empirical analysis of the value of the delivery options.

EXAMPLE 7-2: Use of the Tail of the Arbitrage

If the cheapest-to-deliver bond has a conversion factor of 1.21, then the amount of additional par value of bonds needed to deliver into the futures when 10 futures contracts are short is:

$$\text{Tail} = \$100,000 \ (1 - 1/CF) \ (\text{number of futures contracts})$$
$$= \$100,000 \ (1 - 1/1.21) \ (10)$$
$$= \$10,0000 \ (1 - .82645) \ (10)$$
$$= \$173,550$$

If the price of the cheapest bond declines 2 points between 2:00 and 8 P.M. on a delivery day (the wild card option), or after trading ceases at the end of the month (the end-of-the-month option), then the futures seller profits by:
$$\$173,550 \ (.02) = \$3,471$$

---

18 The existence of these delivery options causes the futures price to sell at a discount to Pc/CF, at least in the month of delivery. For additional discussion of the delivery options, see Meisner and Labuszewski, "Treasury Bond Futures," pp. 569–577.; Arak, Goodman, and Ross, "Cheapest to Deliver Bond," pp. 49–74; and the subsequent sections of this chapter.

19 To use the end-of-the-month option, the arbitrageur equates the par value of the cash and the futures on the last futures trading day. This strategy allows the arbitrageur to take advantage of either price increases or price decreases in the cash market without incurring any risk. See Arak and Goodman for a description of the process. Marcelle Arak and Laurie S. Goodman, "Treasury Bond Futures: Valuing the Delivery Options," *The Journal of Futures Markets*, Vol. 7, No. 3, 1987, pp. 269-286.

20 Arak, Goodman, and Ross, "Cheapest to Deliver Bond," pp. 49–74.

Quasi-Arbitrage as an Alternative to a Short-Term Investment

T-bond futures quasi-arbitrage is equivalent to creating a synthetic short-term cash instrument. Thus, the purchase of a long-term cash T-bond and the sale of a T-bond futures contract should theoretically provide a return similar to a cash T-bill. If the return on this synthetic instrument is greater than the return on a short-term T-bill, then executing the quasi-arbitrage is beneficial. However, the discussion above shows that the delivery options on the T-bond futures contract are valuable to the seller of the futures contract. Consequently, anyone who institutes a quasi-arbitrage transaction also must employ these delivery options in order to receive the full value from the short futures position. Since the futures price is lower due to these delivery options, calculating the synthetic short-term interest rate without including the option values typically shows the quasi-arbitrage strategy to be inferior to the short-term instrument.

T-BOND FUTURES ARBITRAGE: EMPIRICAL EVIDENCE AND DETERMINING THE VALUE OF THE DELIVERY OPTIONS

Arbitrage Results with the Cost of Carry Model

Resnick and Hennigar[21] investigate the existence and size of T-bond futures arbitrage profits by using daily data. This study includes the effects of the cost of carry model and the quality option, but does not consider the other delivery options. The fair value of the arbitrage position from their equation is then compared to the actual value. The analysis includes transactions costs.

Approximately 46 percent of the daily observations tested implied that arbitrage profits were possible. The average net profits for *all* observations were $66.50 per $100,000 contract, which includes the unprofitable arbitrage transactions. However, 10 of the observations in early August 1980 accounted for three-quarters of the total profit, possibly due to a *Wall Street Journal* error in the recorded price of the cheapest-to-deliver cash bond. Removing these outliers reduces the average net profit to $17.67 per contract. Even so, these results suggest that T-bond futures arbitrage is profitable even before the wild card and end-of-the-month delivery options are considered.

Examining the results in terms of length of time of the arbitrage shows that no particular arbitrage length is more profitable than another. However, an analysis of the size of the arbitrage profits in relation to the level of interest rates does indicate a relationship. Figure 7-6 illustrates the following results: the profits from a T-bond futures arbitrage are larger when the interest rate is high (above 10%) than when the interest rate is low (below 10%). In fact, when interest rates are high, the average net profit is positive, and when rates are low, the average net profit is negative. However, this relationship concerning the level of interest rates and arbitrage profits may relate simply to the greater variability in interest rates when these rates are above 10%; in other words, the greater the variability, the

---

21 Resnick and Hennigar, "Relationship Between Futures and Cash Prices," pp. 282–299.

FIGURE 7-6: T-Bond Arbitrage Profits by Interest Rate Level

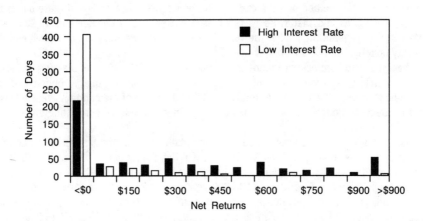

Source: Adapted from data in Bruce G. Resnick and Elizabeth Hennigar, "The Relationship Between Futures and Cash Prices for U.S. Treasury Bonds," *The Review of Research in Futures Markets*, Vol. 2, No. 3, 1983, pp. 282-299. "Discussion," pp. 300–313.

greater the "noise" in the market, creating less information and more risk. Alternatively, the level of interest rates may be related to the value of the remaining delivery options.[22]

The Resnick and Hennigar results show that arbitrage profits are available for T-bond futures, although these profits typically are not large. Moreover, the other delivery options are ignored in this study. On the other hand, Arak and Goodman[23] state that simply using futures and cash prices and coupon investment returns provides an annualized implied repo rate of return for arbitrage that historically has been 250 basis points *below* the actual financing rate for much of the 1980s. In other words, the futures price has been too *low* to provide adequate returns for arbitrage when the delivery options are ignored.

---

22 Unfortunately, intraday cash bond prices typically are not available for T-bond arbitrage studies. The daily cash and futures prices employed in this analysis have a timing difference of 30 to 60 minutes, which may adversely affect the results. James Hoag (in the discussion to Resnick and Hennigar, 1983) states that using dealer bid/ask quotes for half-hour intervals in comparison to corresponding futures prices decreases the apparent opportunities for obtaining arbitrage profits; he found that only 7 percent of the possible bid/ask situations provided arbitrage profits when the half-hour data was employed.

The T-bill rate is employed by Resnick and Hennigar as a proxy for the repurchase rate; repo rates tend to be higher than T-bill rates according to traders, but others claim that the results are not affected by the T-bill/repo substitution (see the discussion to Resnick and Hennigar, "Relationship Between Futures and Cash Prices," pp. 300–315).

23 Arak and Goodman, "Treasury Bond Futures," pp. 269–286.

The Value of the Quality Option

The quality option is valuable to the arbitrageur because the cheapest bond changes as interest rates change. Thus, the arbitrageur increases profits by selling the bond currently held and buying the cheapest bond. These opportunities occur because of the biases in the conversion factor method and the cash market preferences. The extent of these biases for different coupons and maturities was discussed earlier in this chapter and in Kane and Marcus.[24] In general, the greater the volatility in interest rates, the greater the value of the quality option.

Benninga and Smirlock[25] examine the quality option and the effect of marking-to-market on the implied repo rates of bond arbitrage. They find that the quality option and the marking-to-market effect increases return by .4% of the value of the bond on average ($400 per contract), although the value of this option changes substantially from one time period to another.

Kane and Marcus[26] determine both a dollar option value for the quality option and the effect of conversion factor risk on the variability of the quality option value. They find that the value of the quality option for four delivery dates from September 1981 to March 1983 varies from $1,390 to $4,600 per $100,000 contract, which translates to 1.9% to 6.2% of the futures price. Moreover, hedgers who ignore the benefits of this delivery option would receive only one-half of the potential reduction in risk. However, Hegde[27] estimates this option is only worth .5% of the average futures price over the last quarter of the contract's life.

Hemler[28] employs three separate techniques to estimate the value of the delivery option from 1977 to 1986. These methods give values from .2% of par to 1.2% of par for the delivery option—that is, $200 to $1,200 per contract, with $200 to $500 being accepted as a fair estimate of this option.[29]

The Wild Card Option

Arbitrageurs use the wild card option to purchase cash bonds when the price declines after the 2:00 P.M. close of the futures market. This option allows arbitrageurs to deliver these bonds into the futures contract at the 2:00 P.M. invoice price. Gay and Manaster[30] examine the optimal delivery strategy related to the wild card option, finding that profits from this

---

24 Alex Kane and Alan J. Marcus, "The Quality Option in the Treasury Bond Futures Market: An Empirical Assessment," *The Journal of Futures Markets*, Vol. 6, No. 2, Summer 1986, pp. 231-248.

25 Simon Benninga and Michael Smirlock, "An Empirical Analysis of the Delivery Option, Marking to Market, and the Pricing of Treasury Bond Futures," *The Journal of Futures Markets*, Vol. 5, No. 3, Fall 1985, pp. 361-374.

26 Alex Kane and Alan J. Marcus, "The Quality Option in the Treasury Bond Futures Market: An Empirical Assessment," *The Journal of Futures Markets*, Vol. 6, No. 2, Summer 1986, pp. 231-248.

27 Shantaram P. Hegde, "An Empirical Analysis of the Implicit Delivery Options in the Treasury Bond Futures Contract," *Journal of Banking and Finance*, Vol. 11, No. 3, September 1988, pp. 469-492.

28 Michael L. Hemler, "The Quality Delivery Option in Treasury Bond Futures Contracts," *Journal of Finance*, Vol. 45, No. 5, December 1990, pp. 1565-1586.

29 Hemler, ibid., explains the difference from the Kane and Marcus, ibid., results by stating that the latter study employs *estimated* term structures and associated volatilities over the period of the analysis.

30 Gay and Manaster, "Implicit Delivery Options, 1986, pp. 41–72.

optimal strategy are significantly positive.[31] Gay and Manaster find that the per contract gain over a naive delivery strategy is $653 to $2,127 after transaction costs when selling to beat the bid price, with the size of the profits depending on the assumption concerning the next day's cash price. The monthly gain over the naive strategy is $0 to $269 when selling to beat the ask price. Bond dealers can take advantage of the bid price opportunities, whereas others are able to execute only at the ask price.

The article concluded that profits are available via the rules given by Gay and Manaster, whereas actual deliveries indicate that suboptimal choices have been made by the arbitrageurs. Moreover, futures prices seem to track the delivery policies of the actual shorts rather than the optimal delivery policies. On the other hand, Kane and Marcus[32] argue that the Gay and Manaster trading rule does not maximize the value of the wild card option for the short. In particular, Kane and Marcus state that bond prices need to decline by more than a given critical value before delivery is optimal, whereas Gay and Manaster maintain that one should deliver if any profit is available.

Kane and Marcus[33] present a valuation model for the wild card option and then determine the value of that option for *simulated* conditions of various volatility levels. They conclude that the value of the wild card option increases: the greater the number of trading days remaining in the delivery month; the greater the volatility of cash prices; and as the difference increases between the conversion factor for the cheapest bond and a conversion factor of one. With a standard deviation of 10% for bond returns and a conversion factor of 1.5, the value of the wild card option is estimated to be $165 per contract. A standard deviation of 20% for bond returns increases the wild card value to $329.

Arak and Goodman[34] include more market realities in the pricing of the futures and cash markets in order to develop their analysis of the wild card option.[35] They find that the wild card option is worth an average of $120, assuming a volatility of cash returns of 18 percent. These values are significantly less than the results for the previous studies. LaBarge[36] argues that the Kane and Marcus results are heavily influenced by two volatile delivery months. When LaBarge employs actual data in the Kane and Marcus model, then the wild card option has value only when large volatilities exist and a high coupon bond is delivered. During low-volatility months the wild card is essentially worthless.

31 Gay and Manaster, ibid., describe the wild card option as a portfolio of put and call options on the optimal bond for delivery. Their article details the considerations and interpretations of their results.

32 Alex Kane and Alan J. Marcus, "Valuation and Optimal Exercise of the Wild Card Option in the Treasury Bond Futures Market," *Journal of Finance*, Vol. 41, No. 1, March 1986, pp. 195-207.

33 Ibid.

34 Arak and Goodman, Treasury Bond Futures, pp. 269–286.

35 Arak and Goodman, ibid., discuss the disadvantages of the assumptions made by Gay and Manaster, "Implicit Delivery Options," 1986, pp. 41–72, and Kane and Marcus ("The Quality Option..." 1986 and "Valuation..." 1986) in determining the value of the delivery options. Essentially, Arak and Goodman state that the previous studies did not treat the cash-futures basis correctly, that the T-bond futures exercise was not correctly modeled, and that one must consider the potential change in the cheapest bond after the market closes. Moreover, Arak and Goodman claim that the 2% to 7% value of the quality option determined by Kane and Marcus is too high, because the same bond was held throughout the period, rather than switching to the cheapest bond as the interest rate changed.

36 Karin Peterson LaBarge, "Does the Wild Card Option Really Have Value?" Center for the Study of Futures Markets, Working Paper No. 186, Columbia University, January 1989.

The End-of-the-Month Option

The end-of-the-month option is often called the implicit put option, because it gives the seller the right to deliver any deliverable cash bond on any of the last seven days of the delivery month while using the closing futures price of the last day of trading (seven trading days before the end of the month). This end-of-the-month option is separated into a "waiting profit" and a "quality profit." The waiting profit is associated solely with changes in interest rates, whereas the quality profit relates to changes in the cheapest bond.

Gay and Manaster[37] find that the average waiting profit is large (more than $800 on average for a five-day wait) but highly variable; the waiting profit is probably due to the general decline in bond prices over the time period of their analysis. The quality profit ranges from $143 to $232 and is statistically significant. Overall there is a value to the end-of-the-month option of $66 (for a one-day wait) to $956 (for a six-day wait) as calculated for the time period in question.[38]

Arak and Goodman[39] explain the factors affecting the end-of-the-month option and then value that option. They find that the end-of-the-month option is worth an average of $88 when the volatility is 12%.

Hegde[40] uses data from 1977 to 1986 to determine that the delivery options have an average value of $539 and a median value of $474 per futures contract, although the value has a standard deviation of $692. The delivery option increases in value the longer one waits to execute the option. The option is worth $126 if executed on the second trading day after futures stop trading, $416 on day five, and $539 if executed on the last trading day of the month.

The Switching Option

The studies that investigate the quality option essentially determine the value of this option by comparing the benefits of changing from an "old" cheapest-to-deliver to the "new" cheapest bond. Typically this comparison is only completed once, with the resultant difference being the measured value of the quality option. The benefits of switching from the "old" to the "new" cheapest bond on multiple occasions, whenever the benefits are larger than the transactions costs, is called the **switching option**. Livingston[41] determines that such switching can eliminate the potential cost that long arbitrageurs bear from the quality option.

---

37 Gay and Masaster, "Implicit Delivery Options," 1986, pp. 41–72.

38 Arak and Goodman, "Treasury Bond Futures," pp. 269–286, state that Gay and Manaster's method for switching to the cheapest bond at the end of the month is oversimplified, since they fail to take into account the optimal pattern of switching bonds.

39 Arak and Goodman, ibid..

40 Shantaram P. Hegde, "An Ex-Post Valuation of the Quality Option Implicit in the Treasury Bond Futures Contract," *Journal of Banking and Finance*, Vol. 14, No. 4, November 1990, pp. 741-760.

41 Miles Livingston, "The Delivery Option on Forward Contracts," *Journal of Financial and Quantitative Analysis*, Vol. 22, No. 1, March 1987, pp. 79-88.

Barnhill[42] finds that the average value of the cumulative switching profits for three-month arbitrages varies from $280 to $1,120, depending on the size of the transaction costs, while the pure quality option profits were only $120 to $250. Barnhill and Seale[43] examine optimal exercise strategies for this switching option.

Conclusions and the Simultaneous Nature of the Delivery Options

The studies that examine the delivery options use different procedures to obtain a value for these options. Consequently, the results vary significantly. Some studies find that the delivery options are worth $500 to $1,000 (or more) in total, per contract. More recent studies value these options at closer to $200 per contract. Moreover, these more recent studies suggest that the quality option provides the vast majority of the total value of the delivery options. In addition to the time period, and hence the volatility of interest rates, as well as the methodology employed, the type of data used in the analysis significantly affects the results. In particular, the use of bid versus ask prices (with an 8/32 spread) causes annualized returns to change from positive to negative values. Others argue that large transactions of $5 million possess spreads of only 1/32 of a point.

In conclusion, the appropriate value of these delivery options on T-bond futures has yet to be determined precisely. A simultaneous model to value all of the delivery options in conjunction with one another would be a useful extension to previous work. In the meantime, the most recent evidence suggests that the delivery options have only minimal value. Moreover, with interest rates near 8% and the volatility of rates being moderate in the later 1980s and early 1990s, the opportunities to use the delivery options effectively is reduced.

MUNICIPAL BOND FUTURES PRICING

The pricing of Municipal Bond Index (MBI) futures is based on the basic cost of carry model, although the muni futures are settled in cash and an Index is employed as the equivalent "cash security." The composition of the Index used to value the futures contract is explained in Chapter 2. The process to value the bonds is completed as follows: Each bond in the Index is priced daily by five municipal bond brokers between 1:45 P.M. and 2:00 P.M. (Chicago time), and also between 10:45 A.M. and 11 A.M. during the futures expiration month. The highest and lowest prices for each bond are dropped, and the remaining three prices are averaged as an appraisal value. This value is divided by a conversion factor in order to standardize each bond for coupon and maturity differences. Thus, the Index is composed of hypothetical 8%, 20-year bonds. These standardizations reduce potential problems when the composition of the Index is changed. Changes in the Index are considered on the 15th and last day of the month; changes occur when bond ratings change and when bonds are inactive. The MBI portfolio changes *entirely* about every three months. This situation complicates the pricing and arbitrage of the futures contract.

---

42 Theodore M. Barnhill, "Quality Option Profits, Switching Option Profits, and Variation Margin Costs: An Examination of Their Size and Impact on Treasury Bond Futures Prices," *Journal of Financial and Quantitative Analysis*, Vol. 25, No. 1, March 1990, pp. 65-86.

43 Theodore M. Barnhill and William E. Seale, "Optimal Exercise of the Switching Option in Treasury Bond Arbitrages," *The Journal of Futures Markets*, Vol. 8, No. 5, October 1988, pp. 517-532.

The use of a conversion factor creates the same type of biases that exist for the T-bond and T-note futures, except these biases are less important for pricing purposes because no cash bonds are delivered. On the other hand, it creates difficulties for arbitrageurs because the futures contract is settled in cash but they have to arrange their arbitrage based on actual bonds. The influence of the tax rate on the effective municipal bond yields also complicates the valuation process.

Hamilton and Koch[44] develop a cost of carry model for MBI futures and explain the influence of the factors that affect the pricing of these futures. Their empirical tests show that the prices of these futures contracts do not consider transactions costs on all of the bonds in the Index. Thus, arbitrageurs may be using cash portfolios that are smaller than the 40 bond futures specifications *or* the arbitrageurs do not revise their portfolios as the composition of the index changes. Kochin and Parks[45] found that the pricing of MBI futures when it started trading in 1985 traded at large discounts to fair values, creating profits for long futures arbitrage. Before transactions costs, profitable opportunities switched several times from long to short futures arbitrage through 1986.[46] After transactions costs, quasi-arbitrageurs in a 25 percent tax bracket typically gained $1,500 to $4,500 per contract through the September 1986 futures expiration.

SUMMARY AND LOOKING AHEAD

This chapter examined T-bond, T-note, and municipal bond futures pricing and arbitrage. The cost of carry model links the futures to the underlying cash prices. This pricing link provides justification to use futures as a hedging mechanism. The conversion factor method creates *one* cheapest-to-deliver bond for arbitrage purposes. However, the pricing and arbitrage of these contracts are complicated by the biases that arise from the conversion factor method and cash market preferences and by valuing the delivery options. Overall, short T-bond arbitrage provides substantial profitable opportunities. Others also need to consider the factors that influence pricing, since (1) speculators need to know the fair price of the futures, and (2) hedgers can use the delivery options if they carry a short futures position into the delivery month. The next chapter examines short-term interest rate pricing and arbitrage.

---

44 Thomas R. Hamilton and Timothy W. Koch, "Cost-of-Carry Trading and Pricing of Municipal Bond Futures," paper presented at the Southern Finance Meetings, San Antonio, 1988.

45 Levis A. Kochin and Richard W. Parks, "Was the Tax-Exempt Bond Market Inefficient or Were Future Expected Tax Rates Negative?" *Journal of Finance*, Vol. 43, No. 4, September 1988, pp. 913-931.

46 The authors did not investigate 1987 and later because of a change in the proposed tax code.

Chapter 8

Short-Term Interest Rate Futures Pricing and Arbitrage

The cost of carry model determines the pricing of Eurodollar and T-bill futures contracts, with the type of financing arrangement being the important consideration affecting pricing. Market participants execute both pure and quasi-arbitrage. Pure arbitrage employs outside financing to obtain risk-free profits, whereas quasi-arbitrage occurs when a security currently in the portfolio is sold and replaced with an identical security for a lower cost. These strategies are important for low cost traders in the cash markets (money center banks for Eurodollars and dealers for T-bills who execute pure arbitrage) and for those who hold Eurodollar time deposits or T-bills in their portfolios (quasi-arbitrage).

In this chapter we will examine the important strategies for Eurodollar/T-bill futures arbitrage and the relevant diagrams and transactions associated with each strategy. Empirical results concerning pricing and the arbitrage transactions also will be discussed. We find that pure arbitrage explains the pricing of futures contracts for nearby expirations. However, using comparisons of futures and forward rates to determine whether arbitrage exists must be made with care.

PRICING SHORT-TERM INTEREST RATE CONTRACTS

The pricing of short-term interest rate futures is important both for the integrity of the market and for users of these contracts. Pricing must be based on rational financial economics criteria, such as the cost of carry mode, for hedgers and speculators to have confidence in the relationship between the cash and futures pricing. In addition, the pricing model provides the foundation for determining whether arbitrage exists in these markets. Potential arbitrage profits are particularly important for the Eurodollar time deposit and T-bill markets because of the large dollar volume of these markets and the widespread use of these instruments.

There are three methods to determine the pricing of Eurodollar and T-bill futures contracts, all of which employ the cost of carry formulation. The first is directly applying the cost of carry equation by using prices of the instruments; this approach is most feasible for T-bill futures. The second is comparing the forward rate to the futures rate.[1] The third is comparing the implied repo (financing) rate to the actual financing rate. Chapter 4 presents the latter two methods. These methods are discussed here before explaining the specific transactions needed to implement an arbitrage with these contracts. Although each method

---

1 Technically, the implied repo rate is relevant for T-bill and T-bond futures only, since repurchase agreements are used for financing these contracts. However, the equivalent concept of the implied financing rate is applicable for Eurodollar futures pricing via term loans.

is based on the same model, convenience of data availability or industry practice often dictates the use of one method over another.

The Cost of Carry Equation

The cost of carry model and arbitrage concepts discussed previously apply directly to short-term interest rate futures contracts. In fact, more exact pricing and therefore lower profit opportunities are likely with short-term interest rate futures because there are fewer difficulties with exact matching of cash instruments with futures delivery requirements (essentially no tracking risk), transactions costs are minimal, and all cash inflow effects are known and occur at the end of the period.

The basic cost of carry concept is applicable for Eurodollar and T-bill futures pricing without adjustment, since there are no intermediate cash flows and a *specific* cash instrument is priced by the futures contract. "Delivery" for Eurodollar and T-bill futures is limited to a two-day period, and the interest received is adjusted depending on which day is employed, eliminating any uncertainty concerning the deliverable instrument.[2] However, the exact specification of the cost of carry concept does differ slightly between T-bill and Eurodollar futures pricing because of the method of interest payment and pricing on the instrument.

T-bill futures pricing employs the basic cost of carry equation $P_{FAIR} = P_C (1 + i)^t$ with i representing the financing rate. The interest received on cash T-bills is due to the difference between the purchase and sales prices; hence, the difference between the current T-bill cash price of P_C and its price when deliverable into the futures contract represents the interest earned on the T-bill. Thus, no specific adjustment needs to be made to account for interest earned.

Eurodollar futures pricing is slightly different. Eurodollar time deposits pay interest on a money market basis related to the original amount deposited. Therefore, the straightforward application of calculating the forward rate *or* the implied financing rate, as covered in Chapter 4, is appropriate.

In general, the specific cost of carry equation that uses prices is *not* employed for short-term interest rate futures pricing because of the necessity for converting interest rate quotes to prices. The more common approach is to use the forward rate or implied financing rate. However, arbitrage calculations typically consider the dollar prices of the instruments.

Using Forward and Implied Financing Rates

A number of market participants, as well as empirical pricing and arbitrage studies, use either the forward rate or implied repo (financing) rate for pricing and arbitrage decisions.

---

2 Recall that Eurodollar futures are settled in cash. Starting with the June 1983 contract, the expiration date of the T-bill futures is set based on the maturity of the one-year cash T-bill. In addition, 180-day and/or 90-day T-bills also are deliverable into the futures contract. Typically, the specific cash T-bill maturity that can be delivered into the futures contract is uniquely priced in relation to the other cash T-bills with similar maturities (maturities within two weeks of the deliverable cash bill). In other words, the additional demand for the deliverable T-bill often drives down its yield in relation to the nearby maturities. Although one can hypothesize that this pricing discrepancy should not occur in *perfect* markets, the evidence shows that futures market activity may have an important effect on this specific T-bill maturity.

The forward rate is determined from the term structure of interest rates to the interest rate implied from the futures price in order to determine whether a significant difference exists between the cash and futures prices. Alternatively, the implied financing rate is compared to the actual financing rate to determine whether the futures pricing is fair or arbitrage exists. Chapter 4 illustrates how to calculate the forward and implied financing rates. Later in this chapter we find that forward and implied financing methods differ in their assumptions of how the arbitrage transaction is financed.

Exhibit 8-1 states the circumstances when short or long futures arbitrage is appropriate *and* the type of transactions needed to implement the arbitrage.[3] For example, a short futures arbitrage is appropriate when the forward rate is greater than the futures rate (i.e., the forward *price* is less than the futures price); thus, the arbitrageur sells the more expensive futures and invests in a longer-term cash instrument. How funds are obtained for financing arbitrage transactions is examined below.

EXHIBIT 8-1: Decision Rules and Strategies for Using the Implied Repo Rate and the Forward Rate

---

Chapter 4 discusses and develops the following rules to implement arbitrage strategies. These transactions are examined in the strategies discussed in this chapter.

- If the implied repo (financing) rate > short-term financing rate* (i.e., if the forward rate > futures rate), then for
  - Short pure arbitrage:
    Obtain funds from borrowing.
    Invest in the six-month, interest-bearing instrument.
    Sell the futures contract.
  - Short quasi-arbitrage:
    Invest in the six-month, interest-bearing instrument from existing funds.
    Sell the futures contract.

- If the implied repo (financing) rate < short-term financing rate* (i.e., if the forward rate < futures rate), then for
  - Long pure arbitrage:
    Obtain funds from borrowing.
    Invest in a three-month, interest-bearing instrument.
    Buy the futures contract.
  - Long quasi-arbitrage:
    Invest in a three-month, interest-bearing instrument from existing funds.
    Buy the futures contract.

---

*For quasi-arbitrage, the relevant risk-free rate is substituted for the financing rate.

---

3 Exhibit 8-1 is a combination of exhibits originally presented in Chapter 4.

ARBITRAGE FOR SHORT-TERM INTEREST RATE CONTRACTS

Arbitrage strategies are particularly important for Eurodollar and T-bill futures because of the large size of these markets and the widespread use of these instruments. In particular, any financial institution or portfolio that employs these instruments as an investment vehicle can obtain the benefits of a quasi-arbitrage strategy to create a synthetic position with futures that earns a higher return than the current cash position.

Arbitrage Issues

An arbitrage transaction is initiated when mispricing exists between the associated futures and cash instruments. The arbitrageur takes equivalent positions in the futures and cash markets, profiting from the discrepancy in the relative pricing between the markets. Since the two positions are equivalent, risk is eliminated.

Arbitrage for short-term interest rate futures is often transacted by pure arbitrageurs; that is, the transaction is executed via borrowed funds. Quasi-arbitrage strategies to obtain higher alternative returns also are employed—for example, when a financial institution already owns the short-term instrument.

Pure arbitrageurs often borrow funds at the overnight financing rate and roll over the overnight loan for as long as the arbitrage transaction is kept in place, rather than obtaining a loan for the entire period. This financing method is particularly relevant for T-bill futures arbitrage. Of course, this procedure creates a risk that the financing rate will change over the term of the arbitrage, causing the transaction to no longer be "risk-free." This practice sometimes is referred to as speculating on changes in the overnight interest rate. Consequently, the method of financing becomes an important consideration for short-term interest rate futures arbitrage.

Pure Arbitrage Strategies

Pure arbitrage occurs when risk-free profits can be obtained without the need for internal funds. Eurodollar and T-bill futures provide excellent examples for examining pure arbitrage, since these contracts have only a two-day window for delivery and no complications affect the pricing and arbitrage relationships.

Conceptually, an arbitrage transaction is profitable when:

$$\text{Purchase price} + \text{costs of financing} + \text{trading costs}$$
$$< \text{sales price} + \text{interest received} \qquad (8\text{-}1)$$

For ease of comprehension, prices and costs are used here rather than comparing interest rates. Actual comparisons are typically completed with interest rates.

Short arbitrage exists when a short futures transaction is implemented as part of the arbitrage strategy, for example, when a six-month T-bill is purchased and a T-bill futures contract is sold.[4] Providing one meaningful simple equation for this relationship is difficult because of the differences between the arbitrage transactions for T-bills and Eurodollar time

---

4 Of course, maturities of other than six months and three months can be executed, and futures expirations other than the nearby contract can be employed for arbitrage purposes. The use of a specific set of dates is chosen to illustrate the relevant concepts in order to make the discussion of arbitrage more comprehensible. See Jones for a general algebraic discussion of arbitrage and alternative returns. Frank J. Jones, "The Integration of the Cash and Futures Markets for Treasury Securities," *The Journal of Futures Markets*, Vol. 1, No. 1, Spring 1981, pp. 33-58.

deposits, and the characteristics of the transactions. For example, T-bills earn interest via the change in price over the holding period, while Eurodollar time deposits earn money market rates on the amount deposited. Moreover, T-bills are delivered into the futures contract, while two separate loans are needed to implement a short Eurodollar arbitrage. The "strategies" described below show the transactions needed to implement arbitrage and how to convert these transactions into dollar amounts to determine potential arbitrage profits.

The implementation of short pure arbitrage depends on how funds are obtained to finance the arbitrage. Eurodollars can be deposited in or borrowed from a major bank in London, or another international banking center. Hence, only the bid-ask spread between deposit and loan rates constitute a transactions cost. Funds for T-bill arbitrage theoretically can be borrowed from a bank, but such arbitrage typically is executed via repurchase agreements. A short sale of a cash T-bill also can be implemented in order to obtain funds. Long pure arbitrage also requires funding, but the type of transactions executed differ.

Quasi-Arbitrage Strategies

Quasi-arbitrage occurs when risk-free profits exist for a combination of cash and futures transactions for which the arbitrageur already owns an equivalent cash security. For example, assume that a financial institution owns three-month cash T-bills. If the institution can obtain an additional profit by (1) selling the currently owned three-month T-bills and (2) creating a synthetic three-month T-bill by using futures contracts and longer maturity cash T-bills, then a quasi-arbitrage opportunity exists. Alternatively, one can think of quasi-arbitrage in terms of returns. A financial institution should choose the transaction that provides the largest risk-free return over the period in question, either the cash T-bill or the synthetic cash-futures T-bill.

Quasi-arbitrage is essentially equivalent to pure arbitrage except for one major factor: the quasi-arbitrageur does *not* have to finance the cash position, since the cash T-bill already is being held in the portfolio. Hence, the relevant comparison becomes the alternative rate of return with the currently held cash instrument, rather than the cost of borrowed funds. The implications of this difference in financing methods is examined in association with the empirical results for T-bill futures arbitrage.

EURODOLLAR FUTURES PRICING AND ARBITRAGE

Eurodollar Futures Pricing

The concepts of Eurodollar time deposit futures pricing and T-bill futures pricing are very similar. This similarity exists because both contracts are based on cash assets with 90 days to maturity and both have a two-day window for delivery/settlement. Differences that exist relate to the characteristics of the two futures and cash markets. In particular, Eurodollar time deposit futures settle in cash rather than in delivery of a cash instrument. Hence, a small risk exists that the futures contract will have a different interest rate than a selected bank Eurodollar time deposit, since the cash settlement price for futures is based on an average rate from eight banks. (Twelve banks are contacted for quotes, but the two highest and two lowest quotes are dropped.) However, the competition for dollar transactions in London is so intense that any difference is only a few basis points.

Eurodollar cash loans and time deposits quote London Interbank Offer Rates (LIBOR) with Eurobanks dominating the cash activity in Eurodollars. The spread between the bid rate (the rate the London bank pays for deposits) and the ask rate (the rate the bank earns on funds loaned out) is typically small, usually $12\frac{1}{2}$ basis points. This spread is consistent regardless of the maturity, as shown by Grabbe.[5] Rates are money market rates. Of course, the loan rate depends on the perceived risk of the borrower. If the borrower is a U.S. money center bank conducting arbitrage, then the risk is considered to be unimportant. Rates to corporations are higher. The Eurodollar futures are based on the bid LIBOR rate, since the futures reflect the *time deposit* rate. Also recall that the Eurodollar futures are based on a $1 million time deposit, whereas T-bill futures track a $1 million *face* value T-bill that sells at a discount.

Eurodollar Futures Arbitrage Strategies

Eurodollar futures arbitrage is transacted simply by borrowing from or lending to a Eurobank in London. Being able to obtain or lend funds in large amounts at small spreads simplifies the arbitrage strategies significantly.

Pure Arbitrage Strategies. Strategy 8-1 illustrates a pure short arbitrage for Eurodollar time deposit futures. Execution of the pure long strategy is shown in Strategy 8-2. Note that these strategies can be implemented by using different dates from those employed here; for example, for the pure short strategy one could initially borrow for one month and lend for four months to correspond to a futures contract expiring in one month. Notice that no funds from the arbitrageur are needed to implement the pure short arbitrage. Hence, a profitable pure arbitrage transaction can be repeated many times until the arbitrage profits disappear when the prices readjust, or until no additional financing is available to the arbitrageur. Example 8-1 illustrates how to calculate potential profits from a short pure Eurodollar arbitrage.

Quasi-Arbitrage Strategies. Quasi-arbitrage strategies are implemented by Eurobanks that deal in Eurodollars. For example, let us assume that banks are borrowing longer-term and lending shorter-term, which is typically the case if they expect interest rates to increase. If futures are expensive (futures rates < forward rates), then a short quasi-arbitrage with futures provides a higher return than the cash market alternative. Similarly, if banks are lending longer-term and borrowing shorter-term in anticipation of lower interest rates, then when futures are cheap (futures rates > forward rates), buying futures provides a higher return than the cash transactions.

Forward/Futures Considerations

There are several considerations that affect the profitability of the Eurodollar arbitrage calculation, especially if it is based on a forward/futures comparison; namely,

- The effect of the financing procedure must be considered: it is possible that overnight financing using LIBOR rates can be employed for arbitrage. Since the forward/futures comparison implicitly employs a term financing rate, the effect of overnight financing would have to be considered in the analysis.

---

5   Orlin Grabbe, *International Financial Markets*. New York: Elsevier, 1986.

STRATEGY 8-1: A Pure Short Eurodollar Arbitrage

The diagrams of the strategies illustrated in this chapter show the *source of the funds received* and *how the funds are invested.* These strategies are executed only if there is a relative mispricing between the future and cash instruments, creating an arbitrage opportunity. *When* these transactions are initiated is stated in the specific strategies listed below the diagrams.

The situation is as follows: futures rate < forward rate (futures price > forward price).

A + B create a *long* forward position for time T + 3 to T + 6.

C is a *short* futures position expiring at T + 3.

A: Invest in Eurodollar time deposits for six months	
B:Borrow funds for three months with a Eurodollar loan at LIBOR	C: Borrow funds for 3 months as of T = 3 with a Eurodollar loan (rate locked-in with a sale of futures at T = 0)

| 0
T | Three Months
T + 3 | Six Months
T + 6 |

At time T (now):

Borrow funds for three months with a Eurodollar loan at LIBOR.

Invest for six months by placing funds in a Eurodollar time deposit.

Sell a futures contract now to *lock in a cheap interest rate (high price)* for Eurodollar time deposits starting in three months.

At time T + 3:

Futures contract expires; daily marking-to-market means one has collected or paid the difference between the original futures rate and the cash maturity rate.

Original three-month loan comes due; pay interest on three-month loan (partially or fully offset by interest earned but not yet collected on six-month time deposit).

Take out new three-month loan at LIBOR (rate locked in from original futures sale).

Consequence: if interest rates rise from T to T + 3, then the higher cost of a new loan is offset from profits on the short sale of a futures contract (and vice versa).

At time T + 6:

Collect interest on six-month time deposit.

Pay interest on second three-month loan.

STRATEGY 8-2: A Pure Long Eurodollar Arbitrage

The situation is as follows: futures rate > forward rate (futures price < forward price).
A + B create a *short* forward position for time T + 3 to T + 6.
C is a *long* futures position expiring at T + 3.

A: Borrow funds for six months with Eurodollar loan at LIBOR	
B: Invest in three-month Eurodollar time deposit	C: Invest in three-month Eurodollar time deposit starting at T + 3 (rate locked-in with a purchase of futures at T = 0)

0   Three Months   Six Months
T   T + 3   T + 6

At time T (now):

Borrow funds for six months with a Eurodollar loan at LIBOR.

Invest for three months by placing funds in a Eurodollar time deposit.

Buy a futures contract now to *lock in a high interest rate (cheap price)* for Eurodollar time deposits starting in three months.

At time T + 3:

Futures contract expires; daily marking-to-market means one has collected or paid the difference between the original futures rate and the cash maturity rate.

Original three-month time deposit comes due; collect interest on deposit.

Take out new time deposit for three months (rate locked in from original futures purchase).

Consequence: If interest rates rise from T to T + 3 then the loss on the long futures position is offset by higher interest on a three-month time deposit starting at T + 3.

At time T + 6:

Collect interest on second three-month time deposit.

Pay interest on six-month loan (partially or fully offset by the interest earned on time deposits).

EXAMPLE 8-1: A Pure Eurodollar Short Arbitrage

The following rates are quoted for Eurodollar time deposits (bid) and loans (ask):

Three-month Eurodollars	8.475–8.60
Six-month Eurodollars	8.575–8.70
Eurodollar futures	91.75

Pure arbitrage transactions:

At time T: borrow funds for three months at 8.60%; invest for six months by placing funds in Eurodollar time deposit at 8.575%; sell a futures contract now to lock in low interest rate for Eurodollar loan starting in three months (loan rate is 12½ basis points above time deposit rate of 8.25%—that is, 8.25% + .125% = 8.375%).

At time T + 3: pay interest on original three-month loan that comes due; take out new three-month loan with an interest rate locked in with expiring futures.

At time T + 6: collect interest on six-month time deposit; pay interest on second three-month loan.

Interest income on six-month time deposit:
$1,000,000 (.08575) (180/360) = $42,875

Interest paid on first three-month loan:
$1,000,000 (.0860) (90/360) = $21,500

Interest on second three-month loan:
$1,021,500 (.08375) (90/360) = $21,387

Net profit: $42,875 – $21,500 – $21,387 = $–12

A loss is created because of the 12½ basis point difference in the time deposit and loan rates.

- The timing of the cash and futures quotes is critical: London time is six hours ahead of Chicago time; hence closing quotes for time deposits are closer in time to the opening of the Chicago Eurodollar futures than to its close.
- Calculation of forward rates when an irregular number of days is employed provides a distorted forward price, since odd day time deposits are not quoted often. Consequently, Eurodollar rates for *monthly* intervals typically are employed to determine the forward rates, even if this is an approximation of the actual length of the time period in question.[6]

---

6 For example, as noted by Kawaller, if today is February 13 and the March Eurodollar futures stops trading on March 18, then the time span from value date to value date is 34 days. One could then calculate a forward rate for 91 days based on cash quotes of 34 and 125 (34 + 91) days. However, using one- and four-month time deposit rates would provide more accurate results because of the liquidity in these rates. Ira Kawaller, "Determining the Fair Value for Eurodollar Futures," *Market Perspectives*, Vol. 6, No. 3, April 1988, p. 1, 3.

- Only certain arbitrageurs have access to Eurodollar borrowings at 12½ basis points above the investment rate, namely financial institutions with good credit risks. Others must pay higher rates, and therefore the likelihood of obtaining arbitrage profits is reduced.[7]
- There could be marking-to-market of the futures, although this is minor in most situations.

T-BILL FUTURES PRICING AND ARBITRAGE

The concepts of pricing T-bill futures are adequately explained in the earlier section on short-term interest rate futures pricing. Since T-bills are deliverable into the futures contract, no pricing risk exists for arbitrage transactions. The interesting aspects of the accuracy of T-bill futures pricing relates to the empirical results, which will be examined shortly.

T-bill futures arbitrage transactions are similar to Eurodollar futures arbitrage in that funds are borrowed and invested. However, the process of implementing these transactions is different for T-bill futures. The typical method to obtain funds for pure arbitrage is to use repurchase agreements. Therefore, this method is discussed here. An alternative method, using a short sale of cash T-bills, is explained in Appendix 8A. Long pure arbitrage and long quasi-arbitrage are also covered in Appendix 8A in order to concentrate on the most important concepts within the chapter.

Short Arbitrage with Repurchase Agreements

The strategy typically employed to implement a short T-bill futures arbitrage is to use repurchase agreements, as illustrated in Strategy 8-3. A repo agreement allows the arbitrageur to sell *temporarily* a cash T-bill in order to receive funds, with the agreement that the T-bill is repurchased after a given period of time. The arbitrageur pays interest on the repo for the time the borrowed funds are in use, whereas the T-bill is used as collateral to guarantee that the funds are repaid. All transactions are completed simultaneously. Although interest is paid on the funds received from the repurchase agreement, the arbitrageur receives interest on the cash T-bill purchased. Hence, the difference between the T-bill and repo interest rates is a critical factor for this type of arbitrage. Of course, the relationship between the rates of the cash T-bill and the T-bill futures contract also is an important factor in determining if an arbitrage should be initiated, as well as determining the size of the arbitrage profits.

Implementing T-Bill Futures Arbitrage with Repos

T-bill futures arbitrage typically is initiated by using repo agreements. Since the repo market is an active and liquid market, it is easy to initiate an agreement for standard maturity dates. Funds for the arbitrage are obtained from executing either a term repo or a series of overnight repos. The term repo is a loan for the entire arbitrage period, in our example a loan for three months. The interest rate paid on the repo agreement is known before the arbitrage transaction is initiated.

---

7 The full bid-ask spread must be included in the numerical analysis, since one borrows funds at the higher rate and invests (lends) them at the lower rate; see Kawaller, ibid.

STRATEGY 8-3: A Short Pure T-Bill Futures Arbitrage with a Repo Transaction

---

The situation is as follows: futures rate < forward rate.

A + B create a *long* forward position for time T + 3 to T + 6.

C is a *short* futures position expiring at T + 3.

A: Buy a six-month cash T-bill	
B: Temporarily sell same six-month T-bill via three-month repo	C: Deliver T-bill into futures at T = 3 months

0 T	Three Months T + 3	Six Months T + 6

At time T (now):

Purchase a six-month cash T-bill.

Initiate a repurchase agreement where the six-month T-bill is temporarily sold in order to obtain funds to pay for the T-bill purchase; the repo requires that the T-bill be repurchased after three months and interest be paid on the use of the funds over the three-month period.

Sell the futures contract that expires in three months.

At time T + 3:

Regain the cash T-bill by executing the repurchase agreement (the T-bill now has three months to maturity).

Pay the interest due according to the repurchase agreement.

Interest received on T-bill obtained via the difference in price from time T to T + 3.

Deliver the original six-month cash T-bill (which now has three months remaining until maturity) into the futures contract.

Alternatively, a series of overnight repos is executed when daily loans are obtained, with the cash T-bill being used as collateral. The interest rate paid on the overnight repos can change daily. Hence, this type of arbitrage is *not* risk-free, but rather depends on the behavior of interest rates over the period of the arbitrage. Hence, the use of overnight repos is essentially speculating on the short-term interest rate. An advantage of using a series of overnight repos is that the arbitrageur can close the arbitrage whenever conditions warrant—for example, when prices change to such an extent that most of the profit potential on the arbitrage transaction is realized. Moreover, overnight repos are a very liquid market and represent the majority of the arbitrage transactions. The overnight repo market is the key financing market because primary fixed-income dealers use this market to finance their holdings of T-bills and T-bonds. The rates on overnight repo transactions are slightly less than the Fed funds rate.

An Example of Short Pure Arbitrage

Example 8-2 provides a basic numerical example of a pure short arbitrage with T-bill futures. The data is taken from late 1982, a time when interest rates were volatile and expectations concerning inflation differed significantly for the three-month versus six-month time periods. The overnight repo rate is employed as the appropriate financing rate for funds. Since this rate is used in our example as the financing rate for the entire three-month period, we are implicitly assuming that the *repo rate does not change*. The example shows that an arbitrage profit of $3,341 was possible before transactions costs by using the overnight repo rate; this profit is due to two factors:

1. The major differences in interest rates between the futures and the six month T-bill, and between the six-month T-bill and the repo rate.
2. The use of the overnight repo rate of 8.25% instead of the term repo rate of 9.7%; use of the latter term repo eliminates this profit.

Short Quasi-Arbitrage

A short quasi-arbitrage transaction by using the same maturity T-bills as in the pure arbitrage example is given in Strategy 8-4. Note that the arbitrage transaction involving the six-month cash T-bill and a short futures contract creates a synthetic three-month T-bill that is equivalent to the three-month cash T-bill originally held in the portfolio. Thus, the new position is equivalent to the old cash position, except that a higher return is earned on the synthetic position.

The factors affecting the existence and size of the quasi-arbitrage profits are the rates on the three- and six-month cash T-bills and the price of the futures contract. Transactions costs typically are not significant, although the initial sale of the three-month cash T-bill originally held in the portfolio does create an extra set of costs in comparison with the pure arbitrage transactions. Alternatively, the financial institution could decide whether the cash-only strategy or the synthetic strategy is better *before* any security is purchased for the portfolio. This alternative return approach reduces transactions costs.

As hinted at above, which alternative return strategy provides a superior return can be determined by comparing the cash three-month rate with the synthetic three-month rate. In general, decisions on whether quasi- or pure arbitrage strategies are profitable can be determined by comparing forward and futures rates, or by determining the implied repo rate, as discussed in Chapter 4.

Example 8-3 provides a basic numerical example of a short quasi-arbitrage transaction. The appropriate quasi-arbitrage trades in this example guarantee a return that is $3,375 higher than the cash-only transaction. Note that this profit is *not* affected by the overnight versus term repo financing assumptions, since the financial institution is choosing between alternative strategies and no funds are borrowed to finance the transaction.

EXAMPLE 8-2: An Example of a Pure Short T-Bill Arbitrage

On September 20, 1982, the following rates were in effect:

90-day cash T-bill bid	7.74%
180-day cash T-bill bid	9.42%
Dec 82 T-bill futures price	90.25

Repo rates: overnight, 8.25%; three-month, 9.70%.

Prices for the T-bill cash and futures positions and the cost of the repo are calculated as follows:*

$$\text{T-bill price} = \text{Face value} - \frac{(\text{discount yield})\ (\text{face value})\ (\text{days maturity})}{360}$$

Interest cost on repo = (principal) (repo rate) (days/360)

Price of the 180-day T-bill = $1MM − (.0942) ($1MM) (180)/360 = $952,900

Price of the 90-day T-bill = $1MM − (.0774) ($1MM) (90)/360 = $980,650

Value of the futures = $1MM − (.0975) ($1MM) (90)/360 = $975,625

Interest cost on repo = ($952,900) (.0825) (90/360) = $19,654

A pure arbitrage transaction is initiated as follows:

At time T: buy six-month cash T-bill; fund purchase with three-month repo transaction; sell futures contract.

At time T + 3: deliver original six-month T-bill into futures contract.

Return on six-month T-bill held for three months (interest received + gain from price difference between cash and futures rates):

Futures price − cost of six-month T-bill = $975,625 − $952,900	= $ 22,725
Interest cost on repo transaction	= $−19,654
Net profit per $1 million transaction (before transactions costs)	= $ 3,071

---

*$1MM = $1 million.

Note: Using the overnight repo makes the implicit assumption that interest rates will remain constant. Moreover, since technically this would be a series of overnight repo transactions, the correct interest is found by determining $P_t\, e^{it} - P_t$ or $952{,}900\ e^{.0825\ (90/360)} - 925{,}900 = \$19{,}858$. Using the term three-month repo rate creates interest of $23,108.

Forward Versus Futures Comparisons

Comparing forward and futures rates has an appeal because the concepts are well understood and the calculations are straightforward. The industry often uses this comparison, or the equivalent implied repo rate comparison, to examine arbitrage possibilities. Many of the empirical studies on arbitrage also examine the forward/futures relationship. However, one must take care if this comparison is made without the proper adjustments, since factors other than just potential arbitrage profits affect the difference in these rates. For example,

STRATEGY 8-4: A Short Quasi-Arbitrage Strategy for T-Bill Futures

In this situation, A + C creates the equivalent of a three-month cash T-bill.

A: Buy a six-month cash T-bill	
B: Create a synthetic three-month T-bill from the relevant trades*	C: Deliver T-bill into futures contract at T = 3 months

0	Three Months	Six Months
T	T + 3	T + 6

At time T (now):
Sell the three-month cash T-bill currently in the portfolio.
Purchase a six-month cash T-bill.
Sell a futures contract expiring in three months.
(The last two transactions create a synthetic three-month T-bill.)

At time T + 3:
Receive interest on the six-month T-bill resulting from the difference in price from time T to T + 3.

Deliver the cash T-bill that now has three months to maturity into the futures contract.

---

*If the synthetic three-month T-bill provides a higher return than the current cash three-month T-bill held in the portfolio, then execute this strategy.

one must determine whether implementing a strategy based on a forward versus futures comparison involves financing (pure arbitrage), or is based on a security that is part of the current portfolio (quasi-arbitrage). Since these two approaches involve different implied financing costs, as well as different transactions costs, implementing an arbitrage transaction is related critically to the assumptions that are implicit in a forward/futures comparison.

Some of the factors affecting the forward/futures differential relate to economic causes, while others relate to difficulties with the data. The major factors are:
- The effect of the financing rate on the profitability of pure arbitrage transactions. Hence, the relationship between the financing rate and the cash rate is important, especially since the empirical evidence shows that futures are priced based on the pure arbitrage model.
- Transactions costs.
- The effect of marking-to-market and varying interest rates on the futures returns.
- The effect of default risk of the cash market and the cost of guaranteeing performance in the futures market.

EXAMPLE 8-3: An Example of a Short T-Bill Quasi-Arbitrage

See Example 8-2 for data, equations, and prices of cash and futures T-bills.

Quasi-arbitrage transactions:
   At time T: sell three-month cash T-bill currently in portfolio; purchase six-month cash T-bill; sell T-bill futures contract for delivery in three months.

   At time T + 3: deliver original six-month cash T-bill into futures contract.

Opportunity loss on original three-month T-bill:
   Face value – cost = $ 1,000,000 – $980,650   = $–19,350

Return on six-month T-bill held for three months (interest received + gain from price difference between cash and futures):
   Futures price – cost of six month T-bill = $975,625 – $952,900   = $ 22,725

Net gain from arbitrage (alternative return strategy)   = $ 3,375

- The effect of differing tax rates between the cash and futures markets.[8]
- Use of improper data for the analysis, such as problems created by
  1. Timing differences between the cash and futures data.
  2. The incorrect use of the bid or ask price in the analysis.[9]
  3. The use of nondeliverable cash T-bills to calculate forward rates; that is, nondeliverable T-bills have different supply-and-demand influences that affect rates.
  4. The use of cash quotes that are not representative of the market or are not liquid at large volume.

Many of the above factors are relevant for empirical T-bill arbitrage results and are discussed in conjunction with these results. Each factor has an effect on how to interpret the futures/forward differential. Moreover, although these factors also affect dollar profits for pure and/or quasi-arbitrage results, empirical arbitrage analysis typically either explicitly considers these individual factors (such as the financing and transactions costs), or interprets the results with these factors in mind (such as the tax effect).

The most important factor affecting the forward/futures comparison is the financing rate. In fact, if we carefully compare the pure arbitrage, quasi-arbitrage, and futures/forward procedures, we find that the interest rates and prices for the instruments used in the arbitrage transactions are basically the same. Only the implied financing rate differs. Another difference between the procedures is that the forward rate model concentrates on the

---

8 The change in the tax laws in 1981 eliminated differential tax effects on T-bill cash versus futures contracts. However, the tax factor was important for analysis of data before 1981.

9 Vignola and Dale show that use of the bid versus the ask price has a significant effect on the mean differences of empirical results. A per-period analysis shows a 6- to 40-basis point difference between the bid and ask arbitrage profits, with the signs of the profits often differing between the bid and ask results. Anthony J. Vignola and Charles J. Dale, "Is the Futures Market for Treasury Bills Efficient?" *Journal of Portfolio Management*, Vol. 5, No. 2, Winter 1978-79, pp. 78-81.

second period of the transaction, whereas the pure and quasi-arbitrage transactions concentrate on the first period of the transaction (the first three months in the examples). Traders emphasize the first period, since this is their holding period. In general, all of the approaches examine the same type of transaction, but the empirical evidence shows that the different assumptions concerning financing costs can be critical in determining whether arbitrage profits exist, and how futures contracts are priced.

EMPIRICAL RESULTS FOR T-BILL FUTURES ARBITRAGE

Pure and Quasi-Arbitrage

Vignola and Dale[10] examine pure and quasi-arbitrage strategies for T-bill futures by employing repurchase and **reverse repurchase transactions**. Table 8-1 shows the key results from the Vignola and Dale study. The fact that nearby pure arbitrage dollar profits and the annualized basis point profits are relatively small indicates that pure arbitrage is the key to the pricing process for nearby T-bill futures.[11] As the time to futures expiration increases, the annualized basis point profits for the pure arbitrage also increases. However, the quasi-arbitrage basis point profits decrease, showing the importance of quasi-arbitrage for pricing

TABLE 8-1: T-bill Arbitrage Results

| | Futures Expirations | | |
	Nearby	First Deferred	Second Deferred
Pure arbitrage:			
Average dollar profits	$268	$704	$2086
Average annualized basis point profits	.105	.174	.323
Short arbitrage opportunities	215	423	479
Long arbitrage opportunities	462	118	28
Quasi-arbitrage:			
Average dollar profits	$342	$555	$713
Average annualized basis point profits	.264	.144	.074
Short arbitrage opportunities	584	437	161
Long arbitrage opportunities	134	229	499

Source: Abstracted from Anthony J. Vignola and Charles J. Dale, "The Efficiency of the Treasury Bill Futures Market: An Analysis of Alternative Specifications," *Journal of Financial Research*, Vol. 3, No. 2, Summer 1980, pp. 169-188.

10 Anthony J. Vignola and Charles J. Dale, "The Efficiency of the Treasury Bill Futures Market: An Analysis of Alternative Specifications," *Journal of Financial Research*, Vol. 3, No. 2, Summer 1980, pp. 169-188.

11 Moreover, these values do *not* consider commissions or bid-ask spread trading costs, the futures and cash prices differ by one hour, and the financing rate may not be a correct reflection of the true financing rate.

purposes for the deferred contracts.[12] In addition, the pure arbitrage trades for deferred contracts are heavily weighted toward short arbitrage opportunities, whereas the quasi-arbitrage results for the second deferred contract emphasize long arbitrage. Thus, the appropriate pricing process and the size of the arbitrage profits depend on the time to futures expiration.

More recent results also support the profitability of T-bill arbitrage strategies. Elton, Gruber, and Rentzler[13] use intraday data to show that the quasi-arbitrage strategy of selling high-priced cash T-bills and constructing a synthetic T-bill position with futures contracts earns additional profits. Hegde and Branch[14] found pure arbitrage profits for short arbitrage and quasi-arbitrage profits for long arbitrage. MacDonald, Peterson, and Koch[15] improve on the Hegde and Branch profits for quasi-arbitrage with filter rules stating when to institute the arbitrage.

In general, the results stated above indicate that futures are overpriced based on the pure cost of carry model, especially for the more deferred contracts. The quasi-arbitrage model indicates that futures are underpriced for the second deferred contract. This discrepancy can be addressed by showing that the two models employ different financing costs. Therefore, one's assumptions concerning financing costs are critical in determining the pricing of futures contracts and whether arbitrage transactions should be undertaken. The effect of financing costs is addressed shortly.

Forward Versus Futures Rates

Rendleman and Carabini,[16] among others, provide an empirical analysis of the forward/futures rate differential for T-bill futures. They found mean absolute *annual* basis point

---

12 One explanation given for the large pure arbitrage profits for the deferred T-bill futures contracts is the existence of differing tax rules for the futures and cash instruments during the time of the analysis (see Arak). Specifically, futures were taxed as a capital asset and hence received capital gains treatment if the contract was held for more than six months, whereas cash T-bills were taxed as an ordinary asset. This tax differential treatment no longer exists. The superiority of the quasi-arbitrage results over the pure arbitrage results for pricing purposes may reflect the lack of a cash T-bill needed for perfect arbitrage. In other words, it is more logical for quasi-arbitrageurs to undertake a less than perfect transaction than for pure arbitrageurs to undertake such a position. Kawaller and Koch note that prior to June 1983 arbitrage was not always possible for deferred expirations, since deliverable cash T-bills were only guaranteed to exist 90 days before the futures expiration. Hence, some of the Vignola and Dale results past 90 days may reflect only the lack of a perfect arbitrage transaction. Beginning in June 1983 the T-bill futures delivery cycle was altered such that any original one-year T-bill could be used to satisfy delivery requirements. Hence, it is likely that after June 1983, pure arbitrage does a better job of explaining the results for contracts with three to nine months to delivery than the results shown here. Marcelle Arak, "Taxes, Treasury Bills, and Treasury Bill Futures," *Federal Reserve Bank of New York*, March 1980. Ira Kawaller and Timothy W. Koch, "Cash-and-Carry Trading and the Pricing of Treasury Bill Futures," *The Journal of Futures Markets*, Vol. 4 No. 2, Summer 1984, pp. 115-124.

13 E. Elton, M. Gruber, and J. Rentzler, "Intra-Day Tests of the Efficiency of the Treasury Bill Futures Market," *Review of Economics and Statistics*, February 1984, pp. 129-137.

14 Shantaram Hegde and Ben Branch, "An Empirical Analysis of Arbitrage Opportunities in the Treasury Bill Futures Market," *The Journal of Futures Markets*, Vol. 5, No. 3, Fall 1985, pp. 407-424.

15 S. Scott MacDonald, Richard L. Peterson, and Timothy W. Koch, "Using Futures to Improve Treasury Bill Portfolio Performance," *The Journal of Futures Markets*, Vol. 8, No. 2, April 1988, pp. 167-184.

16 Richard Rendleman and Christopher Carabini, "The Efficiency of the Treasury Bill Futures Market," *Journal of Finance*, September 1979, Vol. 34, No. 4, pp. 895-914.

differentials of 24.6, 10.9, and 11.3 for the first three expirations, *before* adjusting for transactions costs. Rendleman and Carabini found that $2,459 per contract per year could be produced by arbitrage transactions for the nearby expiration before transaction costs. Transactions costs create a band for no-arbitrage opportunities, thereby reducing both the number and the size of the profitable transactions. After transactions costs, the authors determine that only about one-third of the daily opportunities fall outside the no-arbitrage band, with *these* profitable opportunities creating mean differences of 8.2, 10.8, and 13.2 basis points per contract for the three expirations, respectively. The results show the importance of transactions costs for the nearby contract. The profits identified with the forward/futures comparisons are quasi-arbitrage profits, since financing costs are not included in the analysis.[17]

In addition to transactions costs, other explanations for the apparent arbitrage profits from the consistent forward/futures differentials that occur both in this and other studies are as follows:

- The effect of differential tax rates on cash versus futures transactions for positions held more than six months (see Arak[18] and Viswanath[19]).
- The effect of daily marked-to-market settlement on futures accounts (see Morgan[20]).[21]
- The effect of the cost of guaranteeing performance (see Kane[22]).
- The effect of liquidity on the size of the differential (see Kamara and Lawrence[23]).

Chow and Brophy[24] examine the importance of the above factors, as well as argue for a "preferred habitat premium." Considering commissions, bid-ask spreads, and margin effects in their analysis, they determine that daily marking-to-market makes only a negligible contribution to the yield differences. After commissions, they calculate an average 25-basis-point forward/futures differential and a 29-basis-point differential for contracts expiring after six months. They subsequently find that taxes account for only 4 to 13 basis points of the 29-basis-point differential. Moreover, they conclude that a differential risk premium due to performance guarantees does not explain any of the difference in forward/futures rates.

17 The authors of the study discount the possibility of pure arbitrage profits due to the charge of 50 basis points for selling short cash T-bills. However, the use of repos and reverse repos for T-bill arbitrage transactions could change this conclusion.

18 Arak, "Taxes, Treasury Bills, and Futures," 1980.

19 P. V. Viswanath, "Taxes and the Futures-Forward Price Difference in the 91-Day T-Bill Market," *Journal of Money, Credit, and Banking*, Vol. 21, No. 2, May 1989, pp. 190-205.

20 George E. Morgan, "Pricing Treasury Bill Futures Contracts," Comptroller of the Currency, June 1978.

21 However, Chow and Brophy argue that daily marking-to-market involves mostly unsystematic risk and therefore should not produce any appreciable differences. Brian Chow and David J. Brophy, "The U.S. Treasury Bill Futures Market and Hypotheses Regarding the Term Structure of Interest Rates," *Financial Review*, Vol. 13, No. 2, Fall 1978, pp. 36-50.

22 Edward Kane, "Market-Incompleteness and Divergences between Forward and Futures Interest Rates," *Journal of Finance*, Vol. 35, No. 2, May 1980, pp. 221–234.

23 Avraham Kamara and Colin Lawrence, "Trading Systems, Liquidity, and Default: Evidence from the Treasury Bill Market," National Bureau of Economic Research (NBER) working paper, September 1987.

24 Brian G. Chow and David J. Brophy, "Treasury-Bill Futures Market: A Formulation and Interpretation," *The Journal of Futures Markets*, Vol. 2, No. 1, Spring 1982, pp. 25-49.

They explain the remaining differential as a "preferred habitat premium." In other words, market participants are willing to pay or receive a premium in order to participate in a given market. Hence, Chow and Brophy are stating that arbitrage opportunities exist, and the existence of arbitrage occurs because of an inability or reluctance of market participants to deal in both the cash and futures markets.

Effect of the Financing Rate

Since financing costs are not included in the empirical studies on the forward/futures differential, it is difficult to state conclusions concerning pure arbitrage based on these studies. However, if pure arbitrage activity is the pricing mechanism for T-bill futures, then the effect of financing is important. Moreover, the Vignola and Dale study examined above shows that both pure and quasi-arbitrage strategies result in profitable opportunities. This section examines the effect of financing on pure arbitrage profits and hence also examines the forces that drive the pricing of T-bill futures.

Kawaller and Koch[25] examine the arbitrage and pricing aspects of the nearby T-bill futures contract by focusing on the financing cost of the pure arbitrage strategy. In fact, the financing assumptions of arbitrage can be employed to explain the different results obtained for pure and quasi-arbitrage transactions, as well as the results for the forward/futures differential studies. The critical financing consideration is whether pure arbitrageurs use term repos or overnight repos to finance their arbitrage positions.

Figure 8-1 shows the effect of assuming a term repo to finance the pure arbitrage transactions versus a series of overnight repos for the financing. These results are startling: the use of the overnight repo rate reduces the net financing cost (or equivalently the forward/futures differential) significantly. Moreover, the overnight repo results show near zero pure arbitrage profits, without even considering transactions costs or the need for a premium due to the riskiness associated with the use of the overnight repo rate.[26] Thus, the overnight repo is the valid financing rate for T-bill futures arbitrage. Moreover, these results show that the forward/futures differential is affected critically by the implied financing rate employed in the analysis: one does *not* have to appeal to transactions costs, margin effects, or performance guarantees to attempt to explain the forward/futures differential.

SUMMARY AND LOOKING AHEAD

This chapter discusses the concepts and strategies associated with short-term interest rate pricing and arbitrage. Pure and quasi-arbitrage procedures are discussed at length, with specific short and long arbitrage strategies illustrated for Eurodollar and T-bill futures contracts. Empirical results for T-bill arbitrage show that pure cost of carry financing dominates the pricing of nearby contracts, although deferred contract profits may exist. In general, the type of financing used to create arbitrage transactions is critical. Part III examines techniques for hedging.

---

25 Kawaller and Koch, "Cash-and-Carry Trading," pp. 115–124.

26 The further the delivery date is from the initiation of the arbitrage strategy, the greater the risk that overnight repo rates will vary significantly, and hence the wider the spread must be to induce an arbitrageur to undertake the transaction. Also note that whenever the term repo rate is greater (less) than the overnight repo rate, then the futures/forward differential is positive (negative).

FIGURE 8-1: Financing Cost of Pure Arbitrage

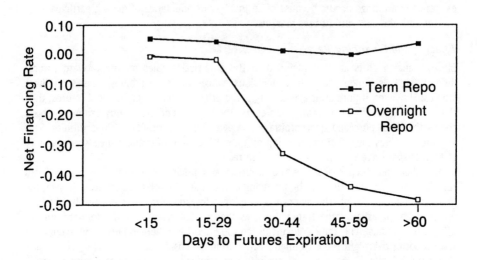

Source: Adapted from Ira Kawaller and Timothy W. Koch, "Cash-and-Carry Trading and the Pricing of Treasury Bill Futures," *The Journal of Futures Markets*, Vol. 4, No. 2, Summer 1984, pp. 115-124.

Appendix 8A
Other T-Bill Arbitrage Strategies

Pure Arbitrage Strategies: Long T-Bill Arbitrage

Long arbitrage exists when a long futures position plus a short-term cash position is cheaper than a longer-term cash position, after adjusting for transactions costs and interest rates. The key to long pure arbitrage strategies is how best to finance the transaction. As with short arbitrage there are three possible methods of financing: a generic borrowing of funds, executing a short sale, or initiating a reverse repo transaction. Since the key factors affecting the existence and size of long arbitrage situations are essentially identical to the short arbitrage transactions, only the reverse repo strategy is presented here.

Long Arbitrage with a Reverse Repo. The typical procedure employed to generate a long pure arbitrage is shown in Strategy 8A-1. A reverse repo is executed to obtain a six-month T-bill, which then is sold to obtain funds; that is, a reverse repo occurs when funds are lent in exchange for receiving a T-bill for security. This transaction is initiated in order to lock in the price of the cash T-bill. In implementing this strategy, the cash T-bill received from the purchase of the futures contract must fulfill the requirements of the reverse repo to facilitate covering the reverse repo at time $T + 3$, otherwise the cash T-bill received via the futures has to be sold and the appropriate cash T-bill needed for the reverse repo purchased. Such a substitution of cash T-bills involves price and liquidity risk and hence affects the desirability of the arbitrage. Thus, the reverse repo acts like a short sale in obtaining funds, with risk occurring when T-bill maturities are not matched exactly.

As with short arbitrage, long arbitrage can be executed for a period longer than the three months given here. Thus, one can obtain funds for, say, one year and buy a strip of futures contracts plus obtaining a three-month cash T-bill; alternatively, one can buy a deferred futures contract and buy a longer-term cash instrument such as a nine-month T-bill. Strips are discussed in Appendix 4A.

Quasi-Arbitrage Strategies: Long T-Bill Arbitrage

A long quasi-arbitrage strategy is illustrated in Strategy 8A-2, in which a synthetic six-month T-bill is created. The strategy is executed if the synthetic six-month T-bill (which is made up of the three-month cash T-bill plus the futures contract) provides an *additional* return above the cash six-month T-bill currently held in the portfolio, after transactions costs are considered.

On the other hand, if the portfolio manager currently has funds and is determining the *best* alternative for placing these funds, then the return on the six-month T-bill would be compared with the return on the synthetic security; in this case the transactions costs are not relevant, since the funds must be invested in one of the alternatives. The procedure outlined above also can be used for arbitrage transactions with deferred futures contracts by either purchasing a longer-term cash T-bill or by purchasing a strip of futures contracts.

STRATEGY 8A-1: A Long Pure T-Bill Futures Arbitrage with a Reverse Repo

In this situation, A + B creates a short forward position for time $T + 3$ to $T + 6$. C is a long futures position expiring at $T + 3$.

A: Execute a reverse repo to obtain a six-month T-bill	

B: Sell the six-month T-bill obtained from the reverse repo to obtain funds	C: Buy a three-month cash T-bill via delivery from the expiring futures contract; use T-bill to fulfill reverse repo

0	Three Months	Six Months
T	T + 3	T + 6

At time T (now), with all transactions completed simultaneously:

Execute a reverse repo to obtain a six-month cash T-bill.

Sell the six-month T-bill to obtain funds.

Use funds to fulfill cash outflow on reverse repo.

Buy futures contract that expires in three months.

At time T + 3:

Receive interest from reverse repo due from time T to $T + 3$.

Receive three-month cash T-bill from expiring futures contract.

Use three-month T-bill to fulfill obligations of reverse repo (the three-month T-bill price is higher than the six-month price, with the difference being the accumulated interest).

STRATEGY 8A-2: A Long Quasi-Arbitrage Strategy for T-Bill Futures

In this situation, B + C creates the equivalent of a six-month cash T-bill.

A: Create a synthetic six-month cash T-bill*

B: Buy a three-month cash T-bill	C: Obtain three-month cash T-bill via delivery from the expiring futures

| 0
T | Three Months
T + 3 | Six Months
T + 6 |

At time T (now):

Sell the six-month cash T-bill currently in the portfolio.

Purchase a three-month cash T-bill.

Purchase a futures contract to expire in three months.

(The last two transactions create a synthetic six-month T-bill).

At time T + 3:

Receive interest from initial cash T-bill via price change from T to T + 3.

Use funds received from maturing cash T-bill to purchase three-month cash T-bill received from expiring futures contract.

At time T + 6:

Receive interest from second three-month cash T-bill via price change from T + 3 to T + 6.

---

*If the synthetic six-month position creates a higher return than the cash six-month T-bill currently held in the portfolio, then execute the strategy.

Part III

Hedging and Risk Management: Concepts and Techniques

Chapter 9

Hedging Concepts

Hedging is undertaken to reduce the price risk of a cash or forward position. The managerial goals of a hedging program are to make a hedging decision and to manage the program. In order to accomplish these goals one must comprehend the concepts, issues, and factors associated with hedging. A discussion of what hedging entails, the hedging process, and hedging strategies provide a foundation of hedging concepts. Examples of the three types of short hedges help to illustrate the concepts and issues associated with hedging. The three types of hedges are: a portfolio hedge, an inventory hedge, and an asset-liability hedge. A portfolio hedge is undertaken when a money manager desires to reduce the risk of a potential price decline for a portfolio of cash assets. An inventory hedge occurs when a market-maker locks in the current value of the asset held in inventory until that asset can be sold. Financial institutions execute asset-liability hedges in order to overcome the effects of differences between either the maturities or the price volatilities of the institution's assets and liabilities.

Long hedges, crosshedges, and changing the effective volatility of an asset are additional applications of futures hedging. A long hedge is undertaken in order to lock in a price for a cash position when the cash position will be initiated in the future. A crosshedge is implemented when the characteristics of the existing futures contracts do not match the characteristics of the cash instrument. Changing effective volatilities of assets is a common portfolio management tool.

Return is also a consideration when hedging. Returns associated with hedging are related to whether the basis gets "weaker" or "stronger." The relationship between risk and return also is examined by hedgers. Finally, the subjective advantages and disadvantages of hedging and the circumstances that would prompt a money manager to hedge are discussed. A focus section examines managerial hedging operations, including the factors to consider when developing, implementing, and controlling a hedge operation. These concepts concerning hedging provide an important foundation for forthcoming chapters on quantitative techniques and procedures for using futures as a risk management tool.

HEDGING CONCEPTS: AN INTRODUCTION

The Objective and Benefits of Hedging

The key to risk management is to determine risk-return objectives and trade-offs. Without a clear understanding of the relevant objectives and trade-offs appropriate for the institution, futures hedging is controversial and can produce unwanted results. Thus, hedging is only a *tool* to achieve clearly defined risk management objectives.

The primary objective of hedging is to reduce the price risk of a current or potential cash position. Those who *must* hold cash inventories, such as bond and currency dealers, routinely reduce their risk by undertaking a hedge position. Financial institutions and pension funds often determine that it is easier and more cost effective to hedge with futures than to restructure their position solely by making cash transactions. In fact, the principal reason for the existence of futures markets is to allow hedgers to transfer their price risk.[1]

The price variability in the financial markets since the mid-1970s has created a surge in volume in the related futures markets. Market participants using futures markets have realized the benefits of reducing price risk (hedgers) or trading on price variability (speculators) provided by these markets. The benefits of risk reduction are so important to many money managers that they employ futures contracts to hedge even when there is no specific futures instrument directly associated with the cash instrument held in their portfolio. For example, corporate bondholders often hedge with T-bond futures in order to minimize the price risk caused by the volatility of long-term interest rates, even though a change in the yield spread between the T-bond and corporate bond yields causes adverse effects for this specific type of hedge.

Hedging benefits society as well as the individual hedger. As outlined in Chapter 1, the ability to transfer risk allows the commodity hedger a more stable estimate of the cost of a product, which translates into a lower and more stable price for the product. Also, users of commodities are able to lock in the future purchase price of the item they need with only a small cash margin "down payment," thereby allowing a reduction in current inventory. This reduction in inventory reduces the cost of business and improves the firm's liquidity, benefits that can be passed on to the consumer. The existence of financial futures allows pension funds to stabilize returns and reduce risk for the pension fund participants, enables financial institutions to reduce risk, and provides the means to create new products in the insurance, loan, and investment arenas.

Hedging also is a tool used to offset the market (**systematic**) risk of stock portfolios. Previously, risk management for common stocks concentrated on diversification to eliminate **unsystematic** risk, but until futures and options contracts on stock index futures came into existence there was no effective means for eliminating most of the systematic risk of a stock portfolio. Alternatively, futures are used to adjust the beta of the stock portfolio to the desired value.

Finally, hedging is extremely important for the proper functioning, long-term liquidity, and open interest of a futures market. Thus, viable futures contracts are linked to commer-

---

1 In some markets speculators provide the risk capital needed for this transfer of risk; however, in the most active financial futures markets both long and short hedgers exist, and speculators provide a time bridge between trades by the long and short hedgers.

cial hedging activity. Although speculative interest provides shorter-term volume, speculative activity can be wavering and uncertain, especially since many speculators hold a position for only a few weeks. Market-makers on the futures floor provide intraday liquidity, but without speculators and hedgers the market-makers soon depart to another pit. Likewise, arbitrageurs provide only limited liquidity for the markets. Hedgers are the key to the market, as is evident when a futures contract stops trading because of a lack of trading volume.

Hedging Concepts

Price Changes and Hedging. In order to understand the basic concepts of hedging, let us assume that we own a portfolio of assets (e.g., stocks and/or bonds). The value of the assets is defined as follows:

$$TV_C = P_C \ N_C \qquad (9\text{-}1)$$

where TV_C = the total value of the cash position

P_C = the price per unit of the cash instrument or asset

N_C = the number of cash units held

Without hedging, the value of the cash position changes over time as the price of the cash asset changes; that is,

$$\Delta TV_C = \Delta P_C \ N_C \qquad (9\text{-}2)$$

If a short position in futures is taken to offset partially or fully the change in the long cash position, we have:

$$\Delta TV_{C\text{-}F} = \Delta P_C \ N_C + \Delta P_F \ (-N_F) \qquad (9\text{-}3)$$

where $\Delta TV_{C\text{-}F}$ = the net change in value

ΔP_F = the change in the futures price

$-N_F$ = the short position on N units of the futures

If the purpose of the hedge is to minimize the net price change (minimize risk), then we have as our objective:

$$\Delta TV_{C\text{-}F} = 0 = \Delta P_C \ N_C + \Delta P_F \ (-N_F) \qquad (9\text{-}4)$$

The next chapter employs this concept to determine the number of futures contracts needed to minimize risk.

Basis, Basis Risk, and Crosshedges. A method for visualizing how hedging affects risk is to examine the basis between the cash and futures position. Basis is the difference between the cash price of the specific instrument one is hedging and the futures price of the futures instrument employed for the hedge (i.e., $P_C - P_F$). Therefore, basis risk is the variability in the basis over time—that is, the variability of the net hedging position. Hedging reduces the price risk inherent in the total price variability of the cash instrument to the variability of the basis; in other words, *hedging exchanges absolute price risk of the asset for basis risk.* For example, if the cash stock portfolio has a standard deviation of 20%, then hedging can reduce the net $(P_C - P_F)$ variability to less than 4% (a reduction of more than 80% of the total variability). This reduction in risk occurs because the futures price change offsets the effect of the cash price change. Figure 9-1 illustrates absolute risk and basis risk by comparing the dollar value of an S&P 500 stock position that is not hedged to a position hedged with S&P futures. Note that the volatility of the hedged position is significantly less than the volatility of the unhedged position. Moreover, the unhedged

FIGURE 9-1: Unhedged vs. Hedged S&P 500 Portfolio

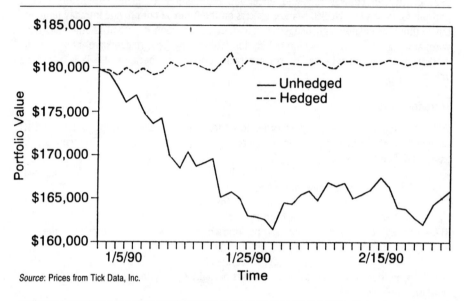

Source: Prices from Tick Data, Inc.

position loses approximately $15,000, but the hedged position's value remains about the same.

If the cash instrument possesses essentially the same characteristics as the futures contract, then the basis risk should be minimal. However, if significant differences exist between the cash and futures characteristics (i.e., if one is executing a **crosshedge** between instruments with substantially different characteristics), then the basis risk often is large. This large basis risk occurs because the futures and cash prices do not move together. In fact, the extent of the basis risk is a critical factor in determining whether a hedge is appropriate for a given situation.

Quantity Risk. Another risk affecting a hedge position is uncertainty over the quantity to hedge. For example, because of weather conditions, a grain farmer is not sure how many bushels of grain will be harvested. A financial institution has similar forecasting problems in anticipating how many certificates of deposit will be purchased by investors. Thus, the fact that N_C in Equations (9-1) to (9-3) can be an uncertain number for some types of hedges creates difficulties in estimating N_F.

Anticipated and Unanticipated Price Changes. It is essential to understand that futures prices reflect the *expectations* of market participants concerning changes in the cash price; that is, futures prices reflect *anticipated* changes in the cash price. In other words, futures are a forward price. Thus, even if current short-term interest rates are at 5%, the forward/futures markets could forecast that short-term rates will be at 6½% within nine months. A hedger who desires to hedge an interest rate position with a futures contract expiring nine months from now is hedging against any change *from the projected forward/futures* rate of 6½%; that is, one can hedge only against *unanticipated* changes not yet reflected in the futures market price. Another way to state this idea is that futures *cannot* protect the hedger against differences between the current interest rate and the *expected* interest rate implied by the current futures price. Note that hedging with futures is equivalent to locking in a forward rate starting, say, nine months from now; it is *not* possible to lock in the *current* interest rate to start in nine months. Similarly, prices of noninterest rate futures contracts reflect expectations concerning future cash price changes. For example, new information or changes in expectations are reflected in stock index futures prices 5 to 30 minutes before they show up in all cash stock prices because of the lower cost and greater liquidity of the futures market. However, this knowledge will *not* help a trader profit in cash stocks, since the *next* trade in the cash stocks (in 5 to 30 minutes) accounts for the change in expectations.

Risk Management. The foregoing discussion emphasizes the primary purpose of futures: the control of risk of the cash position. Risk is described in terms of price change, a change in the basis, Equation (9-2), and unanticipated price changes. Each concept reflects the same need, to control risk. Hence, the first decision is *whether* the portfolio manager or firm wishes to avoid unanticipated price changes. Hedging eliminates most of the effect of these price changes, but it also eliminates potential positive returns. The risk preferences of the potential hedger dictates whether hedging is appropriate for this situation or whether the cash asset's absolute price variability is tolerable.

Avoiding Losses: Sell or Hedge?

A typical question concerning hedging is, "Why should I hedge when I can sell the cash asset if I expect prices to decline?" In fact, selling the cash asset is preferable in some circumstances.[2] The principal rule for deciding whether to make a transaction in the cash market or to hedge in the futures market is:

If you can accomplish your goal *effectively* in the cash market, then complete your transaction in that market.

The key to this rule is the word "effectively." In many situations one or more of the following factors causes difficulties if the transaction is completed in the cash market:

- Liquidity: the cash market for a given asset often is not liquid for large trades. Thus, the portfolio hedger who sells or buys the cash asset, or the dealer who shorts the asset, causes a significant price change in that security when liquidity does not exist. There is no liquidity problem for trades in most (near-term) financial futures contracts.
- Cost: the commissions and size of the bid-ask spread in the cash market often cause the cash transaction to be expensive relative to the same transaction in the futures market. For example, trades in a stock portfolio cost ten times the equivalent trade in futures.
- Execution: a futures transaction is initiated more quickly than a cash transaction due to liquidity reasons.
- Short selling: a short sale in the cash market typically is expensive. For example, a short sale of a cash T-bill costs approximately 50 basis points per year. Moreover, the same

---

2 In fact, dealers do *not* have a choice: they *must* have an inventory of the cash asset to act as a dealer. Thus, dealers often use futures for hedging.

exact T-bill maturity has to be replaced when the short is covered—which is often a difficult and expensive process.
- Internal policy or government regulations: these factors can prevent the desired cash market transaction. For example, a portfolio manager often is required to have a given minimum percentage of assets in bonds rather than in cash or short-term securities, or a financial institution may be prevented from shorting a cash security to obtain an effective cash market hedge.
- Credit risk: creating a forward or short sale in the cash market often involves an implicit credit risk on the part of the participants. Futures transactions are completed with the clearinghouse, virtually eliminating the credit risk problem.

Strategies for Hedging

Hedging typically is associated with reducing risk (reducing price volatility). However, those who employ futures markets have different strategies and different goals in order to implement a hedging program. Market participants practice four overlapping strategies:
- Reduction of risk: the primary use of futures for hedging is to reduce the price variability associated with the cash asset position. Naive, regression, and duration methods determine the appropriate number of futures contracts for a hedge position. The objective of the regression and duration methods is to minimize the risk associated with a cash position. Chapters 10 to 12 discuss these methods.
- Selective hedging: hedging only during those time periods when a forecast determines that the cash position will lose money is called selective hedging. If the forecasts are correct, then risk is minimized during the hedged periods; meanwhile the asset earns positive returns during the unhedged periods. If the forecasts are incorrect, then risk is not reduced. Many institutions employ some type of market timing to decide when to use selective hedging.
- "Speculating on the basis": when the returns from the hedge are a consideration in whether the hedge will be undertaken, then this approach is equivalent to predicting the change in the basis during the hedge period. The considerations in predicting hedge returns are discussed later in this chapter.
- Optimal risk-return hedging: the optimal hedge decision considers both the reduction in risk *and* the return from the combined cash-futures position. Such an optimal position is associated with portfolio analysis and is discussed in Chapter 10 and Appendix 10A.

The above strategies also can be designated as passive or active strategies. A passive strategy is independent of cash market price/interest rate expectations. Passive strategies depend on the risk attitude of the hedger and the volatility of the cash markets. Active strategies require a forecast of future cash prices/interest rates for implementation. The forecast helps the money manager decide when and how much of the cash position to hedge. Thus, an active hedging strategy readjusts the hedging position over time.

The "reduction of risk" strategy listed above is a passive strategy. "Selective hedging" and "speculating on the basis" are active strategies. The "optimal risk-return" strategy can be either a passive or active strategy depending on whether the risk attitude of the hedger or the forecasts of the cash market determine the size of the hedge position.

The Hedging Process

The examples presented below illustrate how hedging entails taking a position in futures that "offsets" the price change in the cash asset. Hence, hedging a current long cash position consists of taking a short futures position. In order to determine whether one should sell or buy futures to initiate a hedge, a potential hedger can follow a two-step process:

1. Determine the exposure of the cash position to potential losses; that is, in what direction must cash prices change in order to create a loss? Thus, a loss occurs for a current long cash position when prices decline, whereas a loss occurs for a short or an *anticipated* cash position when prices increase.
2. Determine whether a short or a long futures position is needed to offset the potential loss in the cash position.

Exhibit 9-1 illustrates the possible situations. The hedging examples in the following sections show how to implement these hedges.

TYPES OF SHORT HEDGES

A **short hedge** exists when a short futures position is undertaken in order to offset adverse price changes in a long cash position. The following discussion illustrates three basic types of risk reducing short hedges.

A Portfolio Hedge

When a money manager forecasts a decline in the price of a portfolio of financial assets *or* does not want the risk associated with those assets, then the money manager can either:
* Do nothing (which creates a loss if the forecast is correct).
* Sell the cash assets.
* Execute a short hedge with a futures contract or alternative hedging instrument.

EXHIBIT 9-1: Initiating Hedging Positions

Cash Position	Cash Market Loss Occurs When:	Change in the Associated Futures Contract	Appropriate Hedge Position
Own (long)	P_C decreases	P_F decreases	Short futures
Short	P_C increases	P_F increases	Long futures
Anticipated long	P_C increases (opportunity loss)	P_F increases	Long futures
Anticipated short	P_C decreases (opportunity loss)	P_F decreases	Short futures

P_C = price of the cash
P_F = price of the futures

Typically, a futures hedge provides benefits over simply selling the asset, as discussed later in this chapter. Hedging the cash asset currently owned is called a **portfolio hedge**.

Example 9-1 presents a case in which a portfolio manager hedges $1 million of Treasury bonds when a money manager expects interest rates to increase. By selling T-bond futures short, the money manager profits on the futures side when prices decline (interest rates increase), thereby partially or totally offsetting the loss on the long cash T-bond position as its price declines. The example shows how the loss of $144,687.50 in the value of the cash bond position is reduced to a net loss of $20,312.50 when the profit from the short sale of the futures contracts is considered. Thus, the hedge reduces the loss on the cash portfolio by nearly 86%. Example 9-2 provides a similar portfolio hedge example for a stock portfolio.

Many basic trade booklets and publications on futures markets present hedging examples by showing a net loss of $0—that is, a situation in which the gain on the futures position *exactly* offsets the loss on the cash position. This situation is equivalent to having a perfect negative correlation of −1.0 between the cash and futures price changes. Although such a situation would be welcome by hedgers, the reality is that such "perfect hedges" do not exist.

An Inventory Hedge

A dealer is a market-maker for an asset or instrument that does not trade on an exchange. The dealer holds inventory of the asset in order to transact trades. For example, bond and

---

EXAMPLE 9-1: A Bond Portfolio Short Hedge Example

A portfolio manager for long-term Treasury bonds forecasts that interest rates will increase over the next few months (bond prices are expected to fall). The money manager holds a portfolio of $1 million ($1MM) of May 2011 bonds. A short hedge is implemented in September when long-term rates are at 7.8% and lifted in February after rates rise to 9.1%.

	Cash	*Futures*
Sept. 16	Holds $1 million par of May 2011 T-bonds, coupon rate 10¾%, yielding 7.8% with a price of 129¹³⁄₃₂	Sells 10 March T-bond futures with a price of 100 (a projected yield of 8.0%)
Feb. 22	Price of bonds has dropped to 114³⁰⁄₃₂ with a yield of 9.1%.	Repurchases 10 March T-bond futures at a price of 87¹⁸⁄₃₂ (with a projected yield of 9.4%)
Change in value:	Loss of $144,687.50 (14¹⁵⁄₃₂ × $1MM)	Gain of $124,375 (12¹⁴⁄₃₂ × $100,000 × 10 or 398 × $31.25 × 10)

Net loss: $20,312.50 (i.e., $144,687.50 − $124,735)

EXAMPLE 9-2: A Short Hedge for a Stock Position

In October 1987, a portfolio manager senses uneasiness in the stock market. The S&P 500 cash index has fallen from 328.08 on October 5 to 298.08 on the morning of October 16. This money manager decides to hedge the stock portfolio, which is structured to resemble the S&P 500 cash index. The following shows the effects of such a hedge only several days later. Note that a loss in the cash portfolio of more than $23 million became a net gain of almost $3 million, since the futures dropped *more* than the cash index.

	Cash	Futures
October 16	S&P 500 cash index at 298.08; portfolio has $100 million of stock	Sells 665 December S&P 500 futures contracts at 300.50 for a value of $99,916,250 (i.e., 665 × 300.5 × 500)
October 26	S&P 500 cash index closes at 227.67, for a portfolio value of $76,378,822 ($100 million × 227.67/298.08)	Repurchases 665 December S&P 500 futures at a close of 220.50 for a value of $73,316,250 (i.e., 665 × 220.50 × 500)
Change in value:	Loss of $23,621,180	Gain of $26,600,000

Net gain: $2,978,820

---

currency markets are dealer markets. These dealers trade billions of dollars in government and corporate bonds and foreign currencies each day. An **inventory hedge** occurs when a market-maker uses futures contracts to lock in the value of their inventory until the market-maker can sell the inventory. On occasion, dealers also lock in the price of assets about to be obtained, especially when bond dealers bid for a new issue of government bonds. Bond and currency dealers routinely use the futures markets to control their risk exposure.

Although the concept and setup for this type of hedge is equivalent to the portfolio hedge discussed in Example 9-1, the motivation differs. Both the portfolio manager and the dealer execute a hedge in order to reduce the price variability of the assets they are holding. However, the portfolio manager could simply sell the cash asset, although the dealer *must* keep the current cash inventory in order to transact business. Hence, the money manager completes the portfolio hedge because futures provide important advantages over simply selling the cash asset, including lower transactions costs and greater liquidity; however, a dealer's futures hedge is used to avoid the problems associated with covering an inventory position in the cash market. In particular, covering an inventory position by short selling a similar cash asset can be difficult to execute, and can be very costly or impossible because of the size of the dealer's position. Alternatively, if the dealer is long on some cash assets and short on others (for example, different bond maturities), then the dealer is naturally hedged for part of the inventory. Example 9-3 shows the classic inventory hedge of the IBM sale of $1 billion of bonds during October 1979, in this case, the dealer avoided a significant loss by hedging.

An Asset-Liability Hedge

Financial institutions and the portfolio hedger have different problems. Whereas the portfolio hedger desires to reduce the price risk of a set of assets, the financial institution is concerned about the *relationship* between its assets and liabilities. Specifically, changes in the financial institution's earnings are caused by the relative effect of a change in interest rates on both the assets and liabilities of the institution. If the cost of funds (liabilities) increases, then this cost is partially or completely offset by the additional return from higher

---

EXAMPLE 9-3: A Dealer's Inventory Hedge: The IBM Underwriting

In October 1979, IBM offered $1 billion of notes and bonds to the financial market, the largest offering in U.S. corporate history. Solomon Brothers and Merrill Lynch were comanagers of the underwriting, heading a group of 227 members. The underwriters' commission on the notes was ⅝% and the bonds provided ⅞%; the spread above the government notes and bonds was only seven and 12 basis points, respectively. Given that the prime rate had increased five times during the previous month, the commission rate and spread were minimal given the risk being undertaken by the underwriters. The sale began on Thursday, October 4, the same day a Treasury auction took place.

On Saturday, October 6, the Fed announced its famous dictum that it was changing its policy from controlling interest rates to controlling the money supply in order to reduce the rate of inflation. That day the Fed increased the discount rate from 11% to 12%. By October 9 the prime rate had increased one percentage point to 14.5%. By October 10 the IBM note yield had increased from 9.62% to 10.65%, and the bond yield had increased from 9.41% to 10.09%.

When the underwriting syndicate was disbanded on Wednesday, October 10, approximately $650 million of the $1 billion offering had been sold, generating $5 million in fees. However, the subsequent loss on the remaining $350 million in unsold notes and bonds was $15 million.

The potential loss on the inventory of bonds from the dramatic increase in interest rates was significantly higher than the underwriting commissions on these issues. Solomon Brothers, which took $125 million of the unsold issue, had hedged its inventory position in the futures market by selling T-bond futures. This hedge undoubtedly allowed Solomon to save a significant portion of its revenues from the underwriting. Since this historic underwriting, dealers in bond issues have routinely hedged their inventory position by employing the T-bond and T-note futures markets.

interest on assets. Thus, the financial institution is naturally hedged for part of the balance sheet. However, many financial institutions find that it is not possible to reduce the volatility of earnings adequately from this natural asset-liability relationship, since assets often are long-term in nature while liabilities are short-term. This situation creates a "gap" in the maturity relationship, which causes changes in earnings when interest rates change. Hedging this maturity gap is called an **asset-liability hedge**.

Example 9-4 illustrates a typical asset-liability problem facing a financial institution and also shows how a futures hedge can alleviate this problem. The example begins by showing the problem that occurs when asset returns are fixed for the long term; however, the liability costs vary over a much shorter period. It then provides an illustration of how a simple T-bill futures hedge can significantly reduce the volatility of a financial institution's earnings by locking in the future cost of the liability. Part IV includes the uses of futures by financial institutions.

USING LONG HEDGES

The Long Hedge Concept

A **long hedge** is initiated when a futures contract is purchased in order to reduce the price variability of an *anticipated* future long position. Equivalently, a long hedge locks in the interest rate or price of a cash security that will be purchased in the future, subject to a small adjustment due to the basis risk. Long hedges are sometimes considered speculative, since the hedger is attempting to offset a *projected* position rather than a current position. However, if future cash inflows can be forecasted accurately, if these funds are invested, and if interest rates are forecasted to decline (prices expected to increase), then executing a long hedge locks in the *current* forward rate existing in the market. Consequently, a long hedge creates profits that offset the subsequent higher price in the cash market. A long hedge also is known as an **anticipatory hedge** because it is effectively a substitute position for a future cash transaction.

The use of a long hedge serves as an effective *temporary* substitute for the purchase of a cash security, where the cash purchase is undertaken in the future. Thus, if interest rates do decline (prices increase) and no long hedge is executed, then the return on the invested funds will be lower than it would be if a hedge were executed. In other words, a long hedge can prevent an **opportunity loss** on future funds to be invested.[3] Other examples of long hedges are when a company that uses, say, wheat or cattle can buy futures to lock in the price they will pay for these commodities in the future, or when a mutual fund or pension fund buys futures for a temporary substitute of a cash transaction to be implemented later. Example 9-5 shows how a long hedge is useful in locking in an effective yield on investment when the funds are not available until a given time in the future. The initiation of a long hedge, as in Example 9-5, is made by management either if the firm

---

3 An alternative method to lock in a future interest rate (price) when funds are not available until later is to buy the financial instrument now (e.g., purchase a cash T-bond) and finance that purchase with borrowed funds until money becomes available. In this way the buyer guarantees the long-term yield on the bond. Whether the futures long hedge or the cash financing method is superior depends on the relationship of the bond yield to the financing rate, plus any difficulties in arranging financing for the cash transaction or convincing the board of directors of the firm to allow such financing.

EXAMPLE 9-4: An Asset-Liability Hedge Example

AAA Savings and Loan has assets in the form of a mortgage portfolio of $500 million, with $300 million of the portfolio having a 9½% fixed rate with 20 years to maturity. The other $200 million in mortgages are variable-rate loans linked to the 90-day T-bill rate plus a 2% premium, adjustable quarterly. For simplicity, let us assume that the liabilities of AAA consist of $500 million of three-month certificates of deposit, where the interest rate is based on the 90-day T-bill rate plus ¾%.

Since the variable-rate mortgages are repriced at the same time and with the same instrument as the liabilities of the S&L (i.e., both are based on the T-bill rate), this portion of the asset-liability mix does not have a pricing risk. However, the fixed-rate portion of the mortgage portfolio is *not* repriced when the cost of the CDs changes in relation to changing interest rates. This creates a significant potential change in the earnings of the S&L as interest rates change.

Part A: Without a Futures Hedge

The three-month T-bill rate is 7% on January 15; this rate changes to 11% by April 15. Note the change in the annualized spread between the fixed-rate portion of the mortgages and the liability interest rate from January to April, causing a significant change in earnings.

	Assets	Liabilities	Annualized Spread
Jan. 15	$200MM variable; 7% T-bill + 2% premium	$200MM 90-day CD, 7¾%	9% − 7¾% = + 1¼%
	$300MM fixed, 9½%, 20 year	$300MM 90-day CD, 7¾%	9½% − 7¾% = + 1¾%
April 15	$200MM variable, 11% T-bill + 2% premium	$2 00MM 90-day CD, 11¾%	13% − 11¾% = + 1¼%
	$300MM fixed, 9½%, 20 year	$300MM 90-day CD, 11¾%	9½% − 11¾% = − 2¼%

Part B: Futures Hedge for Fixed-Rate Mortgages

T-bill futures are sold to offset the higher cost of the CDs *to be issued* during July, the CDs being the cost of funds to the S&L. Thus, the hedge is executed in order *to avoid higher costs* from the new CDs.

Example continues

EXAMPLE 9-4: Continued

	Cash Liabilities	Futures
Jan. 15	Current cost: $300MM 90-day CDs at 7¾%	Sell to hedge cost of new CDs in April: 300 Sept. T-bill futures at 92.60, or 7.40%
April 15	CD's issued: $300MM 90-day CDs at 11¾%	Buy back futures: 300 Sept. T-bill futures at 88.90, or 11.10%
Net (three months):	($300MM) (4%) (1/4 year) = –$3 MM	(300 futures) (370 basis points) ($25 per basis point) = +$2.775MM

Net loss with hedge: $.225MM
Net loss without hedge: $3MM

The net loss shows the *higher cost of funding* for the financial institution. Note that the hedge given here offsets the higher CD cost for only one quarter, since the T-bill futures are 90-day instruments and a one-to-one hedge between the cash CDs and the T-bill futures is executed. Also, the hedge is not perfect: the cost on the CDs increases more than does the T-bill futures rate, creating a net loss of $.225MM on the combined net position; *however*, this loss is significantly less than the $3MM that would occur without any hedge.

---

wishes to reduce risk substantially, *or* if the firm has a better forecast of future interest rates than is available from the forward rate (selective hedging).

Disadvantages of a Long Hedge

Disadvantages of a long hedge are as follows:

- If the financial manager incorrectly forecasts the direction of future interest rates and a long hedge is initiated, then the firm still locks in the futures yield rather than fully participating in the higher returns available because of the higher interest rates.
- If rates increase instead of fall, then bond prices will fall, causing an immediate cash outflow due to margin calls. This cash outflow will be offset only *over the life of the bond* via a higher yield on investment, or from a higher bond price if the bond recovers in the market and is sold. Thus, the net investment is the same, but the timing of the accounting profits differs from the investment decision.
- If the futures market already anticipates a fall in interest rates similar to the decrease forecasted by the financial manager, then the futures price reflects this lower rate, negating any return benefit from the long hedge. Specifically, one hedges only against *unanticipated* changes that the futures market has not yet forecasted. Hence, if the eventual cash price increases only to a level *below* the current futures price, then a loss

---

EXAMPLE 9-5: Example of a Long Hedge

A greeting card company anticipates a large inflow of funds at the end of January when retail outlets pay for the stock of cards sold during the holiday season in December. Management intends to put $10 million of these funds into a long-term bond because of the high yields on these investments. The current date is November 1 and the financial manager of the greeting card company projects that the long-term interest rate will fall significantly by the time the firm receives the funds on February 1. Thus, unless a long hedge is initiated now, the financial manager believes the return on investment will be significantly lower (the cost of the bonds significantly higher) than is currently available via the futures market.

Objective of the long hedge: to benefit from the high long-term interest rates, even though funds are not currently available for investment.

Date	Cash Market	Futures Market
Nov. 1	Bonds at $86^{20}/_{32}$ to yield 9.96%; 8% coupon, 12 years to maturity; $10MM to invest February 1	Buy 100 March T-bond futures at $87^{16}/_{32}$ as a long hedge (9.4% projected yield)
Feb. 1	Receive $10 MM; buy $10MM of T-bonds at 100 to yield 8%	Sell futures at $100^{2}/_{32}$ to cover long position (yield 7.9%)
Change	Opportunity loss: $1,337,500 ($10MM × $13^{12}/_{32}$%)	Gain: $1,256,250 ($100,000 × 100 × $12^{18}/_{32}$%)

Net change: $1,256,250 − $1,337,500 = −$81,250
Net yield with futures hedge: 9.83%

The example shows that the purchase of the T-bond futures contracts creates a gain for the futures instrument and that this gain is used to offset most of the higher future cash T-bond price. To look at it another way, the gain obtained on the futures transaction increases the total yield so it approaches the projected yield given by the futures market on November 1. Although the net loss of $81,250 on the long hedge shows the hedge is not perfect, this is significantly less than the opportunity loss of $1,337,500 that occurs without any hedge position.

---

occurs on the long hedge. Consequently, an increase in return from a long hedge in comparison to the future cash market investment occurs only if the financial manager is a superior forecaster of future interest rates. However, the long hedge does lock in the currently available long-term futures rate (or a close approximation of this rate), thereby reducing the risk of unanticipated changes in this rate.

• Financial institutions are prohibited from employing long hedges, since their regulatory agencies believe long hedges are similar to speculation, and these agencies do not want financial institutions to be tempted into affecting the institution's return with highly leveraged "speculative" futures positions.

CROSSHEDGES AND CHANGING VOLATILITIES OF AN ASSET POSITION

Crosshedges

A crosshedge occurs if the characteristics of the cash asset underlying the futures contract differs from the cash instrument being hedged. A number of factors affect the degree of a crosshedge for a given position. The extent of a stock portfolio crosshedge is affected by the relative stock composition and relative stock weights of the cash and futures positions; any differences in the dollar size between the cash and futures positions also affect the hedge. For a T-bond futures hedge, one must consider the effect of the coupon, the time to maturity of the cash position, whether the bond possesses default risk, and the relative size of the underlying cash position. If any of these factors differ from the characteristics of the futures contract or the cheapest-to-deliver cash bond for pricing the futures, then a crosshedge exists. The extent of a crosshedge can be measured by the size of the correlation coefficient between the changes in value of the cash and futures position. The lower the correlation coefficient, the greater the difference in the two positions. When a low correlation exists, the futures contract is not a good instrument to use for hedging purposes.

Crosshedges arising from some of these characteristics, such as coupon differences, have a minimal effect on the performance of the hedge when the cash and futures prices still move nearly in tandem. Crosshedge factors affecting the volatility of the position (e.g., the maturity of the cash bond) are dealt with by adjusting the number of futures contracts employed in the hedge (as shown in the next chapter). However, the effect of a quality difference, such as hedging corporate bonds with Treasury bond futures, depends on whether there is a major change in the perceived risk in the economy during the hedge period, which would significantly alter the basis. Consequently, the difficulty of overcoming crosshedge effects depends upon the particular characteristic(s) that differ between the futures and cash positions, whether the factors remain stable over time, and the economic environment at the time of the hedge.[4, 5]

In reality, most hedges involve some type of a crosshedge risk, since the cash asset typically differs from the underlying cash instrument priced by the futures contract. The greater the deviation of any of these factors from the underlying cash instrument, the greater the basis risk. For example, the effect of a large change in the shape of the term structure needs to be considered when the maturities of the cash bond and the cheapest-to-deliver bond for the futures contract differ. The creation of the T-note futures contracts with shorter maturities was undertaken in order to provide a more appropriate hedging vehicle under these circumstances. Also note that care must be taken when hedging the prime rate. Because the prime is an administered rate, it does not usually change in the same manner as market rates; in fact, the prime rate is slow to react to downward changes in interest

---

4   For example, hedging one currency with the futures contract of another currency often causes significant crosshedge risk because of the differing economic conditions in the two countries.

5   Liquidity also can be an issue in *measuring* the basis for a given security, since thinly traded issues often have reported prices that differ from their true prices, especially when the market changes but the thinly traded issue does not trade. Moreover, cash prices typically are reported in terms of bid prices and ask prices rather than transaction prices, and the newspaper prices occur at a different time of day than the close of the futures market; both of these factors affect the *apparent* stability of the basis.

rates. Hence, it is sometimes difficult to hedge the prime in an effective manner, especially over the short term.

Example 9-6 shows a crosshedge between a cash portfolio mimicking the S&P 100 cash index and the S&P 500 futures contract. As shown in the example, crosshedges create net gains or losses that often vary to a greater extent than is the case when the characteristics of the futures and cash securities are nearly equivalent. Many of the hedging applications examined in Part IV involve recognizing and dealing with crosshedge characteristics effectively. The hedging techniques discussed in the remaining chapters of Part III also help reduce crosshedge risk.

Adjusting Risk: Altering Effective Volatilities

An important use of futures markets is to change the *effective* volatility of a cash position. For example, selling a T-bond or stock index futures contract reduces the effective volatility of the cash position, whereas buying futures increases the effective volatility of a bond or stock portfolio. In other words, selling bond futures shortens the effective maturity of a bond. Similarly, buying bond futures increases the price sensitivity of the position to changes in interest rates, creating a position that acts like a bond with a longer maturity. A

EXAMPLE 9-6: Example of a Crosshedge

A major pension fund holds $50 million in stocks, with the portfolio configured to match the S&P 100 index. The fund's money manager forecasts an increase in volatility in the market, which increases the probability of a major market decline. To reduce risk the money manager sells S&P 500 futures. Although the S&P 500 futures do not match the S&P 100 price movements exactly, the money manager decides that this type of crosshedge is the best strategy to use in this situation.

Date	Cash Market	Futures Market,
Jan. 12	Stock portfolio of $50 million, with the S&P 100 = 325.09	Sell 287 June S&P 500 futures, with the S&P 500 futures = 348.20 for a value of $49,966,700
April 26	The S&P 100 declines to 315.82 for a portfolio value of $48,574,240 = $50MM (315.82/325.09)	Buy back the S&P 500 futures at 335.25 for a value of $48,108,37
Change	Loss of $1,425,760	Gain of $1,858,325 = 287 × 500 × (348.20 − 335.25)

Net gain: $432,565

The crosshedge generates a gain of $432,565. The large deviation between the loss in the cash portfolio and the futures gain shows the relative ineffectiveness of this crosshedge.

bond portfolio manager often wants to change the volatility of a bond portfolio when the interest rate forecast indicates a change in rates and the portfolio manager wishes to act on this forecast. Decreasing volatility by selling futures reduces losses when rates increase; on the other hand, increasing the effective volatility of the bond position by buying futures increases gains if interest rates decrease. Of course, these strategies also decrease and increase the risk of the bond portfolio, respectively. Correspondingly, selling stock index futures decreases the beta of a portfolio, whereas buying futures increases the portfolio's beta.

Chapter 13 illustrates ways to determine the number of futures contracts to buy or sell in order to change the effective volatility of a bond or stock position. Chapter 13 also discusses techniques whereby futures are employed to turn a bond position into an equivalent T-bill position while providing returns higher than returns available in the current T-bill position.

RETURNS, BASIS, AND CASH FLOWS

Returns and Hedging: Considering the Basis

The sole objective of a "pure" hedging model is to reduce the variability of the cash position as much as possible. This approach is consistent with the objective of minimizing risk, which is the cornerstone of many hedging techniques and examples. However, most hedgers also consider the effect of the hedge on the returns of the position.

When one considers the potential effect of the hedge on returns, it is enticing to concentrate (incorrectly) only on convergence and whether there is a **positive** or **negative basis**—that is, whether $P_C - P_F > 0$ or $P_C - P_F < 0$. If these were the only relevant factors, then a negative basis—in combination with a short hedge—would produce a positive return when the prices converged at expiration. Thus, the cash price would increase to equal the futures price at the expiration of the futures contract. Similarly, a positive basis would produce a negative return for a short hedge. These relationships are shown in Figure 9-2. However, this scenario is *guaranteed* only if the underlying cash position is the cheapest-to-deliver instrument—that is, if no type of crosshedge exists and the position is held until the expiration of the futures contract.[6]

In order to determine whether the returns from a crosshedge will be positive or negative, the hedger must examine the *direction of the change* in the basis *in conjunction with* the question of whether a positive or negative basis exists. An example of this situation is a crosshedge between a corporate bond and a T-bond futures contract. In order to simplify terminology, the effect of the direction and type of basis (positive or negative) for a crosshedge is described in terms of a **weaker** or **stronger basis**. A weaker basis occurs when the cash price increases less or falls more than the futures price. Consequently, a "weaker" basis means that the difference between the cash and futures prices becomes less positive or more negative. A weaker basis in conjunction with a short hedge generates negative returns. Thus, for a short hedge, the long cash position loses more than the short futures position gains (or the cash gains less than the futures loses). Conversely, a "stronger" basis occurs when the cash price increases more or falls less than the corresponding futures price.

---

6   This explanation also assumes the hedger owns the cash asset. If the asset is being financed, then the basis should equal the net financing cost, as discussed in Part II.

FIGURE 9-2: Positive and Negative Basis Effects on Return

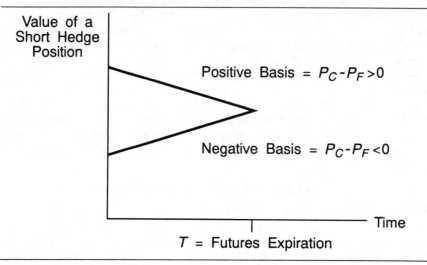

In this situation the basis becomes more positive (or less negative), since the cash position gains more than the futures position loses (or loses less than the futures gain). These relationships are described in Exhibits 9-2 and 9-3 and in diagram form for a short hedge in Figure 9-3.

FIGURE 9-3: The Effect of Basis Changes on the Value of a Short Hedge

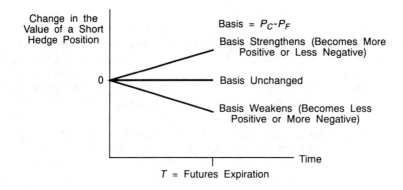

EXHIBIT 9-2: Hedge Position and Returns		
Type of Hedge	*Basis Weakens*	*Basis Strengthens*
Short hedge	Returns < 0	Returns > 0
Long hedge	Returns > 0	Returns < 0

Since yields change in opposite directions to prices, when an upward sloping curve (i.e., a positive basis) exists, then losses occur for a short hedge if the yield curve flattens out (the basis weakens). Similarly, when a downward sloping yield curve flattens out, then a short hedge provides positive returns because the negative basis strengthens.[7, 8]

In conclusion, the attempt to determine hedge returns by forecasting whether the basis will strengthen or weaken is considered by some practitioners before entering into a hedge. The temptation to consider this type of basis trading as the *primary* factor dictating *when* to place the hedge must be guarded against so that the primary objective of risk reduction is implemented immediately. Management and hedge traders should realize that reduction in price risk is more important than a small improvement in return through basis changes.

Marking-to-Market and Cash Flows

The discussion of margins and marking-to-market in Chapter 3 shows that the futures account balance fluctuates as prices change. The change in the account balance affects the overall return of the position since earnings can be withdrawn to earn interest, while losses require additional infusion of cash to meet maintenance margin calls. The additional cash infusions cause a loss on interest on these funds unless T-bills are used to cover the margin calls.[9] Hill, Schneeweis, and Mayerson[10] and Elton, Gruber, and Rentzler[11] show that the net effect of interest earned/paid on margin accounts is small, approximating 2% of the entire return.

On the other hand, the cash flows resulting from marking-to-market require the liquidity management of funds. Earnings need to be invested in a timely manner. Additional funds

---

7 Another reason for a change in the basis is a change in the short-term financing rate employed for arbitrage between the futures and cash positions. This change in the cost of funds to arbitrageurs is the major factor affecting the difference between the futures price and the cheapest-to-deliver cash instrument. Consequently, the basis changes as the financing rate changes.

8 Basis movements also affect our conclusion concerning the ability of the hedge to reduce risk. Thus, when the basis changes over the life of the hedge, which is typical, then the convergence of P_C and P_F creates an imperfect hedge.

9 Recall that T-bills or similar assets can be used to cover both initial margin and maintenance margin calls. The hedger earns the interest on the T-bills. If funds are not available to cover margin calls, then cash must be borrowed, thus creating an interest expense.

10 Joanne Hill, Thomas Schneeweis, and Robert Mayerson, "An Analysis of the Impact of Mark-to-Market in Hedging with Treasury Bond Futures," *The Review of Research in Futures Markets*, Vol. 2, No. 1, 1983, pp. 136-159.

11 E. J. Elton, M. J. Gruber, and J. Rentzler, "Intra-Day Tests of the Efficiency of the Treasury-Bill Futures Market," *Review of Economics and Statistics*, February 1984, pp. 129-137.

EXHIBIT 9-3: Effect of Weakening and Strengthening of the Basis

BASIS MOVEMENT		EFFECT			
Basis = $P_C - P_F$	Price Movements	Type of Hedge	Type of Basis	Direction of Basis	Return
"Weakens"	P_C increases less or falls more than P_F	Short	$P_C - P_F > 0$ (positive)	Narrows	Negative
			$P_C - P_F < 0$ (negative)	Widens	Negative
		Long	$P_C - P_F > 0$ (positive)	Narrows	Positive
			$P_C - P_F < 0$ (negative)	Widens	Positive
"Strengthens"	P_C increases more or falls less than P_F	Short	$P_C - P_F > 0$ (positive)	Widens	Positive
			$P_C - P_F < 0$ (negative)	Narrows	Positive
		Long	$P_C - P_F > 0$ (positive)	Widens	Negative
			$P_C - P_F < 0$ (negative)	Narrows	Negative

can be deposited in the account to avoid margin calls; moreover, a line of credit may be needed to borrow funds to cover losses. A liquidity management model for margin balances can be used to implement this endeavor. Kolb, Gay, and Hunter[12] show how an adaptation of a cash management model used by corporate finance managers is applicable to liquidity management for margin balances. Such a model determines the probability of a margin call, given an initial margin balance and the variability of futures prices. Alternatively, the manager can assign a desired probability of a margin call and the model shows the required margin balance and/or the length of time before additional funds are needed. Such a model would reduce criticisms of unmanaged cash outflows by the firm's directors.

If marking-to-market timing effects are considered to be an important factor affecting the hedge, then the manager can "tail" the hedge. Tailing adjusts the size of the hedge for marking-to-market effects. See Kawaller and Koch[13] and Kawaller[14] for examples of tailing a hedge position.

MAKING THE HEDGING DECISION

The Advantages and Disadvantages of Hedging with Futures

There are a number of advantages to employing a futures hedge as a tool for risk management:

- Hedging with futures provides a risk management tool that usually reduces the price variability of a cash position significantly; if an unwanted risk exposure in the asset position exists, then hedging is recommended.
- Futures provides an inexpensive and easy-to-use instrument for hedging purposes, especially in comparison with hedging in the cash market.
- Long-term hedges are possible with futures contracts, unlike transactions for most cash forward markets; for example, one can hedge out to three years with T-bond futures and four years with Eurodollar futures but less than one year by using interest rate forward contracts.
- Futures can alter the net effect of the cash position quickly; for example, financial institutions that desire to change their maturity structure can do so almost immediately with futures, while it could take many months to change the maturity structure by solely employing cash transactions. Quick executions also become important in fast-moving markets, such as during the October 1987 adjustments in the stock and bond markets. In these situations futures markets operate and provide continuous trading, whereas making a trade in the cash markets may be difficult or impossible.
- Some hedges are possible only in the futures market (e.g., a NYSE stock index hedge).
- One can avoid an adverse cash market impact due to liquidity problems by hedging with futures when the cash security has a thin market or when there is a large cash position. For example, a dealer in bonds often has difficulty in adequately hedging the firm's

---

12 Robert W. Kolb, Gerald D. Gay, and William C. Hunter, "Liquidity Requirements for Financial Futures Hedges," *Financial Analysts Journal*, Vol. 46, No. 3, May-June 1985, pp. 60-68.

13 Ira Kawaller and Timothy Koch, "Managing Cash Flow Risk in Stock Index Futures: The Tail Hedge," *Journal of Portfolio Management*, Vol 15, No. 1, Fall 1988, pp. 41-44.

14 Ira Kawaller, "Hedging with Futures Contracts: Going the Extra Mile," *Journal of Cash Management*, July-August 1986, pp. 34-36.

inventory position if only the cash market is employed, since the trading of moderate-size cash positions often affects the price of the cash security.

Disadvantages also exist when hedging with futures:

- A cash, forward, or futures hedge offsets the cash position, *whether* the cash price changes in an unfavorable *or* a favorable direction; thus, a short hedge loses money on the futures side if the cash market rises.
- Margin calls occur if the futures market goes in the opposite direction than expected, causing a cash outflow and possibly the need for a cash line of credit. Most importantly, margin calls necessitate an understanding of the objective of the hedge by upper management.
- Accounting treatment of the hedge may differ from the tax or regulatory treatment. Thus, interim futures gains may be taxed, or futures losses may appear on accounting statements, while the changes in the cash position are not considered until the sale of the asset.

SUMMARY AND LOOKING AHEAD

This chapter examined the qualitative aspects of hedging. Examples of various types of hedges were provided and risk management considerations discussed. This material provides a foundation for using futures markets as a hedging tool. Quantitative hedging tools are examined in Chapters 10 through 12, with applications of risk management with futures covered in Part IV.

FOCUS 9-1: The Basics of a Risk Management Program

In order to develop and initiate a risk management program, the potential hedger must have a risk management procedure and a plan to institute a hedging program for the institution. Knowledge concerning which hedging techniques to employ, characteristics of the cash market securities, and specific information on how to set up appropriate hedge positions are critical to a properly executed hedge (and are covered in subsequent parts of this book). However, the procedure and steps of a risk management program are the first items a hedger must consider in preparing for a hedge program.

Risk Management Procedures

The basic steps of a risk management procedure are as follows:

1. **Identify the extent and the nature of the risk exposure.** One determines the relative size of the unhedged risk in relation to the capital of the firm and the total loss potential. Moreover, the balance sheet of a financial institution possesses a different type of risk than does a portfolio of assets, and therefore a different program of action is required. An ability to obtain accurate price forecasts reduces risks and maximizes returns without hedging; however, futures hedging is employed to reduce the risks when accurate forecasts are not available.
2. **Decide on the appropriate objectives for the firm and the hedging program, especially the relevant risk-return trade-off.** Since a hedge affects both the risk and the return of the firm or portfolio, the financial manager must decide whether the return sacrificed to achieve the desired risk posture is acceptable, or whether a partial or no hedge position is more appropriate. Unless the manager knows the objectives of both the firm and the hedging program, actual hedges can provide results contrary to those expected.
3. **Develop a procedure to monitor and measure the risk.** The portfolio manager must be able to determine accurately any changes in the risk posture of the cash position in order to decide whether to hedge the risk and, if so, when.
4. **Determine whether a futures contract exists that can reduce risk, and by how much.** Calculate the relationship between the asset's price movements and the futures' price movements, as discussed in Chapters 10 and 12.
5. **Check for tax and regulatory implications of the hedge.**
6. **Determine the relevant hedge position and set targets and parameters to aid the hedging decision.** Chapters 10 and 12 provide methods for calculating the hedge position. Targets benefit the monitoring process and avoid problems of speculation and concentration of trading power. Parameters help the hedger determine whether the hedge is acting as anticipated.

Focus continues

FOCUS 9-1: Continued

7. **Determine the appropriate futures expiration to employ in the hedge by considering the following factors:**
   - Use the first expiration month that follows the expected termination of the cash market transaction. (This factor is the most important one.)
   - Provide flexibility by choosing a later expiration if the exact closing month is unknown or uncertain.
   - Choose an expiration with sufficient liquidity such that entering and exiting the market does not cause undue price distortions.
   - Determine whether any consistent basis changes occur in the delivery month so that one benefits from these basis movements.

Implementing a Hedging Program

The risk management procedure given above provides an outline of the decisions and information needed to construct a viable hedging decision. However, before starting an active program, the following steps are needed to initiate a hedging program.

1. **Obtain enough knowledge concerning the concepts and strategies of hedging that a successful hedging procedure can be implemented, including organizing a viable plan on paper.** Rushing into a hedging program without sufficient planning or knowledge can be disastrous for the effectiveness of the program. A hedging program needs to be developed *before* it is required.
2. **Obtain the approval of management and the board of directors.** The approval procedure is an educational process, especially for management and board members who have a limited financial background. Convincing them that futures hedging is a conservative technique can be difficult, especially if their general knowledge of futures is based on speculative concepts and the knowledge that futures markets are volatile. Understanding futures markets and how hedging helps the firm is essential to the approval process; if the financial manager is not confident of the hedging techniques and procedures, then the board will be skeptical.
3. **Undertake paper trading or trading on small positions.** "Playing the game" with small stakes is a beneficial approach to understand how the mechanics of the markets work and how futures react to new information in relation to the cash markets. Many hedgers say that paper trading proved to be the most beneficial part of their learning process.
4. **Generate the appropriate and required systems and procedures for internal operations, controls, accounting, and computer systems.** To achieve an effective hedging program on a consistent basis one needs an appropriate internal operations system. Control is needed to make sure that no one person can jeopardize the firm by speculating. Accounting and computer systems can be purchased from consultants who specialize in these areas.

Focus continues

FOCUS 9-1: Continued

---

5. **Obtain a line of credit for daily mark-to-market purposes, and generate links to the exchange floor.** Margin calls require a line of credit or a procedure to wire funds to the firm executing the trades. Potentially large hedging programs should establish a relationship with a floor trader so that fast, accurate transactions and market information are obtained, and so that commissions are minimized.

EXHIBIT 9-4: Primary Risk Management Uses

This exhibit shows the varied risk management uses of futures markets by providing a list of such uses segregated according to type of institution or trader. This list suggests that the time and effort needed to institute a hedging program can be justified by providing the institution with much greater flexibility in financial matters, especially in the control of their risk posture.

Fixed-Income Dealer

1. Sell futures to hedge securities inventory
2. Buy futures to lock in cost of future securities
3. Increase trading flexibility; arbitrage; intramarket spreads

Investor

1. Lock in yields on future cash flows
2. Protect the value of purchased instrument
3. Reduce or lengthen the "interest rate maturity" of a fixed-rate security
4. Create synthetic money market instruments

Banks

1. See uses of a Fixed-Income Dealer and Investor (above)
2. Adjust the interest rate maturity GAP between assets and liabilities
3. Lock in cost of funds or returns on future loans

Savings and Loans

1. See uses of Banks (above)
2. Lock in rates on money market certificates and other funding vehicles
3. Hedge value of mortgage portfolio
4. Hedge value of mortgages to be resold in the market

Exhibit continues

EXHIBIT 9-4: Continued

Security Underwriters

1. Protect value of issue until sold
2. Provide information about expected future rates and values

Insurance Companies

1. See uses of Investors (above)
2. Hedge the outflow of policy loans from rising interest rates

Pension Funds

1. See uses of Investors (above)
2. Use futures to lock in yields on projected cash inflows
3. Short-term protection of long-term investments

Corporate Treasurer

1. Hedge borrowing cost
2. Lock in returns on excess cash
3. If using "shelf registration," same uses as Security Underwriters

Source: "Inside T-Bill Futures," Chicago Mercantile Exchange, p. 12.

Chapter 10

The Naive and Regression Hedging Techniques

A major objective of the hedger is to determine the number of futures contracts (the hedge ratio) that provides the best risk-return trade-off. However, the complexities in obtaining this optimal hedge ratio causes hedgers to calculate the hedge ratio that minimizes the basis risk of the position. Equations are given to show how to calculate the naive, conversion factor, and regression-based hedge ratios to minimize risk.

The most popular technique to determine a hedge ratio is based on regression analysis. The minimum variance hedge ratio is developed from the general portfolio model. Empirical evidence concerning this model is presented for T-bonds, corporate debt, T-bills, currencies, and stock indexes. These results show that the hedging effectiveness of futures is very high in most circumstances.

The last section of the chapter examines the effects of an instability in the hedge ratio over time. In particular, if hedge ratios are highly unstable, then the hedging effectiveness measure obtained from past periods can be an incorrect estimate of the current hedging effectiveness. Appendix 10A presents a risk-return methodology to determine the optimal hedge ratio.

NAIVE HEDGE RATIOS

Figures in Parts I and II show the historical volatility of various financial instruments. These price changes create risk for portfolios of cash assets. Offsetting as much of the change in the cash price as possible is the goal of quantitative techniques of **hedge ratio** management, where a hedge ratio is the ratio of the futures to the cash position that reduces risk. These techniques range from the naive method of finding the ratio of the total values of the cash portfolio to the futures contract to the more sophisticated techniques of employing portfolio/regression analysis and duration. The simpler hedge ratio techniques are discussed in this section, with the remainder of the chapter concentrating on the portfolio/regression method. Chapters 11 and 12 examine the duration method.

What Is a Minimum-Risk Hedge Ratio?

A simplified explanation of a hedge ratio is the ratio of the change in the cash price to the change in the futures price. This definition of "relative price volatility" allows the hedger to determine how many futures contracts must be employed in order to minimize the risk of the combined cash-futures position. We can develop this simplified hedge ratio by assuming that the goal is to offset *completely* the adverse price change from the cash position for any *one* time period. Consequently, the cash price change in combination with the futures price change is zero if the risk is eliminated:

$$\Delta P_C + HR\ \Delta P_F = 0 \qquad\qquad (10\text{-}1)$$

where   HR = the hedge ratio between the futures and cash instruments that forms a
                    one-period perfect hedge to eliminate risk
         ΔP_C = the cash price change per unit for the period
         ΔP_F = the futures price change per unit for the period

Solving for HR, the hedge ratio, we find the value of the ratio that causes a net change of zero for the combined cash and futures position:

$$HR = -[\Delta P_C / \Delta P_F] \qquad\qquad (10\text{-}2)$$

The purpose of determining the hedge ratio is to reduce the basis risk between the cash and futures price changes. The minus sign in Equation (10-2) refers to taking the opposite position in the futures as compared to the cash asset. For example, a futures contract is sold to offset the change in a *long* cash position, creating a short hedge. Often, for convenience, this minus sign is left off the equation for the hedge ratio. Consequently, in the simple world shown above, where one concentrates only on the beginning and ending price of the period, *and* the ending price can be perfectly forecasted, the hedge ratio reflects a simple measure of the relative change in the price of the cash and futures instruments (the "relative volatility").

Equation (10-2) is based on the assumption that the total values of the futures and cash instruments are equal. To adjust for unequal total values, we calculate the number of contracts, N, needed for the hedge position:

$$N = (HR)\ TV_C / V_F \qquad\qquad (10\text{-}3)$$

where   N = the number of futures contracts for the hedge
           TV_C = the total value of the cash position
           V_F = the underlying cash value of one futures contract
         TV_C / V_F = the scale adjustment for the relative size of the cash and
                    futures position

The objective of finding the appropriate hedge ratio and the resultant number of futures contracts is to obtain a futures hedge position that offsets exactly the relative price changes between the cash and futures instruments. For example, for a $300,000 cash bond position where the cash price changes by two points for every futures change of one point, the hedge ratio from Equation (10-2) is –2 and the number of short T-bond futures contracts needed to offset the cash price change is

$$N = -2\ (\$300,000 / \$100,000) = -6$$

We can easily show that the cash and futures positions for this perfect hedge have equal changes in total *value* by comparing the cash and futures positions:

$$(\Delta P_C)\ (TV_C) = (\Delta P_F)\ N\ (V_F) \qquad\qquad (10\text{-}4)$$

For our example,

$$(2)\ \$300,000 = (1)\ (6)\ \$100,000$$

A more realistic situation occurs when one realizes that futures hedges cannot eliminate all risk. Recall the discussion in Chapter 9 concerning basis risk. In particular, hedging allows us to substitute basis risk for the absolute price risk of the cash asset, where basis risk refers to the variability of the cash price minus the futures price. Thus if the change in the basis is less than the change in the cash price, then hedging reduces the risk of a cash-only position. In the above example the change in the basis for the total position is zero, which creates a perfect hedge that *eliminates* risk.

Naive (Traditional) Hedging Techniques

The Naive Methods. Several simple methods exist to determine a hedge ratio and the number of futures contracts needed for a hedge. The first naive method is used exclusively for debt instruments. The hedge ratio is found by taking the ratio of the par value of the cash instrument and dividing by the par value of the futures contract. This is the traditional **one-to-one hedge** ratio method for debt instruments:

$$HR_1 = \text{Par value of each cash instrument/Par value of futures} \qquad (10\text{-}5)$$

$$N_1 = (\text{Total par value of cash/Par value of one cash instrument}) (HR_1) \qquad (10\text{-}6)$$

where HR_1 = the hedge ratio for the first naive method

N_1 = the number of contracts for the first naive method

For example, if the portfolio to be hedged involves $50 million of bonds, each with a $1 million par value, then 500 futures contracts are needed for the hedge [i.e., from Equation (10-5), HR_1 = $1,000,000/ $100,000 par for the T-bond futures = 10, and, from Equation (10-6), N = 50 × 10 = 500]. This method is based on the assumption that equal dollar movements occur between the cash and futures positions for each $100,000 par value of the bond.

An adjustment to the one-to-one debt method, which also provides a naive method for stock and currency hedges, employs the current prices of the cash and futures instruments:[1]

$$HR_2 = \text{Cash price per unit/Futures price per unit} \qquad (10\text{-}7)$$

$$N_2 = (\text{Total cash value/Underlying value of one futures contract}) (HR_2) \qquad (10\text{-}8)$$

The cash and futures prices for debt instruments in Equation (10-7) are calculated as a percentage of par, and par values are used in Equation (10-8) for debt positions. This method is equivalent to taking the ratio of the total *investment* values of the two instruments, whereas the one-to-one debt method in Equations (10-5) and (10-6) employs the total *par* values of the instruments. If the cash and futures prices change in proportion to the level of their prices, then the investment value method is more accurate than the one-to-one debt method.

Practitioners sometimes use a naive one-to-one hedge ratio rather than a more sophisticated method when the cash position is nearly equivalent to the characteristics of the futures contract; more complicated hedges do require more sophisticated methods. Practitioners sometimes prefer the one-to-one approach because the results often are as good as the more sophisticated hedge ratio methods when simple hedges are involved. The empirical results in a later section show that more sophisticated methods create hedge ratios that are often near one when the cash and futures positions are equivalent.

---

1   See Asay and Schirr; Gay and Kolb; and Gay, Kolb, and Chiang. Michael Asay and Gary Schirr, "Determining a Hedge Ratio: Two Simple Approaches," *Market Perspectives: Topics on Options and Financial Futures*, Chicago Mercantile Exchange, Vol. 1, No. 2, May 1983, pp. 1, 5-6. Gerald D. Gay and Robert W. Kolb, "The Management of Interest Rate Risk," *Journal of Portfolio Management*, Vol. 9, No. 2, Winter 1983, pp. 65-70. Gerald D. Gay, Robert W. Kolb, and Raymond Chiang, "Interest Rate Hedging: An Empirical Test of Alternative Strategies," *Journal of Financial Research*, Vol. 6, No. 3, Fall 1983, pp.187-197.

Disadvantages of the Naive Methods. Although the above naive methods are simple to use and often are reasonably accurate for cash positions with characteristics similar to a given futures contract, difficulties exist with these methods for many situations in which the naive methods do not adequately account for changes in the basis of the cash/futures position. These difficulties are as follows:

• Bonds with different maturities and coupons have different relative volatilities. In such a case, the basis risk created by a naive hedge ratio method is much greater than necessary. A similar situation exists when the composition of the cash stock position differs from the futures index.

• T-bill or Eurodollar hedges for cash instruments with maturities other than 90 days need to consider the effect of the *dollar* change on the portfolio rather than just the change in interest rates or basis points. In particular, the following tabulation shows the *dollar* change for both a $1 million cash position with a varying number of days until maturity and a $1 million 90-day futures contract, given a 1% change in interest rates:

Maturity of Cash Instrument	Cash Instrument	Futures Instrument
1 year	$10,000	$2,500
6 months	5,000	2,500
3 months	2,500	2,500
1 month	833	2,500

Thus, if one hedges a six-month cash T-bill with the 90-day T-bill futures contract then a 1% change in interest rates causes a $5,000 change in value of the $1 million six-month cash T-bill, but only a $2,500 change in the 90-day T-bill futures contract. Thus, dollar equivalency rather than equating the interest rate change between the cash and futures positions is relevant in this situation; equating dollar changes necessitates a two-to-one hedge ratio for this six-month cash vs. three-month futures example.

• For crosshedge situations, such as using T-bond futures to hedge a corporate bond position, the relationship between the *risky* corporate debt and the *default-free* Treasury debt is not considered by the naive methods. Similarly, hedging an over-the-counter stock portfolio with the blue-chip MMI futures index creates a significant basis risk due to the different types of market risks.

More sophisticated methods attempt to overcome the naive methods' inability to adjust for basis changes.

Dollar Equivalency Hedge Ratios

A **dollar equivalency hedge** ratio equates the dollar change in the cash instrument to the dollar change in the futures contract. The initial section on "What is a Minimum-Risk Hedge Ratio?" demonstrates the importance of thinking about hedge ratios in terms of dollar equivalency. One can expand upon this concept by determining the factors that affect the relative changes in the futures and cash prices.

The most important of these factors for debt securities are the relative maturities and the relative price volatilities of the cash and futures instruments. Thus, if a bank wishes to hedge a six-month certificate of deposit position with the 90-day Eurodollar futures, then the ratio of the relative maturities of these instruments (180 days/90 days = 2) and the relative volatilities of the two securities (perhaps CDs are 1.5 times as volatile as Eurodollars) are multiplied together to determine that a hedge ratio of three is needed for this dollar equivalency hedge.[2] For longer-term instruments, the duration of the instruments are employed to consider the effect of the relative maturities and volatilities (as discussed in Chapters 11 and 12). Similarly, for stock and currency positions, the relative volatilities of the cash and futures positions are relevant.

In essence, the dollar equivalency method considers the factors needed to equate the futures price change and the cash price change. The difficulty of this method is to measure the appropriate relationships between cash and futures for the period in question. The following methods attempt to measure these relationships.

The Conversion Factor Hedge

A **conversion factor hedge** employs the conversion factor method for long-term debt instruments to determine the appropriate hedge ratio. This method reduces the problem of maturity differences between the cash and futures instruments that exist for the naive methods. Chapter 7 describes ways to use the conversion factor method to determine the invoice value of cash T-bonds/T-notes that are delivered into these futures contracts; namely, the conversion factor method explicitly considers the coupon and maturity of the cash debt instrument in relation to the specifications of the relevant futures contract. Conversion factors also are found in tables provided by the exchanges. The conversion factor hedge is promoted in practitioner literature as being superior to the naive methods.

One determines the conversion factor hedge ratio in the following manner:

$$HR_{CF} = CF \qquad (10\text{-}9)$$

$$N_{CF} = CF \ (\text{Total par value of cash/Par value of one futures}) \qquad (10\text{-}10)$$

where HR_C = the conversion factor hedge ratio

   CF = the conversion factor

   N_{CF} = the number of futures contracts needed for the CF hedge

However, this method also has problems. First, changes in the term structure of interest rates adversely affect this method. Second, a crosshedge risk exists when corporate bonds are hedged. Third, the biases from the conversion factor method, as described in Chapter 7, causes problems.[3] Using the CF method *assumes* that the factors considered by this

---

2   Technically, such a hedge should involve a strip of two sequential futures expirations so that the equivalent six-month period is effectively hedged. If two T-bill or Eurodollar futures contracts with the same expiration are employed to hedge the six-month CD *and* a change in the shape of the term structure occurs (the relative forward rates for the adjacent three-month periods changes), then an uncovered basis risk would exist.

3   Arak and Goodman show why the conversion factor method is biased: (1) the method causes low-coupon, long maturity bonds to appear to be more valuable than high-coupon, short-maturity bonds; (2) the CF method calculates the yield on all bonds to the *call* date, which favors the low coupon bonds; in reality, lower coupon bonds trading at a discount should be valued to *maturity* since at the current level of interest rates these bonds will not be called; and (3) the CF method does not consider the fact that bonds trading at a premium trade at a lower price (have higher yields) than par bonds because investors are not willing to take a capital loss as maturity approaches. The beneficial capital gains tax treatment that existed before 1987 typically caused lower coupon bonds to have higher prices (lower yields) than if the tax effect did not exist; however, this benefit was not significant enough to offset the other biases. Marcelle Arak and Laurie S. Goodman, "How to Calculate Better T-bond Hedge Ratios," *Futures*, February 1986, pp. 56-57.

method accurately represent the relative prices of the different bonds in relation to the futures contract, and that the various bonds have an equal percentage sensitivity to a change in interest rates. In actuality, the CF method incorporates biases and thus futures prices move in relation to the cheapest-to-deliver bond.

THE REGRESSION PROCEDURE

Introduction

The related concepts of diversification and portfolio analysis have been applied to common stocks for decades in order to reduce risk and obtain an optimal risk-return combination, respectively. However, both diversification and portfolio analysis, when applied solely to cash assets, still leave a significant amount of risk in the portfolio. Hedging with futures allows the portfolio manager to remove most of this remaining risk.

Finding a method to determine the best hedge ratio has generated interest in both the academic and practitioner communities. In general, an **"optimal" hedge ratio** means the appropriate ratio of the futures position to the cash position that provides the best risk-return combination for the specific hedger. Figure 10-1 shows the efficient set, labeled CD, that provides the positions with the best available return at each level of risk; other nonoptimal available portfolios are below and to the right of curve CD. Curves I_1, I_2, and I_3 represent the hedger's risk-return trade-off curves; I_1, I_2, and I_3 are called the hedger's indifference curves, since each curve describes which risk-return combinations provide the same utility to the hedger. One wants to be on the highest indifference curve possible, since such a curve maximizes return in relation to risk. Point O shows the optimal combined portfolio of the cash asset and the futures position that *maximizes* the total utility of the hedger, since point O is the tangency of the highest indifference curve I_2 with the efficient set.

The optimal risk-return hedge ratio concept has been refined to identify a **minimum variance hedge ratio.** The reasons for using the minimum-variance ratio rather than an optimal ratio are that it is easier to derive, easier to understand because one variable (risk) rather than two variables (risk and return) are employed, determined empirically with minimal effort, does not require indifference curves for the hedger, and corresponds to the risk minimization concept often associated with hedging. Figure 10-1 denotes the minimum variance hedge ratio as b*. Appendix 10A discusses a closed-form equation to obtain an optimal risk-return hedge ratio.

The Minimum Variance Hedge Ratio

Ederington[4] and Johnson[5] employ portfolio theory to derive the mathematical model that defines the minimum-variance hedge ratio (HR) as the proportion of the futures to the cash position that minimizes the net price change risk. The variance of the price changes of the

---

4   L. H. Ederington, "The Hedging Performance of the New Futures Markets," *Journal of Finance*, Vol. 34, No. 1, March 1979, pp. 157-170.

5   L. L. Johnson, "The Theory of Hedging and Speculation in Commodity Futures," *Review of Economic Studies*, Vol. 27, No. 3, 1960, pp. 139-151.

FIGURE 10-1: Portfolio Risk-Return Curve

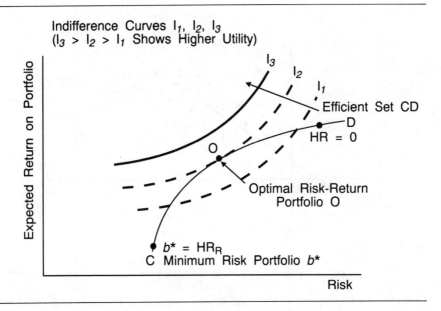

hedged position measures the price change risk. Although percentage price changes (rates of return) are advocated by some, most practitioners use price changes. The use of price changes, percentage price changes, or price levels is examined in a later section.

The minimum-variance hedge ratio is found by solving the following equation:

$$b^* = HR_R = \rho_{C,F} \, \sigma_C/\sigma_F \qquad (10\text{-}11)$$

where $b^* = HR_R =$ the minimum-risk hedge ratio

σ_C and $\sigma_F = \sigma(\Delta P_C)$ and $\sigma(\Delta P_F) =$ the standard deviations of the cash and futures price changes, respectively

$\rho_{C,F} = \rho(\Delta P_C, \Delta P_F) =$ the correlation between the cash and futures price changes

Note that the HR represented in Equation (10-11) is the product of the correlation between the cash and futures price changes *and* the relative volatility of the cash and futures instruments. These measures are determined by using all of the observations in a given period (e.g. weekly data for the last six months).

Figure 10-2 also explains the minimum-variance hedge ratio concept. This figure illustrates the regression line obtained by minimizing the sum of the squared deviations from the line; the slope of this regression line, $\Delta P_C/\Delta P_F = b^*$, is the hedge ratio. [Compare this equation to Equation (10-2).] Deviations from the regression line are called residuals, which constitute the basis risk that is not hedged.

The following section interprets the minimum-variance hedge ratio. Then empirical evidence concerning the size of the hedge ratio and the effectiveness of this ratio to reduce

---

FIGURE 10-2: Illustrating the Regression Hedge Ratio Approach

---

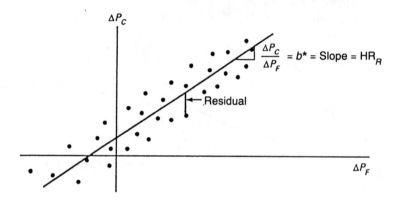

$$\Delta P_C / \Delta P_F = b^* = slope$$

---

price change variability will be examined. Finally, various factors affecting hedge ratios will be discussed, including what problems to avoid when analyzing these ratios.[6]

Interpreting the Minimum Variance Hedge Ratio and the Hedging Effectiveness

The Hedge Ratio. The hedge ratio defined in Equation (10-11) determines the minimum-risk hedge position. Thus, Equation (10-11) is equivalent to point $b^* = HR_R$ in Figure 10-1. Alternatively, if one wishes to maximize expected return, then using $HR = 0$ is appropriate, which is at the top of curve CD. The points between $HR = 0$ and $HR_R = b^*$ provide different risk-return combinations associated with varying degrees of risk. Here we concentrate on the minimum-risk position because of its widespread use and ease of calculation.

Equation (10-11) shows that the size of the minimum variance hedge ratio depends upon two factors: the correlation between the cash and futures price changes and the relative volatility of the cash and futures price changes. The minimum-variance hedge ratio does not have to be near one, unlike the one-to-one naive hedge ratio. In fact, if the

---

6 Gay and Kolb, ibid., provide a simple comparison of some of the methods discussed in this chapter, as well as discussing the factors affecting their effectiveness. Clayton and Navratil, and Pitts critique the Gay and Kolb article. These criticisms note that the Gay and Kolb duration example employs perfect information, whereas the portfolio (regression) method assumes inferior information in comparison to what was available when the regression hedge ratio was determined. Ronnie J. Clayton and Frank J. Navratil, "The Management of Interest Rate Risk: Comment," *Journal of Portfolio Management*, Vol. 11, No. 4, Summer 1985, pp. 64-66. Mark Pitts, "The Management of Interest Rate Risk: Comment," *Journal of Portfolio Management*, Vol. 11, No. 4, Summer 1985, pp. 67-69.

EXAMPLE 10-1: Hedge Ratio and Hedging Effectiveness Calculations

Date	S&P 500 Futures	S&P 100 Cash Index	ΔP_F	ΔP_C	$(\Delta P_F)^2$	$(\Delta P_C)^2$	$(\Delta P_F)(\Delta P_C)$
01/05	328.60	312.48					
01/12	348.20	325.09	19.60	12.61	384.16	159.01	247.16
01/20	336.35	319.99	-11.85	-5.10	140.42	26.01	60.44
01/27	328.60	312.48	-7.75	-7.51	60.06	56.40	58.20
02/06	334.25	308.01	5.65	-4.47	31.92	19.98	-25.26
02/13	336.45	310.58	2.20	2.57	4.84	6.60	5.65
02/21	333.30	307.45	-3.15	-3.13	9.92	9.80	9.86
02/28	336.70	312.48	3.40	5.03	11.56	25.30	17.10
03/07	340.90	316.64	4.20	4.16	17.64	17.31	17.47
03/14	341.50	317.33	0.60	0.69	0.36	0.48	0.41
03/21	342.00	321.08	0.50	3.75	0.25	14.06	1.87
03/28	345.90	323.17	3.90	2.09	15.21	4.37	8.15
04/04	343.10	321.29	-2.80	-1.88	7.84	3.53	5.26
04/11	345.20	322.51	2.10	1.22	4.41	1.49	2.56
04/19	339.60	320.45	-5.60	-2.06	31.36	4.24	11.54
04/26	335.25	315.82	-4.35	-4.63	18.92	21.44	20.14
Sum of column			6.65	3.34	738.8825	370.0214	440.568
Sum squared			44.2225	11.1556			

$$b* = \frac{\Sigma \Delta P_F \Delta P_C - (\Sigma \Delta P_F \, \Sigma \Delta P_C)/(N - 1)}{\Sigma \Delta P_F^{\,2} - (\Sigma \Delta P_F)^2/(N - 1)}$$

$$b* = \frac{440.57 - (6.62)(3.34)/14}{738.88 - 44.22/14}$$

$$= .597$$

$$R^2 = \frac{[\Sigma \Delta P_F \Delta P_C - (\Sigma \Delta P_F \, \Sigma \Delta P_C)/(N - 1)]^2}{[\Sigma \Delta P_F^{\,2} - (\Sigma \Delta P_F)^2/(N - 1)] \, [\Sigma \Delta P_C^{\,2} - (\Sigma \Delta P_C)^2/(N - 1)]}$$

$$R^2 = \frac{[440.57 - (6.65)(3.34)/14]^2}{[738.88 - 44.22/14] \, [370.02 - 11.16/14]}$$

$$= .709$$

standard deviations of the cash and futures price changes are nearly equivalent, then the hedge ratio is *less* than one, since the correlation is always less than one. Thus, in addition to the relative volatility of the cash and futures instruments affecting the hedge ratio, the *association* (correlation) between the cash and futures price changes is critical in formulating the appropriate minimum-variance hedge ratio.

The importance of the correlation coefficient can be shown by examining the extreme situations. At one extreme the hedger may own the same cash asset that is driving the futures price; in this case, the hedge ratio is near one. At the other extreme, if one calculates a hedge ratio for two instruments that have a low correlation, then the hedge ratio will be near zero. For example, attempting to hedge the Bolivian bolivar with Japanese yen futures produces a hedge ratio near zero, since the correlation is close to zero.

Hedging Effectiveness. Equation (10-11) is equivalent to the equation for the slope of the regression line between changes in the futures price (the independent variable) and changes in the cash price (the dependent variable). This relationship conveniently leads to a measure for the minimum variance **hedging effectiveness** of the model, e*, where the hedging effectiveness measures the proportion of the variability of the cash price changes that can be offset by the futures price changes. Based on our definition, hedging effectiveness is measured by the coefficient of determination, R^2, which is the measure of fit of the regression equation

$$
\begin{aligned}
e* &= [\text{var}(\Delta P_C) - \text{var}(\Delta H)]/\text{var}(\Delta P_C) \\
&= 1 - [\text{var}(\Delta H)/\text{var}(\Delta P_C)] \\
&= 1 - [\text{basis risk/cash asset risk}] \\
&= R^2
\end{aligned}
\tag{10-12}
$$

where   e* =   the hedging effectiveness
        var =   variance
        ΔH =   change in value of the net hedged position with futures (i.e., the change in the basis)

Interpretation of R^2 is straightforward. If a regression analysis determines that $R^2 = .85$, then a futures hedge eliminates 85% of the variability in the cash price changes. Note that Equation (10-12) determines the ratio of the basis risk from the hedge to the total cash asset price risk; 1.0 minus this remaining basis risk ratio equals the hedging effectiveness.[7]

R^2 determines the **ex-post** hedging effectiveness when the minimum variance hedge ratio, $b* = HR_R$, is employed. When the same cash and futures instrument are used, then the hedging effectiveness is typically large. However, hedging effectiveness is often a low number for cross hedges with nonsimilar commodities. Thus, the minimum-variance hedge ratio can be unstable over time for crosshedges. This instability is discussed shortly.

---

7   The total dollar variance created by employing the minimum variance hedge ratio is:
$$\sigma_{b*}^2 = X_C^2 \, \sigma_C^2 \, [1 - \rho_{C,F}^2]$$

where σ_{b*}^2 = total dollar variance when the minimum variance hedge ratio is used
        X_C = the total amount of the cash holdings

For hedges with a large coefficient of determination ρ^2, it is obvious that the variance of the hedged position is only a fraction of the variance of the cash positon. We also can show that the hedging effectiveness can be measured by the variability of the residual errors terms (the basis risk) divided by the variability of the total cash position; that is,
$$e^* = [X_C^2 \, \sigma_C^2 - \sigma_{b*}^2] \, / \, X_C^2 \, \sigma_C^2 = \rho_{C,F}^2$$

The Number of Futures Contracts. In the initial section of this chapter we derived a general formulation for the total number of futures contracts needed for a hedge, based on the concept of wanting to offset the total change in value of the cash position with the total change in the futures short position—that is, Equations (10-2) and (10-3). We found that the number of futures contacts needed for the hedge is

$$N = [-\Delta P_C/\Delta P_F]/[TV_C/V_F] \tag{10-13}$$

where N = the number of futures contracts

TV_C = total cash value being hedged (par value for debt instruments)

V_F = the underlying futures value per contract (par value for debt)

TV_C/V_F = the scale adjustment for the relative size of the cash and futures positions

Since the portfolio/regression hedge ratio finds the *average* $\Delta P_C/\Delta P_F = b^* = HR_R$, then

$$N_R = HR_R \,[TV_C/V_F] \tag{10-14}$$

where HR_R = the hedge ratio measuring the relative volatility of the cash and futures prices

Calculating the Hedge Ratio and Hedging Effectiveness from Raw Data

Since the hedge ratio is the slope of the regression line and the hedging effectiveness is the R^2 value from the regression, the standard regression technique is used to find these values when only the raw data are available. Equations (10-15) and (10-16) are the standard equations from regression analysis that are used to calculate the b^* and e^* values, based on the change in price of the cash and futures data. The b^* and e^* values can be calculated from Equations (10-15) and (10-16) with a calculator, the correlation and standard deviations can be determined from the data so that Equations (10-11) and (10-12) can be used, or a spreadsheet program can be employed to calculate b^* and e^* directly. Example 10-1 provides an example of how to employ the following equations to determine b^* and e^*.

$$b* = \frac{\Sigma \,\Delta P_F \,\Delta P_C - (\Sigma \,\Delta P_F \,\Sigma \,\Delta P_C)/(N-1)}{\Sigma \,\Delta P_F^{\,2} - (\Sigma \,\Delta P_F)^2/(N-1)} \tag{10-15}$$

$$e* = R^2 = \frac{[\Sigma \,\Delta P_F \,\Delta P_C - (\Sigma \,\Delta P_F \,\Sigma \,\Delta P_C)/(N-1)]^2}{[\Sigma \,\Delta P_F^{\,2} - (\Sigma \,\Delta P_F)^2/(N-1)]\,[\Sigma \,\Delta P_C^{\,2} - (\Sigma \,\Delta P_C)^2/(N-1)]} \tag{10-16}$$

where N = the number of observations.

THE EVIDENCE ON HEDGING EFFECTIVENESS AND HEDGE RATIOS

During the 1980s a significant number of articles and research reports were written on the hedging effectiveness and minimum-variance hedge ratios for various cash positions. Most of these studies concentrated on financial futures. These investigations examined the relative size of the hedging effectiveness value, whether the hedge ratio varied from one, how these factors changed as the size of the observation period changed or as the nearby versus deferred futures expirations were employed, and the behavior of b^* and e^* for crosshedges. The studies employed here examine specific issues of interest concerning hedge ratio determination and also provide evidence for specific instruments. Other hedge ratio studies can be found in the literature.

Treasury Bonds

Hegde[8] determines the hedging effectiveness and hedge ratios for a number of different instruments. Table 10-1 shows Hegde's results for the T-bond and T-note hedges using T-bond futures. The hedging effectiveness values of these hedges shown in Panel A range from .59 to .97 for the T-bonds and from .36 to .82 for the T-notes. The effectiveness ratios at or above .79 show that a large percentage of the price variability can be hedged; in fact, 21 of the 24 bond positions with maturities of 15 years or greater have effectiveness values of at least .79. The worst hedging effectiveness values for these instruments are related to the change in the shape of the term structure during this period and the periodic substitution of new cash bonds. Problems with the relative timing of the cash and futures quotes also may have contributed to the poorer results. In addition, Table 10-1 shows that T-notes have a much higher effectiveness value for the two-week intervals than for the one-week intervals. These results are typical in that hedges with longer observation periods typically possess higher effectiveness values.

The T-bond hedge ratios shown in Panel B of Table 10-1 are below one for the first period of the analysis and above one for the second period; however, all but one of the T-bond hedge ratios are insignificantly different from one. Six of the eight T-notes ratios *are* significantly different from one, because the maturities of the T-bond futures and T-note cash instruments are substantially different.

The results in Table 10-1 also show that the hedging effectiveness values improve from period I to period II. Hegde discusses how a greater volatility of prices causes a higher volume of trading, which in turn makes the market more liquid. Greater liquidity causes gains in operational efficiency and strengthens the relationship between the cash and futures market. Since period II had a greater volatility of interest rates, larger values for hedging effectiveness should follow. The results in Table 10-1 bear out this hypothesis.

Corporate Debt

Although corporate bonds are an important security, the corporate debt futures instrument never becomes a liquid contract. Thus, one must use T-bond or T-note futures to hedge corporate debt issues. Hill and Schneeweis[9] employ T-bond futures to hedge corporate bond *indexes* in order to examine the resultant hedging effectiveness and the size of the minimum-variance hedge ratios. Table 10-2 shows their results for two-week hedges, using both the near-term futures contract and the Merrill Lynch bond indexes, with different bond coupon levels and for two time periods in the late 1970s.[10] The hedging effectiveness results shown in Table 10-2 are very high, with all but one R^2 value being above 73%. In addition, the values for the more volatile 1979 period are higher than for the earlier period.

---

8 Shantaram P. Hegde, "The Impact of Interest Rate Level and Volatility on the Performance of Interest Rate Hedges," *The Journal of Futures Markets*, Vol. 2, No. 4, Winter 1982, pp. 341-356.

9 Joanne Hill and Thomas Schneeweis, "Risk Reduction Potential of Financial Futures for Corporate Bond Positions," in *Interest Rate Futures: Concepts and Issues*, edited by Gerald D. Gay and Robert W. Kolb, Robert F. Dame Inc., 1982.

10 The article includes results for both time periods combined into one data set, for three other futures expirations, for values for the means and standard deviations, and for mortgage futures. These results are comparable to the ones presented here.

TABLE 10-1: T-bond Hedge Results

Panel A. Hedging Effectiveness (e* = R²)

Instrument	Cash Maturity (Yrs.)	Futures Expiration (Mo.)	One-Week Hedge[a]		Two-Week Hedge[a]	
			I	II	I	II
T-bond	15	6-9	.735	.923	.586	.955
		21-24	.700	.878	.860	.972
T-bond	24	6-9	.832	.919	.860	.972
		21-24	.790	.893	.846	.889
T-note	5	6-9	.358	.426	.562	.820
		21-24	.315	.357	.551	.772
S&P LT Govt.	15	6-9	.829	.904	.867	.962
Index		21-24	.793	.881	.860	.870

Panel B. Hedge Ratios (b* = HR_R)

Instrument	Cash Maturity (Yrs.)	Futures Expiration (Mo.)	One-Week Hedge[a]		Two-Week Hedge[a]	
			I	II	I	II
T-bond	15	6-9	.964	1.057	.943	1.199
		21-24	1.023	1.082	1.039	1.275
T-bond	24	6-9	.840	1.072	.887	1.032
		21-24	.891	1.110	.969	1.108
T-note	5	6-9	.395	.626	.466	.910
		21-24	.419	.601	.508	.965
S&P LT Govt.	15	6-9	.517	.668	.531	.652
Index		21-24	.551	.692	.583	.677

[a] Period I is from January to September 1979; period II is from October 1979 to June 1980.

Source: Shantaram P. Hegde, "The Impact of Interest Rate Level and Volatility on the Performance of Interest Rate Hedges," The Journal of Futures Markets, Vol. 2, No. 4, Winter 1982, pp. 341-356.

TABLE 10-2: Treasury/Corporate Bond Hedging Results

Merrill Lynch Index[a]	8/1977 – 1978[b]		1979	
Coupon Level	$e^* = R^2$	$b^* = HR_R$	$e^* = R^2$	$b^* = HR_R$
High-Quality Corporate				
6 %–7.99 %	.849	1.05	.919	1.49
8 %–9.99 %	.829	1.01	.982	1.58
Medium-Quality Corporate				
6 %–7.99 %	.760	0.73	.765	1.19
8 %–9.99 %	.736	0.85	.975	1.64
High-Quality Utility				
4 %–5.99 %	.563	1.24	.904	1.53
6 %–7.99 %	.875	1.27	.841	1.28
8 %–9.99 %	.846	1.00	.824	1.25
Medium-Quality Utility				
6 %–7.99 %	.761	1.22	.767	1.39
8 %–9.99 %	.786	1.26	.675	1.28
10 %–11.99 %	.741	1.20	.775	1.27

[a] Merrill Lynch High-Quality includes ratings AAA and AA; Medium-Quality includes ratings A and BAA.
[b] Number of observations: 1977-78 (20); 1979 (15).

Source: Abstracted from Joanne Hill and Thomas Schneeweis, "Risk Reduction Potential of Financial Futures for Corporate Bond Positions," in *Interest Rate Futures: Concepts and Issues*, edited by Gerald D. Gay and Robert W. Kolb, Robert F. Dame Inc., 1982.

Hill and Schneeweis[11] examine hedging results for two-week hedges with *individual* corporate issues. These hedging effectiveness results are much worse than for the indexes of bonds reported in Table 10-2. The R^2 values for individual bond hedges range from 2% to 25%, with most of the effectiveness measures being below 12%. The major reason for these poor results seems to be the risk characteristics of the individual bonds. This type of risk *cannot* be hedged with a T-bond futures contract.[12]

11 Joanne Hill and Thomas Schneeweis, "The Use of Interest Rate Futures in Corporate Financing and Corporate Security Investments," *Proceedings of the International Futures Trading Seminar*, Vol. 7, 1980, pp. 72-93.

12 This result corresponds to McEnally's findings regarding individual cash bonds discussed in Chapter 6, where up to 50 percent of the variability of individual bond prices were associated with the specific bond's characteristics. Moreover, the use of GNMA futures also seems to affect the results adversely, since a comparison of the GNMA futures hedges for the Merrill Lynch indexes in this article with the equivalent indexes for T-bond future hedges in Hill and Schneeweis, ibid. "Risk Reduction...", shows a decline of 25% to 30% (and sometimes much more) in the hedging effectiveness measures. In addition, timing differences between the individual corporate issues that do not trade frequently and the futures prices also would distort the results.

Kuberek and Pefley[13] provide additional corporate hedging results with T-bond futures by employing monthly hedges with the first six T-bond futures expirations. Figure 10-3 shows that the hedging effectiveness for these hedges is higher than for the previous studies. This figure also shows that A rated bonds lose about 6% for the effectiveness values as compared to the AAA-AA bonds, as would be expected given their higher default risk. In addition, the hedging effectiveness decreases as one moves from the nearby contracts to the more distant deferred contracts. Kuberek and Pefley use a more general regression procedure to adjust data for differing variances, increasing the precision of their results.

T-Bills

Ederington's article[14] is credited as the catalyst that initiated the use of regression studies to determine the hedge ratio and hedging effectiveness for various futures markets. After Ederington derives the hedging model from the two-asset portfolio model, he empirically analyzes the hedging results for 90-day T-bills, GNMAs, wheat, and corn. The hedging effectiveness measures for these contracts are mostly above 65% for both the two-week and

---

FIGURE 10-3: Corporate Bond Hedging Effectiveness

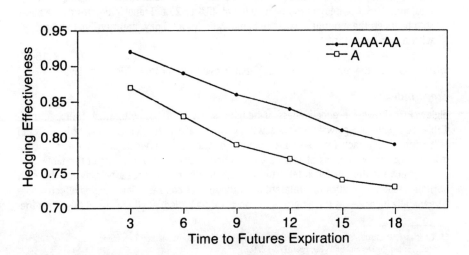

---

13 Robert C. Kuberek and Norman G. Pefley, "Hedging Corporate Debt with U.S. Treasury Bond Futures," *The Journal of Futures Markets*, Vol. 3, No. 4, Winter 1983, pp. 345-353.

14 Ederington, ibid.

four-week hedges for all the markets except T-bills; the T-bill contract have R^2 values ranging from 27% to 14% for the two-week hedges and from 74% to 37% for the four-week hedges. Franckle[15] discovers two problems with the T-bill hedging results determined by Ederington; namely,

- Ederington unknowingly employed a weekly index of daily values for the cash T-bill data, which smoothes out the daily fluctuations for the cash T-bill data, creating a lower R^2 value than justified. Thus, the use of smoothed data via the weekly averages conceals much of the variation in the cash prices. Once this error is corrected (in conjunction with one incorrect data point in the original data) the two-week nearby hedge improves from a 27% effectiveness value to a 68% value.[16]

- Ederington did not adjust the hedges to consider the declining maturity of the cash T-bills. Thus, a 90-day cash T-bill becomes a 76-day T-bill after two weeks have elapsed; similarly, after four weeks a 90-day bill becomes a 62-day T-bill. Treasury bills that have a shorter maturity also have less variability in price and thus have an imperfect correlation with the 90-day futures contract. This declining maturity affects the hedging effectiveness of the results: in one of the four cases R^2 decreases by 10% after the correct adjustment, but it decreases by less than 2% in the other cases.[17] More important, the maturity adjustment affects the size of the minimum-variance hedge ratio. Franckle finds that adjusting for the maturity effect with corrected data causes a decrease in the minimum variance hedge ratio by a factor of 20% to 25%. Franckle derives the relationship between the minimum-variance hedge ratio for a 90-day maturity T-bill and a T-bill with n days to maturity:

$$_nb^* = [n/90] \, _{90}b^* \qquad (10\text{-}17)$$

where $_nb^*$ = the minimum variance T-bill hedge ratio for maturities of n days

Stock Indexes

Figlewski[18] shows the effectiveness of hedging stock portfolios with stock index futures. Table 10-3 shows Figlewski's results with various cash portfolios and the S&P 500 and NYSE futures contracts for observation periods of one day, one week, and two weeks. Data from the last seven months of 1982 are employed to generate the results in the table. The hedge ratios for the portfolios tend to be substantially below one, especially for the cash portfolios that are significantly different from the futures contract. The hedging effectiveness e^* generally increases as the length of the observation period lengthens. Note that Over-the-

15 Charles T. Franckle, "The Hedging Performance of the New Futures Market: Comment," *Journal of Finance*, Vol. 35, No. 5, December 1980, pp. 1272-1279.

16 The nearby four-week hedge did not improve. Ederington's results showed an R^2 value of 74% for this hedge. This high value can be related to the variability of the cash rates for the time period, which overwhelmed the negative effect of the smoothed index numbers. The R^2 values for the deferred contact in Ederington's analysis was much smaller for the four-week hedges; however, Franckle only examines the nearby contact effects.

17 The decline in hedging effectiveness due to declining maturity must be tempered by the fact that the shorter maturity positions have less variability overall. Thus, the hedges for the T-bill positions with declining maturities had 15% to 42% less variability overall than the constant maturity positions, even though the former had somewhat lower R^2 values.

18 Stephen Figlewski, "Hedging with Stock Index Futures: Theory and Application in a New Market," *The Journal of Futures Markets*, Vol. 5, No. 2, Summer 1985, pp. 183-200.

TABLE 10-3: Stock Index Hedging Results

Cash Portfolio	Unhedged	Futures	Portfolio Beta	One Day b*	One Day e*	One Week b*	One Week e*	Two Weeks b*	Two Weeks e*
S&P 500	24.2	S&P 500	1.00	0.65	0.77	0.85	0.95	0.85	0.96
		NYSE	0.99	0.61	0.78	0.85	0.93	0.84	0.95
NYSE	23.2	S&P 500	1.00	0.60	0.75	0.80	0.94	0.82	0.95
		NYSE	0.99	0.56	0.75	0.81	0.91	0.82	0.95
AMEX	23.2	S&P 500	1.33	0.41	0.45	0.69	0.70	0.81	0.83
		NYSE	1.36	0.37	0.41	0.68	0.64	0.82	0.85
NASDAQ	19.6	S&P 500	0.84	0.29	0.33	0.57	0.66	0.57	0.66
OTC		NYSE	0.87	0.25	0.28	0.57	0.62	0.58	0.71
DOW 30	24.1	S&P 500	0.85	0.67	0.76	0.83	0.92	0.85	0.95
		NYSE	0.83	0.64	0.79	0.84	0.92	0.85	0.95

Source: Adapted from Stephen Figlewski, "Hedging with Stock Index Futures: Theory and Application in a New Market," *The Journal of Futures Markets*, Vol. 5, No. 2, Summer 1985, pp. 183-200.

Counter and American Stock Exchange portfolios are not effectively hedged with these futures contracts for the one-day and one-week observation periods. However, the other hedge relationships do have high R^2 values.

Currency Futures

Most currency futures studies employ data from the 1970s to examine hedging effectiveness. Daigler[19] shows that the more recent volatility in currencies can be hedged with currency futures, as long as a futures contract exists in that currency's denomination. Table 10-4 provides a summary of the hedging results for the Canadian dollar, the Japanese yen, the German mark, and the British pound. Six-month periods from 1980 through 1986, with weekly observation periods, are used in the analysis. The hedge ratios are near one and the hedging effectiveness measures are 83% for the Canadian dollar and over 92% for the other currencies.

Table 10-5 shows whether other currencies can be hedged with currency futures. The same time period and weekly observation length are employed here as in Table 10-4. The British pound futures crosshedging results with other European currencies are relatively low, with all of the cross-currency hedging effectiveness values being below 50%. The results for the non-European countries are even worse, with *none* of the hedging effectiveness values above 25%. The German mark futures crosshedging results with the stronger European currencies (the Belgian franc, the French franc, the Italian lira, and the Netherlands guilder) averages above 75% for each currency. The results for Greece and Spain are less impressive, but still average above 50%. Note that these results suggest that the mark futures is an excellent hedging tool for most of the European currencies that do not have futures contracts. The crosshedging results for the non-European countries are poor, with the hedging effectiveness results below 25% and often below 10%.

TABLE 10-4: Average Biweekly Currency Hedging Results

Country	b*	e*
Canada	0.892	0.831
Germany	0.985	0.941
Japan	0.940	0.928
U.K.	0.979	0.934

Source: Robert T. Daigler, "Hedge Ratio Instability for Currency Futures," working paper, Florida International University, 1991.

---

19 Robert T. Daigler, "Cross Currency Hedging Results: Implications for EEC Unification and LDC Trade," working paper, Florida International University, 1990. Robert T. Daigler, "Hedge Ratio Instability for Currency Futures," working paper, Florida International University, 1991.

TABLE 10-5: Average Cross Currency Hedging Results: 1980-86

	British Pound		German Mark	
	b*	e*	b*	e*
European Countries				
Belgium	0.612	0.383	0.890	0.777
France	0.665	0.422	0.919	0.832
Greece	0.500	0.275	0.643	0.513
Italy	0.575	0.373	0.831	0.802
Netherlands	0.648	0.435	0.945	0.911
Spain	0.632	0.459	0.714	0.673
Other Countries				
Australia	0.223	0.215	0.239	0.256
Argentina	−0.039	0.067	0.000	0.043
Brazil	0.034	0.030	0.020	0.025
Canada	0.152	0.160	0.138	0.185
Hong Kong	0.087	0.086	0.153	0.115
Israel	0.044	0.042	0.126	0.042
Mexico	0.171	0.048	0.133	0.032
Singapore	0.202	0.221	0.212	0.275
South Africa	0.254	0.219	0.282	0.215
Taiwan	0.035	0.035	0.023	0.025
Uruguay	−0.160	0.058	−0.201	0.075

Source: Robert T. Daigler, "Hedge Ratio Instability for Currency Futures," working paper, Florida International University, 1991.

Conclusions Concerning the Empirical Evidence

The preceding studies concerning the regression method for determining hedge ratios and hedging effectiveness, in conjunction with other studies on these topics, provide the following conclusions:

- When the cash asset has characteristics that are nearly identical to the cash underlying the futures contract then $R^2 = e*$ is large (often more than 90%) and the hedge ratio is near one.
- The hedging effectiveness improves when the cash instrument is more volatile.
- Longer observation periods (e.g., when two-week periods are used) provide larger hedging effectiveness values.
- Crosshedge results (e.g. using currency futures) provide very low $R^2 = e*$ values when the characteristics of the cash and futures instruments differ.

An important consideration for all of the previous studies is that *historical* data are employed to determine the hedge ratios and hedging effectiveness measures. If these results are used to determine the appropriate hedge ratios and effectiveness for *future* time periods, then the hedger is assuming that the relationships are stable over time. A later section examines the stability of hedge ratios over time.

CONSIDERATIONS IN DETERMINING A HEDGE RATIO

This section examines application considerations when employing the minimum-variance hedge ratio concept. These considerations include the use of price changes instead of price levels, the characteristics of the hedge period and nature of the data, and problems with reported cash data. These factors are important since a correct statistical analysis is needed in order to ensure that the results of the investigation are valid.

Data Considerations

Using Price Changes, Percentage Changes, or Price Levels. Practitioners typically employ price *changes* to implement the regression procedure so as to obtain the minimum-variance hedge ratio. This is especially true when hedge ratios for long-term debt futures are determined, since long-term debt issues are priced in terms of the *percentage* of par value. Using price changes corresponds to the intention of equating the *dollar* change in the cash asset to the *dollar* change in the futures contract, as shown earlier in this chapter. Percentage price changes are advocated by some academicians in order to reduce the effect of a nonconstant variance on the regression procedure. Such an adjustment is beneficial when large price changes occur for the data in question. However, using percentages equates the *percentage* changes between the cash and futures positions, not the dollar changes. An adjustment to the hedge ratio b* must be made to convert a hedge ratio that minimizes net percentage changes to one that minimizes net dollar changes. Hill and Schneeweis[20] find that price changes and percentage changes provide comparable R^2 values.[21]

Using price *levels* instead of changes or percentage changes incorporates **serial correlation** into the results; that is, the assumption of no correlation in sequential time series data for the regression model is violated. Serial correlation causes the R^2 value that measures the hedging effectiveness to be much larger than its true value, and the slope coefficient of the regression (the hedge ratio) to be erratic from one sample to another. For example, when Dale[22] employed price *levels* to examine the hedge results for currency futures, he obtained R^2 values of 98% and 99%. Hill and Schneeweis[23] find that the true values are closer to 70% to 80%.

20 Hill and Schneeweis, ibid., "The Use of Interest Rate Futures . . ."

21 Using percentage changes is equivalent to using rates of return. However, the rate-of-return terminology is seldom used with futures because of the implication that an "investment of funds" is needed for the futures position, which is not the case. One advantage to using the rate of return terminology is that the mean-variance efficient set used for cash only portfolio analysis, as developed earlier in this chapter, employs rates of return.

22 Charles Dale, "The Hedging Effectiveness of Currency Futures Markets," *The Journal of Futures Markets*, Vol. 1, No. 1, Spring 1981, pp. 77-88.

23 Joanne Hill and Thomas Schneeweis, "The Hedging Effectiveness of Foreign Currency Futures," *Journal of Financial Research*, Vol. 5, No. 1, Spring 1982, pp. 95-104. Joanne Hill and Thomas Schneeweis, "A Note on the Hedging Effectiveness of Foreign Currency Futures," *The Journal of Futures Markets*, Vol. 1, No. 4, Winter 1981, pp. 659-664.

The Number of Observations. Too few observations, especially if there are outliers in the data, typically cause difficulties in obtaining a true estimate of the hedge ratio. The difficulty of this data problem is that conclusions are obtained based on an inadequate sample size, and perhaps an inappropriate sample. The hedger wants to determine a hedge ratio that is valid for all time periods, not merely to fit a specific set of historical data. Theoretically, a larger number of observations reduces any inaccurate estimate of the hedge ratio. Statistically speaking, 30 observations are typically the norm used to obtain a reasonable estimate of the population hedge ratio. Although fewer observations are acceptable, a small number of observations (e.g., ten) often causes instability in the hedge ratio and a less accurate hedging effectiveness value. The question of unstable hedge ratios over time will be examined shortly.

The Length of the Time Intervals. The length of the intervals for the observations in the hedge period affects the hedge ratio and the hedging effectiveness. It is generally accepted that employing a one-day interval for each observation provides relatively poor hedging effectiveness. In fact, empirical studies often avoid one-week hedge ratios for the same reason, although such hedge lengths are used by practitioners. Two- and four-week hedge intervals are common in hedging studies, although one must be careful of the effect of convergence on the results as the interval length approaches one month or longer. Moreover, these longer time intervals require the use of several futures contract expirations to obtain a sufficient number of observations for the sample period.

The Normality of the Data. The regression procedure is based on the assumption that the error terms form a normal distribution. Although small deviations from normality are not critical for the regression procedure, a large number of observations beyond two and three deviations from the mean (or one very *large* deviation such as the October 19, 1987 crash value) would create serious problems for the validity of the regression hedge ratio procedure. One way to reduce the effect of larger error terms on the hedge ratio and hedging effectiveness measures is to employ absolute-value regression analysis. Although this method is not popular, it does avoid the problem created by the typical least-squares regression of squaring each deviation from the regression line.[24]

Using Historical Data

One must take care in the preparation and use of historical data for hedge ratio analysis. A major consideration is whether the *reported* cash data provides an appropriate value for the true cash price. In particular, there can be a timing difference between the closing cash price and the closing futures price. This effect is most prevalent for long-term debt instruments, currency prices, and smaller stocks.

A major factor affecting the timing of cash and futures debt issues is that the futures close at 2 P.M. Central time, while the cash market remains open the rest of the afternoon. Hence, closing cash prices can reflect information not impounded in the closing futures prices. This timing difference often adversely affects the calculation of hedging effectiveness

---

24 One might argue that the assumption of a normal distribution of the price changes is not a critical factor, as long as both the cash and futures prices change in a comparable manner across time. However, situations with large cash price changes also usually have the *largest* errors from the regression line, since timing problems between the cash and futures instruments and unusual price relationships for these atypical situations often exist.

values. For example, if one examines the cash T-bond prices in the Chicago Board of Trade Statistical Annual, one finds that cash prices often change more than futures prices, especially during significant market moves. The futures do not adjust to the cash market price until the opening on the following trade day. Thus, one must take care in using cash prices by determining the timing of the close of these prices. Some services use the 2 P.M. price of the cash market as the day's "close," whereas other services use the last trade of the day; obviously, the former price is more appropriate for hedge ratio analysis due to the timing factor. Other futures have similar problems, such as currencies futures that close between 1:00 and 1:30 P.M., depending on the currency.

Liquidity in the cash issue also can have a major effect on the timing of the last trade. For example, a bond that does not trade frequently can possess a reported 2 P.M. "closing" price that is not representative of its true price at the time, simply because it did not trade after interest rates changed. Alternatively, illiquid issues can trade at inappropriate prices *because* they are not liquid. For example, the corporate bond issues reported in *The Wall Street Journal* are for odd lots traded on the bond exchange; often these issues trade ten or fewer bonds on a given day. The major action in these corporate bonds occurs off the exchange by institutions, who trade thousands of the most liquid bonds in a day. Hence, the prices reported in *The Journal* often are poor representations of the true closing prices for these issues.

Another consideration is that a reported price may not be a trade price. Specifically, Merrill Lynch provides a "matrix pricing" service for corporate bonds where bond traders input either a trade price or a "representative" price for each issue. The "representative" price is input for issues that do not trade near the time that prices are put into the matrix. If these representative prices are not accurate representations of what the true trade price would be for that bond, then the regression analysis impounds larger errors than would actually occur if trade data were available.

Finally, another critical factor when historical data are employed is whether the hedge ratios are stable over time. Authors of hedge ratio studies have assumed that the hedge ratios and hedging effectiveness are in fact stable. The use of the historical regression values implicitly assumes that other time periods would provide the same results. In fact, when fundamental conditions change, the cash/futures relationships can change, or statistical problems may exist. The next section examines the considerations for hedge ratio instability, whether such instability exists, and the potential effect of such instability on hedging effectiveness.

HEDGE RATIO INSTABILITY

If the relationship between the cash and futures price changes varies from one period to the next, then the hedge ratios also are unstable. Using historical data and the regression model to measure the hedge ratio and hedging effectiveness implicitly assumes that the cash/futures relationship does remain stable over time. This section examines the potential effect of unstable hedge ratios on both basis risk and the hedging effectiveness measure when the regression procedure is employed, and then shows the extent of unstable hedge ratios for currency data.

The Effect of Unstable Hedge Ratios on Hedging Effectiveness

Both empirical research and practitioner application of the regression model has implicitly assumed that the hedge ratio is stable over time. In this case, the hedge ratios derived by employing data from time period t are deemed to be relevant measures for hedging purposes for subsequent time periods. However, if hedge ratios are unstable over time, then additional basis risk exists that is not apparent by simply applying the regression model to ex-post data without any adjustment for the changing nature of the hedge ratio. This additional basis risk means that the R^2 value representing the traditional ex-post hedging effectiveness measure is upwardly biased due to the inappropriate hedge ratio.

Let us designate R_{t+1}^2 as the hedging effectiveness measure from using the hedge ratio b_{t+1} for data from $t + 1$, and R_t^2 as the hedging effectiveness measure from using the hedge ratio b_t for data from $t + 1$. Then the upward bias in the typical ex-post R_{t+1}^2 value when hedge ratios are unstable is determined by finding $\Delta R^2 = R_{t+1}^2 - R_t^2$. These relationships are shown as

Data from Period t	Data from Period (t + 1)
	$b_{t+1} \longrightarrow R_{t+1}^2$
b_t ————————————$\longrightarrow R_t^2$
	$\Delta R^2 = R_{t+1}^2 - R_t^2$

Daigler[25] shows that the bias in the hedging effectiveness measure when historical data are employed to determine the hedge ratio *and* when the hedge ratio b_t is unstable over time is determined by

$$\Delta R^2 = \Delta b_t^2 \left(\sigma_F^2 / \sigma_C^2 \right) \tag{10-18}$$

where ΔR^2 = the bias in the hedging effectiveness measure from unstable hedge ratios

Δb_t^2 = the change in the hedge ratio from the measurement period to the subsequent period

σ_F^2 / σ_C^2 = the standard deviation ratio (squared) of the futures and cash price changes

Consequently, if hedge ratios are unstable over time, then the use of the hedge ratio from the previous period results in an upwardly biased R^2 value for hedging effectiveness. Conceptually, if b_{t+1} is the minimum variance hedge ratio during time $t + 1$, then any other hedge ratio b_t that has a different slope to the regression line has a larger sum of squared errors and thus a lower R^2 value. Hence, a bias occurs when the historical hedging effectiveness measure based on b_t is used to estimate the current hedging effectiveness.

Examining Currency Hedge Ratio Instability

Daigler[26] examines the instability of hedge ratios by employing weekly currency cash and futures prices changes for the period 1980 through 1986 in order to generate semiannual hedge ratios both for currencies that have futures contracts and for currencies without futures. Tables 10-6 and 10-7 show the average minimum-variance hedge ratio per period, b_{t+1}^*, the absolute value of the change in the minimum variance hedge ratio from the

25 Daigler, ibid., "Hedge Ratio Instability . . ."

26 Daigler, ibid.

previous period, $|\Delta b_t|$, the hedging effectiveness value for period $t + 1$, $e^* = R_{t+1}^{*2}$, and the bias in the hedging effectiveness that exists when the hedge ratio is unstable over time, ΔR^2.

Table 10-6 shows that the bias in the R^2 values for hedges using the same cash and futures currencies are essentially nonexistent (namely, about 1%). However, Table 10-7 indicates the difficulty that can arise when crosshedges are obtained. In this case, the resulting *average* bias for the hedge effectiveness measures are much larger, ranging from 12% to 28% per period for the yen futures, with individual period biases (not shown here) *often* being above 20%. Moreover, most cross-currency results possess several periods where the variability in price changes are actually *increased* by using the previous period's hedge ratio as compared to using a no-hedge strategy.

The existence of unstable hedge ratios means that the use of past hedge ratios to estimate future hedge ratios and the use of minimum-variance hedging effectiveness measures must be undertaken with greater care for crosshedging situations. Previous researchers implicitly assumed that the hedge ratios obtained from past data provide an appropriate hedge ratio for subsequent periods, and that the minimum-variance hedging effectiveness measure is an unbiased value of the true hedging effectiveness. Since unstable hedge ratios increase the basis risk of the hedge (i.e., reduce the hedging effectiveness) compared with the typical minimum-variance results, the hedger may need to reevaluate the firm's analysis procedure for hedging.

SUMMARY AND LOOKING AHEAD

This chapter examined the issues and techniques relating to risk reduction hedging strategies. The following hedge ratio procedures were examined: naive ratios, the conversion factor method, the dollar equivalency concept, and the minimum-risk procedure developed from regression analysis. The difference between the optimal model and the minimum-variance model was explored, empirical evidence relating to the regression method was presented, considerations in determining the regression hedge ratio were discussed, and the effects of unstable hedge ratios over time examined. Appendix 10A examines alternative methods to find hedge ratios. Chapters 11 and 12 explore the uses of duration for cash debt and futures hedging. The concepts and problems relating to the duration method are explored and evidence concerning this method is given.

TABLE 10-6: Hedging Effectiveness Bias:
Same-Currency Hedging Results

Country	b_{t+1}	$\lvert \Delta b_t \rvert$	e^*	ΔR^2
		Average Results per Period		
Canada	0.892	0.112	0.831	0.017
Germany	0.985	0.072	0.941	0.010
Japan	0.940	0.078	0.928	0.009
U.K.	0.979	0.056	0.934	0.005

Note: $\Delta R^2 = \Delta b_t^2 \left[\sigma_F^2 / \sigma_C^2 \right]$
Source: Robert T. Daigler, "Hedge Ratio Instability for Currency Futures," working paper, Florida International University, 1991.

TABLE 10-7: Hedging Effectiveness Bias:
Crosshedging Results

Country	b_{t+1}	$\lvert \Delta b_t \rvert$	e^*	ΔR^2
		Average Results per Period		
Japan vs.				
Australia	0.315	0.366	0.275	0.121
Belgium	0.652	0.313	0.360	0.133
Italy	0.641	0.399	0.416	0.219
Netherlands	0.734	0.365	0.443	0.175
Spain	0.556	0.345	0.319	0.281
France	0.721	0.389	0.398	0.183
Germany vs.				
Australia	0.239	0.215	0.256	0.112
Belgium	0.890	0.145	0.777	0.047
Italy	0.831	0.100	0.802	0.024
Netherlands	0.945	0.085	0.911	0.014
Spain	0.714	0.166	0.673	0.087
France	0.919	0.087	0.832	0.018

Table continues

TABLE 10-7: Continued

Country	Average Results per Period			
	b_{t+1}	$|\Delta b_t|$	e^*	ΔR^2
UK vs.				
Australia	0.223	0.172	0.215	0.060
Belgium	0.612	0.309	0.383	0.092
Italy	0.575	0.250	0.373	0.078
Netherlands	0.648	0.250	0.435	0.078
Spain	0.645	0.237	0.458	0.123
France	0.665	0.241	0.422	0.057

Note: $\Delta R^2 = \Delta b_t^2 [\sigma_F^2/\sigma_C^2]$
Source: Robert T. Daigler, "Hedge Ratio Instability for Currency Futures," working paper, Florida International University, 1991.

Appendix 10A
Risk-Return Hedging Models

This appendix discusses a hedging model that employs both return *and* risk in order to determine the appropriate hedge ratio. Closed-form equations for this risk-return hedge ratio and the measure of hedging effectiveness provide benefits over a full-fledged portfolio model, but the instability of the historical return values cast doubt on the model's usefulness from a practical standpoint unless the hedger is a good forecaster.

Risk Minimization Versus a Risk-Return Model

The discussion of the regression model to determine the minimum-variance hedge ratio and the resulting hedging effectiveness value presented in this chapter begins by examining the risk-return aspects of the general portfolio model. We then determine that the *minimum-risk* position on the portfolio's efficient risk-return set can be obtained by finding the slope of the regression line between the changes in the futures prices and the changes in the cash prices. Using this approach assumes that the hedger desires to *minimize* risk, and thus minimize the return of the hedged position as well. In reality, the hedger may wish to create a hedged position that lies on the efficient set but provides a different risk-return combination. In other words, return also is an important consideration for many hedgers.

The portfolio model allows the hedger to choose any risk-return combination on the efficient set. However, determining the appropriate risk-return choice for a particular hedger involves deriving the individual's indifference curves that specify that individual's trade-off between risk and return.[1] Finding these trade-off curves is very difficult, if not impossible. Moreover, the calculations involved in determining the best risk-return position on the efficient set (the position where the highest indifference curve is tangent to the efficient set) are complicated and require a computer program dedicated to this task.[2]

---

1 Anderson and Danthine examine the portfolio approach to hedging and derive an equation that determines "the benefit of being able to trade futures." This expression is based on the investor's risk aversion, that is, one must essentially determine the indifference or risk-return trade-off curves for the hedger. Koppenhaver also develops an indifference curve model, with his model based on varying the hedger's risk aversion factor to determine the effect on the results. R. Anderson and J. Danthine, "Cross Hedging," *Journal of Political Economy*, Vol. 89, No. 6, December 1981, pp. 1182-1196. G. D. Koppenhaver, "Selective Hedging of Bank Assets with Treasury Bill Futures Contracts," *Journal of Financial Research*, Vol. 7, No. 2, Summer 1984, pp. 105-119.

2 Several computer programs exist to determine the efficient set and the weights (hedge ratios) for various portfolio risks. Two microcomputer products generating useful results are PMSP and AAT. The PMSP program determines the relevant weights for a given standard deviation or an expected return. The AAT model allows the user to input a risk-return ratio for the risk preference of the individual into the model. A hedger can use these programs to obtain risk-return hedge ratios, assuming the risk and return inputs to the model are reasonable estimates of the actual risk and return values that occur during the time period.

An alternative to using the portfolio model is to employ a **risk-return hedging model.** The model presented below provides an easy to calculate risk-return hedge ratio and a value for the associated hedging effectiveness. However, this simplification also creates some problems. The following discusses the risk-return hedge model, evidence concerning the model, and difficulties associated with the model's use.

The Concept of a Risk-Return Hedging Model

Howard and D'Antonio[3] develop a **closed-form** risk-return hedging model that can be implemented easily, although the model is more complicated than the risk minimization hedging models.[4] The basic idea of the Howard and D'Antonio risk-return model is shown in Figure 10A-1. Parts A, B, and C of Figure 10A-1 show a cash security S, a tangency point T that represents the optimal combination of the cash and the futures positions, and a risk-free asset with a rate of return i; M is the minimum variance point. Risk is shown on the horizontal axis as the standard deviation, while return is on the vertical axis. The risk-free asset is joined to the cash asset S via a broken line, whereas the risk-free asset is joined to the cash-futures portfolio T by a solid line.

The hedger can choose to be at any risk-return combination on line iS or line iT simply by varying the proportion of the funds placed in the risk-free asset i versus the funds placed in either S or in T.[5] Note that line iT has a superior risk-return combination to line iS for any given standard deviation in parts A and C of the figure; that is, the return is higher for any given amount of risk for line iT as compared to line iS. The extent of the difference between these lines shows the benefit of using futures relative to using only the cash security. In part B of the graph, the cash security S and the tangency portfolio T are equivalent; thus, in this case there is no benefit to using futures contracts.

The quantitative expression that determines the hedge ratio on a risk-return basis is as follows:

---

3 Charles T. Howard and Louis J. D'Antonio, "A Risk-Return Measure of Hedging Effectiveness," *Journal of Financial and Quantitative Analysis,* Vol. 19, No. 1, March 1984, pp. 101-112. Charles T. Howard and Louis J. D'Antonio, "Treasury Bill Futures as a Hedging Tool: A Risk-Return Approach," *Journal of Financial Research,* Vol. 9, No. 1, Spring 1986, pp. 25-40.

4 Adjustments and comments on the following model are made by Chang and Shanker, Gjerde, and Howard and D'Antonio. Chang and Shanker ("Hedging Effectiveness ...") include margins and transaction costs in their model, as well as developing separate models for four separate situations involving long, short, and synthetic futures positions. Gjerde develops two models: the first includes margins and transactions costs and the second includes a measure for the individual's attitude for the trade-off between risk and return. Jack S. K. Chang and Latha Shanker, "Hedging Effectiveness of Currency Options and Currency Futures," *The Journal of Futures Markets,* Vol. 6, No. 2, Summer 1986, pp. 289-306. Jack S. K. Chang and Latha Shanker, "A Risk-Return Measure of Hedging Effectiveness: Comment," *Journal of Financial and Quantitative Analysis,* Vol. 22, No. 3, September 1987, pp. 373-376. Oystein Gjerde, "Measuring Hedging Effectiveness in a Traditional One-Periodic Portfolio Framework," *The Journal of Futures Markets,* Vol. 7, No. 6, December 1987, pp. 663-674. Charles T. Howard and Louis J. D'Antonio, "A Risk-Return Measure of Hedging Effectiveness: Reply," *Journal of Financial and Quantitative Analysis,* Vol. 22, No. 3, September 1987, pp. 377-381.

5 This description is equivalent to the development of the Capital Market Line, which is a fundamental concept associated with portfolio analysis.

FIGURE 10A-1: A Graphical Depiction of Risk-Return Hedging

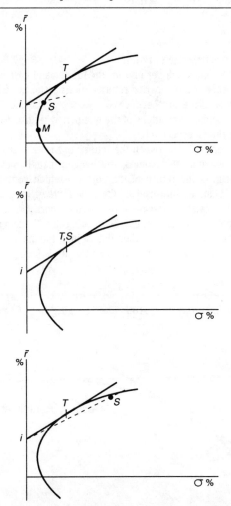

Source: Charles T. Howard and Louis J. D'Antonio, "Treasury Bill Futures as a Hedging Tool: A Risk-Return Approach," *Journal of Financial Research*, Vol. 9, No. 1, Spring 1986, p. 28.

$$B^\star = (\lambda - \rho)/\gamma\pi(1 - \lambda\rho) \qquad (10A\text{-}1)$$

where
$\lambda = \alpha/\pi = [\bar{r}_F/\sigma_F]/[(\bar{r}_C - i)/\sigma_C]$

$\alpha = \bar{r}_F/(\bar{r}_C - i)$

$\pi = \sigma_F/\sigma_C$

$\gamma = P_F/P_C$

i = the risk-free rate of return

P_F, P_C = the current price per unit for the futures and cash securities, respectively

$\bar{r}_F, \bar{r}_C$ = the expected one-period returns in respect to price for the futures and cash securities, respectively

σ_F, σ_C = the standard deviations of the one-period returns for the futures and cash securities, respectively

ρ = the correlation between the returns of the cash and the futures positions

The measure of hedging effectiveness, the hedging benefit per unit of risk (HBS), is determined by comparing the return of the portfolio which contains futures to the cash portfolio that does not contain futures: HBS finds the *increase* in returns for a given amount of risk. Figure 10A-2 shows the increase in returns for a portfolio on line iT as compared to the equivalent risk portfolio return on line iS; dividing this "hedging benefit at point T" by the standard deviation of these portfolios determines the hedging benefit per standard deviation, called HBS. This gain per unit of risk measure is found as follows:[6]

FIGURE 10A-2: Illustrating HBS: The Hedging Benefit per Unit of Risk

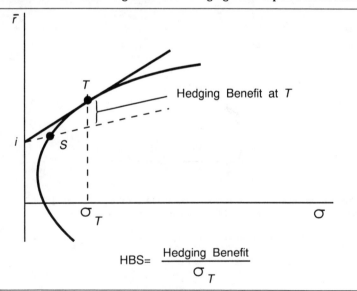

$$HBS = \frac{\text{Hedging Benefit}}{\sigma_T}$$

---

6 Note that HBS approaches ∞ as ρ approaches one.

$$\text{HBS} = \left\{ \sqrt{[(1 - 2\lambda\rho + \lambda^2)/(1 - \rho^2)]} - 1 \right\} [(\bar{r}_C - i)]/\sigma_C]$$ (10A-2)

Interpreting the Model

This risk-return hedging model has several characteristics that provide insights into its performance. The risk to excess return (or risk-return) relative λ is a critical parameter that influences both the hedge ratio and the hedging effectiveness of this model. λ shows the relative attractiveness of using futures versus employing only the cash position. When λ is less than 1, the futures position provides less excess return per unit of risk than the cash position offers, creating benefits for a short futures position. When λ is greater than 1, the futures position provides a greater excess return per unit of risk than the cash position. $\lambda < 1$ is the typical futures hedging situation.

The relationship of λ to ρ is also an important factor in determining the optimal risk-return hedge ratio. Assuming $1 - \lambda\rho > 0$, when $\lambda < \rho$ then $B^* < 0$ and a short hedge is appropriate; when $\lambda > \rho$ then $B^* > 0$ and a long futures position is beneficial. Hence, not only is the correlation coefficient ρ important for hedging, as in the risk minimization case, but the relationship of the risk-return relative λ to ρ affects the results. Moreover, the measure of hedging effectiveness, HBS, depends significantly on both 1 and ρ.

In order to illustrate the relationship of the various factors in determining the hedge ratio and hedging effectiveness, let us assume that $\bar{r}_C - i = 4\%$, $\lambda = .05$, $\rho = .75$, $\sigma_C = 20\%$, and $\lambda = \pi = 1$. By using Equation (10A-1) we find that the risk-return hedge ratio is $-.73$ and HBS = .091. Hence, the hedger would short .73 contracts per unit of the cash instrument and the benefit of using futures (HBS) would be an increase in expected returns of 9.1 basis points per unit of risk for the hedged portfolio in comparison to the unhedged cash position. If the risk of the hedged portfolio is kept the same as the cash position (i.e., $\sigma_C = 20\%$), then the benefit of hedging would be an increase in return of 1.82% (i.e., 20% × .091).

The Evidence Concerning Risk-Return Models

T-Bill Hedging. Howard and D'Antonio[7] test their risk-return hedging model by hedging cash Treasury bills with maturities ranging from four to 48 weeks with T-bill futures. Hedge ratios based on one-week observations and the associated risk-return HBS hedging effectiveness measures are calculated, using data from September 1977 to April 1982. The sample data represent 243 weekly observations separated into ten subperiods.

The first test determines the risk-return hedge ratio and the hedging effectiveness by using perfect foresight. Thus, the values for Equations (10A-1) and (10A-2) are calculated by assuming the hedger knows the relevant values of the equation for the period the hedge is implemented. Note that this perfect foresight method is the same procedure typically used when the risk-minimizing regression procedure is employed.

The average values for the key variables over the ten subperiods for the perfect foresight method are as follows: $\lambda = .531$, $\rho = .780$, and HBS = .252. Since the risk-return relative $\lambda < 1$ and $\lambda < \rho$, a short hedge is appropriate. The ρ of .780 shows that a reasonable association exists between the cash portfolio and the futures contracts, since the risk-minimizing hedging effectiveness would be $\rho^2 = R^2 = .61$. The risk-return hedging effectiveness

---

7   Howard and D'Antonio, ibid., "Treasury Bill Futures . . ."

HBS value of .252 indicates that a short futures position increases the hedged return by 25 basis points for each unit of risk when compared to the cash-only position. An average maturity of 35 days for a cash portfolio translates into an improvement from a 12.26% return without a futures hedge to a 17.26% return with the hedge!

Using historical data rather than perfect foresight to determine the parameters of the risk-return hedge ratio and the hedging effectiveness provides completely different results concerning the ability to hedge effectively on a risk *and* return basis. Specifically, the average HBS obtained by employing historical data is only .014, implying that little or no risk-return hedging benefit exists when historical data are employed to determine the parameters for the hedge. The culprit in this analysis is , the return relative. The R^2 between the historical and actual α is only .02; thus, the return relative is not stable over time, and thus all of the other calculations are adversely affected.

Howard and D'Antonio then retest the data with the assumption that $\alpha = 0$, and hence $\lambda = 0$. This approach is equivalent to risk minimization, but uses the risk-return equation. Using $\alpha = 0$ implies that the futures price is an unbiased estimate of the subsequent cash price. The HBS is somewhat better in this case, with HBS = .036, although obviously significantly less than the perfect foresight results of HBS = .252. Finally, a naive one-to-one hedge is examined. In this case HBS is .064.[8]

The results of the Howard and D'Antonio study show the *potential* benefits of hedging on a risk-return basis and the disadvantage of using historical data to formulate the hedge ratio. Thus, although risk-return hedging using this index model is very successful with perfect foresight, the instability of the return relative over time makes the use of historical data almost useless in obtaining benefits from hedging on a risk *and* return basis.

Alternative Hedging Devices. Chang and Shanker[9] use the risk-return hedging model for an interesting application that does not require the use of forecasts or historical data to determine the parameters of the model. Using weekly currency futures and options data, Chang and Shanker examine which market provides a superior hedging device on both a risk and return basis. They develop risk-return hedging effectiveness models based on the Howard and D'Antonio model formulation for four cases that include margins and transactions costs. Their results show that the hedging effectiveness of the futures contract is higher than the effectiveness of the option contract for the majority of the situations examined. They conclude that options will not supplant futures as a hedging device. Conversely, options possess certain characteristics that futures do not; hence, futures will not replace options.

---

8   Several difficulties exist for the Howard and D'Antonio T-bill risk-return study. First and foremost, most of the cash T-bill returns are the result of amortization over time and hence cannot be hedged; only the price changes caused by interest rate changes can be hedged. Second, the use of cash T-bills as the spot instrument can reduce the benefit of the method, since the risk-free asset (a one-week T-bill) and the spot instruments (4- to 48-week T-bills) often have responded similarly to external economic forces. Third, the authors do not make adjustments for changes in maturity for the cash instruments; Franckle shows that this shortcoming affects minimum-risk hedging results. Fourth, the use of one-week hedges can adversely affect hedging results because correlations often are smaller for shorter-term hedges. Charles Franckle, "The Hedging Performance of the New Futures Market: Comment," *Journal of Finance*, Vol. 35, No. 1, March 1980, pp. 157-170.

9   Chang and Shanker, ibid., "Hedging Effectiveness . . ."

Examining the Characteristics of the Risk-Return Hedging Model

The risk-return hedging model developed by Howard and D'Antonio provides an extension of the risk minimization models discussed previously. The model can be a very beneficial technique for comparing alternative hedging instruments, as shown in the Chang and Shanker currency study. Unfortunately, several aspects of the model reduce its usefulness as a hedging technique. First, the reliance of the model on a stable return relative across time essentially eliminates the use of historical data to determine the hedge ratio. Second, the model claims to abstract from utility/indifference considerations, but in reality it does not completely solve the individual's risk-return trade-off decision. Finally, one must determine the objective of the hedge in order to examine its effectiveness. A few comments on each of these factors shows how they affect the risk-return model.

The Unstable Return Relative. The results of the risk-return model show that the instability of the historical return relative is the key factor in the poor risk-return hedging effectiveness values. On the other hand, use of perfect foresight provides large positive benefits to the hedger. Hence, the technique is valid, but obtaining superior inputs to the model can be difficult. As shown in the chapter, using historical data in the risk minimizing regression method typically has minimal effects on hedging effectiveness, as long as the instrument being hedged is similar to the cash security underlying the futures instrument. Consequently, the instability of the return relative may be the key factor that keeps the risk-return hedging method from being implemented on a large scale.

Risk-Return Trade-offs. Although the model claims to eliminate the risk-return trade-off decisions of the hedger, in fact the hedger must still determine what risk-return combination is most appropriate for the situation at hand. However, this risk-return index model is still easier to implement than the complete portfolio model, since the latter requires the hedger to choose the value of an ambiguous risk parameter that delineates the hedger's trade-off between risk and return. Gjerde,[10] Anderson and Danthine,[11] Koppenhaver,[12] and Stein[13] provide more involved portfolio models for hedging. Gjerde does have a closed-form risk-return index hedging model, although it does require the risk parameter to be chosen. The other models are complete portfolio models.

Objective of the Hedge. Finally, one must determine the objective of the hedge in order to choose the correct procedure for calculating a hedge ratio. A pure risk minimization objective suggests a regression or duration approach is appropriate. Howard and D'Antonio argue that (risk-return) hedging is not successful because the empirical risk-return hedging effectiveness results are poor. As noted above, it is the instability of historical data that creates the poor results, not the concept of risk-return hedging. Moreover, if a major objective of the hedger is to protect the cash position against *unanticipated* changes in value (which may be the culprit of the unstable relative returns), then a properly formulated risk-minimizing hedging program will succeed in meeting this objective.

---

10 Gjerde, ibid.

11 Anderson and Danthine, ibid.

12 Koppenhaver, ibid.

13 Jerome Stein, "Spot, Forward and Futures," *Research in Finance*, Vol. 1, 1979, pp. 225-310.

Chapter 11
Duration and Immunization

Duration and the related risk-reduction technique of immunization are popular cash market methods that provide the user with information concerning the volatility of bonds and ways to hedge the cash bond portfolio, either with or *without* the use of futures contracts. Moreover, duration provides a means for determining the price change of a bond for a given change in interest rates.

Duration combines all effects of changes in interest rates on bond prices into one number. Specifically, duration considers the effects of time until maturity, coupon rate, and the yield to maturity on the price change of a bond, given a change in the market interest rate. Duration also measures the relative price sensitivity of bonds to changes in interest rates. Thus, the longer the duration, the greater the price change of the bond to a given change in interest rates. Consequently, bonds with longer durations are more volatile.

Immunization uses duration to guarantee a minimum target rate of return on the bond portfolio if the assumptions of the duration procedure are met. A consideration in determining the final portfolio value, either with or without immunization, is the role of the reinvestment rates on the cash flows received from the bond's coupon and principal payments. The role of these reinvestment rates is examined to show their effects. In addition, the importance of the planning horizon for the immunization process and the assumptions of duration are discussed.

Contingent immunization allows the portfolio manager flexibility in managing the bond portfolio to enhance returns, while still relying on a minimum floor return to guarantee payouts. The key features of contingent immunization end the chapter, while Appendix 12A discusses how to measure and control immunization risk.

DURATION: THE CONCEPTS

Duration is a risk management tool for fixed-income securities. Duration identifies the risk of a bond, provides a tool for changing the risk of a bond portfolio, and through immunization provides a means for eliminating most risk. Duration is also used with futures in the next chapter to control the risk of a bond portfolio.

Factors Affecting Interest Rates

The bond theorems state that for a given change in interest rates:
1. Longer-term bonds change more in price than shorter-term bonds; that is, bond price volatility is *directly* related to the time to maturity.
2. Higher coupon bonds change less in percentage terms than lower coupon bonds; that is, bond price volatility is *inversely* related to the coupon.

Consequently, the price change of a bond is affected by *both* the maturity and coupon of the bond. Moreover, when longer-term bonds have higher coupons, the coupon effect on the price partially offsets the maturity effect. This combined maturity-coupon effect creates difficulties in determining *which* bonds are more volatile; in other words, maturity is an outdated method for measuring the relative volatility of bonds. In addition, the timing of the cash flows, the size of the coupon, and the realized reinvestment rates are also determinants of relative volatility. **Duration** overcomes the shortcomings of using only maturity as the relevant factor affecting volatility and price change by incorporating all of the above factors to determine the relative volatility of a bond.

Duration and Its Uses

Duration quantifies the relative volatility of a fixed-income instrument, incorporating the timing of the cash flows, the size of the payments, and reinvestment effects. Duration has become a popular technique for bond professionals because it is easy to use and it has a multitude of applications. Duration is employed to:

- Approximate quickly the price change of a bond or bond portfolio for *any given* change in interest rates.
- Summarize in one value the cash flow characteristics of bonds (i.e., the coupon, maturity, and yield effects), thereby providing a measure of the relative volatility of bonds.
- Achieve specific bond portfolio objectives, such as immunizing the portfolio against adverse interest rate effects.

Spreadsheets can be employed to accomplish the same objectives without using duration measures. However, duration has become popular among professionals because it is used without relying on more sophisticated computer programs and because this easily understood relative measure of volatility allows quick decision making. Liebowitz[1] states that bond portfolio managers turned to duration starting in the late 1970s because of a number of factors:

- Higher interest rates and a broader range of coupons made average maturity a less satisfactory measure of average life.
- There was a greater volatility in interest rates, which made a comparison measure of volatility necessary.
- An intermediate-term corporate bond market was developing.
- The increased focus on short-term rate of return and performance measures required new decision-making tools.
- Greater flexibility in the management of maturity necessitated better measures of volatility.
- Use of computer tools for bond portfolio management became standards in the industry.

Calculating Duration

Macaulay Duration. Macaulay developed the most popular measurement of duration, which is calculated by determining the ratio of the sum of the *time-weighted* present values

---

1   Martin L. Leibowitz, "How Financial Theory Evolves into the Real World—or Not: The Case of Duration and Immunization," *Financial Review*, Vol. 18, No. 4, November 1983, pp. 271-280.

of the cash flows to the total present values of the cash flows. Mathematically this concept is presented as follows:

$$D = \frac{\Sigma \text{ time weighted present values}}{\text{total present value}}$$

$$D = \frac{\sum_{t=1}^{M} t\, PV_t}{\sum_{t=1}^{M} PV_t} \qquad (11\text{-}1)$$

where D = the duration of the instrument or portfolio

t = the unit of time, typically measured in years

M = the maturity of the bond, in terms of the number of periods

PV_t = the present value of the cash flows received at time t

A more descriptive definition of the Macaulay duration given in Equation (11-1) is the weighted *average time* to each bond payment (coupon and principal), where the weights are the size of the present values of each of the payments as a percentage of the total present value of all the payments. This definition is shown mathematically as:

$$D = \frac{\sum_{t=1}^{M} t\, C_t / (1+i)^t}{\sum_{t=1}^{M} C_t / (1+i)^t} = \frac{\sum_{t=1}^{M} t\, C_t / (1+i)^t}{PV_B} \qquad (11\text{-}2)$$

or equivalently as

$$D = \sum_{t=1}^{M} t\, w_t$$

such that

$$w_t = \frac{C_t / (1+i)^t}{\sum_{t=1}^{M} C_t / (1+i)^t} = \frac{PV_t}{\sum_{t=1}^{M} PV_t} = \frac{PV_t}{PV_B}$$

where C_t = coupon amount per period, with C_M being the coupon plus principal

i = yield to maturity (interest rate in the economy for similar risk bonds)

w_t = the weights, as defined by the size of the present values of each of the payments as a percentage of the total present value of all the payments

PV_B = the present value of the bond based on the yield i

Describing the Duration Process. The denominators of Equations (11-1) and (11-2) are simply the present value of the bond. The numerator is the sum of: the individual present values for each coupon payment multiplied by the associated time until payment. Thus, duration is measured in units of time, typically years. Duration is the point in time at which the total present values of the cash flows of the bond before the duration value equal the total present values of the cash flows after the duration value. Figure 11-1 illustrates this point, with the dark areas of the cash flows representing the respective present values.

The key aspect of Equation (11-2) is the time factor t. The multiplication of t by the associated present values in the numerator of the duration equation causes t to be *the* critical variable affecting the duration value, as shown in Example 11-1. The procedure to calculate duration, as given by Equation (11-2) and illustrated in Example 11-1, is as follows:

1.   Find the present value of each cash payment—that is, the coupons and principal.

FIGURE 11-1: Duration: Equating Cash Flows

A.

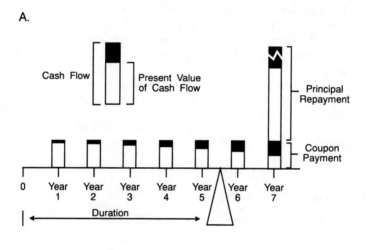

B.

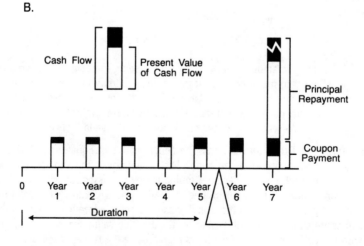

2. Time weight the present values by multiplying each present value by the time period. This procedure associates each cash flow value to time.
3. Calculate the duration by taking the ratio of the time-weighted present values to the total present value of the cash flows of the bond.

Recall that a zero-coupon bond pays a given principal amount at the maturity date, with no intervening coupon payments. The advantage of a zero-coupon bond is that no reinvestment rate risk exists; thus, the promised yield to maturity is the actual compound yield to maturity if the bond is kept until it matures. A zero-coupon bond has a duration equal to its maturity, since all of the weights (cash flows) are zero until the face value is paid at maturity. A bond with a duration D *acts like* a zero-coupon bond with maturity M. Moreover, the duration of a coupon-paying bond is always less than the maturity of that bond. Also, duration decreases as the frequency of the coupon payments increases.

The duration for bonds paying coupons semiannually also is calculated from Equation (11-2), with t = 1, 2, ... measuring the half-year periods (that is, t = 1 equals six months, t = 2 equals one year, etc.). Correspondingly, the coupon and yield values used in Equation (11-2) are measured semiannually as half the annual value. The resultant durations are

---

EXAMPLE 11-1: Calculating Duration

A bond has a 10 percent coupon that is paid annually, the bond matures in five years, and the yield to maturity for an equivalent bond is 14%. The following table uses Equation (11-2) to calculate duration for the bond in question. Each term in the equation is specified in the table.

(1) Time Period t	(2) Cash Payment C_t	(3) PV Factor $1/(1+i)^t$	(4) Present Value $(2) \times (3)$ $PV=C_t/(1+i)^t$	(5) Time-Weighted Present Value $(4) \times (1)$ $t\,PV_t$
1	100	0.87719	87.72	87.72
2	100	0.76946	76.95	153.89
3	100	0.67497	67.50	202.49
4	100	0.59208	59.20	236.83
5	100	0.51936	51.94	259.68
5	1000	0.51936	519.36	2,596.80
Total			862.67	3,537.41

$$D = \frac{\Sigma \text{ time weighted present value}}{\text{total present value}}$$
$$= 3{,}537.41 \,/\, 862.67$$
$$= 4.10 \text{ years}$$

calculated in six-month periods. Typically this duration value is converted to years simply by dividing by two.

   A Closed-Form Duration Measure. An alternative equation to calculate duration is given by Chua.[2] This alternative approach has the advantage of being a closed-form equation; that is, it does not have to be summed over the series of cash flow payments. Equation (11-2) is tedious to manipulate without a spreadsheet. Equation (11-3) shows the "relative" simplicity of using this closed-form equation for duration:

$$D = \frac{C \left[\dfrac{(1 + i)^{M+1} - (1 + i) - iM}{i^2 (1 + i)^M} \right] + \dfrac{FM}{(1 + i)^M}}{PV_B} \tag{11-3}$$

where F is the face value of the bond, in dollars.

   As with Equation (11-2), the annual coupon and yield are divided by two for semiannual coupon bonds, with M reflecting the number of six-month periods; the resultant duration is then divided by two to obtain an annual duration value. Example 11-2 numerically illustrates the calculation of duration by means of Equation (11-3), which is a closed-form equation.[3]

Related Duration Measures

Two related terms often used in conjunction with the Macaulay duration given by Equation (11-2) are **modified duration** and **dollar duration.**

$$\text{Modified duration} = \frac{D}{(1 + i)} \tag{11-4}$$

Modified duration is used to calculate the percentage change in price of a bond for a given change in yield, as shown below. Dollar duration is employed to determine the *dollar* price change in a bond when yields change, where dollar duration is defined as:

$$\text{Dollar duration} = \text{modified duration } (P_B) \tag{11-5}$$

where P_B is the current price of the bond. Dollar duration is important because the *dollar* price change is the relevant value for hedging purposes.

Implementing Duration

The longer the duration of a bond, the greater the price sensitivity of that bond to a given change in interest rates. The effect of a change in interest rates on the price of the bond is found by the simple relationship:

$$\Delta P_B = -D \, P_B \, \Delta i \tag{11-6}$$

where ΔP_B = change in the price of the bond
$\quad\quad\quad D$ = (Macaulay) duration of the bond
$\quad\quad\quad P_B$ = current price of the bond

2   Jess H. Chua, "A Closed-Form Formula for Calculating Bond Duration," *Financial Analysts Journal,* Vol. 40 No. 3, May-June 1984, pp. 76-78.

3   Other closed-form duration measures are given by Babcock and by Caks, Lane, Greenleaf, and Joules. Moser and Lindley extend the concept to coupons paid within the period. Guilford C. Babcock, "Duration as a Weighted Average of Two Factors," *Financial Analysts Journal,* Vol. 41, No. 2, March-April 1985, pp. 75-76. John Caks, William R. Lane, Robert W. Greenleaf, and Reginald G. Joules, "A Simple Formula for Duration," *Journal of Financial Research,* Vol. 8, No. 3, Fall 1985, pp. 245-249. James T. Moser and James T. Lindley, "A Simple Formula for Duration: An Extension," *Financial Review,* Vol. 24 No. 4, November 1989, pp. 611-615.

EXAMPLE 11-2: Calculating Duration by the Closed-Form Approach

Equation (11-3) presents a closed-form method for calculating the duration of a bond. Using the information on the bond from Example 11-1 we find:

$$\frac{C\left[\dfrac{(1 + i)^{M+1} - (1 + i) - iM}{i^2 (1 + i)^M}\right] + \dfrac{FM}{(1 + i)^M}}{PV_B} \tag{11-3}$$

$$D = \frac{100\left[\dfrac{(1 + .14)^{5+1} - (1 + .14) - (.14)(5)}{(.14)^2 (1 + .14)^5}\right] + \dfrac{(1000)(5)}{(1 + .14)^5}}{862.67}$$

$$D = \frac{100\left[\dfrac{2.1950 - 1.14 - .7}{.0196 (1.9254)}\right] + \dfrac{5000}{1.9254}}{862.67}$$

$$= (940.70 + 2596.86) \,/\, 862.67$$

$$= 4.10$$

Although the closed-form approach still requires the calculation of the present value of the bond to determine the denominator of the equation, this value is obtained easily with the use of most calculators.

Δi = forecasted change in the interest rate

Interest rates and bond prices are inversely related, which is the reason for the negative sign in front of duration in this equation. Although Equation (11-6) is the relationship often given to determine the price change of a bond, in reality it is a simplification, and it becomes less accurate for higher interest rates. A more accurate equation is as follows:[4]

$$\Delta P_B = \frac{-D \, P_B \, \Delta i}{(1 + i)} = - \text{ modified duration } (P_B) \, (\Delta i) \tag{11-7}$$

An equivalent expression to Equation (11-7) for the dollar price change of a bond is determined by using dollar duration:

$$\Delta P = - \text{ (dollar duration) } \Delta i \tag{11-8}$$

The *percentage* change in price of a bond is found as follows:

$$\% \, \Delta P_B = \frac{\Delta P_B}{P_B} = \frac{-D \, \Delta i}{(1 + i)} = - \text{ modified duration } (\Delta i) \tag{11-9}$$

---

4   One can see how Equation (11-6) is only an approximation by realizing how the equation is developed. The effect of a change in interest rates on bond prices is determined by taking the derivative of the price of the bond with respect to the interest rate, i.e. dP_B/di. This results in the equation $dP_B/P_B = -D(di)/(1 + i)$, or when changes are used and the equation rearranged, $\Delta P_B = -D \, P_B \, \Delta i \,/(1 + i)$. Obviously, the level of interest rates affects relative values given by Equations (11-6) and (11-7). In addition, *both* equations are approximations when large changes in the interest rate occur, since the derivative finds the slope of the line that is *tangent* to the *nonlinear* bond price relationship, resulting in the instantaneous change in price rather than the average change in price. Hence, the larger the change in interest rates, the larger the error in the duration measure. This relationship is explored later in this chapter and in Chapter 12.

If the bond has semiannual coupons (cash flows are determined semiannually to determine duration), then (1 + i) in Equations (11-7) and (11-9) must reflect a *semiannual* yield, *regardless* of whether or not the duration value is converted to years. Similarly, if the cash flows are paid every three months, then (1 + i) would reflect this payment schedule by the adjustment i = annual yield/4.

The simplicity of Equations (11-6) to (11-8) allows a user to *approximate* quickly the effect on the price of a bond for numerous potential changes in interest rates. These equations also show why duration is considered a relative measure of volatility among a number of bonds, since a larger duration value translates into a larger change in price. Example 11-3 shows the effect of a potential change in interest rates on the bond price.

Duration Relationships

Duration is superior to time until maturity as a price sensitivity measure, since duration considers both time to maturity *and* coupon payments. The relationships between duration and the factors influencing it are as follows:
Duration is longer:
- For bonds with a longer time to maturity.
- For bonds with a lower coupon.[5]
- As the yield to maturity decreases.[6]

Table 11-1 and Figure 11-2 show how duration varies as the coupon rate and years to maturity change. As can be seen, for a specific maturity an increase in the coupon rate causes a decrease in the duration, although the decline is not dramatic. For example, in Table 11-1 duration drops from 10.74 to 8.89 for the 20-year bond. For a specific coupon rate, an increase in the time until maturity increases the duration measure significantly. For example, a 5% coupon bond increases duration from 1.95 years to 10.74 years as the maturity increases from 2 to 20 years. The largest durations occur with the combination of the longest maturities and the lowest coupons.

Another beneficial characteristic of duration is that the duration of a portfolio of fixed-income securities is calculated easily from the durations of the individual securities. Thus:

$$D_P = \sum_{i=1}^{n} w_i D_i \qquad (11\text{-}10)$$

where D_p = the duration of the portfolio of securities
w_i = the weight (proportion) of funds in security i
D_i = the duration of security i

This linear association between individual securities and the portfolio of securities simplifies calculations and promotes the implementation of bond strategies involving interest rate forecasts.

---

5 Smaller coupons cause the more distant time periods to be relatively more important (in comparison with the distant time periods for larger coupons) both as a percentage of the total present value of the cash flows of the bond and the total time-weighted value. This situation occurs because of the discounting effect, as noted in Chapter 6.

6 The yield is important since the discount rate determines the compounding effect. As the discount rate increases, the more distant payments become less important, causing the duration value to fall, and vice versa.

EXAMPLE 11-3: Determining the Price Change with Duration

Using the information from Example 11-1, we have a bond with a duration of 4.1 years, a current price of $862.67, and a yield of 14%. If we forecast an immediate drop in interest rates of 30 basis points then the forecasted change in the bond price is as follows:

$$\Delta P_B = -D\ P_B\ \Delta i \tag{11-6}$$
$$= -4.1(\$862.67)(-.0030)$$
$$= \$10.61$$

Equation (11-7) gives a more accurate result:

$$\Delta P_B = -D\ P_B\ \Delta i\ /\ (1 + i) \tag{11-7}$$
$$= -4.1\ (\$862.67)\ (-.0030)/(1.14)$$
$$= \$9.31$$

The *percentage* change in price is determined as follows:

$$\%\Delta P_B = -D\ \Delta i\ /\ (1 + i) \tag{11-9}$$
$$= -4.1(-.0030)/(1.14)$$
$$= .0108 = 1.08\%$$

These equations show that bonds with longer durations are affected to a greater extent by a given change in interest rates. Thus, duration is used as a ranking device to determine which bonds change most in price when interest rates change.

TABLE 11-1: Bond Duration Values for a 7% Yield

Years to Maturity	Coupon Rates				
	.05	.08	.10	.12	.14
2	1.950	1.925	1.909	1.895	1.881
5	4.488	4.281	4.170	4.074	3.991
10	7.661	7.044	6.759	6.536	6.358
15	9.648	8.741	8.367	8.091	7.880
20	10.741	9.746	9.365	9.095	8.893

A simple strategy using duration is to buy bonds with long durations when interest rates are expected to decline (prices increase), since these bonds would increase *more* in price than bonds with shorter durations. Similarly, when rates are expected to increase, then one can switch to shorter duration bonds. Moreover, the use of duration allows the money

FIGURE 11-2: Durations vs. Bond Maturity and Coupons

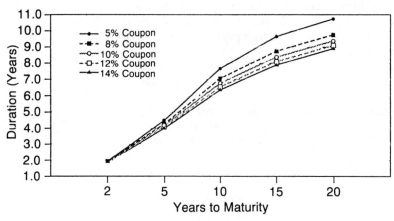

Source: Table 11-1

manager to realize that duration provides more information than simply using maturity; for example, a shorter-term low coupon bond can actually have a larger price change than a longer-term high coupon bond. A money manager concentrating on maturity effects alone could not be this precise.[7]

Convexity

Duration is based on the concept of *small* changes in yields. Consequently, an important factor affecting the usefulness of duration is **convexity.** Convexity is the effect of the curvature of the graph representing the relationship between the bond price and interest rates, as shown by curve BB' in Figure 11-3. Duration is interpreted as the (approximate) slope of the line that is tangent to this bond price curve BB' at the current interest rate. This slope is designated as D in Figure 11-3; that is, D is the line tangent to BB' at interest rate i_1. In this context, duration is defined mathematically by Equation (11-11) for small changes in P_B and i:

$$D = \frac{-\Delta P_B/P_B}{\Delta i/i} \qquad (11\text{-}11)$$

---

7   The portfolio concept of maximizing returns relative to the risks also can be applied to durations: One can maximize yields relative to the duration of the portfolio. Duration is used in the mortgage-backed security field as well as with traditional bonds. However, owners of mortgages often prepay their loans, causing complications in using duration to measure adequately the relationship between changes in interest rates and changes in the mortgage-backed security value. Another application of duration is matching the durations of assets versus the duration of liabilities, rather than to matching the cash flows of assets and liabilities. The assumptions of duration, as examined shortly, show that duration and cash flows may not provide equivalent answers.

FIGURE 11-3: Convexity

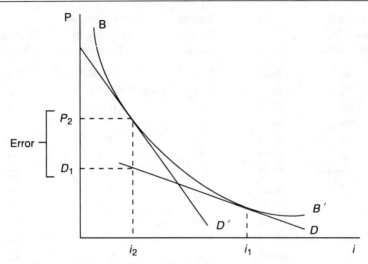

As the interest rate changes from i_1 to i_2, the duration (which is approximated by the slope of the line tangent to BB') changes from D to D'. $P_2 - D_1$ represents the error if D is used to calculate the change in price when D' is the appropriate value.

More precisely, we could use derivatives to show:

$$D = \frac{d(P_B)/P_B}{d(1 + i)/(1 + i)} \qquad (11\text{-}12)$$

where $d(\ ) = $ **derivative.**

Thus, duration is defined in economic terms as the elasticity of price changes to yield changes—that is, the effect of a percentage change of yields on a percentage change in price.[8]

The importance of convexity is that only very small (infinitesimal) changes in the interest rate are appropriate when the slope is used to approximate the price change of the bond. More specifically, Figure 11-3 illustrates that as the yield changes from i_1 to i_2, the slope to the nonlinear bond price curve changes. Thus, as interest rates change, duration changes, since duration is represented by the changing slope of the line tangent to the bond price curve. If the yield changes significantly, the duration also changes significantly. Consequently, using the original duration, D creates an error in the estimated price change because of the *change in the slope* of the tangent line; the size of the error is shown to be $P_2 - D_1$ in Figure 11-3. In this situation it is obvious that the portfolio manager *must constantly recalculate duration* in order to determine the price volatility, as well as to *rebalance the bond portfolio* to achieve the desired duration. Table 11-2 shows how

---

8   The elasticity approach to duration helps to explain the concept and difficulties of duration. However, calculating duration by elasticities is difficult and often inaccurate.

TABLE 11-2: Effect of Convexity on Bond Price Changes[a]

Change in Interest Rate, Basis Points	Price	Percent Change in Value	Percent Change Estimated by Duration	Error Due to Duration
+300	80.26	−19.7%	−24.3%	−4.6%
+250	83.02	−17.0	−20.2	−3.2
+200	85.96	−14.0	−16.2	−2.2
+150	89.11	−10.9	−12.2	−1.2
+100	92.48	− 7.5	− 8.1	−0.6
+50	96.11	− 3.9	− 4.0	−0.1
No change	100.00	NC	NC	0.0
−50	104.20	4.2	4.0	0.2
−100	108.72	8.7	8.1	0.6
−150	113.62	13.6	12.1	1.5
−200	118.93	18.9	16.2	2.7
−250	124.69	24.7	20.2	4.5
−300	130.96	31.0	24.3	6.7

[a] Calculations are based on a 30-year bond with a current yield of 12 percent.

convexity distorts the estimate of the size of the price change of the bond when large interest rate changes occur and duration is not recalculated.

Whereas duration is defined in Equation (11-12) by means of the derivative of P_B in terms of i, convexity is explained in terms of the second derivative. Thus, the slope of curve BB' in Figure 11-3 is the first derivative of the nonlinear price-interest rate relationship, whereas the second derivative (convexity) represents the *rate of change in the slope*. The existence of convexity means higher order derivatives are needed to account for the change in price, especially when the change in yield is large—that is, when one cannot rebalance the portfolio of bonds quickly enough to overcome the effect of the change in duration. The procedure for hedging against convexity effects is given in Chapter 12.

More Complicated Duration Measures

The previous discussion demonstrated how convexity causes difficulties in using duration when large changes in interest rates occur. Another problem for the Macaulay duration measure exists when the *shape* of the yield curve changes, since the Macaulay duration is based on the assumption of a flat yield curve that undergoes only parallel shifts. (A subsequent section in this chapter examines these issues and their effects.)

If one wishes to calculate a more complicated duration figure that considers the convexity effect, then a higher order duration must be determined (see Goodman and

Vijayaraghavan[9]). Bierwag[10] examines alternative duration measures for more complicated yield curve shapes and term structure shifts. In general, the more complicated duration measures employ a specific type of shape/shift in the yield curve to define mathematically a new duration measure. One technique is to use an additive or multiplicative shift in the term structure; for example, let the short-term interest rate vary 1.3 times as much as the long-term rate. Bierwag[11] shows that more complicated duration values do not vary significantly from Macaulay duration except for high coupon or long maturity bonds. Chapter 12 shows how (Macaulay) duration-convexity hedges are employed to mitigate the problems created by yield curve shifts.

IMMUNIZATION

The Concept

An important goal of any large pension or insurance fund is to guarantee now what the value of a portfolio will be in a given future time period, with that value occurring *regardless* of how interest rates change. Equivalently, the fund wants to obtain a *predetermined* annual rate of return on funds invested (which is typically a rate equal to the current yield to maturity). **Immunization** achieves these objectives. Immunization exists if the total value of the portfolio at the end of the investment period equals the ending value expected at the time of purchase. If a portfolio is immunized, then changes in interest rates will *not* affect the ending value of the portfolio. In other words, immunization eliminates the risk of a change in bond portfolio value due to a change in interest rates. Therefore, the funds needed to pay off a future liability will be available from the assets available, regardless of the behavior of future interest rates.[12]

Immunization is straightforward when the fund owns zero-coupon bonds. In this case, the ending value of the bonds is known with certainty (if the bonds do not have default risk), since there are no coupons to reinvest. However, only a limited number of originally issued zero coupon bonds exists. Moreover, those created by brokerage houses include an extra cost that makes their yield to maturity too low to be used by funds.

Immunization for coupon-paying bonds is based on the natural trade-off between the price change in the value of the bonds and the reinvestment rate effect of the cash flows when a given change in the interest rate occurs. Specifically, if the portfolio manager adjusts the structure of the portfolio so that any potential adverse changes in the bond value are offset with beneficial changes in the reinvestment rate (and vice versa), then the portfolio is immunized. The variability in the reinvestment rate is known as **reinvestment risk.** Duration is employed to help determine the appropriate structure of the portfolio in order to immunize its value. The concept of duration also is used by financial institutions to equate the duration of their assets with the duration of their liabilities, creating a matched or immunized balance sheet.

9   Laurie S. Goodman and N. R. Vijayaraghavan, "Generalized Duration Hedging with Futures," *The Review of Futures Markets*, Vol. 6, No. 1, 1987, pp. 94-108.

10 Gerald O. Bierwag, *Duration Analysis: Managing Interest Rate Risk.* New York: Ballinger Press, 1987.

11 Gerald O. Bierwag, "Immunization, Duration, and Term Structure of Interest Rates," *Journal of Financial and Quantitative Analysis*, Vol. 12, No. 5, December 1977, pp. 725-742.

12 The discussion of immunization assumes the use of Treasury bonds, since the potential default risk of corporate bonds is not considered.

The Reinvestment Rate Effect

In order to immunize a portfolio, the money manager must deal with the dual problems of a loss in the value of the portfolio if interest rates increase and with the reinvestment rate problem of having unknown and inconsistent rates of return when investing the proceeds from bond coupons and principal payments. This trade-off between bond value and reinvestment returns is the key to immunization.

The reinvestment rate over time has a significant effect on both the ending value and the realized compound yield to maturity (RCYTM) for a portfolio. Table 11-3 provides an example of the effect of the reinvestment rate on the final portfolio value and on the RCYTM when different interest rates and investment horizons are considered for a ten-year, 10% coupon bond. The effects of the change in interest rates given in Table 11-3 are shown in Figure 11-4.

Figure 11-4 shows the dollar change in the price of the bond and the dollar change in reinvestment returns for an increase and decrease in interest rates. The time t the position is held, in conjunction with the change in interest rates, determines the net profit or loss on the bond position. The same results are shown in Table 11-3. The top panel of Table 11-3 has the fund's investment horizon of ten years equal to the maturity of the bond. The middle column of this top panel states that the *future* interest rate associated with the reinvestment returns of the coupons will equal the original yield to maturity of the bond, that is, the future reinvestment rate equals 10%. This situation causes the *RCYTM to equal the initial return on investment of 10%.* However, when the future reinvestment rate immediately falls to 8% (the left column of the table), then the rate of return obtained from reinvesting the coupons is *less* than the original YTM of 10%. This coupon reinvestment effect causes the terminal value from the total investment to be less than the return initially expected (i.e., less than the original YTM), causing the actual RCYTM to fall to 9.33%. Likewise, an increase in the reinvestment rate to 12% after the bond is purchased (the right column of the table) results in higher reinvestment returns for the coupons than expected, creating a RCYTM of 10.71%. Obviously, the variability in the final RCYTM values and the terminal value ratios given in Table 11-3, which range from a RCYTM of 9.33% to 10.71% as the reinvestment rate assumptions change, can cause a wide range of total dollar amounts for pension funds that deal in hundreds of millions of dollars.

The other panels of Table 11-3 show situations in which the investment horizon is not equal to the maturity of the bond. When the investment horizon is 15 years, then the principal of the bond must be reinvested after 10 years, along with continual reinvestment of the coupon payments. The middle panel of Table 11-3 shows the compounding effect of reinvesting proceeds at various interest rates for the 15-year time horizon. For an interest rate of 8% the RCYTM for the 15-year horizon falls to 8.89%, which compares unfavorably with the 9.33% RCYTM for the ten-year, 8% reinvestment rate horizon as well as unfavorably with the original expected 10% YTM. On the other hand, a subsequent interest rate of 12% increases the RCYTM for the 15-year horizon to 11.14%.

The five-year horizon in the final panel of the table shows a reversed picture from the 15-year horizon, with an 8% interest rate providing lower reinvestment returns on the coupons, but with this adverse effect being more than offset by the capital gains from the higher bond value obtained after five years as the result of the lower interest rate. Likewise,

TABLE 11-3: Investment in Ten-Year 10% Coupon Bond
Priced at Par of $1,000

	Future Reinvestment Rate		
	8%	10%	12%
10-Year Horizon:			
Coupon receipts	$1,000	$1,000	$1,000
Accumulation from coupon reinvestment	489	653	839
Total value of coupons	1,489	1,653	1,839
Repayment at maturity	1,000	1,000	1,000
Total terminal value	$2,489	2,653	$2,839
Terminal value ratio[a]	2.489	2.653	2.839
Realized compound YTM	9.33%	10.00%	10.71%
15-Year Horizon			
Value of bond at maturity			
(See "10-Year Horizon" terminal value)	$2,489	$2,653	$2,839
Accumulation from reinvestment			
of bond proceeds for 5 years	1,195	1,669	2,246
Total terminal value	$3,684	$4,322	$5,085
Terminal value ratio[a]	3.684	4.322	5.085
Realized compound YTM	8.89%	10.00%	11.14%
5-Year Horizon			
Coupon receipts	$ 500	$ 500	$ 500
Accumulation from coupon reinvestment	100	129	159
Total value of coupons	600	629	659
Price of bond	1,081	1,000	927
Total terminal value	$1,681	$1,629	$1,586
Terminal value ratio[a]	1.681	1.629	1.586
Realized compound YTM	10.67%	10.00%	9.43%

[a] The realized compound yield is found from the equation

$$RCYTM = (\text{terminal value ratio})^{1/N} - 1$$

for N periods (using semiannual compounding is used).

Note: All calculations are based on semiannual coupons and yields to maturity.

Source: Richard McEnally, "How to Neutralize Reinvestment Rate Risk," Journal of Portfolio Management, Vol. 6, No. 3 Spring 1980, pp. 59-63.

FIGURE 11-4: Reinvestment Rate Effect

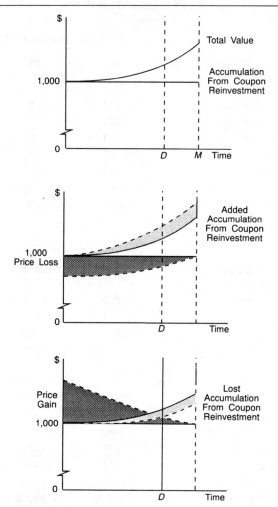

M is the maturity of the bond and t indicates the holding period of the bond. The solid line equals the total value of the bond returns plus the reinvestment returns *before* a change in interest rates. The broken lines and hatched areas show the effects of a change in interest rates on bond price and reinvestment returns.

D is the duration of the bond. When the duration equals the holding period, the change in the bond price equals the change in reinvestment returns; that is, the bond returns are immunized. At time periods other than D the price change does *not* equal the change in reinvestment returns.

Source: Richard McEnally, "How to Neutralize Reinvestment Rate Risk," *Journal of Portfolio Management*, Vol. 6, No. 3 Spring 1980, pp. 59-63.

the higher 12% interest rate provides larger reinvestment returns but generates a capital loss when the bond is sold. These examples show that the relationship between the investment horizon and the maturity (duration) of the bond must be considered *in conjunction with* the reinvestment rate in order to determine the RCYTM and the relevant investment strategy.

RCYTM and Immunization

The effect of the reinvestment rate, the horizon (holding period) of the fund, and the duration on the realized compound yield to maturity is conveniently summarized by Babcock[13] as follows:

$$RCYTM = (D/H) \, (YTM) + (1-D/H) \, (ARR) \qquad (11-13)$$

where

RCYTM	=	realized compound yield to maturity
D	=	duration
H	=	horizon period
YTM	=	yield to maturity on the bond or bond portfolio
ARR	=	average reinvestment rate

This equation shows that the RCYTM is a weighted average of the YTM and the reinvestment rate, with the weights being determined by the relationship between the duration and the horizon period. Moreover, when the *duration equals the horizon, then the RCYTM equals the YTM.* In this case the portfolio is *immunized.*

Equation (11-13) shows that an immunized portfolio is possible for a properly chosen duration and horizon. For example, Table 11-4 gives the terminal value and RCYTM for the bond used in Table 11-3, with the additional knowledge that the horizon period equals the duration of the bond at 6 1/2 years. Both the terminal values and the RCYTM for the various assumed reinvestment rates in Table 11-4 show that the effect of changing the reinvestment rate is exactly offset by the change in the value of the bond. Thus, setting the horizon period equal to the duration immunizes the portfolio.[14] This relationship is also shown in Figure 11-4, where part B shows graphically how the additional funds received from a higher reinvestment rate offset the loss from the decline in the value of the bond; part C shows the same effect when the loss from a lower reinvestment rate is offset by the gain in the value of the bond.

A later section in this chapter discusses the effects of violations of the duration assumptions employed to implement immunization on the results of the immunization process. Considering these effects is crucial to a successful risk management program. One of the assumptions of the Macaulay duration is that only parallel shifts in a flat yield curve exist. Fisher and Weil[15] *prove* that a portfolio of bonds with a duration equal to the length of the desired holding period is immunized against a parallel shift in a flat yield curve. A simplified

---

13 Guilford C. Babcock, "Duration as a Link between Yield and Value," *Journal of Portfolio Management*, Vol. 10, No.4, Summer 1984, pp. 58-65.

14 The RCYTM in Table 11-4 differs from 10% by several basis points because the actual duration is 6.545 years rather than 6.5 years, and because of the effect of convexity.

15 L. Fisher and R. L. Weil, "Coping with the Risk of Interest Rate Fluctuations: Returns to Bondholders from Naive and Optimal Strategies," *Journal of Business*, Vol. 44, No. 4, October 1977, pp. 408-431.

**TABLE 11-4: Reinvestment Rates and Immunization with a
Ten-Year 10% Coupon Bond Priced at Par of $1,000**

	Future Reinvestment Rates		
	8%	**10%**	**12%**
6½ Year Horizon			
Coupon receipts	$ 650	$ 650	$ 650
Accumulation from coupon reinvestment	181	236	294
Total value of coupons	831	886	944
Price of bond	1,060	1,000	945
Total terminal value	$1,891	$1,886	$1,889
Terminal value ratio	1.892	1.886	1.889
Realized compound YTM	10.04%	10.00%	10.02%

Note: All calculations are based on semiannual coupons and yields to maturity.

Source: Richard McEnally, "How to Neutralize Reinvestment Rate Risk," *Journal of Portfolio Management*, Vol. 6, No. 3 Spring 1980, pp. 59-63.

example of this relationship is shown when zero-coupon bonds are employed. Since the duration of a zero-coupon bond equals its maturity, we can substitute maturity for duration in the immunization statement $D = H$ to obtain $M = H$; in other words, when the maturity of a zero-coupon bond equals the holding period, then the portfolio is immunized against a change in interest rates. Of course, such a statement must be true unless the bond issuer defaults, since no reinvestment problems occur and the bond pays its principal at maturity.

EVIDENCE CONCERNING DURATION AND IMMUNIZATION

Table 11-5 provides empirical evidence on the ability of duration to achieve immunization, as based on a study in Bierwag, Kaufman and Toevs.[16] A ten-year horizon period is used, with annual revisions made in the portfolio to adjust for changes in the duration value. Column 3 in the table shows the difference between the return promised by the immunization strategy at the beginning of the period and the actual returns achieved. Column 3 shows that duration provides results within 15 basis points of the promised return. Duration consistently outperformed a simple maturity matching approach, with duration being closer than maturity matching to the promised yield 80% to 93% of the time. However, the inclusion of commissions and taxes would adversely affect these results. The original article

16 Gerald O. Bierwag, George Kaufman, and Alden Toevs, "Duration: Its Development and Use in Bond Portfolio Management," *Financial Analysts Journal*, Vol. 39, No. 4, July-August 1983, pp. 15-35.

TABLE 11-5: Promised and Realized Returns for
Alternative Portfolio Immunization Strategies
(Ten-Year Planning Periods, 1925-1978)

	Return			Percentage of the time:	
	(1)	(2)	(3)	(4)	(5)
Immunization Strategy	Promised (Annual Average)[a]	Realized (Annual Average)	Realized Minus Promised	Closer to Promised than Maturity Strategy	Within 5 Basis Points of Promised
1925–1949					
Macaulay duration	3.697	3.552	– 0.145	93	13
Maturity	3.697	3.465	– 0.232	—	0
1940–1963					
Macaulay duration	2.257	2.214	– 0.043	79	50
Maturity matching	2.257	2.214	– 0.043	—	36
1954–1978					
Macaulay duration	4.064	4.026	– 0.038	87	80
Maturity matching	4.064	4.234	+ 0.170	—	13

[a] Ten–year yield to maturity at date of purchase.
Source: Adapted from Gerald O. Bierwag, George Kaufman, and Alden Toevs, "Duration: Its Development and Use in Bond Portfolio Management," *Financial Analysts Journal*, Vol. 39, No. 4, July–August 1983, pp. 15–35.

compares the performance of the Macaulay duration measure to more complicated measures, and the conclusion suggests that the Macaulay measure provides equivalent results. Consequently, the benefit-cost ratio obtained from implementing more involved duration measures seems to be small.

Using data from 1975 to 1985, Bierwag, Kaufman and Latta[17] show that more recent data mirror the results in Table 11-5. In addition, they find that using a two-factor duration process to reduce risk, rather than simply using the Macaulay duration, improves the performance of the immunization process 75% to 90% of the time.

ASSUMPTIONS OF DURATION AND IMMUNIZATION

The process of immunization described in the chapter states that an immunized bond position is obtained by simply holding a bond position that has a duration equal to the

17 Gerald O. Bierwag, George G. Kaufman, and Cynthia M. Latta, "Bond Portfolio Immunization: Tests of Maturity, One- and Two-Factor Duration Matching Strategies," *Financial Review*, Vol. 22, No. 2, May 1987, pp. 203-220.

investment horizon. However, several caveats are needed before implementing the duration and immunization techniques. These caveats show that duration and immunization require active management and the use of sophisticated analysis in order to obtain optimal results.

Portfolio Structure

The first consideration occurs when a fund holds a portfolio of fixed-income investments rather than a single bond. Whether calculating an average duration for the bond portfolio causes difficulties in obtaining a useful value for duration or immunization depends upon the structure of the portfolio and the slope and behavior of the term structure of interest rates, as elaborated on below. Even more difficult problems arise for investments with more complicated cash flow arrangements, such as those involving repayment and repricing clauses—for example, mortgage instruments.

A One-Time Immediate Adjustment to Interest Rates

The duration and immunization techniques are based on a one-time *immediate* adjustment in interest rates, rather than on continuous and numerous changes in rates. The discussion of convexity in the chapter illustrates that the actual process of interest rate change that occurs in the economy necessitates a frequent recalculation of the duration value for accuracy, and therefore a subsequent rebalancing of the portfolio in order to keep the duration equal to the investment horizon for immunization purposes. If adjustments are not made, perfect immunization no longer exists and the RCYTM varies from the expected return. Moreover, the impact of transactions costs needs to be considered so the benefits of rebalancing are not negated by commissions and trading costs.

A Schedule of Horizons

The third consideration is that the fund's investment horizon often is a schedule of horizons; for example, a series of horizons is needed to meet the pension or insurance needs of different age groups. One could calculate a single horizon by determining the duration of the liabilities for the pension fund or insurance company needs and then use this figure as the investment horizon. As with the duration of bonds, a horizon duration would need to be recalculated periodically.

Term Structure Behavior

The fourth caveat concerns the behavior of the yield curve, which is a major factor affecting the duration/immunization process. In particular, the Macaulay measure of duration is based on a flat yield curve, where only parallel shifts in the yield curve are allowed. The importance of a flat yield curve to obtain accurate results for duration and immunization rests with the effect of changes in the forward rates of the term structure on the calculation of duration. In other words, we can define duration in terms of the individual discount forward rates, as shown in Equations (11-14) and (11-15), rather than in terms of one yield to maturity as is done in the Macaulay definition of duration:

$$D = \frac{\displaystyle\sum_{t=1}^{M} t\, C_t / (1 + R[0,t])^t}{\displaystyle\sum_{t=1}^{M} C_t / (1 + R[0,t])^t} \qquad (11\text{-}14)$$

where $R[0,t]$ is the actual cash discount rate for the cash flow to be received at time t.

A long-term interest rate $R[0,t]$ can be separated into the current short-term cash rate plus a series of forward rates; that is,

$$R[0,t] = (1 + R[0,1]) (1 + r[1,2]) (1 + r[2,3]) \dots (1 + r[t-1,t])^{1/t} \qquad (11\text{-}15)$$

This designation helps us to visualize the effects of changes in interest rates on duration. In particular, changes in the location or shape of a curved term structure cause *unequal* changes in the forward rates $r[i, i + 1]$. Thus, the changes in the discount rates $R[0,t]$ do not equal, nor are they uniquely related to, the change in the yield to maturity. Moreover, a given change in the discount rate or in the forward rate is consistent with a variety of changes in the yield to maturity, and a given change in the yield to maturity is consistent with a variety of patterns in the discount rate changes. Thus, *there is no one unique relationship.* Since our simple Macaulay duration is calculated by using the yield to maturity, this Macaulay duration value provides accurate results *only* when the change in the yield to maturity is appropriately measured—that is, *when a flat yield curve exists.* The resultant problem for the immunization process is evident: if changes in a nonflat yield curve cause inaccurate duration values, then the changes in the total terminal value due to the reinvestment rate do not offset the change in the bond price. In this case immunization does not occur because duration is not measured accurately.

Statistical Processes

Another approach to the assumption concerning the effect of the shape of the yield curve on duration is to examine the statistical or **stochastic process** describing the behavior of changes in the term structure of interest rates. Differing statistical processes have different effects on how the yield curve shifts and changes shape. For example, one stochastic process designates that short-term interest rates are twice as volatile as long-term rates. The Macaulay measure of duration used here employs a stochastic process where a flat term structure curve exists, where forward rates change randomly, and where all forward rate changes are equal. In fact, any single factor duration method is based on the assumption that all changes in the forward rates are perfectly correlated, otherwise a multiple factor duration process is needed. More complicated stochastic processes of term structure behavior and their related durations are given in the appendix of Bierwag, Kaufman and Toevs.[18] However, there is some question whether the more complicated measures of duration provide more accurate results, especially since we do not know the actual statistical process that determines the behavior of interest rates.

---

18 Bierwag, Kaufman, and Toevs, ibid.

Arbitrage Profits

A final criticism of the Macaulay measure of duration is that it does not satisfy the equilibrium condition of no arbitrage profits, since owning high coupon bonds provides larger returns than owning low coupon bonds of the same duration, assuming a flat yield curve with only parallel shifts. In other words, even though two bonds have the same volatility (duration), a higher coupon bond provides a higher return. Again, more complicated duration measures describe more realistic interest rate behavior, but the simplicity of the Macaulay duration measure often becomes the dominant measure in practice.

CONTINGENT IMMUNIZATION

The Concept of Contingent Immunization

Leibowitz and Weinberger[19] develop an extension of the simple classical immunization technique which is discussed in the chapter. This extension, called contingent immunization, provides active bond managers flexibility in their trading decisions with the objective of obtaining above-average returns, while providing a guaranteed minimum rate of return. This process has been received favorably by the investment community via fixed-income funds offered by Salomon Brothers.

The parameters affecting the risk and return of contingent immunization are the minimum return desired and the specification of the horizon time *range* identifying *when* the minimum acceptable return can be achieved. The key concept of contingent immunization is to switch from an active trading mode to an immunized mode if/when the projected realized YTM falls to the floor (minimum) return for *all* time periods in the horizon range. The time period when the fund is switched into the immunized mode is known as the trigger point. Figure 11-5 shows the relationship between contingent immunization and classical immunization in terms of the present yield (identified as "0" on the X-axis versus the minimum floor immunized return.[20]

The Trigger Point

Leibowitz and Weinberger[21] provide specific information on the relationship between the trigger point which identifies when to switch to the immunization mode and the factors affecting this trigger point. These factors are the minimum return and the horizon range. Reducing the minimum return required provides flexibility for trading by moving the immunization trigger point away from the present yield to maturity. However, a lower floor return entails greater risk when poor forecasting of interest rates occur. Similarly, using a

---

19 Martin Leibowitz and Alfred Weinberger, "Contingent Immunization—Part I: Risk Control Procedures," *Financial Analysis Journal*, November-December 1982, pp. 17-31. Martin Leibowitz and Alfred Weinberger, "Contingent Immunization—Part II: Problem Areas," *Financial Analysts Journal*, January—February 1983, pp. 35-50. Martin Leibowitz and Alfred Weinberger, "The Uses of Contingent Immunization," *Journal of Portfolio Management*, Fall 1981, pp. 51-55.

20 Contingent immunization is similar to buying a call option. If bond prices increase, then profits increase, with the cost of the option being the potential loss of return as defined by the difference between the classical immunized return and the contingent minimum immunized return.

21 Liebowitz and Weinberger, ibid., "Contingent Immunization - Part I..." and "The Uses of Contingent Immunization."

FIGURE 11-5: Contingent Immunization

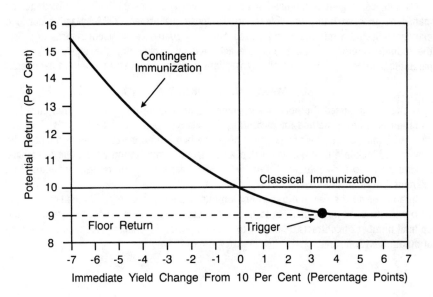

range of investment horizons rather than a specific horizon also moves the trigger point curve away from the present yield.

Disadvantages and Problems

The potential disadvantages of contingent immunization include:
- Many portfolio managers tend to be more conservative when the floor constraint for an immunized return exists. Simulations suggest that this constraint causes an average give-up of 70 basis points from what a fully active portfolio manager could achieve.
- Problems exist when switching from active management to the immunized mode: liquidity and marketability of the current and potential bonds for the portfolio plus transactions costs are the most serious of these problems. "An initial trigger warning system" often is used to notify the portfolio manager of impending immunization, allowing the manager to switch gradually into other bonds.
- As the horizon period declines, the flexibility of active bond management decreases significantly, often forcing immunization. This lack of flexibility is due to the restrictions imposed by the minimum immunized return and the horizon range, in association with the short horizon period.

- The problems related to the assumptions of duration (discussed in the previous section) and to immunization risk (covered in Appendix 11A) also exist here; thus, immunization risk arising from twists in the yield curve could cause the actual return to be below the target return.[22]

Overall, contingent immunization combines two goals sought by many fixed-income managers: an opportunity to achieve returns above the present YTM by active portfolio management and a minimum immunized return to guarantee sufficient returns to satisfy the fund requirements. These goals are achieved by augmenting the typical risk-return parameters inherent in most security transactions with the floor return as a third parameter.

SUMMARY AND LOOKING AHEAD

This chapter discussed the bond management techniques of duration and immunization. Duration provides a method for measuring the relative volatility of a bond as well as the effect of a change in interest rates on the price of a bond. Immunization allows the portfolio manager to lock-in a final portfolio value. Contingent immunization allows one to manage a bond portfolio for additional return while still keeping a floor return. Appendix 11A examines immunization risk.

In addition to the use of duration and immunization by cash portfolio managers, those who wish to use futures markets to hedge can use the duration model to determine the optimal number of contracts to employ to hedge a portfolio. Chapter 12 examines the uses of duration with futures.

---

22 Leibowitz and Weinberger claim that this risk was 24 basis points from 1958-75, substantially higher than the immunization results given in the body of the chapter. One may structure the immunized portfolio with cash flows near the investment horizon, which minimizes the immunization risk.

Appendix 11A
Immunization Risk

O ne may immunize a bond portfolio for a given target rate of return if the duration equals the holding period *and* if only parallel shifts in a flat yield curve occur. When immunization exists, changes in the price of the bond are offset by changes in the reinvestment returns. However, if large interest rate changes occur before rebalancing then convexity causes differences between the target immunized return and the actual rate of return on the portfolio. Convexity and nonparallel shifts in the term structure create immunization risk.

The Concept of Immunization Risk

Immunization risk occurs when the actual statistical (stochastic) process that determines the behavior of interest rates differs from the simple unrealistic process used for Macaulay duration and the associated immunization process. Thus, immunization risk is a function of the relationship among:
1. the planning period (horizon) of the investment,
2. the cash flow characteristics of the fixed-income investments, and
3. the actual stochastic process of interest rates.

Noting that items (2) and (3) may be used to define an accurate measure of duration *if* (3) was known and could be measured precisely, we could use this new duration measure to guarantee that immunization risk would be zero when the planning period equaled the duration. However, since the stochastic process that determines the behavior of interest rates is not known, immunization risk needs to be measured and controlled.

A simple approach to minimize the immunization risk is to choose individual securities with durations that are as close as possible to the investment horizon. This strategy minimizes the effect of differences between the bond price change and the reinvestment returns. In fact, if the bond is a zero-coupon bond then no immunization risk occurs.

Measuring Immunization Risk

A more specific approach to immunization risk than portfolio restructuring was developed by Fong and Vasicek,[1] who devised an equation to measure the immunization risk due to changes in the shape of the term structure curve. When a change in the shape or **twist in the yield curve** does occur, immunization may not be possible, e.g. for a given twist from downward to upward sloping, it would be possible to have both a loss in the value of the bond (as long-term rates increased) *and* a decline in the reinvestment rate (as short-term rates decreased). Fong and Vasicek showed that a change in the terminal value of a portfolio

---

1 . H. Gifford Fong and Oldrich Vasicek, "The Tradeoff Between Return and Risk in Immunized Portfolios," *Financial Analysts Journal,* September-October 1983, pp. 73-78.

when a yield curve twist occurs is given by equation (11A-1), while the immunization risk
per se is measured by equation (11A-2):

$$\Delta I_H = - M^2 \, \Delta_S \qquad\qquad (11A-1)$$

where ΔI_H = change in the ending value of the immunized portfolio

Δ_S = change in the slope (twist) of the term structure

M^2 = measure of the immunization risk, as based on the structure of the
portfolio, with:

$$M^2 = \sum_{t=1}^{m} (t - H)^2 \, C_t \, (1 + r[t,t+1])^{-t} \, / \, PV_B \qquad\qquad (11A-2)$$

where t = the time periods of the payments, with t=1,...m

H = the horizon period

C_t = payment at time t

r[t,t+1] = forward interest rate at time t

PV_B = present value of the bond

Equation (11A-1) shows that the terminal value of the portfolio is affected by M^2 and Δ_S.
M^2 depends on the structure of the cash flows of the portfolio, while Δ_S depends only on
the behavior of the term structure of interest rates. The portfolio manager can affect the
quantity M^2, which in turn determines the risk of the portfolio when a change in the slope
of the term structure occurs. Also note that M^2 is similar in nature to our general definition
of duration, except that it is affected by the individual *unequal* forward discount rates
r[t,t+1] and M^2 is the weighted *variance* of the time to payment around the horizon date.
When payments are widely dispersed in time (such as a "barbell" portfolio of very short and
very long bonds), then M^2 is large. When the payments occur near the horizon period (such
as with zero coupon or deep discount bonds) then M^2 is small. Both types of portfolios are
immunized against parallel shifts in a flat yield curve, but they react quite differently to
twists in the yield curve. In particular, a twist causes significant risk for a barbell type
portfolio.

Chapter 12

The Duration Hedging Technique

Using duration to determine the appropriate futures hedge ratio is an alternative to the regression-based method for fixed-income investments. The duration-based hedge ratio considers the relative volatilities of the cash and futures instruments by computing the durations of these instruments. Here we develop the duration-based hedge ratio, then compare and contrast this approach to the regression methodology.

Duration is used for a number of different types of hedges, including portfolio, anticipatory, asset-liability, and immunization hedges. Empirically, the duration approach is superior to naive methods. However, no studies have compared the regression and duration procedures.

Unfortunately, there are difficulties with the basic duration-based hedge ratio. Large yield changes and changes in the slope or shape of the yield curve are two important problems that can create errors for duration hedge results. Convexity is the cause of these errors, and a duration-convexity hedge procedure is developed as an alternative to the duration-only approach.

APPLYING DURATION CONCEPTS TO FUTURES HEDGING

Introduction

Duration provides an alternative technique to regression in order to determine an appropriate hedge ratio for fixed-income investments. Based on the duration concept developed in Chapter 11, one can find the hedge ratio that minimizes the net price change from the combined futures/cash position, given that the assumptions of the duration model are met. Recall that duration includes time until maturity, coupon, and the level of interest rates to determine the effect of a change in interest rates on the price of the relevant fixed-income instrument. Thus, the relative durations of the cash and futures instruments are the key elements in the **duration-based hedge** model.

A difficulty with the use of cash immunization for hedging covered in Chapter 11 is that changes in interest rates, time, or the shape of the term structure often forces the portfolio manager to rebalance the portfolio. Rebalancing adjusts for changing durations in order to benefit fully from immunization. This rebalancing of the portfolio to keep the desired duration often creates large transaction costs and/or is difficult to implement when there are thin cash markets. The use of futures contracts to adjust durations significantly reduces these costs and liquidity problems.

The Development of the Duration Model for Hedging

In Chapter 11 we state that the basic objective of hedging is to find a hedge ratio that offsets the price change in the cash instrument with the price change in the futures position; that is,

$$\Delta P_C + (HR)\ \Delta P_F = 0 \tag{12-1}$$

where ΔP_C = the price change of the cash instrument

ΔP_F = the price change of the futures instrument

HR = the futures hedge ratio

or, equivalently, that the appropriate hedge ratio to eliminate or minimize the net change in the combined cash/futures value is

$$HR = -\Delta P_C / \Delta P_F \tag{12-2}$$

where the minus sign stands for a futures position that is opposite the cash position. Thus, if one owns the cash asset, then a manager would short futures.

The regression model finds the "appropriate hedge ratio" illustrated in Equation (12-2) by determining the "*average* relationship" between the ΔP_C and the ΔP_F" via the slope of the regression line such that the variance of the errors around the regression line is minimized. The duration-based hedge method determines the hedge ratio by minimizing the *net change in wealth* of the hedger. Expressed another way, regression inputs historical price changes in order to minimize the variability of the net hedge position over the period of the hedge, whereas the duration method employs the relative volatilities of the cash and futures instruments as measured by duration in order to minimize the net price change between the initiation and termination of the hedge.[1]

The price change equation developed in Chapter 11 describes the effect of a change in interest rates on the price of a debt instrument when duration is used to measure volatility:

$$\Delta P_C = -D\ P_C\ \Delta i\ /\ (1 + i) \tag{12-3}$$

We can then develop the duration-based hedging model in terms of instantaneous changes by using derivatives and Equation (12-3):[2]

$$dP_C = -D_C\ P_C\ di_C\ /\ (1 + i_C) \tag{12-4}$$

$$dP_F = -D_F\ P_F\ di_F\ /\ (1 + i_F) \tag{12-5}$$

where d ($\cdot$) stands for the derivative of the associated variable,

dP_C, dP_F, and di represent ΔP_C, ΔP_F, and Δi respectively, from

Equations (12-2) and (12-3). In addition,

D_C, D_F = the durations of the cash and futures instruments

P_C, P_F = the prices of the cash and futures instruments

i_C, i_F = the interest rates (yields) associated with the cash and futures positions

If we assume that the change in the cash and futures interest rates di_C and di_F are equally sensitive to a change in the risk-free interest rate (i.e., $di_C/di_F = 1$), then we can

---

1   Toevs and Jacob show that the regression and duration models are equivalent when the horizon of the hedge is instantaneous and when regression uses forecasted values. Alden L. Toevs and David P. Jacob, "Futures and Alternative Hedge Ratio Methodologies," *Journal of Portfolio Management*, Vol. 12, No. 3, Spring 1986, pp. 60-70.

2   The small parallel changes in the yield curve, which is an assumption of duration, relate to the use of calculus for the derivation of the duration and duration-based hedge ratio equations. This factor is discussed in more detail later in the chapter.

take the ratio $dP_C/dP_F = \Delta P_C/\Delta P_F = HR$ stated in Equation (12-2) to derive the duration-based hedge ratio, resulting in:

$$HR_D = \frac{D_C \, P_C \, (1 + i_F)}{D_F \, P_F \, (1 + i_C)} \qquad (12\text{-}6)$$

The number of contacts needed for a hedge which follows the format for the previous hedge ratio methods, is:

$$N_D = HR_D \text{ (total par value of cash/par value of one futures contract)} \qquad (12\text{-}7)$$

Some formulations of Equation (12-6) include a minus sign to indicate a futures position that is opposite the cash position. The duration of the futures contract is determined by finding the duration of the cheapest-to-deliver bond. In addition, recall from our previous discussions of duration that i_F and i_C are measured in terms of *six-month yields* for bonds issuing coupons semiannually.

Incorporating Relative Sensitivities

Equation (12-6) is the most common formulation of the duration hedge ratio. However, if one wishes to incorporate unequal sensitivities of the cash and futures interest rates to a change in the risk-free rate, then we must determine the sensitivity of Equations (12-4) and (12-5) to a small change in the risk-free interest rate i_{RF}. We then substitute these results into Equation (12-2) in order to obtain the duration formulation for the hedge ratio. The result is a refined hedge ratio, as follows:

$$HR_{D2} = \frac{D_C \, P_C \, (1 + i_F)}{D_F \, P_F \, (1 + i_C)} \, RS \qquad (12\text{-}8)$$

where RS is the relative sensitivity of the cash market yield to the futures market yield, given a change in the risk-free rate; that is,

$$RS = \frac{di_C/di_{RF}}{di_F/di_{RF}}$$

In most cases, the interest rates relative sensitivity is obtained from a historical analysis of the instruments in question. Such an analysis reduces the advantage of the duration method over the regression method since Equation (12-6) does not employ historical data.[3]

The interest rate's relative sensitivity to the risk-free rate can be important when the default risk between the cash and futures instruments differ, when the term structure curve is not flat, or when the term structure has a nonparallel shift in conjunction with significantly different durations for the futures and cash instruments. However, since the calculation of the relative sensitivity is complicated and typically not determined in practice, Equation (12-6) is usually employed for duration-based hedging, even though HR_D would include some bias. Moreover, the assumptions of a flat yield curve and nonparallel shifts impounded in the calculation of the duration values in Equations (12-6) and (12-8) can cause inaccurate hedge ratio results in any case.

---

3   A more involved derivation of the duration hedge model is found in Kolb and Chiang, who call the model the "price sensitivity" approach to hedging. Robert Kolb and Raymond Chiang, "Improving Hedging Performance Using Interest Rate Futures," *Financial Management*, Vol. 10, No. 4, Autumn 1981, pp. 72-79. Robert Kolb and Raymond Chiang, "Duration, Immunization, and Hedging with Interest Rate Futures," *Journal of Financial Research*, Vol. 5 No. 2, Summer 1982, pp. 161-170.

Example of a Duration Hedge

Example 12-1 shows how to use Equations (12-6) and (12-7) to calculate the hedge ratio and the number of contracts needed for a short hedge. Since both the cash and futures are based on T-bonds, we assume that RS in Equation (12-8) is equal to one; that is, the relative sensitivity of the cash and futures yields to a change in interest rates is the same. Example 12-2 shows the effect of the duration hedge when cash and futures prices decline—namely, that the hedge eliminates more than 96% of the loss in the cash bonds.

Considerations in Implementing the Duration Model

Two considerations in implementing the duration hedge model are the effect of unstable input values on the hedge ratio and whether current or expected input values should be employed in the model. Instability in the input values over time can cause a change in the hedge ratio, thereby necessitating a change in the number of futures contracts employed for the hedge.

If the cash instrument is a close substitute for the cheapest-to-deliver futures instrument, then the input ratios of P_C/P_F and $(1 + i_F)/(1 + i_C)$ in the model will not change significantly over time. If the cash instrument is not the cheapest, then volatile values for P_C/P_F and $(1 + i_F)/(1 + i_C)$ can occur. The stability of D_C/D_F depends on the characteristics of the instruments, the size of the change in interest rates, the length of time until the termination of the hedge, and the extent of violations of the assumptions of a flat yield curve and nonparallel shifts in the yield curve. Thus, the stability of the durations is related to the effects of convexity. The final section of this chapter examines these effects and a duration-convexity hedge procedure.

Kolb and Chiang[4] indicate that the application of the duration-based hedge ratio given in Equations (12-6) and (12-8) requires future *expected* values for the input variables as of the *termination* date of the hedge. Toevs and Jacob[5] qualify this statement by maintaining that anticipatory hedges should use expected values, whereas a short hedge for a currently held asset should use the current values for the cash instrument and the expected values for the duration of the futures instrument based on the (expected) delivery date. The use of expected values in the duration model is associated with the *cash flows* of the relevant instrument when the cash instrument is actually held, and thus the effect of convergence on the results is eliminated. *However*, forecasting the value of these variables can be difficult. Consequently, in practice hedgers often use the current values of the input variables. The effect of using current values in place of expected values for anticipatory hedges is related to the same factors noted above for unstable hedge ratios over time; that is, major differences occur only when the cash and cheapest-to-deliver instrument have significantly different characteristics.

Example of an Anticipatory Duration Hedge Ratio

Example 12-3 calculates a duration-based hedge ratio for an anticipatory hedge, based on a given set of input data. Since it is an anticipatory hedge, the *expected* future values for the

4 Kolb and Chiang, ibid. "Improving Hedging Performance . . ."

5 Alden L. Toevs and David P. Jacob, "Interest Rate Futures: A Comparison of Alternative Ratio Methodologies," Morgan Stanley Research Report, June 1984.

EXAMPLE 12-1: Determining a Duration Hedge Ratio

Current portfolio value	$10,000,000
Cash instrument to be hedged	T-bonds: 12% of May '05
	YTM: 10.4%
	Price: 113:24
	Duration: 7.75
Number of bonds at current price	
($1,000 Face Value)	8,791
T-bond futures*	Price: 81–8
	YTM: 10.8%
	Duration: 8.36

The duration hedge ratio is as follows:

$$HR_D = \frac{D_C \, P_C \, (1 + i_F)}{D_F \, P_F \, (1 + i_C)} \qquad (12\text{-}6)$$

$$= \frac{(7.75) \, (113.8) \, (1.054)}{(8.36) \, (81.25) \, (1.052)}$$

$$= 929.58/714.57$$

$$= 1.300$$

For this example, $(1 + i_F) = 1.054$ and $(1 + i_C) = 1.052$, since the bonds have semiannual coupons.

$$N_D = HR_D \text{ (total par value of cash/par value of futures)}$$
$$= 1.300 \, (\$8,791,000/\$100,000)$$
$$= 114.28$$
$$= 114 \text{ contracts}$$

---

* The cheapest-to-deliver cash bond is assumed to be a 14% bond due in 20 years with a conversion factor of 1.5875. The futures price is determined by finding the present value of the bond for the relevant time to maturity and then dividing by the conversion factor.

---

cash and futures interest rates (YTM), prices, and durations are used with Equation (12-6) to determine the duration hedge ratio. (In practice, many hedgers use current rather than expected values.) Inasmuch as both the cash instrument and futures contract are based on T-bonds, we assume that the relative sensitivity of the cash and futures yields to a change in interest rates given in Equation (12-8) equals one.

The hedge ratio calculated in the example is 1.273, which shows that the hedger should buy 1.273 T-bond futures contracts for each $100,000 of cash T-bonds. When the size of the cash position is considered, we find that the number of contracts to use for the hedge is $N_D = 112$. Example 12-4 shows the dollar results of implementing this duration-based

---

EXAMPLE 12-2: Results of a Duration Hedge

	Cash Market	Futures Market
March:	Portfolio value: $10 million Current cash T-bond price: 113:24 Total bonds of $1,000 par value: 8,791	Sell 114 T-bond futures contracts at 81–8 Value of futures: $9,262,500
June:	Price per bond: 102:6 Value of bonds: $9,010,775	Buy back 114 futures contracts at a price of 72–23 Value: $8,311,312
Gain/loss:	($989,225)	$951,188

Net loss: ($38,037)
Percentage of loss offset: 96.2%

---

hedge ratio. Specifically, the opportunity loss of $526,229 in the cash position is offset by the gain in the short futures position, *eliminating* the entire loss!

In this example, the duration-based hedge provides a near perfect hedge. However, if the cash instrument characteristics differ significantly from the cash instrument underlying the futures contract, the term structure behaves differently than assumed by the duration procedure and/or large changes in the interest rate occurs, then the efficiency of the duration-based method deteriorates.

EXAMINING THE DURATION-BASED HEDGING MODEL

Comparing the Duration and Regression Models

The duration hedging model differs from the regression model in two fundamental ways:
1. How relative volatilities are determined:
   - The duration model uses the *duration values* of the cash and futures instruments to determine the relative volatilities of these instruments, which in turn are employed to obtain the relevant hedge ratio for *minimizing the net price change* of the combined futures/cash position.
   - The regression model uses *historical price changes* for the futures and cash instruments to determine their relative volatility such that the hedge ratio *minimizes the variance* of the net futures/cash position.
2. Assumptions concerning the data:
   - The duration method assumes that the expected future input values for the duration, price, and yield variables for an anticipatory hedge are correct, and that

EXAMPLE 12-3: Determining an Anticipatory Duration Hedge Ratio

Expected cash inflow (June)	$10,000,000
Cash instrument to be hedged (semiannual coupons)	T-bonds: 12% of May '05
	Current YTM (March): 10.4%
	Current price: 113:24
Number of bonds if purchased at the current price ($1,000 face value)	8,791
Expected values for cash instrument in June	Expected YTM: 9.73%
	Expected price: 119:23
	Duration at expected YTM: 7.92
March T-bond futures price*	81–8
Expected position in T-bond futures in June*	Expected price: 86–6
	Expected yield: 10.0%
	Duration at expected YTM: 8.62

The duration hedge ratio is as follows:

$$HR_D = \frac{D_C \, P_C \, (1 + i_F)}{D_F \, P_F \, (1 + i_C)} \tag{12-6}$$

$$= \frac{(7.92) \, (119.719) \, (1.050)}{(8.62) \, (86.188) \, (1.0487)}$$

$$= 995.58/779.12$$

$$= 1.278$$

For this example $(1 + i_F) = 1.049$ and $(1 + i_C) = 1.0487$, since the bonds have semiannual coupons.

$$N_D = HR_D \text{ (total par value of cash/par value of futures)}$$
$$= 1.278(\$8,791,000/\$100,000)$$
$$= 112.34$$
$$= 112 \text{ contracts}$$

---

* The cheapest-to-deliver cash bond is a 14% bond due in 20 years with a conversion factor of 1.5875 for March and 1.5840 for June. The futures price is determined by finding the present value of the bond for the relevant time to maturity and then dividing by the conversion factor.

interest rate behavior is described by a flat yield curve with small parallel shifts in the term structure.

- Regression assumes the hedge ratios based on historical data are good estimates of the hedge ratios over the hedge period—that is, that the associations between the futures and cash price changes remain stable.[6]

---

6 Geske and Pieptea present a combined regression/duration method for hedging. The futures implied interest rate is regressed with the cash rate to identify the interdependency between the futures and cash position. This information then is used in combination with the sensitivity of the fixed-income portfolio to interest rate changes as measured by duration to obtain the hedge ratio. Robert L. Geske and Dan R. Pieptea, "Controlling Interest Rate Risk and Return with Futures," *The Review of Futures Markets*, Vol. 6, No. 1, 1987, pp. 64-86.

EXAMPLE 12-4: Results of an Anticipatory Duration Hedge

	Cash Market	*Futures Market*
March:	Anticipated cash inflow during June: $10 million	Buy 112 T-bond futures contracts at 81–8;
	Current cash T-bond price: 113:24	Value of futures: $9,100,000
	Total bonds of $1,000 par value if purchased now: 8,791	
June:	Funds received and invested: $10,000,000	Sell 112 futures contracts at 86–6;
	Price per bond: 119:23	Value: $9,653,000
	Total bonds purchased: 8,352	
Gain/loss:	March cost: $9,998,707.50	March purchase: $9,100,000
	June cost (of 8,791 bonds): $10,524,936	June sale: $9,653,000
	Opportunity loss: $526,229	Gain on futures: $553,000

Net gain $26,771

Percent of opportunity loss offset with duration hedge: 100%

Advantages and Disadvantages of the Duration Method

The duration method possesses advantages and disadvantages in comparison with other hedge ratio methods. The advantages of the duration method are:

- It is superior to naive hedge ratio methods because duration provides a logical procedure to minimize the net change in price over the period of the hedge. In particular, the duration method considers the relative volatilities of the futures and cash instruments, whereas the naive methods ignore this valuable information.
- The duration procedure can provide near-perfect hedge results if the violations of the assumptions of duration are minimal, or if the hedge ratio is periodically recalculated and the hedge rebalanced. By comparison, the regression method requires stable hedge ratios over time and no violations of the assumptions of the regression model in order to minimize the variance of the price changes of the hedged position.[7] Stable hedge ratios for the regression method are less likely for crosshedges.

---

7   The regression method can use *forecasts* of the inputs to determine the hedge ratio rather than historical data, although this approach is not typically used.

- The duration model typically is employed when there is no history of price changes since the regression procedure employs historical data. For example, when new bond issues are sold that have maturity, coupon, and/or default risk characteristics differing from existing issues, then historical data cannot be used to model a regression procedure, but duration can provide accurate results.
- The duration method is a more convenient method to use when the analyst wishes to adjust the model; for example, when call provisions affect the volatility of the bond, or when the analyst wants to model the basis.[8]

The disadvantages of the duration method are:

- Major deviations from the assumptions of duration cause large net hedging errors, at least if frequent rebalancing is not undertaken.
- Accurate forecasts of the inputs for an anticipatory hedge as of the termination date are difficult to achieve.

The Uses of Duration for Hedging Purposes

There are a number of different hedging operations that employ duration. Table 12-1 lists each of these types of hedges, its purpose, how duration is used in the hedge, and the procedure for the hedge operation. Each of these hedges is discussed below. Most of the futures strategies noted here also can be accomplished solely in the cash market; however, cash market transactions often are more expressive, are hampered by liquidity problems, and cannot be transacted as quickly as futures trades.

Portfolio and Inventory Hedges. A portfolio manager protects the current value of a cash bond position by a sale of futures—that is, a short hedge. Cash bond positions are held by bond funds (a portfolio hedge) or by dealers (an inventory hedge).[9] Duration determines the volatilities (price responses) of the bond and futures instruments to a given change in interest rates. These relationships are used by Equations (12-3), (12-4), and (12-5) to determine the price change of the bond, and are employed to calculate the duration-based hedge ratios found in Equations (12-6) and (12-8).

Anticipatory Hedges. A purchase of futures contracts (a long hedge) locks-in the bond price/yield available now for cash that is not received until some time in the future. As with the portfolio hedge, duration determines the volatility of the cash and futures positions. The inputs to the hedge ratio formulations of Equations (12-6) and (12-8) are the *future expected* values of these variables.

Asset-Liability Hedges. Asset-liability hedges are executed in order to reduce the variability of earnings for a financial institution. One method for accomplishing this goal is to adjust the cash flows of the assets and/or liabilities such that the duration of the assets equals the duration of the liabilities. This cash-only procedure is similar to the immunization process discussed in Chapter 11. A second procedure for reducing earnings variability is to

---

8   See Toevs and Jacob, ibid. "Futures and Alternative ...", for their views on the superiority of the duration methodology.

9   In Chapter 9 we distinguished between a portfolio and inventory position as follows: a portfolio of bonds is a long-term investment, and such bonds can either be sold or hedged when interest rates are expected to increase. An inventory position is a short-term holding by dealers and hence cannot be sold until there is a demand for these issues.

TABLE 12-1: Hedging Operations Using Duration

Type of Hedge	Purpose of Hedge	Use of Duration	Procedure
Portfolio or inventory	To preserve the value of cash bonds currently owned	Considers volatilities of cash and futures positions; see Equations (12-6) and (12-8)	Short futures using current values for the inputs (expected values for the futures duration can be used)
Anticipatory	To lock-in the available price or yield for funds to be received in the future	Considers volatilities of cash and futures positions	Purchase futures using future expected values for the inputs to Equations (12-6) or (12-8)
Asset-liability	To reduce the variability in earnings of a financial institution	Considers relative volatilities of the assets and liabilities	(1) Set *cash* duration of assets = cash duration of liabilities (2) Adjust current asset or liability durations by purchase or sale of *futures*
Cash immunization	To lock-in a target rate of return or ending portfolio value	Duration used as a measure of zero coupon equivalency	Set cash duration = investment horizon
Futures immunization	To lock-in both the current value and the reinvestment rates in order to guarantee the ending portfolio value	Considers volatilities as in the portfolio hedge	Short T-bond futures to lock-in bond value; purchase short-term futures to lock-in reinvestment rates
Adjust the duration of a portfolio	(1) To adjust the volatility of a portfolio to respond to a change in interest rates (2) To rebalance a cash-immunized portfolio (3) To create a cash/futures portfolio that mimics an immunized portfolio	To measure the volatilities of the positions	Buy/sell futures to reach the desired duration value; method described in Chapter 13
Immunized hedge	To lock-in *anticipated* rates until funds are received, then immunize the cash portfolio	Duration used in cash immunization	Buy futures to lock in yield; lift buy hedge when funds are received and then immunize the cash portfolio.
Asset allocation	To change the amount of funds allocated to bonds in a stock/bond portfolio	To measure the effect of a change in interest rates on the value of the portfolio	Buy/sell futures to reach desired exposure to Δi; see Chapter 13 for method

adjust the durations of the assets and/or liabilities by the appropriate long or short futures hedges (see the "adjusting durations" procedure below).

Cash Immunization. Immunization is undertaken to "guarantee" a target rate of return or ending portfolio value for the fund. This target return/ending portfolio value is locked-in when the duration of the portfolio is set equal to the investment horizon; that is, i.e. D = H. In this context, duration measures the equivalent maturity of a zero-coupon bond. The "guaranteed return" for the fund is based on the trade-off between the change in the bond's value and the change in the reinvestment returns for any given interest rate change.

Futures Immunization. Futures can be employed to generate a combined cash/futures immunized portfolio similar to the cash immunization procedure. This **"futures immunization"** strategy involves locking-in both the current value of the bond *and* the reinvestment rates on the coupons to be received, the overall objective being to guarantee the ending portfolio value. Such a strategy involves both short and long hedges. A short T-bond hedge locks in the bond value, as noted in the portfolio hedge description, whereas long hedges in T-bill or Eurodollar futures lock-in the reinvestment rates on the coupons. Futures immunization differs from cash immunization in that the former locks-in the present value for the current cash portfolio. However, the latter strategy requires the duration of the cash portfolio to equal the horizon. The difficulty with the futures immunization strategy is that a limited number of futures expirations exist to execute the long hedges. Hence this strategy is not typically advocated by practitioners. Also note that simply instituting a short portfolio hedge to protect the bond value does *not* achieve immunization, since the reinvestment returns are not locked-in by the portfolio hedge.

Adjusting the Duration of a Portfolio. Changing the duration of a current bond portfolio is undertaken for three possible reasons: (1) to increase/decrease the duration in order to benefit from a forecasted change in interest rates; (2) to rebalance a cash portfolio originally immunized in order to reequate D = H after changes in interest rates or time have caused duration no longer to be equal to the horizon; and (3) to create a combined cash/futures portfolio with an adjusted duration that mimics a cash-only immunized portfolio. Note that futures are typically more effective than cash transactions in changing the duration of portfolios because of lower transaction costs, greater liquidity, and quicker execution of trades. Chapter 13 discusses methods for determining the number of futures contracts needed to change the effective duration of the bond portfolio, which are related to the first two reasons given above.

The cash/futures strategy which mimics a cash-only immunization strategy is preferred to a cash-only strategy when more flexibility is desired in choosing cash bonds for the portfolio rather than requiring the cash bond portfolio duration to equal the horizon. Moreover, since duration decreases as the level of interest rates increase, there are few bonds with durations above ten years when rates are high (see Fong[10]). Little[11] develops a cash/futures immunization model for flat yield curves, concluding that: (1) small (local)

---

10 Gufford H. Fong, "Portfolio Construction: Fixed Income," in *Managing Investment Portfolios: A Dynamic Process,* John L. Magin and Donald L. Tuttle, eds. Boston: Warren, Gorham, and Lamont, 1983.

11 Patricia Knain Little, "Financial Futures and Immunization," *Journal of Financial Research,* Vol. 9, No. 1, Spring 1986, pp. 1-12.

changes in interest rates are consistent with cash/futures immunization *only* if the number of futures contracts employed lies within a critical range; (2) immunization for large (global) changes in interest rates is *impossible* if the cash/futures portfolio contains a long position in futures, but is possible in some cases for short futures positions. The marking-to-market cash flow effects of futures help to create these difficulties for the cash/futures strategy. These conclusions show that there are different considerations for the cash-only and the cash/futures immunization strategies.[12]

An Immunized Hedge. Chance[13] describes a procedure that guarantees an ending portfolio value when funds are not available for a given amount of time. This procedure is called an **immunized hedge** because it combines a futures hedge with the cash immunization procedure. The strategy involves implementing a long bond futures hedge now in order to lock-in the yield until the cash is available for investment. The subsequent cash investment is then implemented so that the cash immunization objective is achieved. Hence, the procedure is a combination of an anticipatory hedge and cash immunization.

Asset Allocation. The goal of **asset allocation** is to change the relative percentages of stocks and bonds, or stocks/bonds/bills, to correspond to the fund manager's projections concerning the desired relative exposure in these markets. Duration is used in this context to determine the current and projected exposure of the bond portfolio to a change in interest rates. The purchase or sale of futures contracts then can be employed to change this exposure and hence to change the effective asset allocation. Chapter 13 describes the concept and procedure for asset allocation in detail.

EVIDENCE ON DURATION-BASED HEDGE RATIOS

Duration Versus Unhedged and Naive Strategies

Gay, Kolb, and Chiang[14] test anticipatory hedges for the basic duration-based hedging model of Equation (12-6) against two naive hedging strategies and a no-hedge alternative.

---

12 Little examines other negative cash flow situations that affect immunization. Chance, "Floating Rate Notes ...", shows how to achieve immunization for a floating-rate note. Chance, "Futures Contracts ...", also develops a cash/futures immunization model, but his model is not restricted to flat yield curves. The empirical tests corresponding to this theoretical model provide the following results:

- One- and two-year holding periods for individual cash bonds/futures are *not* immunized.
- Three- to five-year holding periods for cash/futures bond positions provide immunized results almost 100 percent of the time. This result is more encouraging than Ingersoll's results, which conclude that cash immunization is *not* possible for five-year holding periods.

Don M. Chance, "Floating Rate Notes and Immunization," *Journal of Financial and Quantitative Analysis*, Vol. 18, No. 3, September 1983, pp. 365-380. Don M. Chance, "Futures Contracts and Immunization," *The Review of Research in Futures Markets*, Vol. 5, No. 2, 1986, pp. 124-140. Jonathan E. Ingersoll, Jr., "Is Immunization Feasible? Evidence from the CRSP Data," in *Innovations in Bond Portfolio Management: Duration Analysis and Immunization*, G. O. Bierwag, G. C. Kaufman, and A. L. Toevs, eds., Greenwich CT: Jai Press, 1983. Patricia Knain Little, "Negative Cash Flows, Duration, and Immunization: A Note," *Journal of Finance*, Vol. 39, No. 1, March 1984, pp. 283-288.

13 Don M. Chance, "An Immunized-Hedge Procedure for Bond Futures," *The Journal of Futures Markets*, Vol. 2, No. 3, Fall 1982, pp. 231-242.

14 Gerald Gay, Robert Kolb, and Raymond Chiang, "Interest Rate Hedging: An Empirical Test of Alternative Strategies," *Journal of Financial Research*, Vol. 6, No. 3, Fall 1983, pp. 187-197.

The naive strategies are: (1) buy ten T-bond futures contracts; and (2) buy $1,000,000/$P_F$ T-bond futures contracts, where P_F is the current futures price.

Table 12-2 shows that the simple duration-based procedure hedged 73% of the total variability of the cash positions. The naive strategies hedged 64% and 57% of the variability, respectively. No comparison to the regression method was given.

Landes, Stoffels, and Seifert[15] examine the duration-based hedging procedure by employing 12 different portfolios of industrial and utility corporate bonds. The portfolios are constructed by various methods, including random selection, coupons, maturities, and ratings. Both two-year and four-year hedges are investigated. The duration-based method averaged a 4% loss for the two-year hedge, whereas the unhedged portfolio averaged a 17% loss. Over the four-year period the duration method actually gained .4% (several portfolios were overhedged, creating gains), whereas the unhedged portfolios averaged a 21% loss.[16]

Duration Versus a Covariance Methodology

Hilliard[17] examines how a duration-based hedge with one or more T-bill futures expirations compares to a hedge based on a previous period's matrix of unexpected changes in cash rates for T-bills (the covariance approach).[18] The covariance method results are compared with duration hedges with equal weights for the expirations, random weights, and for the

TABLE 12-2: Duration Versus Naive Methods: Hedge Results

Absolute Change in Wealth	Unhedged	Naive 1	Naive 2	Duration Hedge
Mean	$80,781	$32,637	$34,538	$25,292
σ	$73,396	$26,075	$31,322	$19,477
Percent reduction in risk		64.47	57.33	73.46

Source: Robert Kolb and Raymond Chiang, "Duration, Immunization, and Hedging with Interest Rate Futures," *Journal of Financial Research*, Vol. 5 No. 2, Summer 1982, pp. 161-170.

15 William J. Landes, John D. Stoffels, and James A. Seifert, "An Empirical Test of a Duration-Based Hedge: The Case of Corporate Bonds," *The Journal of Futures Markets*, Vol. 5, No. 2, Summer 1985, pp. 173-182.

16 Although the duration method was superior to the unhedged position for these corporate bond portfolios, several adjustments could improve the accuracy of the individual portfolio results. First, hedge ratios were rounded to the nearest integer for $1 million positions, creating errors of up to one-half a contract. Such rounding is necessary for actual positions but distorts the accuracy of the method when "small" positions of $1 million are employed. Second, no adjustments for the relative sensitivity between the T-bond and corporate rates were made [the RS in Equation (12-8)]. Relative sensitivity is important when quality differences exist.

17 Jimmy E. Hilliard, "Hedging Interest Rate Risk with Futures Portfolios under Term Structure Effects," *Journal of Finance*, Vol. 38, No. 5, December 1984, pp. 1547-1569.

18 The monthly matrix of unexpected changes is based on the deviation from the previous month's rates. This method provides superior results to the use of a pure expectations approach of computing deviations from the forward rates. Choosing the better method may have introduced some bias into the results.

first deferred contract only.[19] The covariance method produces hedging results that are consistently superior to the duration methods; that is, the net hedging results are consistently 25 percent to 50 percent better than the duration-based methods.

For the short-maturity T-bill data used in the above tests, the duration model provides inferior results to a covariance approach that uses multiple futures contracts. However, these results do not test the typical use of duration: to determine the volatility of long-term fixed-income securities. Until more complete tests are implemented, money managers must judge for themselves whether a duration, regression, covariance, or duration-convexity methodology provides the best technique for hedging interest rate contracts. The duration-convexity approach is examined in the following section.

DIFFICULTIES WITH AND SOLUTIONS TO THE DURATION HEDGE MODEL[20]

The Problems

The often used duration-based hedge ratio shown in Equation (12-6) creates two significant problems for obtaining accurate hedging results. First, large changes in yields cause deviations from the expected net hedging results when the duration of the cash and futures instruments differ significantly from one another. Second, changes in the shape or slope of the yield curve cause hedging errors if adjustments to the Macaulay duration equation given in (12-6) are not made.[21]

The causes and effects of these problems are explained below. The solutions to these problems are: (1) to use a more complicated measure of duration, and/or (2) to hedge with several different types of futures contracts simultaneously.

Convexity and Large Yield Changes: The Concept

Using duration to calculate a hedge ratio assumes that only small yield changes occur and that rebalancing takes place after any nontrivial change in yields. In reality, the convexity of the bond price-yield relationship creates errors for duration when large yield changes occur.

Convexity refers to the *change* in dollar duration given a change in yield.[22] An alternative description of convexity involves the *squares* of time, whereas duration involves simply time. That is, if we express modified duration as:

---

19 The duration procedure determined the hedge ratio. The allocation of the hedge among the three futures expirations then was made on an equal and random basis.

20 This section draws from Goodman and Vijayaraghavan. Their 1987 article discusses some of these topics in a more mathematical context. Laurie Goodman and N. R. Vijayaraghavan, "Generalized Duration Hedging with Futures Contracts," *The Review of Futures Markets*, Vol. 6 No. 1, 1987, pp. 94-108. Laurie Goodman and N. R. Vijayaraghavan, "Combining Various Futures Contracts to Get Better Hedges," *Advances in Futures and Options Research*, Vol. 3, 1988, pp. 257-268.

21 These problems with duration create significant hedging errors when long-term fixed-income securities are hedged with T-bill or Eurodollar futures, as suggested in Kolb. The hedging relationships discussed here emphasize futures hedging. One also can hedge a cash fixed-income instrument with a short position in another cash instrument. However, a short cash hedge often suffers from a lack of liquidity and much higher transactions costs. Robert Kolb, *Understanding Futures Markets*, 2d ed., Glenview, IL: Scott Foresman, 1988.

22 Dollar duration is defined in Chapter 11, where dollar duration = modified duration (P_B) and modified duration = duration/$(1 + i)$. Convexity is briefly discussed in that Chapter and in more detail later in this chapter.

$$\text{Modified D} = \sum_{t=1}^{N} \frac{t \, w_t}{(1 + i)} \qquad (12\text{-}9)$$

where   t = time
         w_t = the fraction of the present value of the cash flow received at time t with respect to the price of the bond
         i = yield to maturity of the bond
then convexity C is expressed as

$$C = \sum_{t=1}^{N} \frac{t^2 \, w_t}{(1 + i)} \qquad (12\text{-}10)$$

Thus, convexity can be termed the **second order moment** of duration since it involves the squares of time.[23]

Figure 12-1 also helps to explain convexity and duration. Curve B_1 in Figure 12-1 shows the relationship between the bond price P_B and yield i for bond B_1. This relationship is curvilinear (convex). The slope of the tangent line T to curve B_1 for the current yield i_C measures the duration of the bond at this interest rate. For a small change in the interest rate i, the corresponding change in the bond price P_B is (approximately) indicated by the slope of the tangent line, as shown by Δi and ΔP_C in Figure 12-1. However, if a large

FIGURE 12-1: The Price-Yield Curve and Duration

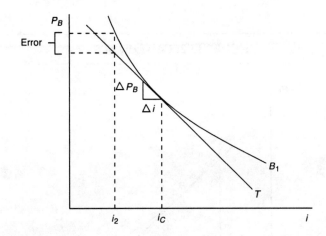

---

23 Chapter 11 defines duration as Σ tw, but here we define *modified* duration as Σ tw/(1 + i). Since modified duration = D/(1 + i), as defined in Chapter 11, the two equations are equivalent. Note that duration considers only the first derivative in determining price change; convexity considers higher derivatives such as slope (second-moment) and curvature (third-moment) effects.

change in interest rates occurs (to i_2), then the slope of the tangent line T no longer represents the duration of the bond B_1 at the new interest rate i_2, since a significantly different tangent line exists at i_2. The change in the duration causes the error that occurs from large yield changes.

When a hedge ratio is determined via Equation (12-6) then the duration of both the cash and futures instruments are considered in the process of offsetting the price change of the cash instrument with the price change of the futures contract. For example, one can attempt to hedge the cash bond B_1 with a T-bond futures contract, where the futures is represented by the cheapest-to-deliver bond B_2. Bond B_2 in Figure 12-2 has the same duration as bond B_1 (the same tangency at rate i_C), but B_2 has a different convexity in relation to changes in the interest rate (the shape of curve B_2 differs from B_1). The figure shows that at the new interest rate i_2 the curvature is greater for bond B_2 than for bond B_1. Figure 12-3 shows that the new tangent lines T_1 and T_2 to bonds B_1 and B_2 at point i_2 (T_1 and T_2 represent the new durations) *differ* significantly from each other *and* from the original tangent line T given in Figure 12-1. Thus, the duration for B_2 has changed significantly more than the duration for B_1. These different size changes in duration cause the duration hedge ratio to vary significantly from before to after the change in interest rates. This large change in the hedge ratio causes errors in the net hedging results.

In conclusion, convexity measures the curvature of the relationship between bond prices and interest rates, with the extent of the convexity determining the potential for changes in the duration of a bond. The figures above show the importance of determining the relative change in duration for cash and futures instruments used in a duration-based hedge when a large change in interest rates occurs.

FIGURE 12-2: Convexity of Bonds

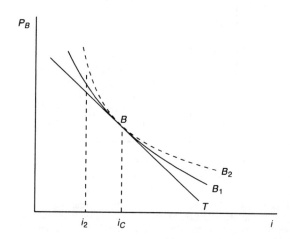

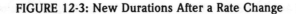

FIGURE 12-3: New Durations After a Rate Change

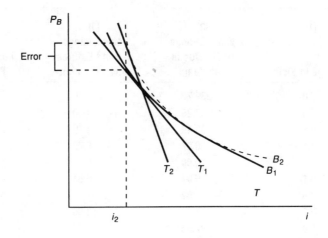

Convexity and Large Yield Changes: An Example

Table 12-3 provides a numerical example of the extent that interest rate changes affect net hedging results when the convexity differs between the two instruments employed in the hedge. The cash instrument being hedged is the 7 1/4 coupon cash bonds due in ten years. The short hedging instrument is a T-bond futures contract. The modified duration of the cash bond is 6.99 years, whereas the modified duration of the cheapest-to-deliver cash underlying the futures contract is 11.52 years (adjusted for the conversion factor). The resultant hedge ratio from Equation (12-6) using current durations is .577.

Column 1 of Table 12-3 lists different possible changes in yields. Column 2 provides the change in value of the cash bond for the associated change in yield and column 3 gives the same information for the short futures position with a hedge ratio of .577. Column 4 shows the net result of the long and short positions. Column 4 illustrates that if the change in yield is relatively small, then the effect on net hedging results is also small. However, large changes in yields create large net losses on the combined hedge position. These large differences are attributable to large changes in the durations of the instruments as interest rates change, and hence to large changes in the resultant new hedge ratios. Columns 2 and 3 of Table 12-4 show the cash and futures durations after adjusting for each interest rate change. Column 4 presents the resultant correct hedge ratio for the new level of interest rates.

The fact that the duration for the futures contract changes significantly more than the duration for the cash bond implies that the futures instrument has a greater degree of convexity. In fact, the convexity for the futures contract is 185.92, whereas the cash bond has a convexity of 61.68. Since the typical duration-based hedge procedure selects a hedge ratio that equates only the effects of the relative *current* durations, changes in the relative

TABLE 12-3: The Effect of Convexity on Hedging Results
(per $1,000 Face Value)

(1) Change in Yield	(2) Value Change of 7¼ Due in Ten Years	(3) Value Change: T-Bond Futures Short Position	(4) Loss on the Portfolio
− 3.0	239.70	− 262.40	− 22.70
− 2.0	152.28	− 159.10	− 6.81
− 0.5	35.49	− 34.79	.70
− 0.1	6.97	− 6.72	.24
0.0	0.00	0.00	.00
+ 0.1	− 6.91	6.61	− .29
+ 0.5	− 33.92	31.99	− 1.93
+ 2.0	− 127.01	113.69	− 13.32
+ 3.0	− 182.56	158.34	− 24.21

[a] Durations:

7 ¼ due in 10 years   D = 6.99 years

T-bond Futures   D = 11.62 years

Note: Hedge ratio from Equation (12–6): .577

TABLE 12-4: Durations and Hedge Ratios as Yields Change

(1) Change in Yield	(2) Duration: 7 ¼ Due in Ten Years	(3) Duration: T-Bond Futures Position	(4) Hedge Ratio
−3.0	7.34	13.70	.440
−2.0	7.22	12.95	.484
−0.5	7.05	11.87	.553
−0.1	7.00	11.59	.572
0.0	6.99	11.52	.577
+0.1	6.98	11.45	.582
+0.5	6.93	11.17	.601
+2.0	6.75	10.19	.677
+3.0	6.63	9.58	.727

FIGURE 12-4: A Multiplicative Change in the Yield Curve

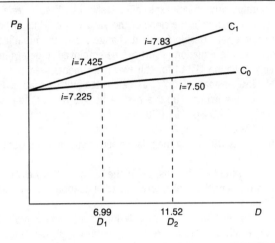

durations create large errors for the hedge procedure *unless* frequent rebalancing is performed.[24]

Changes in the Yield Curve

Changes in the slope or shape of the yield curve also adversely affect duration-based hedging results. The effect on the hedging results depends upon the extent and type of change in the yield curve. Let us assume a **multiplicative** relationship for the slope of the yield curve between the change in duration and the change in interest rates; interest rates change more for longer-duration instruments than for shorter-duration ones. Figure 12-4 shows this relationship as a change in the slope of the interest rate-duration curve from C_0 to C_1 for the two instruments employed in the above example. Specifically, this figure shows that as the interest rate changes by 20 basis points for the shorter-duration instrument, it simultaneously changes by 33 basis points for the longer-duration (futures) instrument.

The effect of having different size yield changes for the two instruments is that the simple duration-based hedge ratio from Equation (12-6) changes as interest rates change. This effect occurs because the simple duration method is based on equal changes in yields—that is, parallel shifts in the yield curve.

Our simple relationship for yield curve slope changes shown in Figure 12-4 is shown mathematically as

$$\Delta i_2 = \Delta i_1\, D_2/D_1 \qquad\qquad (12\text{-}4)$$

where Δi_2 = change in yield for the longer-term instrument

Δi_1 = change in yield for the shorter-term instrument

---

24 Any change in the cheapest-to-deliver cash instrument is ignored in this analysis, although significantly different convexities would still exist. Regardless, the concept being portrayed here is still relevant.

D_2 = the duration for the longer-term instrument

D_1 = the duration for the shorter-term instrument

Consequently, this multiplicative relationship effectively describes the *relative sensitivities* of the security yields to a change in the slope of the yield curve. Thus, if Equation (12-11) appropriately describes the relationship for yield changes, then the modified relative sensitivity duration model given in Equation (12-8) can be employed to determine the appropriate hedge ratio. Using Equation (12-8) for the two instruments used previously creates a new hedge ratio of .350, instead of .577, as calculated with Equation (12-6). The net hedging result with the new hedge ratio is a perfect hedge, whereas the .577 hedge ratio creates a net difference of $5.04 per $1,000 value for the small changes in interest rates represented in Figure 12-4.

There are two difficulties with using the relative sensitivity model described by Equation (12-8):

- One must know the extent of the change in the slope of the yield curve in order to determine the relative sensitivity of interest rates. Equation (12-11) defines only one possible relationship.
- The relative sensitivity relationship works only for small changes in yields. Larger yield changes are still adversely affected by convexity, as previously described.[25]

Summarizing the Problems and Proposing a Solution

The effect on duration-based hedging models when changes in yields and/or changes in the slope or shape of the yield curve occur are summarized as follows:

- If changes in yields are *small* and yield curve shifts are *parallel* between rebalancings of the portfolio, then the simple duration-based hedge model of Equation (12-6) performs well.
- If yield changes are *large* while yield curve shifts are *parallel*, then both duration and convexity affect the hedging results. The simple duration model does not work well, but one can use *two* futures instruments simultaneously to hedge against duration and convexity effects, as explained below.
- If yield curve shifts are nonparallel, small, and have a *known* relationship, then the relative sensitivity adjustment given in Equation (12-8) is useful. If the yield change is in terms of the shift in the slope of the yield-duration curve, then Equation (12-11) defines the relative sensitivity relationship. Unfortunately, as a rule we do not know the form of the change in the shape of the yield curve, and thus there are difficulties in estimating the true relationship for the relative sensitivities. Alternatively, hedging against both duration and convexity reduces most of the effect of a small change in the slope of the yield curve.
- If there are yield changes (either large or small) in *conjunction* with changes in the slope of the yield curve (small changes only), then hedging with two futures instruments simultaneously can reduce or eliminate *both* duration and convexity effects.
- If the *shape* of the yield curve changes (as, for example, when the curve changes from upward sloping to downward sloping) or when large shifts in the slope of the curve

---

25 Essentially, the relative sensitivity duration model adjusts for convexity when *small* yield changes occur, but does not adequately adjust for convexity when large yield changes occur.

occur, then "higher-order" moments than duration and convexity affect the hedging results. In this case, more than two futures instruments are needed for accurate hedging results. See Goodman and Vijayaraghavan[26] for a mathematical development of these higher-order moments.[27]

The above summary states that, in general, using two or more futures instruments to hedge against duration *and* convexity effects provides superior hedging results compared with using only one futures instrument to hedge against duration effects. While using the one-instrument duration hedge is simple and minimizes transaction costs, it is accurate only for the first case listed above. Using more than two futures instruments to hedge provides more accurate results, especially for changes in the shape of the yield curve, but this technique is more expensive and requires more complicated analysis. Consequently, hedging against duration and convexity provides a compromise that is reasonably accurate for most situations.

A Two-Instrument Futures Hedge for Duration and Convexity

The procedure to implement a two-instrument futures hedge to counteract both duration and convexity effects is straightforward. One simply solves the following two equations simultaneously for X_1 and X_2:

$$X_1 D_1 + X_2 D_2 = D_3 \qquad\qquad (12\text{-}12)$$

$$\text{and} \quad X_1 C_1 + X_2 C_2 = C_3 \qquad\qquad (12\text{-}13)$$

where D_i = durations of instruments 1, 2, 3
C_i = convexities of instruments 1, 2, 3
X_i = market values of instruments 1 and 2

Here, 1 and 2 are the futures hedging instruments and 3 is the cash bond to be hedged. To solve Equations (12-12) and (12-13) simultaneously, simply solve each equation separately for X_1 and then set the two resulting equations equal to one another and solve for X_2. Substituting X_2 back into either of the previous equations provides the value for X_1. Solving Equations (12-12) and (12-13) simultaneously gives the following result:

$$X_1 = \frac{C_2 D_3 - C_3 D_2}{C_2 D_1 - C_1 D_2} \qquad\qquad (12\text{-}14)$$

$$X_2 = \frac{C_3 D_1 - C_1 D_3}{C_2 D_1 - C_1 D_2} \qquad\qquad (12\text{-}15)$$

Example 12-5 shows how to find the hedge ratios X_1 and X_2 in Equations (12-14) and (12-15). Example 12-6 shows the dollar hedging results for the hedge ratios. The hedging results show that a duration-convexity hedge is superior to a duration-only hedge for both a yield change and a slope change. Note that the relative sensitivity adjustment used in Equation (12-8) does *not* have to be determined in the duration-convexity hedge in order to achieve the superior results.

---

26 Goodman and Vijayaraghavan, ibid,. "Generalized Duration . . .".

27 The three most common effects on the hedging results from changes in the term structure are attributable to level changes, slope changes, and curvature changes. This section concentrates on the level changes and small slope changes by examining duration and convexity hedging. Larger slope changes and curvature changes are examined via the third derivative, which corresponds to using three futures instruments with different underlying cash maturities for hedging purposes.

EXAMPLE 12-5: Determining a Two Instrument Hedge Ratio

The following information has been determined:

Instrument	Yield	Duration	Convexity
7¼ due in ten years	7.225	6.99	61.68
Five-year T-note futures*	6.86	4.22	19.99
T-bond futures*	7.50	11.52	185.92

The 7¼ cash bond is to be hedged; the two futures instruments are used as the hedging instruments. Find the two-instrument hedge ratio.

(A) The Simultaneous Equation Approach:

Substituting into Equations (12-12) and (12-13) we obtain

For duration: $X_1 (4.22)$ $+ X_2 (11.52) = 6.99$
For convexity: $X_1 (19.99)$ $+ X_2 (185.92) = 61.68$
 Solving for X_1 in each equation: $X_1 = (6.99 - 11.52\ X_2)/4.22$
                                                                  $X_1 = (61.68 - 185.92\ X_2)/19.99$
Equating these two equations: $(6.99 - 11.52\ X_2)/4.22 = (61.68 - 185.92\ X_2)/19.99$
Solving for X_2: $X_2 = .218$ (hedge ratio for the T-bond futures)
Substituting back into either equation:
                          $X_1 = 1.063$ (hedge ratio for the T-note futures)

(B) The Direct Solution Approach:

Using Equations (12-14) and (12-15) we obtain:

$$X_1 = \frac{(185.92)(6.99) - (61.68)(11.52)}{(185.92)(4.22) - (19.99)(11.52)} = \frac{589.03}{554.30} = 1.063 \quad \text{(hedge ratio for the T-note futures)}$$

$$X_2 = \frac{(61.68)(4.22) - (19.99)(6.99)}{(185.92)(4.22) - (19.99)(11.52)} = \frac{120.56}{554.30} = .218 \quad \text{(hedge ratio for the T-bond futures)}$$

---

* The cheapest-to-deliver for the T-note futures is the 6 5/8 due in five years; the cheapest for the T-bond futures is the 7 1/2 due in 24 years.

Panel A of Table 12-5 provides the duration and convexity values for Eurodollar, Ten Year T-note, and T-bond futures contracts.[28] Duration increases as the maturity of the cheapest-to-deliver cash underlying the futures contract increases, but at a slower rate than convexity increases. Panel B of Table 12-5 presents the relevant duration-convexity hedge ratios per dollar of cost by using the futures instruments in Panel A; various maturities of cash instruments are presented in the table.

---

28 These values are for the cheapest-to-deliver bond as of August 18, 1986.

EXAMPLE 12-6: Hedging Results for a Two-Instrument Hedge

From Example 12-5 we know that each $1,000 of the 7¼ cash bond needs to be hedged with $X_1 = HR_1 = 1.1063$ or $1,063 of the T-note futures, and $X_2 = HR_2 = .218$ or $218 of the T-bond futures. These are market values, not face values.

For a 50-basis-point increase in all instruments (a "medium" parallel shift), the following occurs per $1,000 of the long cash instrument:

Instrument	Δ Yields	ΔP per $1,000	HR	Total ΔP
7¼ cash bond	.50	$-33.92	—	$-33.92
T-note futures	.50	+21.10	1.063	22.43
T-bond futures	.50	+55.44	.218	12.09
Net hedging result:				$+ 0.60

The net hedge results for a .50 basis point yield change using the basic duration-based hedge (see Table 12-4) is −$1.93. Thus, the two-instrument hedge ratio is superior.

For a slope change we have the following result:

Instrument	Δ Yields	ΔP per $1,000	HR	Total ΔP
7¼ cash bond	.20	$-13.79	—	$-13.79
T-note futures	.12	+ 4.90	1.063	5.21
T-bond futures	.33	+35.24	.218	7.68
Net hedging result:				$- 0.90

This result compares to a net change of $5.04 using the basic (one-instrument) duration model.

Examining Panel B of Table 12-5 one sees that the proportion of T-note futures increases as the proportion of Eurodollar futures falls in the three- to eight-year cash maturity range. Similarly, the T-bond proportion increases as the T-note proportion falls in the eight- to 20-year range. These results are logical relationships based on duration concepts.

However, convexity effects can create nonintuitive hedge combinations. For example, a duration-convexity hedge for a short-term cash position when the T-note/T-bond futures combination is used often requires a *long* T-bond futures position. The long T-bond position is needed in order to remove the extra convexity created by the short T-note futures position. Thus, hedges that appear to be nonintuitive at first actually are set up to obtain the correct balance of *both* duration *and* convexity effects.

TABLE 12-5: Duration and Convexity for Futures Contracts

Panel A: Duration and Convexity Values

Futures Contract	Duration[a]	Convexity[a]
Eurodollar	0.23	0.10
T-note	4.97	33.48
T-bond	8.70	122.54

Panel B: Duration-Convexity Hedge Ratios Using Futures Contracts

Underlying Cash Maturity (Years)	Eurodollar Futures	T-Note Futures	T-Note Futures	T-Bond Futures	Eurodollar Futures	T–Bond Futures
			(Per Unit Dollar of Cash)			
2 years	−5.00	−0.11	−0.79	0.21	−6.88	−0.03
3 years	−7.00	−0.27	−1.09	0.25	−9.38	−0.08
4 years	−6.73	−0.46	−1.24	0.24	−10.72	−0.14
5 years	−5.74	−0.74	−1.41	0.21	−12.15	−0.23
8 years	1.58	−1.65	−1.47	−0.05	−12.65	−0.52
10 years	8.69	−2.36	−1.34	−0.32	−11.62	−0.75
20 years	51.33	−5.80	0.15	−1.89	1.32	−1.84
30 years	106.98	−9.89	2.53	−3.95	21.82	−3.14

[a] Using interest rates and cheapest–to–deliver instruments available when calculated.

Note: Negative signs indicate positions opposite the cash position, i.e. a short position if the cash is long.

Source: adapted from Laurie Goodman and N. R. Vijayaraghavan, "Generalized Duration Hedging with Futures Contracts," *The Review of Futures Markets*, Vol. 6 No. 1, 1987, pp. 94–108.

One also can determine hedge positions that create a net positive convexity or duration position rather than the net zero positions employed in our discussion. Thus, if a money manager has an opinion on the *direction* of interest rates, then a nonzero convexity and a zero duration position is desired. Computer programs are more efficient in determining such positions than hand calculations.[29]

---

29 Changes in the cheapest-to-deliver instrument can change the relative hedge ratio, as shown in Goodman and Vijayaraghavan, ibid., "Generalized Duration . . ." Such changes are more prevalent when the maturity of the cash instrument differs from the underlying cash maturity of the futures contract, such as for a 30-year bond. This situation relates to the degree of stochastic risk inherent in the cash versus futures portfolio, as discussed in Chapter 11 and Appendix 11A.

SUMMARY AND LOOKING AHEAD

This chapter developed and explained duration-based hedge ratio procedures, provided examples and evidence concerning these procedures, and showed the various strategies for employing duration for hedging. The difficulties inherent in using a simple duration method for hedging, such as convexity, can be overcome by employing two futures instruments concurrently to improve upon the basic duration procedure.

Part IV of the book examines a number of applications of hedging to real world problems. Applications of hedging and risk management include uses of futures for portfolios of assets, dealers, financial institutions, corporations, and insurance companies.

Part IV

Applications of Futures to Risk Management

Chapter 13

Futures and Portfolio Management

The increased volatility of stock and bond markets in the past decade has made the management of these assets difficult. Therefore, devising strategies for dealing with stock and bond portfolio risk and return by using futures contracts has become a popular method to deal with these management difficulties both quickly and cheaply.

Bond applications to futures markets include adjusting the risk of the bond portfolio by using duration and creating synthetic instruments to enhance return. Employing futures to adjust bond durations manages the risk of a bond portfolio. If the duration is reduced, then the sensitivity of the portfolio to changes in interest rates declines. Similarly, if the duration is increased, then the portfolio sensitivity increases. Futures can change this sensitivity quickly and inexpensively. Synthetic securities are generated by an appropriate combination of futures and cash instruments. Synthetic securities often provide a higher rate of return than a similar cash instrument.

Stock applications using futures include using stock index futures to adjust the beta risk, using futures to manage portfolio cash flows and the activities of money managers, and portfolio insurance. Stock index futures are used to alter the risk of a stock portfolio by adjusting the effective beta of the portfolio; that is, hedging reduces the market risk of a portfolio. Pension fund sponsors can use futures to separate the functions of timing the market and the selection of individual issues. Such a separation of functions helps to manage large inflows and outflows of cash and to smoothe the transition from one money manager to another. Portfolio insurance is a strategy that attempts to keep the portfolio value from falling below a given floor while still allowing the portfolio to participate in market rallies. Portfolio insurance products were one of the fastest growing products on Wall Street until the crash of October 1987, when they did not adequately protect the portfolio value from the market decline.

A combination strategy employing stocks, bonds, and T-bills is called asset allocation. Asset allocation strategies are a form of active portfolio management where the portfolio manager changes the makeup of the portfolio between stocks, bonds, and cash to benefit from the manager's forecasts of these markets. These strategies are performed faster and cheaper by employing futures contracts. Diversification with commodity futures contracts is another combination strategy.

PENSION AND INVESTMENT FUND APPLICATIONS

An Introduction

An important and growing application of financial futures markets is the use of stock and bond futures contracts for portfolio management. The size of stock and bond portfolios, the increased risk management sophistication of portfolio managers, the volatility of interest rates and stock prices, and the issuance of billions of dollars of Treasury bonds and notes to finance the federal deficit all have contributed to the increased usage of futures contracts.

The basic concepts and applications of futures hedging to reduce the risk of portfolios are straightforward, as shown in Chapter 9. Here we concentrate on more sophisticated risk and return applications of futures contracts, such as changing the **beta** of a stock portfolio in order to adjust risk, changing the duration of a bond portfolio, portfolio insurance, and asset allocation. The use of futures to accomplish these strategies often provides a lower-cost alternative and a faster adjustment to achieve the stated goals than a similar strategy in the cash market. The benefits of futures for portfolio management are especially important when the fund has multiple external money managers. In this situation the pension fund can decide to make changes in the asset allocation of the funds, initiate portfolio insurance, or hedge the portfolio without disrupting the asset choice or trading activities of the individual money managers.

The Investment Philosophy of Corporations and Insurance Companies

The success of the corporation's pension fund is important for reasons other than the pension benefits it provides to the workers. Pension fund earnings also directly affect the earnings of the parent corporation, since the earnings of the fund determine the amount of cash the corporation must place into the pension fund from the corporation's revenue.

The investment portfolio also is important to insurance companies, because these companies count on investment earnings to provide a majority of their profits for the firm. Thus, the premiums received from insurance contracts are invested in long-term securities, with the intention that the premiums plus part of the investment earnings will be used to pay off future claims. The remaining earnings from the investments constitute the profits to the insurance company.[1]

The applications of futures for pension fund and insurance investments parallel the uses for general bond and stock portfolio management. Applications that are more unique to

---

1   The benefits that pension funds and life insurance companies are required to pay their constituents can be predicted with an acceptable degree of accuracy by actuaries. Information concerning factors such as worker attrition, life expectancy, retirement ages, early retirement programs, and inflation are employed to forecast future needs. Of course, inflation is the most difficult factor to forecast. With an estimate of future cash flow needs, pension funds and insurance companies then can determine the required rate of return and cash inflows to meet these needs.

pension fund and insurance uses relate to the management of large additions and reductions to the portfolio, as well as pension fund activities such as switching money managers. The Employee Retirement Insurance Security Act of 1974 (ERISA) has been interpreted to allow the use of futures markets as part of a prudent investment strategy, as long as futures are employed in association with an overall diversification strategy and are not used to increase the riskiness of the fund. Many of the larger pension funds and insurance companies now employ futures as part of their overall investment strategy.

The remaining sections of this chapter examine fixed-income, stock, and combination strategies that employ futures markets for portfolio management. These strategies implement concepts developed in previous chapters.

FIXED-INCOME APPLICATIONS

Adjusting Bond Durations[2]

Purchasing a T-bond or T-note futures contract increases the sensitivity of the combined asset/futures portfolio to a change in interest rates, thereby increasing the effective duration; selling long-term debt futures decreases the portfolio sensitivity to interest rate changes and thus decreases the duration.[3] A money manager who adjusts the duration of the portfolio as forecasts of the direction of interest rates change could accomplish this strategy more effectively by using futures contracts. Specifically, the alternative of changing the cash position of the fund—for example, selling bonds and holding T-bills if prices are forecasted to move lower—is not typically a feasible alternative for a fund since restrictions on portfolio composition often hamper the bond manager. Moreover, such a major change in the bond portfolio is expensive in terms of transaction costs, liquidity costs, and potential short selling and tax costs.

In general, a careful choice of the number, position (long or short), and type of futures contracts allows the money manager to replicate the duration of any pure cash bond portfolio. Thus, the specific price reaction of a bond portfolio to a change in interest rates is dictated by adjusting the duration of the bond portfolio with futures contracts. Reducing the duration of the bond portfolio is equivalent to short hedging. Thus, hedging decisions for bonds are essentially duration decisions.[4]

---

2   The difficulties of using duration in conjunction with futures contracts are covered in Chapter 12. The following discussion relates to the *application* of futures to adjust bond duration. The example and application concepts given here follow "Concepts and Applications: Using Interest Rate Futures in Pension Fund Management," The Chicago Board of Trade, pamphlet, 1987.

3   Note that purchasing futures *always* increases the sensitivity of the combined cash/futures portfolio, *regardless* of whether the duration of the futures position is less than or greater than the duration of the original cash position. The reason is that futures do not require any investment of funds. Thus, the value of the combined position changes to a greater extent with futures than without them, making the portfolio more sensitive to interest rate changes. A similar situation is true for the sale of futures contracts; that is, a sale decreases the sensitivity regardless of the relative durations of the futures and cash instruments. *Averaging* durations is appropriate only when all the positions involve a cash investment of funds *or* when only futures are employed.

4   Recall that the Macaulay duration measure assumes a flat-yield curve with parallel shifts to the term structure. When nonparallel shifts occur, the Macaulay measure of duration provides biased results. Consequently, the relationship of a cash portfolio with a given duration value to a futures-adjusted portfolio with the same calculated duration depends on the type of interest rate shift that occurs and the cash flow characteristics of the two portfolios (i.e., the cash and futures-adjusted portfolios can act differently when a nonparallel shift in the term structure occurs). See Chapters 11 and 12 for in-depth discussions of this topic.

The first step in changing a bond portfolio's duration is to find the **basis point values** (BPVs) for the current cash portfolio, the target duration adjusted portfolio, and the futures contract. The BPV is the *total* dollar price change that is associated with a one-basis-point change in the interest rate. Thus, BPV is related to the dollar equivalency concept described in Chapter 9. The BPV is determined from equation (13-1), which employs duration to calculate the change in the value of the portfolio resulting from a change in interest rates of one basis point:

$$BPV = (D) \ (PMV) \ (.0001) \ / \ [1 + (i/k)] \qquad (13\text{-}1)$$

where   BPV = basis point value

D = duration, typically the Macaulay duration

PMV = the portfolio market value

i = the annualized yield to maturity

k = the number of payments per year; that is, k=2 for semiannual coupons

.0001 = one basis point (.01 percent).

Note that equation (13-1) is simply the rephrasing of the equation given in Chapter 11 for a ΔP due to a Δi; that is, $\Delta P = -D \ P \ \Delta i/(1 + i)$. The formulation in equation (13-1) is employed more frequently in the practitioner community because of its ease of use in finding the number of required futures contracts.

The determination of the BPV for the *current cash* portfolio, which includes individual cash bonds, is calculated in one of two ways:

- The composite duration of the portfolio is determined, if ease of calculation is the primary factor;
- The BPV for each bond is calculated and the weighted sum of the individual BPVs is determined, if greater accuracy is important.

The BPV of the *target* portfolio is determined by plugging the duration desired by the portfolio manager into equation (13-1). Finally, the BPV for the futures contract is found by obtaining the duration associated with the cheapest-to-deliver cash bond, since this bond is the one tracked by the futures market in the pricing process. The futures BPV on a *per contract* basis is then determined by dividing the BPV of the cheapest-to-deliver cash bond by the appropriate conversion factor:[5]

$$BPV \ of \ futures = \frac{BPV \ of \ the \ cheapest\text{–}to\text{–}deliver \ cash}{conversion \ factor} \qquad (13\text{-}2)$$

Given the relevant BPVs from equations (13-1) and (13-2), the number of futures contracts needed to obtain the desired portfolio duration is determined as follows:

$$N = \frac{BPV \ target - BPV \ current}{BPV \ futures} \qquad (13\text{-}3)$$

where the target and current BPV values are in total dollar values for the portfolio, and the BPV futures value is per contract.

Example 13-1 shows how the above concept is applied in order to adjust a bond portfolio duration. In particular, the example shows how to increase the effective duration from the current cash portfolio value of 4.6 years to a 10-year duration. Since interest rates move in the forecasted direction (downward) for the example, the longer duration increases

---

5   Since multiplying the futures price by the conversion factor changes a futures price into a cash price equivalent (Chapter 7), one finds the relevant futures price BPV by dividing the cash price by the conversion factor.

EXAMPLE 13-1: Changing the Duration of a Portfolio

On January 2, an internal pension plan manager expects a steep decline in bond yields over the next two-month period. The manager's conviction concerning the decrease in yields is so strong that the duration of the fixed-income portfolio is more than doubled. Because the underlying portfolio is tied to a broad-based bond index, and since the internal manager wants to avoid disrupting the externally managed cash bond portfolio, futures contracts are purchased in order to increase the duration of the portfolio rather than buying bonds.

Data Inputs	January 2	February 28
Portfolio duration	4.6	
Target duration	10	
T-bond futures price	85-00	94-26
Cash portfolio value	$100,000,000	$104,535,095
BPV (basis point value) of T-bond futures (cheapest-to-deliver cash)	$115.61	
Portfolio yield to maturity	9.27%	

There are three steps to be followed. See Equation (13-1) for steps 1 and 2 and Equation (13-3) for step 3.

1. Convert cash portfolio duration to a BPV:

$$\frac{4.6}{(1 + .0927/2)} \times \$100,000,000 \times .0001 = \$43,962$$

2. Convert target portfolio duration to a BPV:

$$\frac{10}{(1+.0927/2)} \times \$100,000,000 \times .0001 = \$95,570$$

3. Determine the number of contracts required to achieve the desired portfolio duration:

$$\frac{(\$95,570 - \$43,962)}{\$115.61} = 446 \text{ contracts}$$

Results	January 2	February 28
Without futures:		
Cash portfolio value	$100,000,000	$104,535,095
Return		4.54%
With futures:		
Cash portfolio value	$100,000,000	$104,535,095
Futures gain ($9^{26}/32 \times 446 \times \$31.25$)		$ 4,376,375
Return		8.91%

Source: "Concepts and Applications: Using Interest Rate Futures in Pension Fund Management," Chicago Board of Trade, pamphlet, 1987, p. 3.

the rate of return on the portfolio. If rates increase, however, then a longer duration provides inferior results to the original (shorter) portfolio duration. This example shows that in addition to being a low-cost and quick way to extend the duration of the cash portfolio, futures allow the portfolio manager to obtain durations that are difficult to structure solely in the cash market, at least without using zero-coupon bonds.[6]

Synthetic Debt Securities and Return

A **synthetic security** replicates a cash security by purchasing a different cash instrument and either buying or selling a futures contract. Creating a synthetic security for long-term debt is very similar to changing the duration of a bond portfolio by using futures. However, the *purpose* of creating a synthetic security is to obtain a higher return than is available for an almost equivalent cash market security, whereas adjusting a bond duration changes the sensitivity of the portfolio to movements in interest rates. This section describes how to generate a synthetic debt instrument and how to compare the returns for such an instrument to a nearly equivalent cash security.

The two basic procedures to create a synthetic debt instrument are:

- To buy a cash T-bill and then buy T-bond or T-note futures in order to generate a synthetic long-term debt instrument.
- To buy a long-term T-bond and sell T-bond or T-note futures in order to generate a synthetic short-term debt instrument.

The primary reason to create a synthetic security is to obtain a rate of return advantage over a cash security with the same duration. Such an advantage is possible to construct if (1) the futures contract is mispriced, (2) futures price changes lead the cash market changes, or (3) differences exist in the price patterns of the cash and synthetic securities because of the differing cash flow characteristics of the two instruments in conjunction with a favorable twist in the shape of the term structure.[7]

Example 13-2 shows how a synthetic security made up of cash T-bills and a long T-bond futures position can outperform a 10-year cash instrument, with both positions having the same duration. The superiority of the synthetic position depends on a beneficial change in the shape of the yield curve. Thus, the combination of a cash T-bill with a duration of three months, with the appropriate number of T-bond futures contracts with a duration of approx-

---

6   There is no conflict between the BPV for futures of $110.80 in Example 13-2 and the $31.25 value of a 1/32-point price change for the T-bond futures contract. The former states the *total dollar* change for a $100,000 par value T-bond with a .01% change in *yield*. This total dollar change is affected by the duration of the bond: the greater the duration, the greater the change in price for a given *yield* change. The 1/32 states the value of the change in *price* for the futures contract. Thus, BPV states the total change in value of the bond per .0001 change in *yield*, while 1/32 simply reflects the price change due to a change in the quotation of the bond (a percentage of par of the bond). Stated differently, a 1% change in yields create a change of 4% to 5% in the price of a longer-duration bond.

7   Mispricing of the futures contract is determined either by (1) comparing the futures price with the price from a theoretical model, or (2) comparing the implied repo rate from the futures arbitrage transaction with the current repurchase rate for the equivalent term. Both procedures are complicated by the pricing effects of the futures delivery options that exist for the bond and note futures. The type of "favorable twist" in the yield curve necessary to obtain superior returns depends on the relative characteristics of the cash and synthetic instruments.

EXAMPLE 13-2: Creating a Synthetic Instrument

A manager has received a $20 million cash inflow and wants to purchase 10-year Treasury notes in order to keep the portfolio duration constant. The money manager expects a flattening of the long end of the yield curve in the next month such that long-term bonds will outperform 10-year notes. A synthetic 10-year security using cash T-bills and T-bond futures contracts is created that will outperform the cash security if these expectations prove to be true, as shown below.

Inputs	January 22	February 21
T-bill yield	5%	5%
10-year T-note yield	7%	6.8%
20-year T-bond yield	8%	7.5%
T-bill invoice price (cash)	98.78	99.18
10-year T-note price (decimal)	101.74	103.15
T-bond futures price	99-01	103-26
BPV for T-bill: $20 MM	$464.60	
BPV for 10-year T-note: $20 MM	$14,185.88	
BPV for T-bond futures	$94.82	

Determine how many futures contracts must be added to the cash T-bill position to replicate the duration of a 10-year security:

$$\text{Number of contracts} = \frac{(10\text{–year BPV} - \text{T–bill BPV})}{\text{T–bond futures BPV}}$$

$$144 \text{ contracts} = \frac{(\$14,185.88 - \$464.60)}{\$94.82}$$

Results	January 22	February 21
10-year cash T-note		
10-year T-note	$20,000,000	$20,277,177
Accrued interest	$ 270,879	$ 390,384
One-month return		1.98%
Synthetic instrument:		
Purchase cash T-bills	$20,000,000	$20,080,988
T-bond futures gain		$ 688,500
One-month return		3.85%

Source: "Concepts and Applications: Using Interest Rate Futures in Pension Fund Management," Chicago Board of Trade, pamphlet, 1987, p. 9.

imately nine years, provides a combined synthetic security with a duration that is equivalent to the cash T-note position. Moreover, a flattening of the long-term portion of the yield curve illustrated in the example generates superior returns for the synthetic security as compared with the cash instrument. This superiority occurs because the synthetic security is made up of a long position in T-bond futures that benefits more from the flattening of the yield curve than does the 10-year cash T-note instrument. That is, the price of the bond futures increases more than the price of the T-note when the yield curve becomes flatter. On the other hand, if the yield curve had become *less* flat, then the synthetic security would have performed *worse* than the cash instrument.[8, 9]

Futures as Synthetic Money Market Instruments

A basic use of T-bill (or Eurodollar) futures for a money market trader is to provide an alternative for investing short-term funds by creating synthetic money market instruments. As an example, let us assume a money manager desires to invest funds for six months in an instrument with the credit risk and liquidity of a T-bill. The various alternatives for such an investment are:
1. Buy a 180-day cash T-bill.
2. Buy two successive 90-day cash T-bills (as one T-bill matures, the funds are used to purchase a second 90-day T-bill).
3. Buy a long-term T-bill and sell it after 180 days, with the sale occurring before the T-bill matures.
4. Buy a 90-day T-bill, and buy a T-bill futures contract now that expires when the cash T-bill expires.
5. Buy a long-term cash T-bill (say a 270-day T-bill) and sell short a T-bill futures now, for a combined synthetic security with a maturity of 180 days (the futures contract would have to expire when the cash T-bill has 90 days left to maturity).

The above six-month investment alternatives include three combinations involving cash securities and two combinations of cash and futures instruments. Several factors affect the final decision for several of the alternatives. Specifically, alternatives 2 and 3 involve price risk, since one must buy or sell the securities before maturity. The price risk causes the final return for these alternatives to be affected by the interest rates occurring within the investment period since a change in interest rates affects the prices of the instruments.

Only alternatives 1, 4, and 5 remain as risk-free strategies. Of course, the basic rule for the money manager is to choose the alternative with the highest rate of return in relation

---

8   The duration of a T-bill, such as in Example 13-2, is simply the maturity of the T-bill. T-bills are zero-coupon bonds since they have no intermediate cash flows. The duration of a zero-coupon bond is its maturity.

9   Changes in carrying costs and potential crosshedges are major factors affecting the basis risk of a synthetic position. Carrying costs are dominant when the cash and synthetic securities have similar characteristics. However, if the durations are significantly different, or the assumptions of the duration procedure are not met, then the crosshedge risk often is the dominating effect. For example, recall from Chapter 11 that a bond portfolio made up of short-term and long-term securities (a "dumbbell" portfolio) changes its duration significantly if a nonparallel change in the shape of the term structure occurs. Although a short hedge for such a situation still shortens the effective duration of the bond portfolio substantially, the behavior of the combined cash-futures position is more difficult to analyze, and acts differently than a pure short-term instrument.

to the risk. Theoretically, if the cash and futures markets are completely linked together, then these three alternatives provide equivalent returns.[10] But the existence of different types of participants in the cash and futures markets, who possess different expectations concerning interest rate behavior, can cause prices and rates in the two markets to diverge. Alternatively, other considerations such as commissions, bid-ask spreads, or liquidity cause a money manager to prefer one alternative over another.[11] If interest rates or costs do differ significantly between the two markets, then one of the three remaining alternatives provides the highest return. In summary, the existence of T-bill futures provides additional investment alternatives with potentially higher returns for those who have the choice of dealing in either the cash or the futures markets.[12]

A Strip of Futures as a Synthetic Instrument

The futures money market alternative described above is extended here to examine the benefits of a strip of futures. Appendix 4A explains strips. A strip of futures is created when one purchases sequential expirations of several T-bill (or Eurodollar) futures contracts. The purchase and subsequent expiration of four sequential T-bill futures provides the investor with a series of four 91-day cash T-bills. Moreover, the total return and price of these T-bills is determined when the four futures contracts are originally purchased. Therefore, one can compare a strip of four T-bill/Eurodollar futures to a one-year cash T-bill/Eurodollar deposit in order to determine which investment provides a better return. Appendix 4A presented such comparisons. Of course, other strips of futures are employed for other investment horizons.[13]

Another use of the futures strip occurs when an institution always desires three-month cash T-bills for liquidity, but forecasts that interest rates are going to drop drastically over the next (say) year. Purchasing the strip of futures now provides higher returns for the one-year period than buying cash T-bills every three months, since the cash T-bills will have significantly lower interest rates (higher prices) after the interest rates decrease. Of course, the relative success of this futures strategy relates to the forecasting ability of the money manager.

---

10 In fact, if markets were perfect and in equilibrium, then all five alternatives would provide the same returns. However, new information and changing expectations cause interest rates to fluctuate, causing price risk for alternatives 2 and 3.

11 For the situation in question, the T-bill futures combinations do have a disadvantage in comparison with the cash alternative. Specifically, since futures contracts expire only four times per year, using futures poses a significant restriction on matching desired maturity combinations. Consequently, for most situations, the money manager would need flexibility for the length of the investment in order to benefit from the futures/cash alternatives as viable investment opportunities. When the maturity is flexible, then the potential higher returns often associated with a futures/cash alternative, or the other potential benefits associated with futures markets listed in the text, could be an important consideration.

12 In addition to the strategies noted here, pension and investment funds use futures to convert stock or bond positions into equivalent short-term, risk-free positions *without* selling the stocks or bonds. The benefits of such an opportunity in terms of commissions and liquidity risk are obvious. The sale of the futures contract is equivalent to an arbitrage position if the cash securities fulfill the specifications of the futures contract. This situation represents a risk-free position where the return is typically equivalent or higher than a short-term, risk-free asset.

13 Since the expiration date of T-bill futures now varies from one expiration month to another, a perfect strip of futures is not attainable. Strips with Eurodollar futures do not have this problem.

Stock Index Arbitrage as a Synthetic Instrument

Stock index arbitrage also creates a synthetic position, as discussed in Chapter 5. Thus, the sale of overpriced futures and the purchase (or ownership) of stocks create a synthetic, risk-free position. The purchase of underpriced futures and sale of stocks from a portfolio also creates a synthetic risk-free position. These synthetic instruments are implemented only if they earn a return above the risk-free rate. Consequently, stock index arbitrage becomes an alternative to money market investments.

STOCK MARKET APPLICATIONS

Hedging and Adjusting Stock Portfolio Betas

The basic procedure for hedging a portfolio of stocks is described in Chapter 9: one sells stock index futures to reduce the potential loss from a decline in stock prices. In Chapter 10 we examined the use of regression analysis using the cash asset and the futures contract to determine the importance of the relative volatilities of the cash stock portfolio and the futures contract in order to maximize the performance of the risk-minimizing hedge.

There is another tool that evaluates the importance of the stock portfolio volatility, namely beta. Beta is the (regression) measure of the relative volatility between the stock portfolio currently held and the relevant cash stock *index*.[14] Consequently, a beta hedge is an alternative method to estimate the *minimum risk* futures hedge ratio. The number of futures contracts needed for the beta hedge is determined by multiplying beta (representing the hedge ratio) times the relative dollar amounts of the stock and futures positions; that is,

$$N_b = (V_S/V_F)\ \beta_p \qquad (13\text{-}4)$$

where N_b = the number of futures contracts for a stock beta hedge

V_S = the value of the stock position

V_F = the value of one futures contract, i.e., the futures price times its multiplier

β_p = the beta of the portfolio

A study by Lindahl, Boze, and Ferris[15] shows that using portfolio betas as discussed here provides less basis risk than employing the minimum variance regression method between the cash portfolio and futures contract.[16]

---

14 Betas were originally developed as a measure of the relative risk of individual stocks versus the market index. A beta is determined by regressing the stock (or portfolio) returns against the stock index returns, with the slope of the regression line being the beta. A portfolio beta also is obtained by finding the weighted average of the individual stock betas:

$$\beta_p = \sum_{i=1}^{n} W_i\,\beta_i$$

where β_p = the beta of the portfolio

n = the number of stocks in the portfolio

W_i = the proportion of the total funds in stock i ($\sum W_i = 1$)

β_i = the beta of stock i

Most investments and security analysis textbooks discuss betas in detail.

15 Mary Lindahl, Ken Boze, and Mike Ferris, "Hedging Market Risk with Stock Index Futures and Options," working paper, The University of Alaska, Fairbanks, 1987.

16 Some hedgers further modify Equation (13-4) by multiplying N_b by the slope of the regression line between the cash *stock* index and the stock index *futures* contract. However, this relationship is near unity and therefore has only a minimal effect on the number of futures contracts used for a hedge. Another consideration is whether β_p changes over time. In general, the betas for large portfolios of stocks are stable over time, whereas

Futures also are employed to *change* the relative riskiness of the portfolio. A small alteration in Equation (13-4) determines the number of futures contracts needed to change the portfolio beta to a different relative riskiness value:[17]

$$N_b = (V_S/V_F) (\beta_t - \beta_p) \tag{13-5}$$

where β_t is the target beta for the portfolio.

If N_b is negative, then a short hedge is appropriate; a positive N_b relates to a long futures position. Example 13-3 shows how to calculate a stock beta hedge and how to change a portfolio beta with the use of futures.

Portfolio Management of Funds

Timing and Selectivity. One example of using futures markets for timing purposes is related to the strategy of creating a synthetic risk-free instrument with futures. Specifically, one sells futures to create an equivalent risk-free position when a market downturn is expected and lifts the futures position when an upturn is anticipated. This use of futures contracts reduces trading and liquidity costs significantly as compared to cash trades, as well as allowing the manager to keep the desired selection of individual securities. Thus, being able to "buy and sell the market" via futures transactions separates the broad asset allocation decision relating to stocks and bonds from the investment decisions for individual assets. In addition, those who have superior selection abilities but minimal market timing abilities benefit from being able to hedge the market. In fact, one money manager can concentrate on market timing via the use of futures while another concentrates on the selection of individual securities. Moreover, once a decision concerning the appropriate relative volatility of the portfolio is made, then that decision is executed via going long or short in futures rather than having to choose the individual securities in accordance with the riskiness of that security.

Additions and Reductions to the Portfolio. Pension funds and insurance companies experience periods when large cash inflows or outflows to the investment funds occur. Futures can benefit the timing process by allowing the money manager to invest (or disinvest) large sums of money without being affected by the liquidity of individual securities. Over time, these individual securities can be purchased or sold and the futures positions covered.

Sponsor Activities. Pension funds typically allocate funds to money managers to invest. The overall investment policy is set by the pension fund and is implemented by the managers.[18] Futures then allow the pension fund unique opportunities to separate the

---

individual stock betas and the betas of portfolios of a small number of stocks do change over time. The interval used to measure the beta (i.e., daily or weekly or monthly returns) and the length of time employed affect the beta measure. Moreover, the portfolio beta can differ between an up-market and a down-market because of the reaction of the individual stocks to bull and bear market factors; see Kawaller for a brief discussion. Investments books examine the question of beta stability in some detail. Ira Kawaller, "The Beta Bogy," *Futures,* July 1987, pp. 64, 66.

17 In effect, the hedge obtained from Equation (13-4) attempts to change the portfolio beta to zero.

18 Sharpe examines the timing and allocation functions of money management. He shows how the pension fund sponsor can separate and allocate these functions to different managers. In particular, the advantages and disadvantages of active versus passive portfolio management are discussed. William F. Sharpe, "Decentralized Investment Management," *Journal of Finance,* Vol. 36, No. 2, May 1981, pp. 217-234.

EXAMPLE 13-3: Stock Beta Hedges

A. Hedging a Stock Portfolio

A wealthy investor wishes to hedge her stock portfolio against a potential downturn in the market until she can decide how to rearrange her portfolio. Currently the stock portfolio is risky, since it includes a large number of high-technology stocks. The beta of the portfolio is 1.4 and the current value of the S&P 500 index is 275.00. The dollar value of the investor's portfolio is $1,250,000. The number of futures contracts needed for a hedge with the S&P futures contract is calculated as follows:

$$N_b = (V_S/V_F)\ \beta_p \qquad\qquad (13\text{-}4)$$
$$N_b = [1,250,000/(275)(500)]\ 1.4$$
$$N_b = 9.091(1.4) = 12.73 = 13 \text{ contracts}$$

B. Adjusting a Portfolio Beta

The investor above decides that her portfolio is more volatile than she desires. She wants to sell the stocks and put the money in utilities and bonds. However, her broker convinces her that the stocks in the portfolio will outperform the market by more than what is warranted by their extra riskiness if products currently in the research stage prove successful. The broker convinces her to keep the individual stocks but to reduce the effective market risk of the stock portfolio to .6β by using futures to reduce the beta of the combined cash/futures portfolio. The number of contracts needed are:

$$N_b = (V_S/V_F)\ (\beta_t - \beta_p) \qquad\qquad (13\text{-}5)$$
$$N_b = [1,250,000/(275)(500)]\ [.6 - 1.4]$$
$$N_b = -9.091\ (.8) = -7.27 = 7 \text{ contracts (short)}$$

---

various functions of the money managers. Separate managers can be hired who excel at market timing and security selection. The fund can override asset allocation, relative riskiness, or market timing decisions made by the individual money managers by employing futures. When managers are changed, futures allow implementation of such a transition.[19]

Portfolio Insurance

The Objective and Concept. The *objective* of portfolio insurance is to "guarantee" a floor for the ending value of the portfolio if the market declines in value while allowing the portfolio to participate in market increases. A portion of the potential returns of an uninsured portfolio are forgone in order to obtain the minimum floor value. Portfolio insurance is useful for pension funds, since their managers do not want the value of their assets to fall below their designated floor, as defined by the present value of their liabilities. Notice that portfolio insurance has characteristics similar to other forms of insurance. For example, fire

---

19 Switching of money managers often creates large pools of cash and/or a wholesale restructuring of the individual securities in the portfolio. Futures ease the difficulties encountered in such transitions.

FIGURE 13-1: Pure Portfolio Insurance

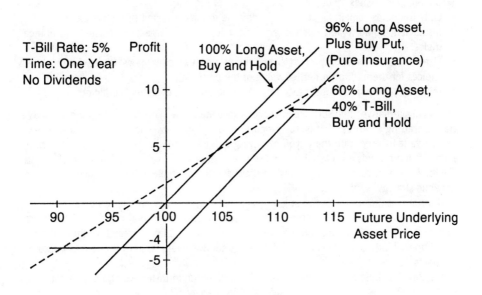

insurance on a house protects the original value of the house to the insurer (for a cost), while any appreciation in the value of the house accrues to the insurer.[20]

Figure 13-1 illustrates the concept of pure portfolio insurance as compared to placing (1) all of one's funds in the asset, or (2) placing 60 percent of the funds in the asset and 40 percent in T-bills. The pure insurance portfolio is best described by buying a put option to guarantee the minimum asset value. A put option allows the buyer to *sell* the asset at a prespecified price (the strike price) until the option expires. There is a cost to buying the put option.

Figure 13-1 illustrates how the initial asset price of $100 changes for the alternative investments described above. In particular, the pure insurance alternative loses a maximum of $4 if the asset price falls ($4 is the cost of the put) but participates in upside gains. The 100 percent long alternative has superior profits on the upside, but larger losses when the asset falls below $96. The 60 percent long-40 percent T-bill alternative creates smaller gains and smaller losses than the 100 percent long case.[21]

---

20 As with homeowners' or auto insurance, one can create portfolio insurance with a "deductible"; that is, the guaranteed floor can be below the current value.

21 One can specify a minimum future value *above* the current portfolio value. In this case, one purchases a put where the exercise price is *above* the current value. The cost of the put is larger since it includes the current value of exercising the put now. The cost of the option typically is reduced by using interest from funds invested in T-bills.

Portfolio Insurance and Dynamic Trading Strategies. Buying puts to obtain down-side protection (one method of obtaining pure portfolio insurance[22]) has the following disadvantages:

- Buying puts creates an ongoing cost (the cost of the put).
- Only the funds remaining after purchasing the put are invested in the cash asset.
- Insufficient liquidity and open interest exist to execute large pure portfolio insurance trades.
- Listed options have only short lives and limited exercise prices (these factors limit choices for the minimum desired value of the portfolio).
- Initiating pure portfolio insurance for a complicated mix of assets is difficult.

As an alternative, the portfolio manager can generate a *synthetic* put option by a **dy-namic trading strategy**; that is, the proportions of the long asset and a risk-free instrument can be varied to replicate the payoff of buying a put and holding the long asset. As prices increase, more funds are placed in the asset. As prices decrease, more funds are placed in T-bills. Unlike buying a put, no cash outlays for the portfolio protection occur when a dynamic strategy is initiated.

Two approaches to implementing a dynamic trading strategy are (1) to buy and sell the asset, (2) to buy and sell futures on the asset. Since transactions costs for futures are one-tenth the size of commissions on the asset itself and liquidity is greater for futures, most institutional funds that implement a dynamic trading strategy employ stock index futures contracts.

Figure 13-2 illustrates the payoffs of a dynamic portfolio insurance strategy in compari-son to a 60% asset and 40% T-bill buy-and-hold strategy. The dynamic portfolio insurance strategy is superior for large price increases and for moderate to large price decreases of the asset. The shape of the portfolio insurance curve is similar to a long asset plus put position, but at a lower cost. The lower cost occurs because the portfolio insurance strategy is replicating a portfolio that is less than fully invested. Thus, on the downside, the loss on the (declining) equity portion of the portfolio is mostly offset by the interest earned on the (increasing) T-bill position.

Futures and Portfolio Insurance. Dynamic portfolio insurance is implemented by using futures. The equity exposure is actively managed by shorting stock index futures contracts as the market declines in order to reduce losses, and to lift part or all of the short hedge as the market increases in value so as to benefit from the upside potential. The extent of the dynamic hedge varies with the market movement and depends on how close the portfolio's value is to the desired minimum value.[23] When the entire stock portfolio is hedged, the portfolio represents a synthetic T-bill. The number of futures contracts to employ for the hedge is determined by using the portfolio beta approach given in equation (13-4).

---

22 Another method of creating equivalent payoffs for pure portfolio insurance is to purchase a call option and invest the remaining funds in T-bills. This strategy generates a payoff curve equivalent to the put strategy in Figure 13-1.

23 This model is similar to the dynamic bond portfolio model of Fong, Pearson, and Vasicek, and bond contingent immunization models. Gifford Fong, Charles Pearson, and Oldrich Vasicek, "Bond Performance: Analyzing Sources of Return," *Journal of Portfolio Management*, Vol. 9, No. 3, Spring 1983, pp. 46-50.

FIGURE 13-2: Dynamic Portfolio Insurance

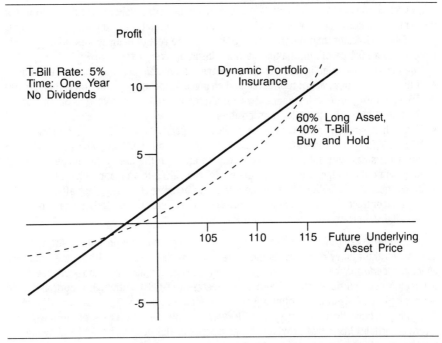

Although the basic dynamic portfolio insurance model is simple to apply, its effectiveness is determined by the care of the portfolio manager in considering the factors that affect the hedge. In addition, if the model is used without market judgment or forecasts, then the size of the futures short hedge simply increases as the market declines and decreases as the market rises. An effective manager realizes when to reduce the risk of the portfolio by either changing the hedge position when the market is overbought, or by changing the minimum floor value (and hence the hedge value) to increase the protection of the portfolio. Hence, the overall performance of a portfolio insurance program ultimately depends on the judgment of the money manager. The ultimate benefit of such a program is to reduce risk in a downward trending market and to provide additional equity exposure in an upward trending market.[24]

---

24 Using futures to implement portfolio insurance is basically a type of asset allocation strategy (which is discussed shortly) except that the key decision for other asset allocation strategies is the asset mix, whereas with dynamic portfolio insurance the asset mix is determined by the floor value and the time horizon. The advantage of undertaking a futures portfolio insurance strategy rather than a static cash asset allocation procedure is that the fund can participate in rallies to a greater extent with portfolio insurance because of the greater equity exposure; in addition, the portfolio typically is protected from significant market declines by the hedging activity. However, to be effective, the futures hedge ratio must be dynamically adjusted to compensate for changing market levels and volatilities. For example, the static cash asset allocation strategy often outperforms the dynamic portfolio insurance strategy when the market declines *rapidly,* since the dynamic strategy cannot change the asset mix fast enough to protect the portfolio against sharp drops in the asset price.

Dynamic Strategies and Market Crashes. Dynamic portfolio insurance was an important strategy employed by funds until the 1987 market crash. At that time stock index futures fell so rapidly that the portfolio insurers could not effectively reduce the exposure of the equity position fast enough by shorting futures contracts. In addition, since futures prices fell much faster than reported cash prices fell, the cost of hedging a position typically represented a 10% premium, making portfolio insurance very expensive.[25]

The market crash highlighted the disadvantages of dynamic portfolio insurance, namely:

- If the hedge strategy is not monitored and changed at the appropriate times, then greater risk exists for portfolio insurance than for alternative strategies involving options or for the traditional cash asset allocation position.
- The option strategy often cannot be replicated effectively with futures, causing larger basis risk for the futures strategy than is desired for the portfolio. The potential for a larger basis risk with futures is associated with errors in the use of the model employed to generate the hedge ratio; that is, the model can calculate an inappropriate hedge ratio or an incorrect volatility value. In addition, the hedging strategy is less effective if the futures contract does not change in correspondence with the underlying cash portfolio (i.e., if a significant amount of basis risk exists).

A Dynamic Portfolio Insurance Model. A dynamic portfolio insurance strategy indicates when the money manager should trade, how much to trade, and how the trade will affect the performance of the portfolio. Portfolio insurance allocates and switches funds between a risky portfolio (stocks) and a risk-free asset (T-bills). Although a portfolio could be invested in T-bills in an amount equal to the minimum floor value desired for the fund, this practice typically leaves very little leeway for investing in assets promising higher returns. Portfolio insurance provides the advantage of the floor value while allowing the fund to trade in the risky assets to obtain higher returns.

Black and Jones[26] present a straightforward application of portfolio insurance that does not involve option pricing theory and does not have a definite expiration date. The Black and Jones model is implemented as follows:

$$eq = m \ (TA - F) \tag{13-6}$$

where   eq = the equity exposure desired

m = the multiple

TA = total assets available

F = the desired floor

The multiple is a function of the total assets, the floor chosen, and the initial equity exposure; that is,

$$m = eq/(TA - F) \tag{13-7}$$

---

25 In fact, Jacklin, Kleidon, and Pfleiderer simulate how a market in which the amount of portfolio insurance is unknown can create a temporary runup in prices and precipitate a market crash. Charles J. Jacklin, Allan W. Kleidon, and Paul Pfleiderer, "Underestimation of Portfolio Insurance and the Crash of October 1987," *Review of Financial Studies*, Vol. 5, No. 1, 1992, pp. 35-64.

26 Fischer Black and Robert Jones, "Simplifying Portfolio Insurance," *Journal of Portfolio Management*, Vol. 14, No. 1, Fall 1987, pp.48-51.

For an example of the above approach let us assume that the total portfolio asset value is $100 million, the desired floor value is $80 million, and the initial equity *exposure* desired is $50 million (50 percent of total assets). An initial multiple of 2.5 is created (the $50 million desired equity exposure divided by the cushion of $20 million). The money manager rebalances after the market moves 2% (the tolerance factor) or, equivalently, when the cushion changes by 2% times the multiple of 2.5 = 5%.

The multiple chosen determines the volatility of the portfolio, with the multiple typically being the ratio of the initial exposure to the initial cushion. The higher the multiple, the faster the portfolio value increases *and* the faster it decreases toward the floor value. Each *trade* brings the exposure back to the same multiple *of the cushion.* As the cushion approaches zero, the exposure approaches zero. The portfolio falls below the desired floor value only if a large drop in asset prices occurs before one is able to make a trade to adjust one's exposure. As the exposure approaches the maximum limit desired in the portfolio, one is fully invested and does not trade. When the exposure is less than the maximum limit, then a significant market move causes the ratio of the exposure to the cushion to differ from the initial multiple desired. When this ratio exceeds some predetermined "tolerance" value, a trade is initiated to bring the multiple back to its initial value. The smaller the tolerance value, the more trades that are executed (and the more commissions generated). Hence, tolerance values often attempt to reduce transactions costs.

In conclusion, portfolio insurance provides a means for creating a floor for the portfolio value (if trading is continuous), while allowing participation in upward trending markets. Although dynamic portfolio insurance did not perform well during the 1987 market crash, and subsequently pension funds lost interest in the tool, some funds recently have returned to using this method to provide structured returns for stock market portfolios.

COMBINATION STRATEGIES

Asset Allocation with Stocks, Bonds, and T-Bills

An asset allocation strategy is an alternative term for active portfolio management. Asset allocators adjust the relative proportions of the portfolio between stocks, bonds, T-bills, and other asset classes when changes in aggregate stock prices and interest rates are forecasted. This strategy has received increased attention in the past few years as money managers attempt to discover methods to enhance short-term portfolio performance. Asset allocation differs from portfolio insurance in that the former typically *reduces* exposure when prices increase (and vice versa), whereas portfolio insurers *increase* exposure as prices rise.

Changes in asset allocations with cash assets cause the typical problems previously discussed that arise from trading costs, liquidity, timeliness, and adjustments to individual asset positions associated with trading cash assets. Employing stock index and interest rate futures contracts reduces these problems for asset allocation. The use of futures contracts to execute asset allocation strategies is a natural extension of cash-only allocation strategies:

* The short- to intermediate-term reallocation of funds between stock and bond portfolios is executed with a lower cost with futures than if attempted in the cash market. In addition, this reallocation is completed with no disruption of the core stock and bond portfolios. For example, when a pension fund employs passive portfolio management (i.e., a core of securities or an index fund is used to mirror the market), then futures

adjust the asset allocation among the different asset categories without requiring the trading of individual cash assets.

- The long-term reallocation of the cash portfolio among stocks, bonds, and T-bills is *initially* undertaken in the futures market in order to avoid the liquidity and timing problems associated with making the adjustments immediately in the cash market. The cash categories then are adjusted when the liquidity of the individual securities allows such changes *and* in conjunction with security analysts' recommendations concerning which individual stock or bond issues to emphasize in the portfolio.
- When a pension fund allocates the assets of the fund to different money managers, then the fund can change the asset allocation exposure itself by using futures contracts. This technique does not unduly restrict the individual stock and bond selections of the individual money managers.

The procedure for implementing an asset allocation strategy using futures markets is straightforward:

1. Determine the amount of cash bonds and stocks one wants to "purchase" or "sell."
2. Find the number of stock index futures to buy/sell by the portfolio beta procedure given in equation (13-4).
3. The BPV (basis point value) and the number of bond futures to buy/sell is determined by using equations (13-1) to (13-3) and the current duration of the bond portfolio.

The performance of an asset allocation procedure is dependent on the timing signals given to change the proportions of the asset categories. Simple timing signals based on publicly available information often provide inferior results. Most asset allocation models employ forecasts of the performance of each asset category based on analysis of the risks and potential rewards of that category. For example, the results from the Kerschner and Pradilla (K&P) model from PaineWebber[27] illustrate how an asset allocation model can improve returns and lower risk. Table 13-1 illustrates how the K&P asset allocation portfolio outperforms both individual asset categories and a static stock/bond/bill strategy.

In conclusion, the benefits of using futures to implement an asset allocation model are that futures provide lower commissions and bid-ask spread costs, and have greater liquidity and market depth. The K&P report concludes that, over the five-year period ending June 1987, a futures asset allocation program would have saved $1.7 million on transactions costs for a $100 million portfolio, *and* would have gained an additional $8.6 million from gains in the basis on the futures trades.

Commodity Futures and Diversification

In order to diversify risks and to enhance returns more effectively, pension funds have added assets previously ignored as potential investments. Such assets include foreign stocks and bonds, metals, real estate, and commodity futures. Futures on foreign stocks and bonds and on metals can be used for hedging and for implementing an adaptation of the asset allocation models discussed above.

---

27 PaineWebber Capital Markets, "The Use of Futures in Tactical Asset Allocation," *Stock Index Options and Futures*, PaineWebber Capital Markets Report, September 17, 1987.

TABLE 13-1: PaineWebber Asset Allocation Model Results
(January 1973 to June 1987)

Asset Category	Annualized Return	Annualized Standard Deviation
K&P PaineWebber Asset Allocated Portfolio	15.99%	9.52%
50% stocks/40% bonds/10% T-bills	11.11%	9.73%
S&P 400	13.06%	16.41%
10-year government bonds	9.28%	8.69%
13- week T-bills	8.86%	0.87%

Source: PaineWebber Capital Markets, "The Use of Futures in Tactical Asset Allocation," *Stock Index Options and Futures*, PaineWebber Capital Markets Report, September 17, 1987.

Buying commodity futures provides a way to participate in the diversification benefits of agricultural and other commodity products. As shown in Chapter 3, Bodie and Rosansky[28] illustrate the benefits of such diversification in reducing risk. In fact, a diversified portfolio of nonfinancial commodity futures contracts provide a risk-return combination comparable to a portfolio of common stocks. Moreover, a portfolio of 60 percent stocks and 40 percent commodity futures possesses the same return as the stock portfolio with two-thirds the risk.

SUMMARY AND LOOKING AHEAD

This chapter examined the uses of financial futures contracts for portfolio management applications. Such applications include asset allocation strategies, portfolio insurance, and adjusting bond durations. Chapter 14 examines applications of futures markets to financial institutions.

---

28 Zvi Bodie and Victor Rosansky, "Risk and Return in Commodity Futures," *Financial Analysts Journal*, Vol. 36, No. 3, May-June 1980, pp. 27-39.

Appendix 13A
How Dealers and Underwriters Use Futures Markets

Dealers and underwriters of bonds and stocks employ futures markets effectively in managing their positions. In fact, dealers and underwriters typically are the largest users of futures contracts, since other alternatives to hedge the price risk of the inventories needed to conduct their business are limited. In addition, bank trading operations and others who must keep inventories employ futures to limit their risk. Dealers also have the opportunity to use futures to initiate arbitrage positions in order to enhance their overall returns.

Basic Uses

The ultimate exposed asset position is borne by dealers and underwriters, especially those trading fixed income securities. Futures are used to hedge these exposed positions. In particular, a dealer makes a market in an asset by keeping the asset in inventory to sell on demand, creating price risk. It is also possible that the demand for particular issues is so strong that the dealer sells more of that specific issue than the dealer has in inventory, i.e., the dealer takes on a short position. Either a long or a short position entails the risk of a major change in the market price level overnight, when the dealer cannot change the inventory level of the position. Such a change in the market often occurs when un-anticipated announcements are made, such as an announcement concerning money supply, politics, or world events. In particular, bond dealers want to be hedged against price changes because they are 98 percent leveraged; any unfavorable announcement could easily bankrupt the firm. In fact, dealers are the largest holders of open interest contracts in many futures markets. Futures are especially useful to dealers because of their liquidity, low cost, and ease in creating a short position.

Futures also are used by dealers when the markets are chaotic within the day and the dealer cannot change the inventory position fast enough in the cash market due to the size of the position. In this case, a 500 T-bond futures contract order covers approximately a $50,000,000 position. Such a position is executed easily in the futures market, but would be difficult or impossible to unwind in the cash market within a short period of time.

In a manner similar to dealers' uses, underwriters employ futures markets to reduce exposure to cash market risk when they sell a large new offering of bonds since this position cannot be disposed of within a few days. This is especially true if the underwriting contract with the corporation guarantees a given interest rate for the bond issue. For example, the IBM sale of $1 billion of bonds outlined in Chapter 9 was set at a guaranteed interest rate by the principal underwriters. Before the October 1979 issue was sold out, the Federal Reserve changed its policy from controlling interest rates to controlling the money supply.

Interest rates rose rapidly; those underwriters who had not hedged their position lost more money from the adverse price change than they gained in commissions. Dealers who purchase large positions from the Treasury auctions have similar problems.

Banks' trading desks are similar in operation to bond dealers, although they are not leveraged to the same extent and their inventory is smaller. However, many banks employ futures in order to reduce the inventory risk of government and municipal bonds and currencies positions.

Using Futures Markets

The use of financial futures contracts by dealers for risk management purposes is critical both for performance and for survival reasons. The size of the bid-ask spreads for trading financial assets are small enough that miscalculations concerning the direction of the market when the inventory position is unhedged would severely affect profits. Moreover, since bond dealers are highly leveraged, any major mistake could easily bankrupt the firm. For example, the bankruptcy of Drysdale Securities, a government bond dealer, shows that trading mistakes can result in bankruptcy for the firm in question and large losses for firms trading with such a firm.

Dealers must be cognizant of their net portfolio risk as well as of the price risk for individual inventory issues. Thus, the combined long and short positions of a dealer's inventory are often significant, causing substantial total price risk, even though the individual issues have small or moderate positions. Such a diversified portfolio requires careful attention in order to determine the overnight or intraday *net* inventory position for effective hedge management. A net duration approach would be appropriate to measure the inventory risk since the portfolio contains bonds with different maturities and coupons.

Bond dealers and bank trading desks are typically very involved with the government quarterly refunding auctions. Such auctions involve billions of dollars of T-bond and T-note issues. Market watchers use these auctions as a determination of the short and intermediate trend for interest rates. Dealers hedge current inventory during these time periods in order to reduce their risk associated with the uncertainty that often exists with refunding. This uncertainty has been compounded in the past several years by the significant involvement of Japanese traders in the U.S. government bond market in combination with the effects of changes in the exchange rate on foreign net returns. Thus, dealers who are successful at predicting intraday trends during normal markets due to supply and demand factors often hedge in the abnormal periods around auctions since external factors often affect the markets at this time.

During auction periods, dealers also need to consider the benefits of hedging due to the additional inventory accumulated during these time periods. Thus, dealers trade bonds vigorously during auction periods, providing the marketmaker function that is the primary reason for their existence. As the dealers accumulate positions in response to money managers rearranging their bond portfolios, they often become overexposed unless sufficient monitoring and hedging of inventory occurs. Given the volatility of the bond markets during auction times, dealers must not become so concerned with the level of activity that they forget the concept of managed inventory positions.

Often dealers hedge *before* an auction by placing an anticipatory futures sell hedge in order to protect against an adverse price reaction if the auction is less successful than generally expected. The hedge is placed before the auction begins, since dealers typically place a bid to purchase bonds and notes directly from the government in order to resell them immediately in the open market. The object of the hedge is to offset the potential adverse effects on their new position if the market falls rapidly once the outcome of the auction is announced. However, the dealer must be knowledgeable concerning the bidding process so that the bid with the government is accepted; if the bid price is too low (no bonds are purchased) *and* the market rallies, then the dealer realizes a loss because there is no cash position to counteract the short futures hedge position.

Block traders for stocks face a situation similar to bond dealers. Block traders sell hundreds of thousands of shares of a stock in one day. When volatile markets occur, block traders find it difficult to execute the blocks at a price that satisfies the trader. Employing stock index futures in this type of situation alleviates the potentially adverse effects of major market movements on the block trading efforts. By 1987 there were over 3,600 block trades consisting of 10,000 or more shares each per day, constituting over one-half of the NYSE volume.

Considerations and Costs of Hedging for Dealers

There are several considerations for dealers when an active inventory hedging program exists. These considerations affect the return, cost, and risk characteristics of the operation:

- Hedging not only reduces the downside risk of the inventory position, it also limits the upside profits if the market rises (falls) when the dealer has a short (long) futures position. Thus, dealers who believe they can forecast the direction of the market, whether it be within the day or for a longer period of time, are hesitant to institute a fully hedged program. However, a fully hedged position for chaotic markets and uncertain time periods often is undertaken.
- The basis risk of the diverse issues that make up the bond portfolios of dealers is difficult to manage, given the variety of maturities, coupons, and types of bonds in the dealer's inventory (i.e., government, corporate, and municipal bonds). The analysis and control of the basis risk of such a portfolio takes a sophisticated computer program and a commitment to the management of the basis risk of the portfolio. A similar situation exists for stock and currency positions.
- The *net* risk position of the firm must be considered for effective risk management. Thus, if the firm is involved with other services, such as brokerage activities and the inventories generated from these accounts, then the risk management function must consider the entire set of activities of the firm rather than just analyzing the dealer function in isolation.

Arbitrage Opportunities

Major dealers and bank trading desks have the opportunity to execute arbitrage transactions in order to enhance the returns of their portfolio of assets. Arbitrage is initiated when an appropriate combination of the cash and futures positions provides a risk-free rate of return which is greater than the T-bill rate. Such possibilities exist if the futures and cash markets are not perfectly integrated. However, the benefits of an arbitrage program typically are restricted to those who take major positions in these markets and who can react quickly during the day to discrepancies between the futures and cash prices.

The profitability of arbitrage transactions are affected by the cost of financing the position as well as the price differential between the futures and cash instruments. In fact, the financing cost is often the factor that dictates the profitability of an arbitrage position. In this regard, if the dealer intends to keep a given size inventory in a security, that position would then need to be financed, regardless if the arbitrage was initiated or not. In this case, one could consider the financing cost of an arbitrage strategy to be negligible, which would enhance the measured profitability of the arbitrage strategy. Arbitrage strategies are examined in Part II.

Futures as Alternatives to Forward and Short-Sale Transactions

Short-selling may be employed by a dealer in order to keep customers when the dealer must make a market in a security, even though the dealer has no inventory in that security. Forward transactions are employed for a number of reasons by financial institutions, corporations, and dealers. For example, a corporation that desires to lock-in the future value of a foreign currency can execute a forward transaction. In addition, there is an active market in forward contracts for mortgage-backed securities to hedge mortgages being packaged for a secondary market sale.[1]

Futures can be employed to create the equivalent to a short-sale or forward transaction. If the futures contract is sold without a corresponding cash purchase then this is equivalent to a cash short-sale for the instrument underlying the futures contract. Futures also can be employed as an alternative to a cash forward transaction, since futures are simply standardized forward contracts.

---

1   A forward transaction may be created in the cash market by either a dealer or the market participant with a purchase of a longer-term security and the short-sale of a shorter-term security, as explained earlier in this chapter. A similar, and less costly, procedure to create the forward transaction is to purchase the longer-term T-bill and then enter a repurchase (repo) agreement where the T-bill is sold for a specified time and then returned to the original owner at a specified price decided upon at the initial sale date. Another method to create a forward commitment is to purchase a T-bill on a when-issued basis, i.e., the T-bill is not purchased until it is actually sold by the Treasury at some later date; however, when-issued transactions typically are for a maximum of several weeks. A cash short-sale may be initiated by obtaining the cash T-bill for the short-sale on a demand basis from the owner (a risky undertaking, since the owner can demand return of the T-bill at any time), or by a reverse-repo transaction.

Chapter 14

Applications of Futures to Financial Institutions

Financial institutions are natural users of interest rate futures contracts. In particular, asset-liability management by financial institutions can be accomplished more easily and quickly with futures instruments. Asset-liability "gaps" are common for financial institutions, with a gap existing when the amount of rate-sensitive assets differs from the amount of rate-sensitive liabilities within a given maturity range. When no gaps exist, then the institution is perfectly matched. Otherwise, interest rate risk exists. Futures are used to manage gaps. One decision explored here is to determine whether specific assets should be hedged (microhedges) or whether the net gap position of the institution should be hedged (macrohedges).

One application of interest rate futures is managing the interest rate cycle; that is— showing how financial futures are employed to manage the asset-liability structure of a bank as the business cycle changes. Specifically, sell or buy hedges are instituted, depending on the slope of the yield curve and the need for liquidity.

Hedging Money Market CD (MMCD) rollovers is one of the easiest and most popular uses of futures markets for adjusting the gap structure of a financial institution. The financial manager employs a short hedge to lock in the cost of funds for the subsequent time period in order to reduce the effect of short-term interest rate fluctuations. A similar procedure is used to hedge the issuance of jumbo CDs. Another application of futures is to institute a sell hedge to create a synthetic fixed-rate loan. This synthetic instrument provides the financial institution with a variable-rate loan, while allowing the corporation to possess a fixed-rate loan.

INTRODUCTION: FINANCIAL INSTITUTIONS AND FUTURES

Factors Affecting Financial Institutions

Earnings of financial institutions are affected significantly by a combination of factors that have increased in importance since the late 1970s:

- Financial institutions possess more short-term liabilities than short-term assets, thus their liability costs increase faster than their return on assets when interest rates increase.
- Deregulation of financial institutions created a competitive environment that encourages institutions to offer new instruments to customers. These instruments often are short-term in nature and offer interest rates that are higher and more volatile than those of savings accounts, which previously provided most of the financial institutions' funds. Specifically, financial institutions sell money market certificates of deposit (CDs) that are tied to the rates of short-term instruments such as T-bills. Moreover, while deregulation

of the liability side of the balance sheet was occurring, the issuance of longer-term fixed-rate loans continued as usual.
- The increasing level and volatility of interest rates created a reduction and instability of earnings.
- The executives of financial institutions did not possess sufficient expertise for effective risk management, mainly because of the highly regulated environment that existed before deregulation.

Because of the above factors, the earnings of financial institutions often are negative when interest rates increase. Since the history of financial institutions is one of stable and positive earnings, this turn of events concerned shareholders, the Federal Reserve, the Federal Deposit Insurance Corporation, and the Comptroller of the Currency.

Financial futures can both alleviate the volatility of earnings of financial institutions and reduce the negative effects of a mismatched asset-liability balance sheet structure. Futures are also tools that help manage the risk environment of the institution, given that a rapid restructuring of the cash balance sheet of such institutions is a difficult and/or costly undertaking when interest rates change. As early as 1981, Sanford Rose[1] claimed that "Banks are damaging their own and their customers' profit potential by failing to see the possibilities of the financial futures markets." In reference to the risk of using financial futures, Richard Sandor states: "Clearly, the main risk is ignorance of risk-management fundamentals and of how current structural change in banking's products requires altering them."[2]

Financial Institutions and Futures

Although a relatively low level of hedging activity by institutions nationwide has been influenced by the significant decrease in the volatility and level of interest rates since 1982, other reasons also are given to explain why futures are used sparingly by financial institutions:
- There is a general fear and lack of understanding of futures markets by some executives and many of the members of boards of directors of financial institutions. This fear is based on a lack of knowledge of the uses and characteristics of futures markets, and the inability to distinguish between speculation and risk management in these markets.
- Accounting effects and regulatory restrictions in the past caused many institutions to delay the implementation of futures. Hedge accounting rules are now available to financial institutions, although these rules still hamper some types of hedging activities. Regulatory requirements mean additional record keeping and reporting burdens for institutions that use futures.
- A short futures hedge creates losses if the cash market value increases. Explaining consistent futures losses to board members can be a difficult undertaking, especially since regulators require that the board authorize all futures trading and take final respon-

---

1 Sanford Rose, "Banks Should Look to the Futures," *Fortune*, April 20, 1981, pp. 185-186, 188, 190-192. Quote on p. 185.

2 Anon., "When You're Trading Interest-Rate Futures, Ignorance is Risk," *ABA Banking Journal*, April 1984, p. 72.

FOCUS 14-1: Deregulation and Its Effects

Deregulation of Financial Institutions

Before the deregulation of interest rate products for financial institutions, individuals received a 4% to 5% return on their savings accounts and did not obtain a return on demand deposits. Although some individuals purchased other assets to hedge against inflation and obtain positive real returns, billions of dollars remained in demand and time deposits. These deposits allowed financial institutions to earn consistent and moderately sized profits by loaning out funds to corporations and individuals. Moreover, these deposits partially subsidized relatively low interest rates for mortgages, automobile loans, and other loans.

During the mid-1970s the distinction between various types of financial service organizations started to blur. Sears made a decision to diversify into numerous financial services, including banking and brokerage (Dean Witter). With its credit card operation and Allstate Insurance, Sears became known as the largest financial services organization in the country. The entrance of brokerage houses into operations typically reserved for commercial banks and savings and loans, plus the advent of money market funds, caused difficulties for these financial institutions. Therefore, traditional financial institutions demanded deregulation to allow them to compete in a changing financial world.

Effects of Deregulation

The combination of higher interest rates associated with increasing inflation rates and various opportunities for individuals to invest at high money market rates caused depositors to withdraw billions of dollars from traditional financial institutions starting in the latter 1970s. The removal of interest rate ceilings restricting what financial institutions could pay on deposited funds allowed these institutions to reclaim and retain funds so they could adequately finance their assets. This deregulation started with the issuance of six-month money market CDs (MMCDs). Various plans to pay interest on checking accounts followed, while deregulation on other MMCD maturities allowed customers additional choices a short time later. As investors became more sophisticated, numerous innovative products offering differing risks and returns were created by financial institutions.

Deregulation worked—too well! It enticed the customers of financial institutions to keep their funds at these institutions. However, the cost of these funds became significantly higher than the old demand and savings deposit rates, creating a significant funds management cost problem.

The short-run shock effect of deregulation on the institutions was severe. Many financial institutions did not know their maturity structure of assets and liabilities, much less the effect that a given change in interest rates would have on their profits. This was a particular problem for smaller and medium-size banks. The resultant need for financial analysis and decision-making similar to corporate financial decision-making was thrust upon an industry not ready or willing to cope with the necessary changes. Bankruptcies and mergers increased significantly. Suddenly the industry wished the "good old days" would return.

The spirit and fact of deregulation continues into the 1990s. Perhaps the most significant change is interstate banking, which allows increased competition among financial institutions. However, institutions outside New York and Chicago are concerned that the money center banks from the major financial cities will buy up the prime local banks and provide "unfair competition" for the remaining banks. Regional banking has emerged as the temporary solution to the threat of the money center banks. With regional banking, two or more states pass laws to allow for mergers across their respective state borders. It remains to be seen whether regional banking can provide the efficiency needed to compete in a global marketplace.

sibility for the program. Consequently, convincing the board of the importance of implementing a hedging program is a critical step.[3]

- Some institutions want to control precisely their risk position arising from gaps. These institutions prefer to avoid futures because of the basis risk involved. Options or other risk management instruments are employed by these institutions.
- Most of the banks not using futures believe they can match their asset and liability structure in the cash market. However, it is doubtful that needed *changes* in the bank's structure can be implemented quickly in the cash market. Such changes may be managed with futures until the cash market adjustments are completed.
- The fact that smaller banks do not adequately measure their effective gaps makes it difficult to formulate a risk management program.
- The costs of starting and administering a futures hedging program are significant, especially in terms of executives' time requirements.[4]

Most of the above difficulties involving futures markets can be overcome or minimized.

ASSET-LIABILITY/SPREAD MANAGEMENT

Asset-Liability Management Concepts

Assets and Liabilities. Financial institutions obtain funds from deposits, savings accounts, and by selling certificates of deposit. They lend out these funds to corporations and individuals, as well as invest funds in T-bills, T-bonds, and municipal bonds. The process of obtaining funds from one segment of the economy and lending funds to another segment of the economy (or obtaining short-term funds and lending on a long-term basis) is known as **intermediation.** This process is the key to asset-liability management as practiced by financial institutions, and is alternatively known as **spread management.**

The maturity and interest rate relationships between the assets of the financial institution (the loans and investments) and the liabilities of the institution (the funds received from depositors plus funds from selling CDs) determine both the profitability and the risk of the bank or savings and loan. Logically, when the average interest rate on the assets exceeds the average rate on the liabilities, then the "spread" is positive and the institution is profitable. When the cost of liabilities exceeds the returns from assets, then the spread is negative and losses occur. Spread management is the control of the assets and liabilities to obtain a desirable rate of return on assets in relation to the risk.

Maturity Structure. The relationships between the maturities of the assets and the liabilities for different maturity ranges have a significant effect on the variability of the earnings of the institution; that is, the maturity relationships are the important factors

---

3 Many institutions employ options rather than futures for their hedging activities, since options have a limited loss feature and thus can be justified to the board with less difficulty. However, the cost of the option represents a disadvantage.

4 A survey by Koch, Steinhauser, and Whigham found that executives desire to keep control and responsibility for the hedge programs within the top structure of management. This consideration emphasizes the importance that top management places on the use of futures to control risk. However, in order to gain expertise, 60 percent of the institutions hired outside consultants and brokers to help implement a hedging program, although many executives expressed concern over the motives and institutional knowledge of brokers. D. L. Koch, D.W. Steinhauser, and P. Whigham, "Financial Futures as a Risk Management Tool for Banks and S&Ls," *Federal Reserve Bank of Atlanta Economic Review,* September 1982, pp. 4-14.

affecting risk.[5] The amount of assets in each maturity range (called **rate-sensitive assets**) typically does not equal the amount of **rate-sensitive liabilities** in the same range. Thus, if interest rates increase in the economy, then a maturity range where more liabilities exist than assets creates a loss when the currently existing liabilities mature and are "rolled over" into new liabilities at a higher cost.[6]

Gaps. The importance of the relative dollar size of the rate-sensitive assets (RSA) to the rate-sensitive liabilities (RSL) in each maturity range is seen by examining a situation where the amounts differ. Exhibit 14-1 presents a breakdown of the RSA and RSL into their major components, with a net RSA–RSL (or "**gap**") given for each maturity range. The maturity ranges less than 90 days possess positive gaps; that is, the values of RSA–RSL are positive. The ranges from 91 days to 180 days have negative gaps. A positive gap has a direct relationship between interest rate changes and earnings: earnings increase when interest rates increase, since more assets than liabilities in a given maturity range are repriced at the current (higher) interest rate. A negative gap has an inverse relationship between interest rates and earnings: earnings increase when interest rates decrease since more liabilities than assets are repriced at the lower interest rate. These associations are shown by the following, with E representing earnings:

		$i+$	$i-$
Positive gap	RSA – RSL > 0	E+	E–
Negative gap	RSA – RSL < 0	E–	E+

Net interest margin (NIM) is often used as the measure of "earnings" for financial institutions. Net interest margin is the difference between interest income and interest expense. Of course, net earnings also would include operating expenses and other charges. For our purposes, we use earnings and net interest margin interchangeably.[7]

The Effect of Gaps on Earnings. An extreme example of how a negative gap for short maturities affects the profitability of a financial institution is shown in Exhibit 14-2. Here a savings and loan association is assumed to have its assets in mortgages with an average yield

---

5 Chapter 11 examines the use of duration as a measure of the sensitivity of a fixed-income asset to changes in interest rates. Therefore, duration can be employed to measure the average asset and liability sensitivities instead of using maturity ranges. Maturities are employed here for several reasons. First, this practice is the convention in the industry. Second, duration ignores the effects of changes in the shape of the yield curve. Finally, most financial institutions concentrate on the effect of the short-term maturity ranges on earnings, rather than the entire asset-liability structure measured by a duration analysis.

6 When rate-sensitive assets and rate-sensitive liabilities are perfectly balanced, then changes in the interest rate have no effect on the earnings stream. The following conditions are needed for a perfectly hedged situation:

   • The spread between the returns generated by the assets and the cost of the liabilities remains stable.
   • The average maturity of the assets equals the average maturity of the liabilities in each maturity range.
   • The distribution of the risk of the asset returns remains the same.
   • The asset-liability maturity ranges include any intermediate cash flows from assets-liabilities that mature later, *or* one analyzes the situation by using duration instead of maturity.

7 Summing the product of the size of the changes in the interest rates for each maturity times the gap for that maturity provides an approximation of the change in net interest margin. The change in the rate of return for the institution is determined by dividing this change in NIM by the amount of assets, or by the capital of the institution.

EXHIBIT 14-1: A Gap Analysis

(000,000s)	Over Night	1-30 Days	31-60 Days	61-90 Days	91-135 Days	136-180 Days
Investments	$1,750	$ 390	$ 484	$1,428	$ 580	$ 440
Loans	—	2,230	1,780	1,802	1,440	1,590
Total rate-sensitive assets:	$1,750	$2,620	$2,264	$3,320	$2,020	$2,030
Money market certificates				$1,50 0		
	—	$1,020	$1,300		$2,610	$1,100
Other liabilities						
	—	530	475	515	900	850
Total rate-sensitive liabilities:	—	$1,550	$1,775	$2,015	$3,510	$1,950
RSA – RSL ("gap")	$1,750	$1,070	$ 489	$1,215	– $1,490	– $ 80

Source: "Inside T-bill Futures," Chicago Mercantile Exchange, p. 13.

of 9.7% and an average maturity of 20 years.[8] The liabilities consist of money market certificates of deposit (60 percent of the total) and savings deposits (40 percent of the total). Panel A shows that the negative gap is profitable when the short-term interest rates for the liabilities are below the interest rates earned on the assets. However, when short-term rates in the economy increase, the cost of new money market certificates of deposit (MMCDs) also increases; that is, MMCDs cost more when the current MMCDs mature and customers reinvest these funds in new six-month MMCDs. This result is shown by the short-term rate increase from 8% in panel A to 14% in Panel B. Thus, the combination of a large negative gap for the short maturity ranges *and* higher liability costs for the short-term MMCDs turn a $2.9 million profit into a $.7 million loss. Equally important as the net loss when liability costs increase is the *variability* in returns as rates change. This significant risk factor is important to an industry that must keep the confidence of both its customers and its shareholders.[9]

8 Although a maturity schedule of the mortgages could be ascertained, using an average maturity is sufficient for this simple example.

9 Another factor that affects earnings variability is changes in the *spread* between the interest rates on assets and the interest rates on liabilities for each maturity range. These interest rates often are affected by different factors, causing changes in the spread. For example, banks may have assets that are prime-based variable-rate loans to corporations and are funded by short-term money market instruments; since the prime rate behaves in a different manner than short-term money market rates, the spread between these instruments varies over time.

EXHIBIT 14-2: The Effect of Gaps on Earnings: An Illustration

A. The Balance Sheet with Low Short-Term Interest Rates

Assets

Category	Amount	Maturity	Average Rate
Mortgages	$100 MM	20 years	9.7%

Liabilities

Category	Amount	Maturity	Average Rate
Savings Deposits	$40 MM	—	5.0%
MMCD	$60 MM	6 months	8.0%

Annualized earnings = $100 MM (9.7 percent) – $40 MM (5.0 percent) – $60 MM (8.0%) = $ 2.9MM

B. The Balance Sheet with High Short-Term Interest Rates

Assets

Category	Amount	Maturity	Average Rate
Mortgages	$100 MM	20 years	9.7%

Liabilities

Category	Amount	Maturity	Average Rate
Savings Deposits	$40 MM	—	5.0%
MMCD	$60 MM	6 months	14.0%

Annualized earnings = $100 MM (9.7 percent) – $40 MM (5.0 percent) – $60 MM (14.0 percent) = $-.7 MM

Managing Gaps

The Risk Factor. As the example shows, the combination of a maturity gap and an adverse interest rate movement causes a decline in earnings. However, an advantageous change in interest rates with the appropriate gap creates an increase in earnings. Thus, if the financial institution can correctly forecast interest rates *and* quickly change its gap structure, then it can profit from both increases and decreases in interest rates.

Unfortunately, it is very difficult to forecast interest rates; moreover, without the aid of financial futures, it is almost impossible to change the structure of the institution's balance sheet quickly. The result is a risk factor for the financial institution's earnings that is associated with the size of the maturity gaps and the size of the change in interest rates. This risk factor became painfully evident to most financial institutions during the volatile interest rate periods of the latter 1970s and early 1980s. Some institutions attempted to restructure the maturities of their assets and liabilities in order to close their gap. This was a difficult undertaking for some institutions and essentially impossible for most savings and loans. Other financial institutions employed financial futures to help control their gaps. Some institutions simply merged or went bankrupt.

The use of futures to restructure the balance sheet is particularly important for savings and loans, since they often must keep their assets on the balance sheet for 10 to 20 years. During the relatively low interest rates of the mid-1980s, savings and loans provided fixed mortgage interest rates at margins of less than 1 percent above variable-rate loans. The question remains as to the long-term balance sheet viability of issuing a majority of fixed-rate loans during low-interest-rate periods. Some economists are asking whether the industry will survive during the next increase in interest rates.

Gaps and Risk Management. The risk resulting from gaps is an important consideration for the asset-liability manager of financial institutions. A complete analysis of the gap situation needs to be made, plus a determination of the appropriate risk posture and forecasting ability of the institution. Only then can the financial executive determine whether the asset-liability structure can be altered, how fast it can be changed, and whether the institution *wants* to change its risk posture. A basic result of this decision making is to determine the appropriate *risk-return* trade-off posture of the firm. Then the asset-liability gap is *managed* to obtain the optimum risk-return position. The management of this gap is critical for the long-run viability of the institution, since a perfectly hedged asset-liability position earns only an 8% return on capital. Since an 8% return is not acceptable for the long-run profit potential of the bank, some risk and maturity gap management must be undertaken. One tool that allows flexibility to adjust the asset-liability mix of the firm quickly to changing economic conditions is financial futures. The typical uses of futures to control the maturity risk of the institution are to hedge the gaps when the direction of rates change, to hedge the money market certificate rollover, and to hedge the issuance of jumbo CDs. These applications are covered shortly.[10]

---

10 *If* the financial institution is naturally hedged between assets and liabilities, then the financial manager must *not* make the mistake of using futures markets for risk control, since there is no maturity risk for this institution. Thus, using futures when the institution is naturally hedged *creates* risk by effectively unhedging the naturally hedged institution. One banking executive in a large regional banking center claimed that futures "were not any good for banks to use"; when pressed, the executive admitted that he had used futures when his bank was naturally hedged.

Factors Affecting Returns and Variability. The increase in the level and volatility of interest rates in the 1970s and 1980s has forced many institutions to manage their gaps. Asset-liability management has shown that the following factors affect the level and variability of earnings:

- Errors in forecasting rates and the appropriate gap sizes have significant effects on earnings, especially because smaller spreads have become available since deregulation.[11]
- Emphasizing interest rate risk by gaps management often causes the financial institution to ignore the credit risk of borrowers. Consequently, credit risk tends to increase as gaps are forced toward zero. Moreover, when institutions take on variable-rate loans to reduce the average maturity of their assets, a significant increase in interest rates can cause financial difficulties for the borrowers, which also increases credit risk.
- The relative movements of asset and liability interest rates for given maturity ranges are not balanced perfectly.[12]
- The accuracy of the model is important. Our discussion is based on a **static model**— that is, one in which no changes in balance sheet amounts during the period are

---

11 Forecasting a multitude of rate changes for the various maturity ranges can be a difficult though rewarding exercise if the forecast is accurate. On the other hand, one may determine the *relative* volatility of the rates in each range to some benchmark and then use this information to develop a modified gap model; this approach reduces some of the difficulties and data problems in forecasting for asset-liability purposes. Moreover, even if the ability to forecast rates is imprecise, a relative volatility analysis shows the risk associated with NIM for various hypothesized changes in interest rates that correspond to a variety of scenarios. Two relative coefficient procedures that measure the effective gap are the piece-by-piece method and the aggregate method. The objective of using one of these procedures to measure the gap is to provide an easier method to forecast the effect of changes in interest rates on NIM. This result is accomplished by relating the changes in rates for each asset and liability to a benchmark rate. Subsequent analysis of the effect of potential changes in the interest rate structure then may be made by simply forecasting the change in the benchmark rate and using that figure in the appropriate NIM equation. Regression equations between each instrument and the benchmark are needed to determine the relative volatility of interest rate effects on NIM. The major benefits of this method are that only one interest rate needs to be forecasted, hence it is easy to determine the effect of a number of different potential interest rate changes on NIM. Disadvantages are that a significant amount of data and data analysis are needed to find the relative volatilities, and that changing or imprecise relationships between the various instruments and the benchmark reduce the accuracy of the forecasts. See both Binder and Dew for additional information. Robert Binder, "New Initiatives in Asset-Liability Management." *Magazine of Bank Administration*, June 1981, pp. 56-64. James Kurt Dew, "The Effective Gap: A More Accurate Measure of Interest Rate Risk." *American Banker*, June 10, 1981, pp. 1+. James Kurt Dew, "The Effective Gap II: Two Ways to Measure Interest Rate Risk." *American Banker*, September 18, 1981, pp. 1+.

12 Factors such as credit risk cause the spread in interest rates between assets and liabilities for each maturity range to change as the economic situation changes. The maturity structure in each maturity range is not exactly matched either, since the maturity of each asset cannot be exactly offset with an equal maturity liability. Moreover, as interest rates change, the supply and demand of many balance sheet items change. Thus, at higher interest rates the demand for MMCDs increases, while consumer and corporate loan demand decreases. Also, when interest rates decrease, the corporate customers want to renegotiate their fixed-rate loans. Another method for determining the relative volatility of the instruments is to employ duration. The procedure is a straightforward application of the duration method discussion in Chapter 11. The relationship between the duration of the assets and the duration of the liabilities gives an idea of the overall maturity gap of the institution. The advantages of a duration approach are the simplicity of using one number in the final analysis and the familiarity of duration to anyone who has dealt with bond maturity management. The disadvantages are that duration is based on a number of restrictive assumptions that adversely affect the results when the yield curve changes shape, and frequent recalculation of the duration value is needed as the data for individual maturity ranges change.

considered, and the changes in interest rates occur at the beginning of the period and remain at the new level for the rest of the period. Dynamic models that allow changes in these factors are more accurate, but require a more complex analysis.

The above factors show that gap management is no easy task. In particular, gap sizes vary constantly. It often is difficult to measure the exact gap, and no one gap is appropriate for all types of economic conditions. However, a concerted effort must be made to monitor and adjust the gaps to correspond to the institution's policy while keeping returns in line with shareholders' expectations.

HEDGING MATURITY GAPS

The following discussion on hedging maturity gaps concentrates on the *factors* affecting these hedges. The methods used to identify the type and size of the appropriate hedge are discussed in Chapters 9 to 13 and therefore are not repeated here. Many financial institutions employ the dollar equivalency hedges described in Chapters 9 and 10 when the cash instrument underlying the futures contract is equivalent to the cash instrument being hedged. If the cash instrument differs in kind from the underlying futures instrument (e.g., CDs versus T-bills), then the relative sensitivities of these instruments to changes in interest rates are determined.[13]

Microhedges and Macrohedges

An institution can hedge either individual assets or the total gap of the institution. This distinction is an important one. A hedging program that deals with the interest rate sensitivity of the balance sheet by hedging *only* the specific instruments associated with the largest gaps is called **microhedging.** The largest microgaps are typically those related to the shorter-term maturities.[14] More sophisticated hedging programs that determine the overall net effect of a change in interest rates on NIM and then hedge the net gap are called **macrohedging** programs. The success of macrohedging depends on the care used to identify the true NIM volatility inherent in the balance sheet and the sophistication of the hedge procedure.

Theoretically, regulators require banks to employ macrohedging procedures, wherein the bank determines the net interest rate exposure for the entire balance sheet, then hedges this exposure. An extreme version of macrohedging is called "blind macrohedging," which occurs when the entire gap is hedged without concern for the maturity or volatility characteristics of the underlying assets or liabilities that make up the maturity mismatch. A blind macrohedge could provide inferior results as compared to a more analytical approach.

Microhedging occurs when specific assets or liabilities are identified to be hedged. The extreme situation for this procedure is "blind microhedging," where hedges are placed on

---

13 When gaps involve a number of different instruments and different maturities, the problem becomes complicated. Some institutions use a combination of short- and long-term futures contracts to hedge intermediate-term gaps. One may use duration or regression to find the sensitivity of the combined futures position to the cash position to determine the appropriate hedge ratio. However, this type of combined futures position creates additional basis risk *if* the shape of the term structure changes, especially if a hump appears in the term structure.

14 Hedging only the shorter-term maturities simplifies the problem of dealing with the maturity and expiration restrictions of the available futures contracts.

specific assets or liabilities without any regard for the relevant gap or effect on NIM. Consequently, blind microhedging often *increases* the risk of the institution.

In reality, many financial institutions use a type of microhedge whereby specific assets or liabilities are hedged with the objective of reducing the effect of interest rate changes on NIM. Regulators accept this type of hedge if there is proof that it reduces NIM exposure to changes in interest rates.

Kolb, Timme, and Gay[15] note that banks use microhedges rather than macrohedges for two reasons. First, bankers associate "hedge" accounting with specific assets or liabilities that can be tracked in price; in fact, many bankers believe that hedge accounting is allowed only when a specific asset (liability) or well-defined set of assets (liabilities) are hedged. Thus, accounting procedures are geared toward microhedging. Second, macrohedging requires a significant amount of information in order to determine the correct gaps. Consequently, the gathering and processing of this information affects the relative cost of macrohedging versus microhedging. Moreover, the information requirements for macrohedging necessitate a centralized operation, whereas a decentralized operation could institute microhedges for each area of control.

Interest Rate Risk, Credit Risk, and Gaps

The effect of three important financial factors must be considered before an optimal hedging program is formulated for financial institutions. These are:
- Timing and selectivity of the hedging program.
- Relationship between interest rate risk and credit risk.
- Extent of bankruptcy risk.

Timing and Selective Hedging. The objective of hedging gaps is to reduce interest rate risk—that is, to reduce the effect of changes in interest rates on NIM. At the extreme, a program to hedge the entire gap could create a perfectly matched balance sheet. Although such a situation eliminates all interest rate risk, it also reduces the rate of return to below average or marginal levels. Hence, it is the function of the financial executive to manage the gap structure in order to achieve the desired balance between interest rate risk and rate of return. In essence, the financial executive must consider timing the implementation of hedges by forecasting interest rates.

Selectively hedging because of correct interest rate predictions provides a superior risk-return relationship for the institution. Unfortunately, there is no simple equation that determines *when* to hedge; such a decision is based on judgment and knowledge of the factors affecting interest rates. However, once a decision is formulated concerning the direction of interest rates, the executive can determine *whether* a futures hedge will benefit the institution and determine the size of the hedge and which futures contracts to use. One compromise to the extremes of either completely hedging the gap position or formulating a purely selective hedging program is to hedge a "core" position on a consistent basis and then use selective hedging on the remaining exposed position.

Credit Risk. The second financial factor affecting the hedging program is the relationship between interest rate risk and credit risk. The historical response of institutions to the

---

15 Robert W. Kolb, Stephen G. Timme, and Gerald D. Gay, "Macro Versus Micro Futures Hedges at Commercial Banks," *The Journal of Futures Markets*, Vol. 4, No. 1, Spring 1984, pp. 47-54.

adverse effect of higher interest rates on negative gaps is to issue more variable-rate loans. Savings and loans changed the majority of new loans from the fixed-rate standard of the late 1970s to variable-rate loans in the 1980s. Banks forced corporations to take variable-rate loans based on the prime rate.

The desired effect of the financial institution to switch from long-term fixed-rate loans to variable-rate loans is a closer match between the maturities of the assets and the liabilities. An unanticipated effect is to increase the credit risk of the institution's customers, since as interest rates increase, the probability that the customers can meet their interest payments falls. Moreover, the highest rated corporations moved to the commercial paper and Euro-dollar markets, since the benefit of a fixed-rate loan to the corporation was no longer in effect.[16] This situation left the banks with inferior customers—that is, the corporations that could not raise funds from the financial markets. Consequently, the process of reducing the size of the maturity gaps in order to decrease the interest rate risk simply increased credit risk.[17, 18]

The savings and loan industry attempted to close the shorter maturity gaps by issuing variable-rate mortgages. Below-market first-year rates, mortgages with balloon payments in five years, and capped-rate variable-rate mortgages were marketed in order to entice the public to choose variable-rate loans. The balloon mortgages initially created a speculative boom in California, and then a bust as the balloons came due before housing values had increased sufficiently to allow the borrower to sell profitably, or to refinance the property.[19]

Overall, variable-rate mortgages seem to have benefitted the borrowers, since they were able to obtain property when rates were high and then benefitted from the decline in rates. When fixed rates declined to below 10 percent, borrowers opted to return to fixed-rate mortgages. While the effect of this behavior on the S&L industry is not yet known, it appears that an increase in interest rates will create another set of problems for the industry, since fixed-rate mortgages are reappearing on the balance sheet in large numbers and borrowers with variable-rate loans may not be able to meet their payments if rates increase significantly.

---

16 The benefit of a fixed-rate loan amounted to protection against increasing rates, but an option to renegotiate if rates fell. The banks would agree to renegotiate in order to keep the corporation's business. Since variable-rate loans no longer had the benefits of a fixed-rate loan, but kept the positive spread above market rates to cover the banker's overhead and costs, corporations decided to raise their own variable-rate funds via the commercial paper and Eurodollar markets.

17 Rose states that there are other effects of variable-rate loans. Since corporations have additional risk from the uncertain cost of funds, they tend to delay or avoid certain capital projects. Also, the additional risk either creates higher product prices or, if prices cannot be increased due to competition, a greater chance the firm will have financial problems, which may affect labor and the returns to stockholders. Sanford Rose, "Banks Should Look to the Futures," *Fortune*, April 20, 1981, pp. 185-186, 188, 190-192.

18 One solution to solve the bank's dilemma is the synthetic fixed-rate loan. A synthetic fixed-rate loan is developed by combining a variable-rate loan with a short position in the futures market. The result is the bank obtains a variable-rate loan that reduces the institution's gap problems, while the corporation receives a fixed-rate loan. This concept is discussed later in this chapter.

19 The below-market first-year rates allowed buyers to qualify for property, even though they could not meet the subsequent payments when interest rates automatically increased. Another feature of the recent variable-rate mortgages is a capped interest rate. Capped mortgages create a type of option to the buyer; this restriction on the maximum change in interest rates adversely affects savings and loans if and when rates increase above the caps.

Bankruptcy Risk. A significant degree of bankruptcy risk for a specific institution often indicates that the financial executives made inappropriate decisions in the past. These decisions may have been related to timing, maturity structure decisions on gap size, credit-worthiness, etc. When bankruptcy is possible, then the ability to institute immediate changes in the gap positions to alleviate this potential catastrophe is unlikely. This situation is another instance in which financial futures are beneficial. For example, a number of savings and loans were in a near-bankrupt situation in the early 1980s when the prime rate was above 20% and fixed-rate mortgages were being financed by six-month money market CDs. An increase of several additional percentage points in interest rates would have created bankruptcy, even for larger institutions. Futures are employed in such a situation to close the adverse gaps until the financial executives believe that the direction of interest rates has reversed.

A specific example of how futures could have helped a bankruptcy case is the situation of First Pennsylvania during 1979. First Penn had rate-sensitive liabilities that exceeded rate-sensitive assets by $1.2 billion. As interest rates rose, the decline in earnings caused the bank's short-term creditors, such as the buyers of CDs, to withhold funds from the bank. This caused the collapse of First Penn such that the FDIC had to bail it out, even though the difficulties could have been reduced significantly by the use of futures for asset-liability management—a technique considered, then rejected, by the officers.

ASSET MANAGEMENT AND THE INTEREST RATE CYCLE

Managing the Investment Portfolio

One part of asset-liability management for financial institutions is to manage the loan-investment portfolio in terms of returns, risk, and liquidity. Changes in the size and composition of the loan and bond investment portfolios occur when there are changes in the economy. Since the location and shape of the yield curve typically changes with the business cycle, the investments with the best returns do not always provide the best risk and liquidity alternative. Moreover, when conditions change, the financial executive does not have sufficient time to alter the structure of the balance sheet to correspond to the changes in the economy. The section below discusses the types of problems that institutions encounter with asset management as the economy changes, and how futures are employed to alleviate these problems.[20]

Common problems encountered by the bank's portfolio manager during critical phases of the business cycle are:
- Lengthening the effective maturities of assets by purchasing long-term bonds when bank loan demand is down in order to obtain higher long-term interest rates.
- Shortening maturities by purchasing short-term bonds when short-term rates are higher than long-term rates.

The existence of the above maturity problems are a result of the business and interest rate cycles. As business activity moves from one phase to another, loan demand changes,

---

20 This discussion assumes the gap structure is analyzed and a maturity mismatch exists. Since such is typically the case, this discussion is relevant for most financial institutions. It also assumes that a microhedging program is in effect for the portfolio division. Since loan and investment portfolio managers are concerned with return, risk, and liquidity factors for *their* portfolio only, concerns about macrogap management typically are left to other divisions in the institution.

and the bank portfolio manager is faced with significant swings in the amount of funds available for investment. In particular, there is a negative relationship between major loans and changes in the amount of liquid assets. The common mistakes given above are a direct result of the changing market environment. Solutions to these problems are discussed below.

The Positively Sloped Yield Curve and the Short Hedge

The phase of the business cycle associated with the maximum easing in money supply is identified by weak loan demand, loan repayments exceeding new loans, high bond prices, low investment yield opportunities, and a positively sloped yield curve. The proper response during this phase is to prepare for the next upsurge in credit demand by building liquidity and keeping maturities short. However, a strong temptation exists to lengthen the investment maturity of the portfolio in order to pick up additional yield, since both loan volume and lending rates have declined. If the portfolio manager is unable to resist the temptation to lengthen maturities to increase yield, then a fall in bond prices in the next phase of the interest rate cycle causes a substantial decrease in the value of the bank's bond portfolio. Moreover, these bonds normally have to be sold at a loss in the next phase of the business cycle in order to meet the bank's liquidity needs for loan demand. If the bank does not sell the bonds, then an opportunity loss exists, since the yield on loans is higher than the yield received on the bonds.

The portfolio manager can overcome the problem of having to sell the longer-term bonds in one period in order to build and maintain liquidity for the subsequent period's increase in loan demand by executing a sell hedge with interest rate futures. Such a hedge protects the bond portfolio against a loss in value if interest rates increase and the portfolio manager must sell the bonds to generate liquidity for loans. Of course, the short hedge also restricts any potential capital gains from a further decrease in interest rates.[21] Moreover, using futures rather than selling the bonds outright allows the portfolio manager to reverse the decision quickly and with minimum cost if a major downward move in interest rates is forecasted.[22] Employing a short hedge also is beneficial for portfolio managers who do not want to realize losses on the bond portfolio by selling the bond, since the futures hedge delays or avoids the losses that the manager does not want to face.

The Negatively Sloped Yield Curve and the Buy Hedge

The second problem encountered by bank portfolio managers is to purchase short-term securities when a negatively sloped yield curve exists. This situation is associated with the

---

21 If high coupon bonds are held, then the portfolio manager can earn returns that are higher than the short-term T-bill rate, with T-bills being the typical security purchased when liquidity is desired. While a futures hedge with a high coupon bond theoretically should provide a higher return than a T-bill position when the yield curve is upward sloping, the existence of basis risk could reduce this return. If return is the primary consideration, a detailed analysis of the basis risk must be undertaken. However, if the bond is deliverable into the futures contract, the portfolio manager can determine the effective return to the delivery date of the futures contract and compare this return to the T-bill rate. See Chapter 7 on T-bond delivery procedure pricing considerations.

22 A disadvantage for institutions not using hedge accounting rules is that the cash bonds are valued at cost, whereas the futures position would be valued at market. The result could be short-term losses and/or an increase in the volatility of NIM.

business cycle phase of maximum tightness in the money supply. At this time most economic indicators are setting new highs, the demand for loans is strong, the Federal Reserve is conducting restrictive monetary policy, the level of bank liquid assets is relatively low, interest rates are relatively high, and bond prices are down. The appropriate strategy during this phase is to extend the maturities of the investment portfolio, locking in the relatively high yields and low bond prices that are available, even though short-term securities provide even higher yields.

The portfolio manager must recognize that during this phase one does not need to maintain a high level of short-term investment securities for liquidity, since liquidity is not needed for loans during the next business cycle phase. During this period liquidity needs to be expended, not built. Moreover, the higher return on short-term securities typically exists for that period only, whereas the return on the longer-term securities is locked in for a much longer time period.

In this phase of maximum cyclical tightness, a long hedge is implemented for one of two reasons:

- To extend the maturities/durations of the current portfolio in order to capture the relatively low price for bonds; executing this maturity extension in the futures market rather than in the cash market reduces transactions costs and provides flexibility for future changes.
- To create an anticipatory hedge so the current high yields can be locked in, even though the funds to purchase these bonds are not available until a later date.[23]

HEDGING CERTIFICATES OF DEPOSIT

The MMCD Short Hedge

The purchase of money market certificates of deposit (MMCD) by the public creates large short-term negative gaps, thereby causing a decline in NIM when interest rates increase. A savings and loan may easily have positive earnings one period and negative earnings the next if short-term rates increase from, say, 7% to 11%. Thus, if the institution believes short-term rates will increase before the current MMCDs mature and are reissued, or if the institution desires to eliminate routinely this MMCD rollover risk, then the future interest rate on these certificates should be hedged.[24] These relationships are shown in Figure 14-1.

Let us assume for simplicity that all MMCDs are issued for six months. The MMCD rate is linked directly to the six-month T-bill auction rate. A short hedge with T-bill futures offsets losses resulting from changes in the MMCD rate between the time the hedge is initiated and when existing MMCDs are rolled over. As the MMCDs are rolled over, the futures are repurchased. The gains on the short T-bill futures contracts resulting from the higher interest rates will offset most of the higher interest expense on the MMCDs. Exhibit

---

23 Bank regulatory agencies do not believe that anticipatory hedges are appropriate, although long hedges may be executed to reduce the risk of the institution in certain circumstances. Moreover, if bond prices decline, the futures loss must be recognized immediately for accounting purposes, whereas the opportunity gain on the cash position is recognized only over the life of the cash investment. The use of hedge accounting rules could alleviate this problem.

24 Much of this section is adapted from Parker and Daigler: Jack W. Parker and Robert T. Daigler, "Hedging Money Market CDs with Treasury-Bill Futures," *The Journal of Futures Markets*, Vol. 1, No. 4, Winter 1981, pp. 597-606.

FIGURE 14-1: MMCDs and Hedging

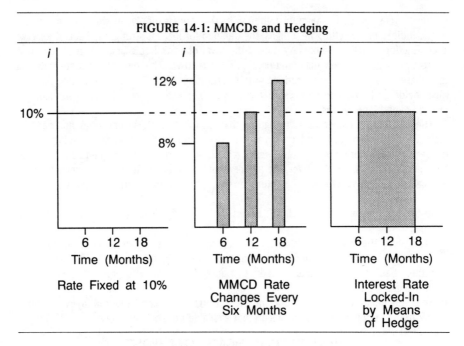

14-3 shows how such a hedge works. Focus 14-2 illustrates the procedure for using T-bill futures for a short hedge of MMCDs.[25]

Considerations in Implementing the MMCD Hedge

Several considerations exist for using T-bill futures to hedge the MMCD position:

- The size of the gap for the period must be forecasted. This undertaking is not easy because a number of factors affect the demand for MMCDs. In particular, the size of this gap is affected by the direction of interest rates and the state of the economy. Moreover, the overall basis risk of the gap is affected by the forecasting error of the amount of MMCDs that will be rolled over.
- The procedure employed for this type of hedge affects the risk of the position. Specifically, the procedure for hedging MMCDs presented in Focus 14-2 assumes that only the following quarter's rollovers are hedged. This only reduces the zero- to three-month gap. Hedging for other gaps is possible if care is taken in setting up the hedge.
- Since the quarterly expirations of the futures contracts are a severe restriction in comparison to the weekly maturities of the MMCDs, the basis risk for the procedure used here is affected, although most of the forward rates typically do not vary significantly from one another.

---

25 This use of interest rate futures markets by national banks is authorized by the Office of the Comptroller of the Currency's revised bank circular No. 79, falling under the category of general asset-liability management hedges.

	January 2	July	December
EXHIBIT 14-3: How a MMCD Hedge Works			
Gap:	$20 million negative gap	$20 million negative gap	$20 million negative gap
6-month MMCDs:	$50 million issued at 8%	$50 million reissued (rolled over) at 9%	$50 million reissued (rolled over) at 10%
NIM effect with no hedge:	No effect	NIM declines by $100,000 over next six months ($20 MM × Δ1% × 1/2 year)	NIM declines by $100,000 over next six months
Futures:	None	Futures sold to lock in December rollover at 9% ($40 MM of 90-day T-bill futures sold)	Futures repurchased at gain of $100,000 to offset increase in MMCD interest rate (locks in 9% effective rate)
NIM effect with hedge:	None	None yet	NIM stays the same over next six months

- If hedge accounting is not employed, then the futures changes affect earnings in the current quarter, while the higher interest cost does not occur until the six-month period after the MMCDs are rolled over. This timing difference could adversely affect the variability of earnings, although it reduces the overall cost of funds during periods when interest rates increase.
- As Jacobs[26] notes, futures prices often include a risk premium or "insurance" cost above the expected spot rate. This extra cost means that the hedge can create a net loss, although this loss is significantly less than the loss of an unhedged position when interest rates increase. In effect, this potential "insurance premium" is the payment required to avoid the risk of unanticipated changes in the future interest rate.[27]

---

26 Rodney L. Jacobs, "Restructuring the Maturity of Regulated Deposits with Treasury-Bill Futures," *The Journal of Futures Markets*, Vol. 2, No. 2, Summer 1982, pp. 183-193.

27 Jacobs, ibid., also discusses the use of T-bill futures to adjust for a *positive* gap caused by a larger amount of short-term loans in comparison to short-term MMCDs. This situation occurs if the bank has loans that are repriced, say, every three months, with LIBOR or the prime rate serving as the relevant interest rate. In this case, a positive gap exists for the zero- to three-month gap, while there is a negative gap for the three- to six-month gap. The positive gap reduces earnings when interest rates decline. In order to reduce the size of this short-term positive gap, the financial manager initiates a *buy* hedge with T-bill or Eurodollar futures.

FOCUS 14-2: A Procedure for Hedging MMCDs

A short hedge with T-bill futures locks-in the cost of future MMCDs so as to avoid the adverse effects of potentially higher future interest rates. The higher cost of the MMCDs is offset by the gain in the short futures position. The following procedure is followed during those quarters when a short hedge with T-bill futures is implemented for six-month MMCDs:

- The amount of the negative (90-day) gap that exists and the amount that the institution *decides* to hedge must be determined. Quarters are used because they represent the typical forecast period for most financial institutions.

- On the first day of the quarter futures are sold to hedge that portion of the gap due to the MMCD rollovers during the quarter. *Two* futures contracts must be sold to hedge each $1 million of cash MMCDs, since T-bill futures are based on 90-day cash T-bills, whereas the MMCDs are six-month instruments. This two-to-one hedge ratio is based on the relative maturity of the cash MMCDs and the futures contract.

- Each week a given portion of the hedged MMCDs is rolled over and reissued. For each $1 million of MMCDs, two futures contracts are repurchased to offset the previous sale. Hence, an increase in MMCD costs due to an increase in interest rates during the quarter (especially large, unanticipated rate increases) are offset by a decrease in futures prices. For each one basis point increase in interest rates the hedge saves $50 in interest expense per $1 million in MMCDs—that is, $1 million $\times$ (1/2 year) $\times$ .0001 = $50.

- The new MMCDs are no longer hedged after they are rolled over. In addition, under the procedure discussed here, MMCDs being rolled over in a quarter other than the current one will not be covered by the hedge. A more encompassing hedge can be devised.

- In general, it is advisable to close out the short positions in T-bill futures only once a week, rather than spreading the closing transactions throughout the week to correspond to the exact issuance date of the MMCDs. The weekly closing is appropriate because the MMCD rate is fixed for the entire week. Monday's closing price of T-bill futures should correspond most closely to the information used to determine the T-bill auction rate, which in turn fixes the weekly MMCD issuance rate. Moreover, closing the shorts only once a week saves on transactions costs if the trades are made in volume.

The decision at the beginning of the quarter to determine whether the bank should hedge the gap is made by one of several methods:

- Automatically hedge each quarter: This procedure reduces the variability of earnings as the institution locks in the future MMCD rates.

- Selectively hedge: based on some mechanical rule that attempts to forecast the direction of interest rates.

- Selectively hedge based on market judgment: Correct selective hedge decisions provide the highest returns since profits based on this method include market forecasting returns. However, incorrect hedge decisions adversely affect the variability of returns as well as earnings themselves.

Two tables that provide the basis for analysis and record keeping purposes are found in Parker and Daigler.* The tables show how to set up the hedge positions and rollovers each week, the unhedged and hedged interest expense, and the relevant futures prices.

---

* Jack W. Parker and Robert T. Daigler, "Hedging Money Market CDs with Treasury-Bill Futures," *The Journal of Futures Markets,* Vol. 1, No. 4, Winter 1981, pp. 597-606.

Models and Results

Maness and Senchack[28] empirically test MMCD hedge strategies for six-month MMCDs. They employ both the basic two-to-one hedge procedure as well as the optimal hedge ratio as derived from historical regression results. The cost reduction and risk of the hedge positions are compared to an unhedged position for a period of rising and falling interest rates, employing hedge lengths of one to 26 weeks, as shown in Table 14-1.

These results show the significant risk reduction benefits of the hedged models as compared with the unhedged position for hedges greater than one week. Hedging reduces the variability of the net cost of rolling over MMCDs by a factor of at least two for the shorter time periods, and a factor of three for hedge lengths of 16 to 26 weeks during the rising rate period. In addition, there is only a minimal difference between the risk for the two-to-one hedge ratio and the optimal hedge ratio, despite the fact that the optimal hedge ratio falls below 1.6:1 in some instances. The cost reduction results in Table 14-1 indicate the obvious; that is, during periods of rising interest rates the hedge saves a significant amount of money, while during periods of falling rates the hedge offsets the lower cost obtained in the cash market.

Speakes[29] suggests a number of related models to determine *when* to implement a MMCD hedge. The models are based on a type of moving average or dollar cost averaging that causes an increase in the size of the futures hedge as interest rates decrease. This contrary trend approach is based on the assumption that, when interest rates deviate from their "normal" range, they will quickly revert direction to return to their normal value.[30] The parameters of the hedge are based on the size of the institution, its exposure to interest rate changes, and a general directional interest rate forecast. Unfortunately, Speakes' limited results do not compare the different hedging procedures to an unhedged position or to a naive hedge, and therefore one does not know how effective the model is on a comparative basis.[31]

Issuing Jumbo Certificates of Deposit

A major source of funding for a bank is the jumbo certificates of deposit (CDs). Selling short-term futures contracts locks in the future rollover rate for CDs in a manner similar to the short T-bill futures hedge for MMCD rollovers. The differences in the two types of hedges are:

---

28 Terry S. Maness and A. J. Senchack, "Futures Hedging and the Reported Financial Position of Thrift Institutions," *The Review of Research in Futures Markets*, Vol. 5, No. 2, 1986, pp. 142–159.

29 Jeffrey K. Speakes, "The Phased-in Money Market Certificate Hedge," *The Journal of Futures Markets*, Summer 1983, Vol. 3, No. 2, pp. 185–190.

30 Unfortunately, economic factors often override the contrary trend concept, at least in the shorter term when most hedges are placed. Thus, inflation, money supply, and deficits affect the trend of interest rates, and these factors tend to exist in major cycles that could provide inferior results for a contratrend procedure. A selective hedging system with superior forecasting ability would provide superior results to this contratrend method. However, the contrary trend method would be less risky than a no hedging policy as long as the procedure is judged over an interest rate cycle rather than only for several quarters.

31 Moreover, Speakes' procedure uses only historical data from the end of rallies, which biases the results since turning points are identified as the only sample observations to examine. A complete analysis would apply these methods to all time periods.

TABLE 14-1: Historical MMCD Hedge Results

	Hedge Length in Weeks	Optimal Hedge Ratio	Cost Reduction in Basis Points		Risk		
			$U - H_2$	$U - H^*$	$\sigma(H_2)$	$\sigma(H^*)$	$\sigma(U)$
Subperiod 1 (rising rates)	1	0.89	5.4	2.4	65.2	54.0	61.7
	6	1.76	30.6	27.0	80.7	77.7	182.7
	11	1.80	64.9	58.6	101.1	97.7	258.7
	16	1.94	94.7	91.8	111.4	111.0	305.9
	21	2.09	119.5	125.1	109.5	108.6	329.0
	26	2.16	142.5	153.6	129.8	127.8	343.8
Subperiod 2 (falling rates)	1	1.08	−14.8	−8.0	52.3	45.0	54.7
	6	1.58	−78.0	−61.7	77.7	70.9	140.2
	11	1.73	−139.0	−120.1	73.3	68.4	181.3
	16	1.76	−181.6	−159.8	93.2	90.3	182.4
	21	1.57	−206.3	−162.1	99.1	88.8	184.4
	26	1.69	−243.3	−206.3	91.1	84.9	202.9

Symbols in the table:

$U - H_2$ = the unhedged less the two-to-one hedged position

$U - H^*$ = the unhedged less the optimal hedged position

$\sigma(H_2)$ = the standard deviation of the two-to-one hedged position

$\sigma(H^*)$ = the standard deviation of the optimal hedged position

$\sigma(U)$ = the standard deviation of the unhedged position

Source: Terry S. Maness and A. J. Senchack, "Futures Hedging and the Reported Financial Position of Thrift Institutions," The Review of Research in Futures Markets, Vol. 5, No. 2, 1986, pp. 142-159.

- One has a choice of whether to use the Eurodollar futures or T-bill futures contracts for a CD hedge.[32] Eurodollar futures often provide a better instrument than T-bill futures for

---

32 Previously a bank CD futures contract traded. The bank CD futures did provide the best association with the cash CD market, but it had less liquidity than the other instruments, as well as some unusual pricing characteristics.

hedging a cash CD position since Eurodollar and CD rates both include a risky component, and therefore their rates are more closely correlated.
- The bank has significantly more control over the issuance of CDs than over MMCDs.
  MMCDs are market-driven instruments and are based on the demand of buyers. CDs are
  issued based on the discretion of the bank's management; in particular, the optimal
  maturity structure of the CDs are determined partially by the decisions of the financial
  executives. Thus, CDs are issued with maturities from three months to one year, depending on the asset-liability structure of the bank and the interest rate in the CD
  market. Futures may aid this maturity structuring process by allowing one to shorten or
  lengthen the effective maturity of the cash instrument by initiating short or long hedges,
  respectively.

Strategies for CD Hedges

Let us assume that the bank wishes to issue six-month CDs; moreover, the bank executives
believe interest rates may increase in the near term, or alternatively they wish to avoid the
potential loss if rates unexpectedly increase. However, the six-month cash CD market is
thin, making the acceptance of a large six-month CD offering at a reasonable interest rate
somewhat doubtful. In this case, the bank could issue three-month CDs and hedge the
rollover interest rate by selling futures that expire in three months. Even if the six-month
CD market were not thin, such a procedure still could be employed if the futures transaction provided a lower cost of funds than could be obtained by issuing six-month cash CDs.

The slope of the yield curve is examined to help decide the best combination of instruments in order to minimize the cost of the bank's liabilities and to provide flexibility in
maturity management. If the yield curve is positively sloped then the bank typically borrows
short-term and invests long-term to obtain a positive return spread. However, this strategy
creates rollover risk for the cost of the borrowed funds. Alternatively, one could create the
following combination:
- Issue a three-month CD.
- Buy a six-month instrument (or invest in a six-month asset).
- Sell short a short-term futures contract expiring in three months.

If the rates associated with these instruments are beneficial to the bank, then a positive
spread is locked in without being affected by the rollover risk. Thus, the above combination
of instruments creates a three-month CD liability and a three-month *net* asset position
(since the last three months of the six-month asset are offset by the short three-month
futures position); the positive spread is locked in *if* the asset and futures have similar
interest rate volatilities.

Negative yield curves present other possibilities. In this situation the bank typically buys
shorter-term assets and funds them with longer-term liabilities to obtain a positive spread.
This situation also causes rollover risk, since if interest rates fall, the spread narrows or
becomes negative. In this case, futures are *purchased* in order to hedge against an increase
in bond prices. The long futures position can be thought of as shortening the maturity of the
liability, or lengthening the maturity of the asset.

SYNTHETIC FIXED-RATE LOANS

Reasons for the Synthetic Fixed-Rate Loan

An interesting application of financial futures contracts for bank management is the **synthetic fixed-rate loan** (SFRL). An SFRL occurs when a variable-rate loan plus short futures hedge has the same cash flow characteristics as a fixed-rate loan. The typical practice is for the lender to provide a variable-rate loan to the corporation, which is preferable to the bank for asset-liability maturity matching purposes. However, the corporation desires a fixed-rate loan in order to eliminate interest rate risk. An SFRL provides benefits to both parties, since the SFRL keeps the variable-rate loan on the books of the bank while the corporate borrower receives a fixed-rate loan. An additional benefit to both the financial institution and the corporation is that the SFRL reduces credit risk by placing a ceiling on the interest rate paid by the corporation.[33]

The SFRL Hedge

A short sale of a short-term financial futures contract, such as Eurodollar or T-bill futures, is all that is necessary to transform a variable-rate loan from a bank into a fixed-rate loan for the corporation. Thus, if interest rates increase, the profits from the short futures transaction offset the higher interest rate costs from the variable-rate loan. Of course, if interest rates fall, the losses on the futures contract offset the *lower* interest costs from the loan. Consequently, except for basis risk, the corporation receives a (synthetic) fixed-rate loan.

One key for the SFRL to work is that the bank must use a market-based instrument to price the loan. The loan rate typically is based on the market instrument index rate plus a premium of, say, two or three percentage points. The index may be T-bills or the Eurodollar LIBOR rate, as long as the index is an instrument traded on the futures market. Using T-bills or LIBOR would entail a shift in policy of most banks, since they usually employ the prime rate as the index for loans. Since the prime rate is not a traded futures instrument, and since the prime has a poor association with market interest rates, hedging a prime-based variable-rate loan creates a significant amount of basis risk.[34] In fact, Dew and Martell[35] state that

---

33 The use of variable-rate loans by banks has driven the most creditworthy corporations to the commercial paper market in order to obtain funds, leaving the higher-risk medium-size firms to obtain loans from the commercial banks. Financial institutions offering an SFRL would obtain a competitive advantage over other commercial banks to obtain larger corporate customers. Corporations prefer the commercial paper market to bank loans since they obtain lower rates from commercial paper than from a variable-rate loan. Actually, large corporations still affect the bank's risk exposure, even when the corporations obtain their funds from the commercial paper market, since the corporations obtain lines of credit from the banks in order to sell the commercial paper. Of course, the corporations use these bank lines of credit if funds are not obtainable from the commercial paper market. Banks would like to regain the large corporations as potential customers in order to broaden their portfolio choices. In fact, one reason for the large loan program to lesser-developed countries during the 1970s and early 1980s was that there was no feasible domestic loan alternative for the banks.

34 Using a market instrument such as Eurodollars to price the variable-rate loan also benefits the financial institution since the lack of association between the prime rate and the actual cost of liabilities to the institution makes asset-liability matching difficult, if not impossible. Thus, using the prime rate instead of a market rate *increases* the volatility of earnings for the financial institution. In fact, the R^2 between the cash CD rate (a major source of funds for the institution) and the prime rate for monthly changes during the volatile 1979-80 period was less than 50% (see Dew and Martell). James Kurt Dew and Terrence F. Martell, "Treasury Bill Futures, Commercial Lending, and the Synthetic Fixed-Rate Loan," *The Journal of Commercial Bank Lending*, June 1981, pp. 27-38.

35 Ibid.

using T-bill futures to hedge a prime-rate loan only eliminates 30% of the risk for weekly repricing and 39% of the risk for monthly repricing.

Implementing the Hedge

An SFRL typically is generated either by the bank or by the corporation. If the bank provides the opportunity for the borrower to receive an SFRL, then the synthetic loan is implemented in one of two ways:

- The bank guarantees a fixed rate for the loan several percentage points above the current short-term rate. The premium above the current interest rate would compensate for the default risk of the loan *plus* the basis risk that the bank is assuming. This alternative is particularly useful if the bank wants to generate a competitive edge over other institutions in the origination of loans for corporations.
- The bank uses its expertise in risk management and futures markets to generate the SFRL; changes in the variable-rate portion of the loan to the corporation are offset by the changes in the futures contract, except for the basis risk. The agreement between the bank and the corporation stipulates that the basis risk is passed along to the corporation. In this case, the price of the loan is the current short-term rate plus a premium for the default risk of the loan; no premium for the basis risk is included.

If the financial institution does not provide SFRLs, then the corporation generates its own SFRL by implementing its own hedges in the futures market. The crucial element in this case is to convince the financial institution that it is in its best interests to use a market-based rate as the base for the variable-rate loan. As noted above, if the prime rate is used by the institution, then the basis risk will make the hedge practically infeasible.

Difficulties with the SFRL Hedge

Several difficulties can exist that would reduce the attractiveness of the SFRL concept for financial institutions:

- The historical practice associated with fixed-rate loans to corporations is as follows: if interest rates increase then the fixed-rate loan remains intact, while if interest rates fall significantly then the corporation asks the bank to renegotiate the loan rate. A renegotiation often is agreed to by the bank to keep the corporate customer happy. Obviously, if a futures hedge is set up to transform a variable-rate loan into a fixed-rate loan, there can be *no* renegotiation of rates unless the bank suffers significant losses, or unless severe and enforceable prepayment penalties exist. This issue could be treated with both legal and educational components, since a "no renegotiation" clause is essential for the effective operation of the SFRL by the financial institution. Alternatively, the futures contract could be assigned officially to the corporation, alleviating any potential that the corporation would attempt to renegotiate the contract.
- The tradition of the banking industry is to use the prime rate as the benchmark for loans. This tradition has survived, even though the prime rate no longer reflects the cost of money to the banking industry. Either prime must be abandoned by the bank in order to institute an SFRL program, or a liquid prime-rate futures must be available in order to hedge against changes in the prime rate.

- The length of the SFRL is limited by the liquidity of the deferred futures contracts and the longest expiration of these contracts.
- The marking-to-market requirements for futures create a daily cash outflow when interest rates fall. From an economic standpoint, negative cash flows are coincident with lower interest rates for the variable-rate loan issued by the bank; thus, subtracting the negative cash flow (due to the futures marking-to-market requirement) from the fixed-rate amount received by the bank nets to the variable-rate amount desired by the bank (ignoring basis risk). Therefore, the bank's management must be able to distinguish between the net economic effect and the separate futures and loan accounts. Alternatively, the futures contract can be assigned to the corporation so it is responsible for the cash flows.
- Without hedge accounting, the effects on the earnings of the bank could vary significantly from quarter to quarter. Thus, the futures price changes would affect earnings in the quarter when they occur, while the effect of the higher earnings from the synthetic fixed-rate loan would be accounted for over the life of the loan. Again, this problem is avoided if the futures contract is assigned to the corporation.

Extensions to the Fixed-Rate Loan Concept

Freeman[36] has outlined two extensions to the basic SFRL concept. The first extension is relevant when the borrower wants to fix the price of the loan immediately, but does not want to use the funds until some time in the future. Real estate developers and certain major manufacturers are interested in this type of a loan. A short hedge from the current period until when the funds are borrowed offsets any changes in interest rates before the funds are needed. The short hedge to lock in the future borrowing rate is equivalent to the short hedge a bank would employ to lock in an interest rate on a CD issue or a MMCD rollover. However, if the bank is actually generating the short hedge for the borrower, then the basis risk for the hedge must be considered for both the pricing process and in terms of whether the loan actually will be executed by the firm.[37]

If the above loan guarantee is for more than three months, then a strip of futures needs to be sold in order to lock in the interest rate. Moreover, if the borrower is uncertain exactly when the loan will be activated, then a strip of futures would allow more flexibility in the timing of the loan activation, although it would create additional basis risk if the actual loan is activated before all the futures contracts expire.[38]

Freeman's second extension to an SFRL occurs when the borrower wants to obtain funds now, but wishes to delay the fixed-rate pricing of the loan until later (hoping that rates will decline). This type of procedure is based on the assumption that the bank *wants*

36 A. Ray Freeman, "Why Not Price Loans Using Financial Futures?," *ABA Banking Journal,* March 1984, pp. 90, 94, 97.

37 Freeman assumes that the bank will provide a fixed-rate loan when the loan finally is initiated, e.g., a loan for one year. Of course, this one-year loan could be an SFRL or a standard fixed-rate loan. In addition, since the decision of when to initiate the loan is determined by the borrower, the bank would need to obtain the funds when the loan is agreed to, and invest the funds in a liquid asset with a similar interest rate sensitivity as the futures contract.

38 Freeman also discusses how to use a buy hedge when the yield curve is inverted and a discrepancy exists between the futures and cash yield curves.

to issue a fixed-rate loan, since the objective of this procedure for the bank is to offset any opportunity loss from a decline in rates. This type of loan is initiated by the bank by issuing a fixed-rate loan at a given premium above the current appropriate futures rate in conjunction with the *purchase* of a short-term futures contract; this combination transforms the fixed-rate loan into a variable-rate instrument to the borrower. The effect of the futures transaction is similar to an anticipatory long hedge, which is used to lock in an interest rate for future investments. In the case at hand, as rates decline the long hedge provides a profit which reduces the net cost of the fixed-rate loan to the borrower, but protects the fixed-rate for the bank.

When the borrower wants to convert the variable-rate loan into a fixed-rate loan (hopefully after rates have declined), the futures contracts are closed out by selling them. Of course, until the futures position is closed, it does entail a significant amount of risk to the borrower since the loan plus futures position is, in effect, a variable-rate loan. Moreover, if the bank is holding the futures position, care must be taken that the firm is creditworthy and the contract is enforceable in relation to the borrower assuming the futures-related costs due to rate changes.

MORTGAGE BANKING AND FIXED-RATE MORTGAGES

A savings and loan association or bank that commits to issuing mortgage loans and then pools these loans in order to sell them in the secondary market within the following six months is involved in mortgage banking operations. When the loans are at a predetermined fixed rate, then the institution takes on the risk that interest rates will increase between the loan origination date and the time at which the loans are pooled and sold. The risk of rising rates (falling loan values) is hedged with a short futures position. Mortgage banking activities for banks is one area in which the regulators allow hedge accounting rules to be employed.

Financial institutions generally are prevented from employing long futures positions, since such positions are identified with anticipatory hedges; regulators view anticipatory hedges as speculating on interest rate movements. However, if the savings and loan is committed to deliver a fixed-rate loan, but that loan has not yet been provided to the borrower, then a long futures hedge is employed to avoid the risk of lower interest rates in case the borrower does not take the loan.

A savings and loan could offer long-term fixed-rate loans to customers while hedging the S&L's variable interest rate risk with futures contracts. However, there are two problems with such a strategy. First, T-bond futures contracts must be employed, since mortgage futures are not active. When major shifts occur in the structure of interest rates, the relationship between T-bond and mortgage rates often diverge, thereby creating significant basis risk. Second, since T-bond futures contracts exist for only a maximum of three years, a long-term hedge has to be periodically rolled over. Such a procedure entails significant risk when the shape of the term structure changes.

SUMMARY AND LOOKING AHEAD

This chapter discussed spread management for financial institutions. Financial institutions employ futures as a tool for adjusting the interest rate risk associated with spread management. Although the term structure and volatility of interest rates cannot be controlled by the institution and the maturity structure of the balance sheet often cannot be changed quickly, the adverse effects of these factors are reduced by employing financial futures. Hedges for specific assets and liabilities of financial institutions also were discussed. Topics included hedging the investment portfolio under positive and negative term structure environments, hedging MMCD rollovers, and the creation of synthetic fixed-rate loans. The following chapter examines the uses of futures markets to corporations and insurance companies.

Appendix 14A
Accounting and Regulation Issues

Banks and Accounting Regulations

The benefits of financial futures for the asset-liability management of financial institutions relate to the ability of futures to reduce the variability of the Net Interest Margin from one period to the next. Put in another way, hedging reduces the bank's overall exposure to changes in interest rates. One major difficulty for banks is that the financial realities of hedging transactions differ from the regulatory (accounting) rules dictated to the banks. Specifically, The Comptroller of the Currency, the regulatory agency of national banks, states that the futures part of hedge transactions must be accounted for by marking the futures transactions to market. Thus, the gains and losses on futures transactions must be recognized in the quarter they occur, rather than as an offset to the cash instrument. Alternatively, the bank may use a "lower of cost or market" accounting procedure, which requires that futures losses are recognized as current losses but futures gains are deferred until the futures position is covered. Since the cash transaction is typically kept on the books at cost, the combined accounting effect of a hedged transaction will be to have significant earnings variability from quarter to quarter as futures prices change, causing reported losses that are larger than actual losses. Of course, this is contrary to the objective of a hedge.

Corporations can use hedge accounting rules formulated under the FASB #80 statement. FASB #80, or hedge accounting, allows the matching of futures transactions with the cash positions they are hedging. This creates offsets such that earnings do not vary for the hedged assets since the futures offset the cash price changes. In fact, swap transactions, which are also used to reduce earnings variability by banks, get favorable accounting procedures to reduce earnings risk while futures transactions do not receive favorable accounting rules by The Comptroller of the Currency.

The Comptroller's position on accounting for hedges is that marking-to-market discourages speculation by showing the effect of futures transactions immediately in the income statement; however, it may also discourage hedging. (While revised rules were considered in 1988, they never were implemented because of the speculation which occurred at Franklin National Bank. However, there is a likelihood that the Comptroller's office will change its position concerning accounting for hedges in the near future.) The effect of the Comptroller's philosophy on banks' actions depends on the attitude of the bank. If the control of financial risk is the most important factor, then a futures hedge strategy may be implemented. If the accounting income reported to shareholders is a major concern, then futures hedging for longer-term positions may be detrimental to shareholders' impressions concerning the (accounting) risk of the bank. Thus, actual financial risk versus reported accounting risk is a factor that each Board of Directors must make. Financial economists would argue that the control of the actual financial risk should take paramount importance.

An alternative to employing the Comptroller's regulations concerning hedge accounting is to bring all transactions to the holding company level of the bank. The public holding company is regulated by the Securities and Exchange Commission, which allows the use of the FASB Hedge Accounting Rules for futures hedge transactions. These rules allow for deferral accounting by amortizing the gains and losses on the futures transactions over the life of the hedge. The benefit of hedge accounting is that it eliminates the fluctuation in income for the *holding* company. However, the *bank's* income statement does not show the effect of the futures hedge position. Depending on the bank, the use of the holding company for hedge transactions may solve the regulatory dilemma.

The FASB Hedge Accounting Rules require two criteria. First, the asset or liability to be hedged is or will expose the institution to price or interest rate risk. Second, the futures contract chosen for the hedge is highly correlated with the cash instrument, is specifically designated as a hedge, and reduces the price or interest rate exposure of the institution. If these criteria are not met then the mark-to-market rules must be employed.

The effect of the accounting restrictions on banks also depends on the type of cash account being hedged. The trading and dealer accounts for the institution are typically marked-to-market daily, which provides an immediate offset between the cash and futures positions. However, the investment accounts are not marked-to-market, creating the dilemma of accounting fluctuations of income discussed above.

The Situation for Savings and Loans

Savings and loans are regulated by the Federal Home Loan Bank Board (FHLBB). The FHLBB realized in 1981 the benefits of using hedge type deferral accounting rules. Therefore, savings and loans are not burdened by the restrictive mark-to-market stipulations that banks face. Since 1981 savings and loans may hedge up to 85 percent of the value of their assets and a wide range of instruments. Before 1981 the savings and loans could only hedge up to the value of their net worth and could only use GNMA futures.

Regulatory Considerations for Initiating a Hedging Program

The Federal Reserve Board and the Comptroller of the Currency provide guidelines for banks that establish futures hedging programs. The Comptroller's guidelines appeared in Circular #79, which appeared in 1979. These guidelines state which policies, limitations, and accounting procedures need to be put into place in order to provide adequate safeguards to avoid speculation in the futures markets by employees. The possibility of zealous or untrained employees actually increasing the risk to the financial institution is the main concern of the regulators. A well thought-out procedure concerning responsibility and accountability is appropriate for the institution. In other words, the bank must demonstrate that those making decisions understand how to use futures markets to reduce risk.

Another difficulty in implementing a hedge program for the executive who is well educated in futures is the regulatory concern and skepticism of the Board of Directors. Since the Board is typically made up of non-finance outside directors, it often is difficult to overcome previous prejudices concerning the inherent riskiness of all futures markets transactions. In other words, the distinction between speculation and hedging becomes an educational process requiring precise explanation during a relatively short Board session.

One report of a large bank seeking approval to begin a MMCD hedge illustrates the executive's difficulty: after one hour of discussion the Board finally was convinced that using one 90-day T-bill futures contract to hedge a 180-day cash MMCD position was an appropriate hedge, but that the second T-bill futures contract *must* be a *speculative* position; recall that two 90-day T-bill futures are needed for a dollar equivalency hedge for a 180-day cash MMCD position. The moral of this story is to start early in educating the Board of Directors and to provide several sources of information to show them the distinctions between hedging and speculation.

Appendix 14B
Analyzing Gaps: Approaches and Difficulties

The Difficulties in Controlling Rate Exposure

Many financial institutions have difficulty in reducing or controlling their interest rate exposure. Four main reasons exist to explain this difficulty:

1. When the term structure of interest rates is downward sloping, losses or reduced earnings occur for most institutions since long-term assets typically are funded by more expensive short-term liabilities. A downward sloping curve existed for the majority of the time from the early 1970s to the early 1980s.
2. During highly volatile periods for interest rates it is difficult to adjust the gaps adequately with only a short lead time.
3. A managed interest rate position often means an increase in the credit risk exposure.
4. Many institutions have problems controlling risk because they do not adequately measure their interest rate exposure.

The macro factors given in (1) and (2) cannot be controlled, but their effect on the institution can be reduced by using futures in conjunction with risk analysis and control. The effect of credit risk listed in (3) can be considered within the context of the asset-liability management of the institution. Thus, the first three factors are important influences on earnings in direct proportion to the degree and success of asset-liability management, whether this management is accomplished solely with cash adjustments to the balance sheet or whether financial futures are employed for hedging purposes. Consequently, the last factor, which notes the difficulty of *measuring* the actual interest rate exposure, is a key ingredient in being able to control the other factors. The remainder of this appendix discusses factors affecting the measurement of interest rate exposure in conjunction with gap analysis.

A Simplified Gap Analysis

The accurate measurement of interest rate exposure is needed to determine precisely the effect of a given change in interest rates on the net interest margin (NIM) of the institution. Summing the product of the size of the changes in the rates for each maturity times the gap for that maturity provides an approximation for the change in net interest margin (earnings change). The change in the rate of return for the institution may be determined by dividing this change in NIM by the amount of assets or by the capital of the institution.

This procedure is static in nature, i.e., no changes in balance sheet amounts during the period are considered and the changes in interest rates occur at the beginning of the period and then remain at the new level for the rest of the period; dynamic models are more accurate but provide additional complexities. In addition, the simplified gap model ignores all gaps after the horizon of the institution, which is an accounting approach to gap analysis. The reason given for ignoring these periods is that no assets or liabilities for the latter periods will be repriced during the analysis period.

Another approach would be to consider the effect on NIM of using a financial economics rational. Here the effect of changes in interest rates for *all* maturity ranges would be considered rather than restricting the analysis to the accounting horizon of the institution. Under this procedure the analysis considers that maturities in excess of the horizon of the institution will eventually have to be repriced at the going interest rate. If the current change in rates is deemed to provide the best current estimate of future rates for periods after the horizon, then from an economic standpoint the effect of these changes needs to be assigned to the current period rather than to the period in which the repricing occurs.

Considerations in Applying the Simplified Model

Although the basic static model seems straightforward, the application of this procedure involves some economic considerations. A potential misapplication of the model is to simplify the process by finding *one* average interest rate change to use for all maturities, then multiplying this rate change by an *average* gap size. This approach does not provide an accurate value for the NIM for two reasons. First, the effect of a changing shape in the maturity (term) structure of interest rates is ignored. Second, the importance of controlling the gaps for each relevant maturity range is not considered. In addition, these two factors tend to interact. The following discussion explains the importance of these considerations, especially for the economic-based model.

Changes in the shape of the maturity structure of interest rates can be significant, since a large relative change in short-term rates (compared to long-term rates) could cause a significantly larger change in net interest margin than if an average interest rate was employed. A related consideration is the relationship between the interest rate changes for assets versus liabilities within each maturity range. Thus, the contractual maturity, i.e., the stated maturity of the item before it is repriced, is not the only relevant factor affecting the interest rate change within a maturity class. For example, for the shortest maturity range the rates for daily Fed funds change more frequently and to a greater degree than changes in rates for daily floating prime rate loans, even though the same maturity for repricing occurs; this difference in repricing causes different overall effects on net income margin. Thus, the exclusive use of the contractual maturity is insufficient to consider the effect of changes in interest rates on income; the *relative rate sensitivity* of the asset versus liability instruments within each maturity range must also be determined to measure accurately the change in net interest margin.

The second consideration in applying the basic model is to separate the effects of the different maturity gaps. If all the gaps for the institution were combined into only *one* average gap value then negative short-term gaps would be offset by positive long-term gaps. This would only be appropriate if changes in the maturity (term) structure of interest rates always form parallel curves. Alternatively, nonparallel shifts would affect the typical negative short-term gaps differently than the positive long-term gaps.[1]

---

1 This discussion shows that serious difficulties exist when a single measure is used for rates or for maturity gaps in order to determine NIM. These difficulties include the use of the typical duration measures. As discussed in Chapters 7 and 11, duration assumes a parallel shift in the interest rate structure, which ignores the typical

While combining the maturity effects for an accounting model would be less devastating than for an economic model, since an accounting model would typically only consider negative gaps, one would still want to separate maturity ranges in order to better evaluate and control the interest rate risk. More importantly, one should realize the implications of choosing a short maturity horizon under an accounting model. Exhibit 14B-1 shows the significance of the institution's horizon on the accounting NIM by presenting an example of a loan repriced each six months, funded by a liability repriced each three months. For the example, a horizon of one month or less creates no change in expected NIM, since neither the asset nor the liability is repriced during this time period. However, for a horizon of one to three months, NIM will decrease as interest rates increase since the liability will be repriced (resold) at the then current market rates while the loan will continue to earn the previously determined six-month fixed interest rate. Finally, for a horizon of three to six months, both the asset and liability will be repriced at the then current interest rates, causing no net effect on NIM for that time range. Thus, for this example, institutions that examine the change in NIM each month would show no change in accounting NIM for the next period of analysis, even when a change in market rates occur; institutions using quarterly or semiannual horizons would show a change in NIM, although no action is required for the last month maturity range since both the loan and CD would be repriced after 5 months. Obviously, the investment horizon is a critical variable affecting accounting NIM, a factor ignored when various maturity gaps are indiscriminately combined into one maturity value or several poorly chosen maturity ranges.

EXHIBIT 14B-1: An Example of Maturity Gaps and Horizons

Asset: $1 million fixed-rate loan repriced each 6 months with the new 6-month CD rate plus 2 points. Matures 5/1, 11/1

Liability: $1 million three month CD, resold (rolled over) each 3 months at the current market rate. Matures 2/1, 5/1, 8/1, 11/1

Date: 6/1

Maturity Range (End of Period)

	0-1 Month	1-3 Months	3-6 Months
Gap	0	RSL > RSA	0
	Neither asset nor liability repriced during maturity range	Liability repriced but asset not repriced during maturity range	Both asset and liability repriced during maturity range

---

situation for asset-liability gap management. Duration assumes the maturities and rates for different ranges are combined into one number, ignoring the significance of the individual ranges. It is evident that any duration procedure that ignores these important factors will give inaccurate results.

Implementing a Gap Model

A primary problem in implementing a gap model is to obtain relevant, accurate data on the size of the gaps for each maturity range and the relevant asset-liability interest rate relationships for each range. The first time such data is collected one usually encounters difficulties in locating the appropriate information. It soon becomes evident that continuing analysis will require procedures to record relevant information for easy access and use. Computer programs have been developed by a number of consultants that will store such information and use the appropriate data in a NIM analysis.

Another consideration in completing the NIM analysis is to forecast accurately changes in interest rates and in the sizes of the gaps at the various maturity ranges. Forecasting a multitude of rate changes can be a difficult, although rewarding exercise if one is accurate. On the other hand, one may determine the *relative* volatility of the rates in each range and use this information to develop a modified gap model; this approach reduces some of the difficulties and data problems in forecasting for asset-liability purposes. Moreover, even if the ability to forecast rates is imprecise, a relative volatility analysis will show the risk associated with NIM for various hypothesized changes in interest rates which correspond to a variety of scenarios.

Forecasting the size of the gaps is easier, although it still can provide inaccurate results. The original model above is static, ignoring potential changes in the balance sheet items during the period of analysis. Such an assumption is highly unrealistic. A more realistic analysis would include the effects of both institutional policies and market conditions. The most difficult part of forecasting quantity changes often relates to customer demand; for example, the change in MMCD positions will be directly linked to the relative level of interest rates, while fixed-rate consumer loans for such items as automobiles will be inversely related to the level of interest rates. Thus, a thorough economic analysis may be needed to forecast accurately certain key gaps.

Changes in Gaps and Rates

As an initial step to include quantity changes, the static analysis may be amended to consider the effect of changes in the gap to obtain a more realistic value for NIM. Another consideration in measuring the NIM is to determine the effect of any change in the relative rates (spreads) between assets and liabilities with the same maturities. Thus, the Fed funds rate and the prime rate will have different relative volatilities.

Relative Coefficient Procedures for Gap Analysis

Two relative coefficient procedures exist to measure the effective gap, the piece-by-piece method, and the aggregate method.[2] The objective of using one of these procedures to measure the gap is to provide an easier method to forecast the effect of changes in interest rates on NIM. This is accomplished by relating the changes in rates for each asset and

---

2 The term effective gap refers to the actual relationships between the relative volatilities of the asset and liability interest rates, including the relative maturities. The contractual gap only examines the maturity or time relationship of *when* the assets and liabilities are repriced. Dew originally presented the nonquantitative foundations of these procedures. James Kurt Dew, "The Effective Gap II: Two Ways to Measure Interest Rate Risk." *American Banker*, September 18, 1981, pp. 1+.

liability to a benchmark rate. Subsequent analysis of the effect of potential (or actual) changes in the interest rate structure can then be made by simply determining the change in the benchmark rate and using that figure in the appropriate NIM equation.

The Piece-by-Piece Method. The piece-by-piece method involves finding the relationships between the rates for *each* asset and liability instrument with the benchmark rate. These relative interest rate coefficients are then multiplied by their associated levels of assets and liabilities to determine the effective gap. The value for the effective gap can then be used to find the change in NIM, given the change in the benchmark interest rate. A regression procedure may be employed to find the historical relationship between the rates and the benchmark. The above procedure requires a number of regression equations to be estimated. An alternative approach to the piece-by-piece method is to separate the relative maturity effect of the instruments from the relative volatility effect.

The Aggregate Method. The second procedure to employ relative coefficients is the aggregate method, which combines the relative rate change effects of the various asset and liability items (weighted by the asset/liability proportions and maturity effects) into one average rate change for the entire balance sheet. A regression between this average interest rate change and the benchmark figure can then be used to help determine the effect on NIM for a given change in the benchmark interest rate. The potential advantage of the aggregate method is that poorly fitted regression equations developed via the piece-by-piece method (i.e., equations with low R^2 values), can be replaced by a better fitting regression line under the aggregate method.

Choosing a Benchmark

In order to complete these methods for determining the gap size and the resultant effect on NIM, one must choose an appropriate benchmark instrument. One consideration is to choose a benchmark whose maturity equals the horizon of the firm. This would relate the relative volatility and maturity effects to the horizon period, thereby directly associating the changes in interest rates to the NIM horizon maturity. Moreover, such a benchmark maturity would be an interest rate that is closely watched by the financial executive. An alternative benchmark would be an instrument with a maturity approximately equal to the weighted average maturity of the gaps of the balance sheet; such a benchmark would tend to mitigate the effects of shifts in the slope of the yield curve on the NIM estimates.[3]

A second consideration in choosing a benchmark is the availability of consistent, accurate information on benchmark rates. Certain cash instruments may not be traded or change frequently, causing inaccurate estimates of current rates; moreover, cash instruments usually change in maturity over time, requiring cumbersome maturity adjustments and frequent changes in the benchmark security. The use of the prime rate as a benchmark

---

3 A benchmark with an average maturity equal to the gap of the balance sheet implies that a duration figure may be an appropriate procedure to determine this maturity and "instrument." However, the problems with cash rates mentioned below would still apply if the duration of cash instruments were used; moreover, using a duration value or some average cash rate across the yield curve would further complicate the analysis and reduce some of the benefits of using a benchmark figure. While duration could be used to determine the average maturity figure, using duration as a key part of a forecast of NIM would cause problems because of the restrictive assumptions concerning the behavior of yield curves, especially if the financial institution had a "barbell" type of portfolio.

is also a poor choice, since the prime is an administered rate rather than a market rate, and is not associated directly with the cost of funds to the institution. On the other hand, a good candidate for the benchmark security is the T-bill futures contract, especially since it has sufficient liquidity and since its 90-day *constant* maturity often matches the horizon of the institution.

Another consideration in using a particular benchmark instrument is the length of the observation period employed to measure changes in rates. Longer periods, say three months, may cause problems for the regression equation if too few observation periods are employed, while it may be difficult to obtain sufficient information on balance sheet items to measure shorter time periods.[4] Ideally, if the above problems can be overcome, the observation period should equal the investment horizon in order to obtain a useful measure of the effect of changes in rates on the NIM.

Finally, and most importantly, the relationship of the benchmark rate to the asset and liability rates must show a strong regression relationship as well as being reasonably constant over time. Statistically, the regressions should possess high R^2 values and constant slope coefficient values. The analyst should also avoid the temptation to use the yields of the instruments in the regression; one should use *changes* in the yields. Using the yield values often violates the underlying assumptions of the regression model, biasing the validity of the results.

The Final Result

The power of the piece-by-piece or aggregate methods is shown when one realizes that the effect on NIM can be determined by simply forecasting the change in the benchmark rate in conjunction with the results from either of the two methods described above. Different estimates of the benchmark rate will give the corresponding effect on NIM. The major benefit of these procedures is that only *one* interest rate needs to be estimated, rather than forecasting rates for each asset and liability item. The relative volatility and relative maturity effects are considered in the determination of the gap, and are found by some combination of historical and maturity repricing relationships; hence, these factors do not need to be considered individually in order to determine the effect of each new estimate of interest rates on NIM.

Assumptions for Gap and NIM Analysis

Before closing our discussion on forecasting changes in NIM, an examination of the basic assumptions of the approaches often used to determine the effect on NIM is appropriate. Since the typical financial institution calculates some form of a static gap, i.e., when interest rates and the structure of the balance sheet remains the same, we will concentrate on the problems associated with a static gap. While these assumptions have been noted previously, it is useful to recall them here in order to emphasize the important aspects of building a NIM model.

---

4   One may decide to use different observation lengths for relative rate calculations versus gap maturities, although relative maturity adjustments for the rate effects would be needed. Such a procedure would provide more observations for the regression analysis.

When a static gap is employed, the effect on NIM is only strictly valid for one point in time; for dynamic considerations other factors also affect NIM:

- The structure of the gap can change over time due to asset-liability changes; thus, forecasts of changes in these asset and liability amounts are beneficial, as discussed previously.
- Changes in the interest rates will occur throughout the period, while static models assume that a change occurs at the beginning of the period and that no other subsequent changes occur. Continuous changes will affect the size of the current period's NIM, although the changes will have no adverse effect on the economic NIM in subsequent periods, as compared to a static model, due to repricing.
- A change in the level of interest rates affects the NIM, since the supply and demand of certain instruments changes as rate levels change. This consideration will affect the forecasts of the new gap sizes.
- The overall effect of a change in interest rates on NIM depends on changes in the shape of the yield curve and in the asset-liability spread relationships. Consequently, the relative volatility of rates for various instruments and the associated rate changes for those maturities are very important factors. Unless these factors are considered, the actual change in NIM will differ significantly from the predicted change.
- Asset and liability amounts within a given maturity range are typically distributed unevenly according to maturity. Therefore, a gap analysis is only strictly valid for a point in time and will change over time. Hence, significant "lumps" in the distribution could be considered as separate maturity ranges.

These dynamic factors are important since they can have a significant effect on NIM. Whether these factors are modeled quantitatively or simply considered subjectively in a gap analysis, their effect on the gap and NIM needs to be evaluated to determine the appropriate managerial decisions for risk-return changes in the assets and liabilities. In particular, effective hedges with futures contracts depend heavily on determining the appropriate effective gap. Logically, the level of sophistication of a particular institution's gap analysis will depend on the objective of the analysis, the availability and accuracy of the data, and the time and resources available for analysis. However, the considerations discussed in this appendix should at least be subjectively considered to determine the effect of management's decisions on current and future NIM values.

Considerations for Regression Analysis

Considerations in the use of regression analysis to determine the relative coefficients are relevant in the determination of the appropriate NIM model. In particular:

- Regression assumes the future relationship between the dependent and independent variables will be the same as the historical relationship.
- Alternatively, one must examine if changes in economic conditions will alter the relative volatility of the rates associated with the dependent and independent variables. While regression will show the average relationship between sets of rates over an economic cycle, the forecasting ability of the equation will be impaired if changes in the relationship occur over time or over the business cycle, and are not adequately considered.

- The length of the observation period should be considered in conjunction with the characteristics of the data. Long periods, say several months or more, can cause significant effects relating to changing maturities for cash securities; in fact, for T-bills a period of only several weeks will affect the volatility of rates because of the changing maturity. When a futures contract is employed as a benchmark, a long time period for the observation length results in either: (a) problems relating to the convergence of the futures contract with the underlying cash, thereby biasing the results, or (b) price adjustment problems if one futures contract is substituted for another contract during the observation period. A long period for observations also ignores any effect of fluctuations in the relationship and rate changes within the observation period. On the other hand, using a short observation period requires more data, more frequent analysis and adjustments, and could result in inappropriate decisions for the longer maturity ranges, since the relationship would be less accurate.

Summarizing Gap Analysis

In summary, gap analysis and the effect of the gap and changes in interest rates on NIM is an extremely important undertaking for the asset-liability manager. One must understand the factors affecting the gap and determine if the institution's risk-return relationship via the current gap corresponds to the firm's objectives. When changes are required, a determination of the relevant gap maturities and instruments to use are the most important factors to employ in order to adjust the gap. Obviously, without an appropriate measurement of the gaps all of these important undertakings would be guesswork. This section has presented the foundations for examining the factors relevant for gap analysis.

There are three procedures to examine gaps and the associated NIM.

- The first is to simulate the effect of potential changes in interest rates for each instrument for each maturity range on NIM. The relevant equations associated with our discussion would be programmed into a computer; forecasts of each instrument's rate and changes in the gaps would be input into the program. The output would show the new gap sizes and the resultant effect on NIM (the overall and/or per maturity range effect). The most important advantage of this method is that accurate forecasts for each instrument and for the gap changes will provide accurate estimates for NIM. Disadvantages are that such accurate forecasts are difficult and a significant amount of input data and forecasts are needed.
- The second method examined is to use regression analysis to obtain relative coefficients via the piece-by-piece or aggregate approaches to determine the effect of changes in the benchmark rate on NIM. Regression equations between each instrument and the benchmark are needed to determine the relative volatility interest rate effects on NIM. The major benefits of this method are that only one interest rate needs to be forecasted and hence it is easy to determine the effect of a number of different potential interest rate changes on NIM. Disadvantages are that a significant amount of data and data analysis are needed to find the relative volatilities, and that changing or imprecise relationships between the various instruments and the benchmark will reduce the accuracy of the forecasts.

- The third method is the use of duration to determine the relative volatility of the instruments by finding a weighted average maturity of the assets and liabilities. The procedure is a straightforward application of the duration discussion in Chapter 11. The relationship between the duration of the assets and the duration of the liabilities will give an idea of the overall maturity gap of the institution. The advantages of a duration approach are: the simplicity of using one number in the final analysis and the familiarity of duration to anyone who has dealt with bond maturity management. The disadvantages are that duration is based on a number of restrictive assumptions that adversely affect the results when the yield curve changes shape, and frequent recalculation of the duration value is needed as the data for individual maturity ranges changes.

The choice of which of these methods is employed depends on the objectives of the institution, its forecasting ability, the amount of historical data available, and the resources to analyze the data. Whichever method is employed, in-depth asset-liability analysis is one of the most critical functions for a financial institution.

Chapter 15

Corporate and Insurance Applications of Futures

Corporate applications of futures include how to lock in the cost of future short-term financing rates, futures as an alternative to cash short-term investments, how to lock in yields on the rollovers of cash investments, and how to hedge inventory costs and foreign exchange exposure. Asset-liability management for corporations is similar to gap management for financial institutions, although differences in the concept and the characteristics of the balance sheet items create differences in the application of futures for this purpose. We also examine the use and difficulties of hedging the issuance of new debt and stock by corporations.

Insurance product applications include the use of futures to manage the cash flows associated with insurance products and loan commitments to private borrowers. Products from insurance companies such as universal life policies, single premium deferred annuities, and guaranteed investment contracts require innovative management of investment funds in order for these products to be both competitive and profitable. Private loan placements often involve forward commitments or other stipulations that need to be hedged in order to remove the risk of changes in interest rates.

CORPORATE ASSET-LIABILITY MANAGEMENT, WORKING CAPITAL, AND FUTURES

Working Capital and Futures

Corporations generate short- and long-term liabilities in order to fund assets. Short-term borrowing and investment is called working capital management.[1] Working capital affects the relative short- and long-term maturity structure of total assets and liabilities, which in turn affects earnings as interest rates change. The considerations for determining whether to finance liabilities with short- or long-term debt are relative flexibility, cost, and the risk of refinancing. Short-term liabilities are more flexible and have a lower cost during low inflationary periods, but they have more refinancing risk. Long-term financing costs are

---

1 Most corporate finance textbooks list the two principal functions of working capital management to be: (1) the adjustment of working capital needs to changes in seasonal, cyclical, and random sales fluctuations, and (2) to help maximize the value of the firm by (a) increasing current assets to the point that marginal revenue equals marginal costs, and (b) to use current liabilities rather than long-term debt to the extent that the cost of capital is reduced.

affected by the timing of the debt issue and are less flexible, but fixed-rate loans do not have any refinancing risk.

Ideally, fixed assets and permanent current assets are financed by long-term liabilities, while *only* the *fluctuating* portion of the short-term assets are financed by short-term liabilities. However, the desire for (1) flexibility and (2) lower current short-term costs, in conjunction with (3) difficulties in forecasting the business cycle, typically result in a much larger amount of short-term liabilities than necessary. In addition, when variable-rate long-term loans are recognized as effectively increasing the amount of *short*-term liabilities, then most corporations have a significant maturity mismatch between their assets and liabilities. This maturity mismatch creates extensive risk and variability in earnings as interest rates change during the business cycle.

Futures are employed to lock in the refinancing costs of debt, as well as to convert variable-rate loans into synthetic fixed-rate loans. Therefore, futures increase the flexibility of short-term financing and help to control changes in the future cost of this type of debt financing. Moreover, the business cycle changes in working capital that managers count on as natural adjustments to help control the effects of maturity mismatches is dealt with more quickly with the use of futures. This timing benefit of futures allows the manager to make interim adjustments to the effective asset-liability structure until more permanent changes due to the business cycle and management action take effect on the balance sheet. However, futures typically are employed only to control short-term costs and risk for the upcoming time period, while fixed-rate long-term debt provides no refinancing risk for the entire life of the debt instrument. Consequently, effective longer-term asset-liability management also needs to consider the maturity/duration relationships between assets and liabilities in a manner similar to the gap management techniques of financial institutions.

Asset-Liability Mismatches

Corporate asset-liability management is similar to gap management for financial institutions. Borrowing directly from gap management for financial institutions, we may summarize the relationship between net balance sheet (interest rate) exposure and earnings sensitivity as follows:

- A negative net balance sheet exposure exists when interest-sensitive assets minus interest-sensitive liabilities is negative. An increase in interest rates reduces earnings. Negative exposure is reduced with a futures sell hedge.
- A positive net balance sheet exposure exists when interest-sensitive assets minus interest-sensitive liabilities is positive. A decrease in interest rates reduces earnings. Positive exposure is reduced by executing a futures buy hedge.

While it is more difficult for corporations to delineate the maturity of many of its assets, the effect of corporate asset-liability maturity differences on earnings as interest rates change is an important factor that should not be ignored. The analysis of the balance sheet by the corporate treasurer must include the factors that determine the net effect of the maturity structure on the firm's earnings:

- The effect of the composition of the instruments being employed for short- and long-term financing. Each source of funds has a different effective maturity and interest rate volatility, which affects the type of futures hedge initiated on the *net* exposure as well as determining the relevant hedge ratio.[2]

- The *economic* rather than the *accounting* balance sheet of the firm is appropriate for determining the effect of interest rate changes on earnings. For example, the timing of the *repricing* of liabilities is the key factor that is important, not when they mature.[3]
- Any special factors affecting the firm or industry must be considered. In particular, if the net working capital exposure relates to seasonal fluctuations, then the interest rate exposure often shifts from a positive value to a negative value during the year. In order to hedge the net exposure, the firm would need a long hedge during part of the year and a short hedge during the rest.[4]

Figure 15-1 shows how the aggregate net working capital exposures of corporations change over time. As the business cycle changes, the net working capital position changes from net positive to net negative. Thus, it is evident that corporations adjust their asset and liability exposure to changes in the business cycle and financial markets. Such changes tend to be related to the liquidity needs of the firms rather than to a desire to forecast short-term interest rates. Futures could be employed to reduce the effect of changes in interest rates on the net exposure position.

MICRO HEDGES OF FUTURES FOR CORPORATIONS

Short-Term Borrowing Costs

A potential increase in short-term borrowing costs arising from the issuance or rolling over of **commercial paper** is locked in with a futures short hedge. If interest rates increase, the profits from the futures short position offset the higher borrowing costs. However, a commercial paper futures contract does not exist; thus, a crosshedge is necessary, which creates additional risk.[5] Those who *buy* commercial paper can lock in the interest rate on an

---

2   Loans from banks are issued at the short-term prime rate, short-term funds are obtained from selling commercial paper or lengthening accounts payable, and long-term funds are raised from bonds, long-term credit lines, and equity. Working capital assets that are sensitive to changes in interest rates are typically listed as: time deposits and negotiable certificates of deposit, short-term Treasury securities and repurchase agreements, other Federal agency securities, commercial and finance company paper, state and local government securities, and bankers' acceptances. Working capital liabilities affected by interest rates are categorized as loans from banks, commercial paper, and other short-term loans. Long-term debt that is repriced on a short-term basis needs to be categorized as a short-term liability for pricing purposes.

3   The financial manager must determine the true economic value of the assets and liabilities, not what is stated on the accounting balance sheet, e.g., depreciation and inventory methods often provide distorted economic values for their associated assets. Such assets need to be restated. Also, many firms may carry inaccurate values (or *no* values) on their balance sheets for such items as leases, swap agreements, and pension fund liabilities. These also must be adjusted to reflect their appropriate economic value.

4   In general, changes in current assets or financing alternatives to offset these seasonal fluctuations often cannot be accomplished rapidly, while effective changes in the interest sensitivity of the balance sheet is changed quickly by using futures transactions.

5   A commercial paper futures contract did exist in the 1970s. It failed for two primary reasons: (1) the price index employed was the interest rate, which meant that the index went *up* when the value of the contract went *down*, causing confusion for some market participants, and (2) a wide range of commercial paper was deliverable against the futures contract, causing the price of the contract to track the cheapest (riskiest) commercial paper issue that was deliverable. The wide range of risk made this characteristic unacceptable to market participants.

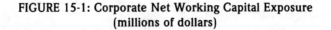

FIGURE 15-1: Corporate Net Working Capital Exposure
(millions of dollars)

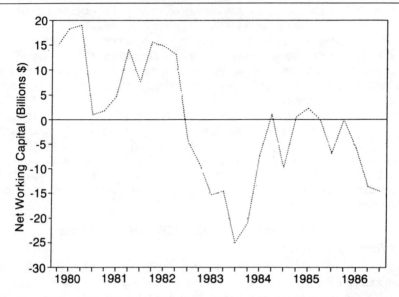

Source: "Quarterly Financial Report for Manufacturing, Mining and Trade Corporations," Federal Trade Commission, 1980-86.

anticipated purchase of commercial paper in the future with a long hedge. Short-term loans based on LIBOR are hedged effectively by the Eurodollar futures contract. The setup of these types of hedges is equivalent to the hedges examined previously.[6]

Short-Term Investment Yields

The interest rate for a new or a rollover investment of a short-term instrument is locked in before the funds are actually invested by executing a buy hedge. Such a hedge is initiated if the cash manager believes interest rates will fall before the investment date. The hedge is instituted for the period between the date the buy hedge is implemented and the date when the new interest rate on the funds is effective.

Futures quasi-arbitrage transactions also are an alternative to typical short-term investments for cash management considerations. An arbitrage transaction can provide a higher

---

6 Since the Eurodollar and T-bill futures contracts are based on 90-day instruments, one must consider the relative maturity as well as the relative volatility of the cash and futures instruments when determining the hedge ratio. If the loan is for one year, then the dollar value of the futures position would need to be four times the dollar value of the cash position in order to obtain dollar equivalency, given the one-year maturity for cash and the three-month maturity for the cash instrument underlying the futures instrument. See Chapter 9 for an additional discussion on this topic.

return than simply investing in an equivalent term cash security. These alternative "synthetic cash instruments" can provide an additional 15 to 50 basis points above the equivalent cash market investment.

Inventory Costs and Foreign Exchange Exposure

Financing Inventory. Inventory is one of the major asset categories associated with working capital management. Inventory hedges are employed as part of an overall macro approach to working capital management, or such a hedge is implemented as a *separate microhedge.*

Commodity Hedging. Another type of inventory hedging is practiced by firms that deal in agricultural commodities. Corporations that employ agricultural products, such as wheat, cocoa, corn, soybeans, etc., routinely hedge their cost of these items in order to stabilize the cost of goods sold and to reduce price risk. Other producers use the metals markets to lock in the cost of copper and silver, the energy markets to guarantee oil prices, and other markets to stabilize the prices of inventory goods such as lumber.[7]

Currency Hedging. The effect of currency fluctuations on the earnings of firms is a subject of great concern to most financial executives. Currency futures allow corporations to hedge against adverse changes in the relative value of currencies due to international trade operations. Without such protection, the profits generated by the sale (or purchase) of the product can be lost due to adverse currency changes. The asset-liability structure of the international division of a corporation also affects earnings. Hence, if the division has a net positive investment in German marks, and the relative exchange rate between the mark and dollar changes, then the dollar change in the value of the division affects the U.S. corporation's earnings. Hedges to reduce the impact of this change in earnings due to the asset-liability structure of the division are implemented in a similar way to working capital hedges instituted for domestic corporations. Books by Grabbe[8] and Riehl and Rodriguez[9] provide an in-depth discussion of foreign currency analysis and transactions.[10]

Long-Term Financing: The Issuance of Securities

Bond Issuance. The issuance of bonds is a good example of how futures are employed to lock in the cost of funds up to the time of the actual sale of the security. From the time the firm decides to raise funds from a sale of bonds until the bonds are actually sold takes six months or more. The delay is related to registration procedures, government regulations,

---

7 The introduction of the Consumer Price Index (CPI) futures contract was heralded as a way to hedge against an overall increase in the price of goods; however, the contract became dormant. If a hedger desires a futures contract to provide an overall hedge against inflation, the Commodity Research Bureau (CRB) futures contract can be employed. The CRB contract is a combination of individual futures contracts, which in effect creates a portfolio of futures contracts on the underlying products.

8 Olin Grabbe, *International Financial Markets*, New York: Elsevier, 1986.

9 Hans Riehl and Rita M. Rodriguez, *Managing Foreign and Domestic Currency Operations*, New York: McGraw Hill, 1983.

10 Grabbe covers all of the instruments that are employed in the foreign currency area, plus he examines the factors and institutions that affect the international financial markets. Riehl and Rodriguez provide complete coverage of the analysis of foreign currencies and how they affect corporations.

and the forming of the underwriting group. During this time period an increase in interest rates could create significantly higher borrowing costs for the firm. In order to avoid higher potential rates, futures are sold so that the profits on the short futures position offset the higher cost of the debt. Of course, if interest rates decrease before the sale, a loss on the futures position occurs, but such losses are offset by lower interest rates on the debt.

Delaying Funding. Futures also are useful when the firm wishes to delay the effective permanent fixed-rate funding of a major project, perhaps to protect its current credit standing, but does not want to risk paying a higher long-term fixed rate when the bonds are eventually issued. The principal operational difference between delaying permanent long-term debt issuance and hedging interest rates while the issue is being registered is simply the longer time involved for the delayed funding. Consequently, one must be more careful about basis risk when delaying issuance, especially if near-term futures contracts are sold for liquidity purposes.

Callable Bonds. Another use of bond futures to manage debt positions is the case of a callable bond that has not yet reached its call date. If interest rates are significantly below the coupon rate for a callable bond then the financial manager would like to call the bonds now and reissue the debt at the current interest rate, since there is a risk that rates will increase before the call date. However, it is not yet possible to call the bonds. A short futures position locks in the current interest rate for the period set up by the hedge as an alternative to calling the bond. Such a position has several advantages. First, futures positions have minimal liquidity problems compared to the alternative of the firm repurchasing some of their own bonds in the open market; moreover, repurchasing the firm's bonds without replacement alters the financing structure of the firm, while replacing long-term debt with short-term financing until new bonds are sold creates interest rate risk. Second, selling a new issue of bonds now to lock in the lower interest rate creates a new level of debt, while the futures position only controls the net cost of the potential new debt. Third, if rates increase again before the new bond issue or the call date, the profits on the short futures position can be taken and the bond issue left in place until rates once again decline.

Fixed to Variable Funding. Futures are employed to turn a fixed-rate debt issue into variable-rate financing. A corporation may want to issue fixed-rate bonds at a high interest rate now in order to guarantee entry into the market, especially if its credit standing is weak and a deterioration in the economic outlook could block the firm's entry into the bond market. Once the bonds are issued, a long position in T-bond futures creates gains if interest rates decline. This effectively turns the fixed-rate bond issue into a variable-rate bond until the futures are covered, allowing the financial manager to benefit from predictions of lower interest rates. Of course, if rates increase, then the effective rate on the bond issue also increases. One advantage of this strategy is that basis risk is no longer a concern, since the corporate bonds already have been issued.

Difficulties of Corporate Debt Hedging. One difficulty for hedging corporate issues is the lack of an active corporate bond futures contract. While a great many dealers of corporate bonds use the T-bond futures markets to hedge against overnight changes in general interest rates, corporate/T-Bond futures hedging can entail a significant amount of basis risk, depending on the rating of the firm. Bonds rated AAA usually are hedged successfully with the T-bond contract. As bond ratings decline so does the relationship of corporate price changes to T-bond price changes.[11] In general, substantial difficulties in hedging lower-rated bonds occur *only* when there is a major economic shift, such as a flight to quality; such a shift typically causes a change in the yield differential between corporate and government debt. To reduce the potentially disastrous consequences of such yield changes, the financial executive must manage the hedge ratio in order to minimize the effect of changing basis risk on the net value of the hedged position.

Synthetic Fixed-Rate Loans. Corporations also obtain longer-term financing from financial institutions. However, in recent years most of these loans have been variable-rate loans, with the repricing of the loans occurring every one to three months. Such loans may have a maturity of several years, but their effective economic maturity is associated with the short-term repricing structure of the loan. Such a loan can be converted into a long-term synthetic fixed-rate loan by selling futures contracts to lock in the interest rate for either the near-term period, or for the length of the loan.[12] Synthetic fixed-rate loans are discussed in detail in conjunction with financial institution hedges.

Equity Financing. Another method of raising long-term funds is to sell equity. As with bonds, equity typically has substantial registration and underwriting delays which amount to six months or more. Hedging against general market declines during this period is possible with one of the stock index futures contracts. However, only a small portion of the variability of individual stock price movements is associated with general market movements, on average amounting to 35% or less of the securities' total price change. Futures cannot be used to hedge against specific stock risk or industry risk, since futures on industries or individual stocks do not exist. Theoretically, large firms that have listed option contracts can use these instruments to partially hedge against individual stock price declines. However, any large issue of equity would be impossible to hedge with individual stock options since sufficient liquidity does not exist.

INSURANCE PRODUCT APPLICATIONS

Introduction

Insurance companies use futures contracts to help manage their products. Insurance regulators have followed the leadership of New York State: as of July 1987, life insurance companies in New York may hedge against 5% of assets. Such transactions must involve contracts that expire within the subsequent 18 months and may *not* include stock index futures or stock options. New York is considering the use of futures and put options by property and casualty insurers. California allows hedging as long as there is evidence of a significant correlation between the item being hedged and the futures contract. The restrictions noted here for New York State (and hence most other states) show that the regulation

---

11 Chapter 10 provides empirical evidence relating to corporate bond ratings and hedging efficiency. While in most environments AAA bond prices act similarly to government bond prices, BBB bonds have significantly more basis risk.

12 If the loan has a maturity longer than the relevant futures expiration (or longer than the farthest *liquid* futures expiration) then one could "stack" the contracts by selling multiples of each futures expiration in order to equal total dollar changes in the cash and futures positions. Thus, a four-year loan could be stacked by doubling up positions on each futures contract that traded out to two years. The difficulty with this approach occurs if the term structure beyond the second year changes in a different manner than the term structure for the first two years. Such a differential change creates additional basis risk.

of insurance companies at the state level has adversely affected the use of futures in this industry.

The applications of futures to insurance products show how insurance companies may provide new products, as well as products at more competitive rates to their customers, without jeopardizing the insurance companies' profits. Such products include forward commitments, guaranteed investment contracts, universal life, and single premium deferred annuity contracts. The latter two products provide variable-rate returns to the policyholder based on quarterly or annual changes in an index. The advantages of these variable-rate policies, especially during greater interest rate volatility, has created a new environment for the management of funds for insurance companies. In fact, insurance companies have had difficulty managing these variable-rate products during volatile rate periods. One method to help control the risk of these products is through the use of futures markets.

Insurance Uses: Investment Products

Hedging Policy Loans. Most whole-life insurance policies allow the owner of the policy the opportunity to borrow cash based on the cash value of the premiums paid into the policy. These loan rates tend to be low compared to individual borrowing rates, although in recent years the rates on newly issued policies have risen significantly. Borrowing on the cash value of the policy provides the borrower with the right to obtain cash at a given fixed interest rate regardless of the going market rate of interest. The likelihood of policyholders availing themselves of this opportunity increases as rates increase. When the cash is borrowed by the policyholders there is a cash drain on the insurance company, an outflow of funds that must be financed at the current rate of interest. A short futures position is employed to hedge against higher interest rates (increasing financing costs).[13]

Universal Life Contracts. Universal life insurance contracts require premiums to be paid periodically, with a portion of the premium being employed as an investment element. Interest on the investment accumulates tax-free until withdrawn, or until it is used to cover future premium payments. The earning payout portion of the policy often is set in relation to an intermediate-term bond index, with the rate changing periodically (quarterly, semiannually, or annually).

Insurance companies must decide the relevant risk and return goals appropriate for this product in order to determine how to invest the premiums that they receive. For a positive yield curve, companies often set the policy return equal to an intermediate-term Treasury bond index, while actually investing the funds in a longer-term corporate bond portfolio. The risks in such an investment philosophy are twofold. First, if yields rise and the yield curve inverts, the company must pay out higher returns to policyholders, even though the investment coupons remain stable *and* the value of the bonds have declined. Second, the relationship between the corporate and government sectors usually deteriorates when the business cycle turns into a recessionary phase. Alternatively, if the funds are invested in short-term instruments when the yield curve is inverted, the policy returns are adequately

---

13 The opportunity to borrow cash at a fixed low rate describes an option. Theoretically, one should hedge an option with an offsetting option. However, purchasing options involves paying a significant premium, which can affect profits adversely when the option hedge is kept for the long-term. Using futures avoids most of this premium cost.

funded at that time but this strategy creates losses when the term structure shifts to an upward sloping yield curve environment.

Using futures in conjunction with a bond portfolio provides some benefits in managing funds from universal life premiums, although risks still exist. Hedging a bond portfolio with futures protects the principal of the portfolio, while generating funds that vary with the short-term interest rate. In fact, a hedged portfolio historically has provided higher returns than cash short-term investments. Such a strategy also provides flexibility for the investment manager, i.e., it allows the manager to change the risk exposure of the investment by deciding how much of the portfolio to hedge. Such changes are made with minimal commission and liquidity costs. If market timing is part of the firm's strategy then this aspect also may be incorporated into the hedge strategy. Of course, changing the amount of bonds to be hedged does affect the riskiness of the strategy. Moreover, changes in the basis risk between Treasury and corporate yields due to business cycle effects cannot be hedged adequately without perfect foresight concerning these changes.[14]

Another aspect of the flexibility of a futures strategy for a Universal Life product is the ability to switch funds to the short end of the yield curve and still simulate long-term bond price changes. In particular, if the yield curve shifts to a downward sloping curve, then: first, the cash bond portfolio is sold and the short futures position covered; second, short-term instruments such as Eurodollar time deposits could be purchased to maximize current return; and finally, T-bond or T-Note futures could be purchased in order to benefit from decreases in the long-term interest rate. This strategy creates larger commissions and perhaps liquidity costs, and would create losses if longer-term rates continued to trend upward, but it is an effective long-term strategy to benefit from eventual increases in bond prices while also covering short-term expenses with the current high short-term rates.

Single Premium Deferred Annuity Contracts (SPDA). The **SPDAs** allow policyholders to pay one premium, receive the rate promised for the given time period, and not pay taxes on the accumulated earnings. When rates reached a historic high in the late 1970s, many policyholders canceled their SPDA policy with one company and purchased an SPDA from another company that offered a higher rate. Since most policies had minimal surrender charges and the tax law allowed such transfers without penalty, the policyholders principal incentive was to obtain the highest available return. The competitiveness that such actions created among insurance companies caused a problem for managing these products. If uncompetitive rates were offered, then the firm lost a significant amount of business. If a high rate was offered, which could not be earned without taking significant risks, then the firm could generate losses over the longer term.

The market environment caused many insurance companies to offer high rates, creating significant risks they did not want. The tendency to structure the portfolio with inherent risks was more pronounced for SPDAs than for universal life policies, since SPDAs had a

---

14 The effect of convergence of the futures and cash depends on whether futures are selling above or below the cash value. If futures are below the cash price then a short futures position results in a cost. The coupon on the bonds less this cost, plus any changes in the basis, are the primary factors affecting the periodic returns on the combined hedge position. These returns historically have been higher than the short-term rate. See Rebell and Gordon, Ch. 18, for a more extensive discussion of these factors in relation to insurance products, including the application of a computer program to evaluate these factors. Arthus L. Rebell and Gail Gordon, *Financial Futures and Investment Strategy,* Dow Jones-Irwin, 1984.

much higher cancellation rate. Thus, the companies would buy long-term instruments when the yield curve was positive and interest rates were low, since the promised return on these investments would be greater than the payout rate. However, if the yield curve shifted upward, then losses would occur as the variable rate on the SPDA increased, but the bonds used to fund this rate declined in value. On the other hand, if the yield curve was inverted and interest rates were high, then the insurance companies invested in short-term instruments to maximize current return and to offer higher rates on the SPDAs. In this situation, when rates declined and the yield curve became upward sloping, the firm did not benefit from an increase in the value of the longer-term bonds but was obligated to pay a higher rate on the SPDAs than could be obtained from the short-term investments.

Futures are employed to help manage these variable-rate SPDA products, although some risk still must be undertaken in order to achieve the desired return. Without futures, the use of a longer-term fixed-income portfolio to fund variable-rate SPDA products creates the problems noted above, since the principal value of the bond varies while the current income from the coupon remains fixed. As with the universal life strategy, using a short hedge with a long-term bond portfolio converts the cash bond position into a fixed principal value and a variable short-term income investment. The return on the variable portion is related to the short-term interest rate, the basis risk, and convergence. These factors are examined to determine the appropriate return obtainable from such a strategy. Of course, the investment manager may attempt to combine the variable-rate futures strategy with a timing strategy to enhance returns, i.e., as rates fall, the hedge could be lifted in order to benefit from higher bond values.[15]

Guaranteed Investment Contracts. A **guaranteed investment contract** pays a guaranteed rate of interest on funds invested for a given period of the contract life, and often the entire life of the contract. These contracts are made between insurance companies, pension funds, and other major investors who desire intermediate-term products. Such rates are determined by the going rate of interest and competitive pressures. The insurance companies face two types of risk with GICs. First, a risk exists that declining rates may occur between the time the fixed-rate is guaranteed by the company and the time the funds are received and invested. Such a situation is hedged with a long position in futures. Second, once the funds are received and invested in bonds, the receipt of coupon payments from these bonds creates a reinvestment risk that interest rates will decline from the GIC rate. Either duration matching or futures transactions is employed to alleviate this risk.

---

15 It may seem that the insurance company should just link the SPDA return to the short-term interest rate. However, historically the SPDA rate often has been guaranteed for one year at a time, with the return related to a bond index. Such a procedure provides higher returns to the insurance company than a short-term rate when the yield curve is upward sloping. More importantly, investors have a multitude of alternatives to obtain the short-term rate. The futures strategy noted here could be refined to employ a strip of futures in order to obtain a yearly rate from the quarterly forward rates. Alternatively, one could stack the futures contracts in nearby or deferred futures, depending on the amount of yield curve risk and forecasting ability one wishes to assume. Analysis of the effect of the coupon returns, the convergence effect, and basis risk determines what additional risks must be undertaken with a futures strategy in order to provide adequate returns to fund SPDA policies. Additional risks to enhance returns include timing the market or switching to short-term instruments when the yield curve is inverted, as explained in conjunction with universal life investment management. Rebell and Gordon, ibid., provide an additional discussion of the use of futures to manage universal life and SPDA investment funds.

Insurance Uses: Loans

Private Placements. Insurance companies invest a major part of their investment portfolio in private loans to corporations. Such loans require an agreement both on the interest rate and the timing of when the loan will begin (the takedown timing). Since such loans provide higher returns and greater certainty of returns than most other investments, insurance companies are eager to provide acceptable terms to the corporation. Of course, the insurance company wants to insure that the return from the loan provides an acceptable spread over their cost of funds. Futures help the insurance company lock in this spread when timing differences exist between when funds are available and when the loan becomes effective. In addition, futures allow the insurance company to provide flexibility concerning the fixed- or variable-rate characteristics of the loan. The following examines several cases regarding timing and rate characteristics.

    Future Loan Takedown. The insurance company may have current funds that are allocated to corporate loans, but the demand for such loans at the going market rate is not sufficient to meet the supply of funds. Assume the funds allocated for such loans have a calculated return that must be earned for the insurance company, which is $2\frac{1}{2}\%$ above the going market rate for T-bonds. T-bond futures are purchased in order to protect the level of return needed by the insurance company. If interest rates decline, the profits from the long futures position offset a lower return on a future loan to a corporation. While waiting to make a loan, the funds should be put into short-term liquid funds so they are not affected by changes in interest rates. However, a significant risk does exist with this strategy: if interest rates increase, then not only does the futures position entail a loss, but the insurance company may not have any customers who are willing to borrow funds at the higher interest rate. In this case the futures contract is rolled forward to future expirations; however, this may involve an additional cost in terms of convergence. On the other hand, without a hedging strategy a decrease in rates creates returns that are insufficient to meet the required return.

    Forward Commitments. Insurance companies make forward commitments at today's rate for both private placements and when obtaining mortgage securities. When the insurance company has not yet obtained the funds for such an investment, and these funds will be acquired at the going rate of interest, then the company has a risk of a fixed-rate loan commitment with a variable-rate financing source. The insurance company may sell futures in order to hedge against higher interest rates until the cost of the funding source is locked in. Of course, basis risk between the Treasury futures issue and the instrument being acquired by the insurance company still exists. The company also may employ the futures market to obtain a consensus viewpoint on forward rates as a guide to determine the appropriate rate to bid for these forward commitments (after any necessary adjustments for credit risk, coupon, and maturity factors).

    Floating-Rate Loans. The corporate client may desire a floating-rate loan when rates are expected to decline in the future. The insurance company can provide a floating-rate loan, at least for several years, by using a long futures contract. Profits from a long futures position would offset a lower interest rate from the loan. Such a strategy may provide competitive advantages in comparison to other financial intermediaries who do not provide such terms. The terms of the loan should include a margin for both credit risk and basis risk. The client should convert the floating-rate loan to a fixed-rate (the long futures positions would be covered) sometime during the period set up for the hedge; however, with an additional cost this period could be extended and the futures hedge rolled to deferred expirations as the initial floating-rate period came to an end. Note that the client does *not* have an *option* to convert to a fixed-rate loan, rather, the client *must* convert to a fixed-rate so that the futures positions are covered before expiration. Only with an additional cost should the client be allowed to keep the floating rate loan in effect.

Fixed-Rate Loans. The insurance company may have funds to lend at a floating rate, but the client wants a fixed-rate loan. This situation is equivalent to the synthetic fixed-rate loans discussed previously, where a futures contract is shorted in order to stabilize the cost of funds. As with most futures positions, such a conversion only is guaranteed up to the expiration of the last liquid futures contract. Beyond that point a risk of convergence cost exists, in addition to any basis risk inherent between the futures contract and the funding source.

Applications for Property and Casualty Insurers

Property and Casualty insurers have more volatility and uncertainty in their cash flows than other insurers; this is due to the type of insurance policies they write. The investment returns for these firms are needed to provide profits when insurance claims create losses. Futures can provide benefits to the investment accounts for property and casualty insurers in a manner similar to the uses described for pension funds and insurance investments. The primary difference is that property and casualty insurers employ municipal securities as a major part of their portfolio in order to reduce the effect of corporate income taxes on their net investment returns. Thus, municipal bond futures are employed in ways that are identical to T-bond futures applications in order to manage these portfolios.

SUMMARY

This chapter examined the corporate and insurance applications of futures markets. Corporate applications include working capital uses and hedging the long-term issuance of securities. Insurance uses of futures relate to product applications unique to the insurance field.

Glossary

Accrued interest The interest that has been earned, but not yet paid, since the last coupon payment date. Accrued interest must be added to the quoted price of a bond to obtain the total cost of the bond.

Accrued interest option The right of the seller to choose when during the delivery month to deliver the T-bond into the futures contract. This choice is affected by the net financing cost.

Amortization of price discount or premium A prescheduled write off or expected change in price resulting from a bond is redemption at par at maturity.

Anticipatory hedge See long hedge.

Arbitrage Obtaining risk-free profits by simultaneously buying and selling identical or similar instruments in different markets. For example, one could buy in the cash market and simultaneously sell in the futures market.

Asset allocation Structuring the portfolio of stocks, bonds, and T-bills to correspond to the forecast of returns and risks in these markets. Futures are employed to change these allocations quickly and inexpensively.

Asset-liability hedge A hedge undertaken by a financial institution in order to offset the variability in earnings caused by maturity or price volatility differences between its assets and liabilities.

Asset-liability management The activity of financial institutions where they manage their investments (assets) in bonds and loans, while minimizing their cost of funds (liabilities) so that the difference between these categories provides a profitable return.

Bank discount interest rate The annualized rate of return based on the *face* value of a security. T-bills are quoted on a bank discount basis.

Basis The difference between the relevant cash instrument price and the futures price (i.e., $P_C - P_F$). Often used in the context of hedging the cash instrument.

Basis point A change in the interest rate of $1/100$ of 1% or .01%. One basis point is written as .01 when 1.0 represents 1%.

Basis point value (BPV) The price change in the debt instrument associated with a one basis point change in interest rates; BPV is used to determine the size of the position to take with futures contracts in order to alter the structure of a portfolio.

Basis risk The variability over time in the basis; alternatively, the risk that remains after hedging with futures.

Bellwether bond The most recently issued and most liquid government bond.

Beta A measure of the relative price movement in the asset (portfolio) in relation to the market movement.

Bond-equivalent yield The annual rate of return on the funds invested in the asset, including both the effect of the interest payment and the capital price change. Bond equivalent yield quotations in the paper assume that no changes in interest rates will occur.

Callable bond A bond that is redeemable by the issuer of the bond during a specific time period. The bondholder is paid the face value of the bond plus a premium for having the bond called. Thus, the issuer is able to repurchase the bond for a price below the current market value if the level of interest rates have decreased.

Carrying charge market When the prices of the deferred expirations are higher than the nearby expirations, causing an upward sloping price structure.

Cash The term "cash" is used in several contexts. Cash or cash instrument refers to the actual asset or the price of the asset, as distinguished from the futures contract; other sources also refer to cash as the "spot" asset. The cash market is where the cash asset trades. Cash settlement is the method for determining the final change in value for certain futures contracts such as stock index futures, that is, cash changes hands rather than having the buyer deliver the asset. Also see "underlying cash asset."

Cheapest-to-deliver The cash security that provides the lowest cost (largest profit) to the arbitrage trader; the cheapest-to-deliver instrument is used to price the futures contract.

Clearinghouse A division of the exchange that verifies trades, guarantees the trade against default risk, and transfers margin amounts. Legally, a market participant makes a futures transaction with the clearinghouse.

Closed-form model An equation providing a one-step solution to the problem.

Commercial paper A short-term financing alternative for corporations, where they sell an unsecured liability maturing in three to twelve months.

Contango The hypothesis that futures are overpriced (short speculators will profit) because hedgers are net long.

Contract specifications or characteristics All the quality, size, pricing, and delivery terms of a futures contract, including which specific cash securities fulfill the delivery obligations of the futures contract.

Convergence The movement of the cash asset price toward the futures price as the expiration date of the futures contract approaches.

Conversion factor hedge Creating a hedge for a long-term debt instrument by using the conversion factor as the hedge ratio.

Conversion factor method The procedure developed to adjust the futures delivery values for different cash T-bonds and T-notes. This adjustment is needed because the bonds (notes) that are eligible for delivery have different maturities and coupons, creating differing cash prices. This method provides a greater pool of cash instruments for delivery and therefore avoids squeezes.

Convexity The curvature in the bond price-yield relationship; convexity creates errors when duration is employed for bond management.

Cost of carry pricing Calculating the appropriate price of a futures contract by determining the costs involved in holding the asset until the futures contract expires. The time value of money is one of these costs.

Crosshedge Hedging when the characteristics of the deliverable instrument (the cash asset underlying the futures) differ from the characteristics of the cash instrument being hedged. The characteristic(s) can differ in terms of quality, maturity, or coupon. Hedging a corporate (risky) bond with a Treasury (no default risk) bond futures is an example of a crosshedge.

Dealer One who functions as a middleman for traders by "making a market" in cash instruments or assets that do not trade on an exchange. The dealer keeps an inventory of the instrument to facilitate buying and selling whenever the market participants need to make a trade.

Default or credit risk The possibility that the issuer of the security will not pay the interest payment or the face value of the bond due to a lack of funds.

Delivery The seller of the futures contract sends the appropriate cash instrument to the buyer of the futures during the futures expiration period. The buyer pays the futures price. Some futures contracts, such as stock index futures, are settled by a cash payment rather than by the physical delivery of the asset.

Delivery options Choices provided to the seller of the T-bond futures contract concerning which bond to deliver and when to deliver it.

Delivery risk The uncertainty concerning *which* cash instrument will be received when the seller of the futures contract delivers the cash asset.

Derivative The procedure from calculus that determines the small change in one variable given a small change in another variable. The value of the derivative of a curve at a given point is the slope of the line that is tangent to the curve at that point.

Designated Order Turnaround (DOT) system The computerized system at the NYSE that allows traders to send buy and sell orders for stocks directly to the floor of the exchange by electronic means, speeding execution time significantly.

Dollar duration Modified duration times the price of the bond; dollar duration is used to determine the dollar price change in a bond for a given change in yield.

Dollar equivalency hedge Equating the dollar changes in the cash position with the dollar changes in the futures position in order to minimize the change in total value. This method employs the relative maturities/expirations and relative volatilities of the cash and futures instruments in order to determine the appropriate hedge ratio.

Duration A measure of the relative volatility of a bond; it is an approximation for the price change of a bond for a given change in the interest rate. Duration is measured in units of time. It includes the effects of time until maturity, cash flows, and the yield to maturity.

Duration-based hedge A futures hedge used to minimize the net price change of a position, where the hedge ratio is determined on the basis of the relative durations of the cash and futures positions.

Dynamic model A model where changes to the input factors over the observation period are allowed to influence the profit results.

Dynamic trading strategy A strategy that changes the proportions of two or more assets as the market price changes.

End-of-the-month option The right of the seller of the futures to announce delivery on any business day of the delivery month after the market stops trading futures, namely the eight business days before the end of the delivery month. The price of the transaction is based on the last day of the futures trade.

Eurodollars A dollar denominated deposit in a bank outside the United States or in an International Banking Facility in the United States.

Ex-post After the fact; the use of historical data to determine an empirical relationship.

Forward contract A private agreement made now to purchase a specified amount of a cash asset at a specific price, with the exchange of the funds and the asset taking place at a specific time in the future. A forward contract, unlike futures, has unique quantity, time until maturity, and other characteristics for each separate forward transaction. Forward contracts typically do not trade.

Forward rate The resulting interest rate obtained from owning a longer-term debt instrument and selling short a short-term cash instrument.

Futures contract A standardized agreement between a buyer and seller for a prespecified quantity of an underlying cash asset. Futures trade until the contract expires, allowing traders to profit from price changes without receiving delivery of the cash asset.

Futures immunization A procedure to lock in both the current value of a bond portfolio *and* the reinvestment rates of future coupons in order to guarantee the total ending portfolio value.

Gap The size of the difference between rate-sensitive assets and rate- sensitive liabilities for a given maturity range.

Guaranteed Investment Contract (GIC) The GIC pays a guaranteed rate of interest for all or part of the life of the investment contract.

Hedge ratio Determining the ratio of the futures to the cash position so as to reduce price risk.

Hedging Reducing the risk of a cash position by taking a position in the futures instrument to offset the price movement of the cash asset. A broader definition of hedging includes using futures as a temporary substitute for the cash position.

Hedging effectiveness The proportion of variability in the cash position eliminated by a futures hedge.

Holding period return A formulation, $(1 + R)$, used to find the ending value of an investment by including both the effect of principal and the return from investing the principal.

Immunization A bond portfolio management technique that "guarantees" a predetermined total value for the portfolio at the end of the investment period regardless of how interest rates change. Thus, immunization provides a stated target annual rate of return for the investment.

Immunized hedge A procedure to lock in interest rates until funds are received; then the funds are invested so that the cash portfolio is immunized.

Implied put option The end-of-the-month delivery option for T-bond futures is equivalent to providing the seller with a put option—that is, the choice of *when* to sell the T-bond at a predetermined price. The holder of the put option profits if the cash T-bond price declines during the end-of-the-month period.

Implied repo (financing) rate The rate of return before financing costs implied by a transaction where a longer-term cash security is purchased and a futures contract is sold (or vice versa).

Initial margin The amount of funds put on deposit by the market participants as a "good faith" guarantee against a loss from adverse market movements. A trader can deposit cash T-bills to meet the initial margin requirement.

Integration of cash and futures markets Integration occurs when these two markets possess sufficient volume such that active arbitrageurs keep the relative prices from these markets in line with one another.

Interest rate parity The no-arbitrage relationship for currency futures that relates the price of the futures to the relative financing interest rates for the two currencies.

Interest rate swap A financial agreement to exchange interest payments of a fixed-rate loan with those of a variable-rate loan.

Intermediation The process where financial institutions obtain funds from one segment of the economy (individual depositors) and lend to another segment of the economy (corporations); or they obtain short-term funds and lend on a long-term basis. Intermediation often causes the amount of rate-sensitive assets to differ from the amount of rate-sensitive liabilities within a given maturity range.

Inventory hedge A hedge used by a market maker in order to reduce the price risk of the marketmaker's inventory of assets until the assets can be sold.

Inverted market When the prices of the deferred expirations are lower than the prices of the nearby expirations, causing a downward sloping pricing structure.

Invoice amount The delivery price the buyer of the bond pays the seller at delivery.

Leverage The magnification of gains and losses by only paying for part of the underlying value of the instrument or asset; the smaller the amount of funds invested, the greater the leverage. For example, buying a house by obtaining a mortgage results in a significant degree of leverage for the owner, since typically the owner pays only 10% to 20% of the purchase price and the mortgage covers the remaining 80% to 90%.

Liquidity The ability to buy or sell a large number of units of a financial asset in a short time period without significantly affecting the price of the instrument.

Long A long position exists when one purchases a futures or cash instrument; it is profitable when the price increases.

Long arbitrage *Buying* futures in connection with a cash market transaction in order to create risk-free profits.

Long hedge Buying a futures contract in order to reduce the price variability of an *anticipated* cash position; alternatively, to "lock in" the price of a cash security that will be purchased in the future. Thus, a long hedge is a temporary substitute for a future cash position.

Macrohedging Hedging the Net Interest Margin.

Maintenance margin The lower limit that the margin account can fall to before the market participant must put up more funds.

Marking-to-market The daily adjustment of the margin balance to account for changes in the market price. If the margin account falls to or below the maintenance margin, then additional funds are needed.

Maturity management The active bond management technique that attempts to increase returns by forecasting interest rates so that the manager can switch from short-term to long-term instruments or vice versa.

Microhedging Hedging specific assets or liabilities on the balance sheet.

Minimum variance hedge ratio The hedge ratio of futures to cash that provides the smallest variance of price changes.

Modified duration The duration of the bond divided by $(1 + i)$; modified duration is used to determine the approximate percentage change in the price of a bond for a given change in the yield.

Money market yield A simple interest rate that adjusts for the number of days the funds are deposited; no compounding exists for these funds; that is, number of dollars × interest rate × number of days held number of days in the year.

Multiplicative relationship A description of the behavior of the yield curve when the slope of the curve changes, causing the rates of long-term bonds to change more than the rates of short-term instruments.

Nearby/deferred contracts The next expiration month is the nearby contract; later expirations are deferred contracts, and futures expiring after one year are distant deferred contracts.

Negative basis Occurs when the cash price is less than the futures price.

Net interest margin (NIM) The amount of "earnings" for the financial institution; that is, the difference between interest income and interest expense. NIM depends on the size and direction of the gap and the relative spread of interest rates between assets and liabilities.

Nominal interest rate The actual market interest rate on fixed-rate securities, which includes the effect of expected inflation. Treasury bills are an example of this rate.

Normal backwardation The hypothesis that futures are underpriced (long speculators will profit) because hedgers are net short.

One-to-one hedge Creating a hedge such that the total value of the futures contracts employed for the hedge equals the total value of the cash instruments being hedged.

Open interest The number of futures contracts that at any given time have both a buyer (long position) and seller (short position). Open interest increases as more positions are taken on both sides of the market; open interest decreases as traders close positions. At expiration, traders settle any remaining open interest positions either by delivery of the asset or by a net cash settlement for contracts not having delivery.

Opportunity loss Forgoing a gain (or a smaller loss) by not taking a specific action or trade.

Optimal hedge ratio The hedge ratio of futures to cash that provides the best risk-return hedge trade-off for the combined position.

Options Contracts that allow the buyer the right (but not the obligation) to purchase (call option) or the right to sell (put option) a given quantity of the cash security at a specific "strike" price for a specific period of time. The strike price of an option is the trade price for the asset if the option is exercised. The strike price distinguishes an option from a futures contract, and results in an initial cost premium over the current value of the option. Options also have a limited loss feature, unlike futures contracts.

Portfolio hedge Hedging assets in order to reduce price risk.

Portfolio insurance A technique that allows participants to benefit from market advances by increasing the exposure to stocks during up markets and providing insurance from market declines by selling stocks during down-markets.

Positive basis Occurs when the cash price is greater than the futures price.

Price limit The daily maximum change in price that may occur for a given futures contract. The price limit often changes over time and varies from one type of futures contract to another. If the price limit is activated, then the next day's limit increases in size.

Program trading Stock index arbitrage, that is, obtaining risk-free profits when the futures price deviates from the forward price by more than transactions costs. In more general terms, program trading is the use of computer programs to execute the purchase or sale of a basket of stocks in order to obtain liquidity and to lower transaction costs.

Pure arbitrage Creating a risk-free profitable transaction using futures and the associated cash instrument by employing external financing (i.e., internal funds are not necessary for the transaction).

Quality option The right of the seller of the futures to deliver *any* cash T-bond (T-note) that meets the specifications of the contract.

Quasi-arbitrage Creating a risk-free profitable transaction with futures and the associated cash instrument by employing internal funds; equivalently, a transaction providing a higher alternative return than an equivalent cash security.

Rate-sensitive assets/liabilities Assets and liabilities that mature, are rolled-over to a new maturity, or are repriced at a given time period in association with a specific rate-sensitive instrument.

Real rate of interest The nominal interest rate less the *actual* inflation rate; the real rate can be positive or negative.

Realized compound yield to maturity (RCYTM) The actual compound return obtained when the actual reinvestment rates for the cash flows are considered.

Reinvestment risk The variability in the interest rate when coupons received are reinvested.

Repurchase (repo) transaction Borrowing funds by providing a government security for collateral and promising to "repurchase" the security at the end of the agreed upon time period. The associated interest rate is the "repo rate."

Reverse repurchase (repo) transaction Lending funds by accepting a government security for collateral and promising to "resell" the security at the end of the agreed upon time period.

Riding the yield curve The guaranteed portion of the return obtained from owning a short-term bond when an upwardly sloping yield curve exists; that is, the increase in the bond's price that occurs as the bond's maturity shortens and therefore the yield decreases.

Risk-return hedging model A procedure that determines a hedge ratio and hedging effectiveness by considering both the risk *and* the return characteristics of the data.

Second order moment The second order of duration is convexity, since convexity consists of the *squared* values of time.

Selective hedging Deciding when to hedge based on a forecast of the direction of the cash market. This method attempts to enhance overall returns but typically causes higher risk because of imperfect forecasts.

Serial correlation A correlation in sequential price changes; it is a violation of one of the assumptions of regression analysis and results in upward biased R^2 values and unstable hedge ratios over time.

Short Selling an instrument without owning it; called a "short sale" when it involves a cash asset because the asset is borrowed (not currently owned) with the promise to buy it back. Short sales with cash assets are often difficult or costly to implement, whereas short futures transactions are easy to implement and inexpensive. Shorts are profitable if the instrument declines in price. If one shorts a futures contract, then either the trader repurchases the contract to cover the short or the trader "delivers the underlying cash asset." When a hedger who owns a cash asset sells a futures contract, then the gains in the short position offset losses in the value of the long cash position.

Short arbitrage *Selling* futures in connection with cash market transactions in order to create risk-free profits.

Short hedge Hedging the value of a currently held cash instrument by selling a futures contract.

Single Premium Deferred Annuities (SPDA) The policyholder pays one large premium which yields a competitive rate of return for a fixed time period (one year) and then the rate changes each quarter or year, based on a defined bond index.

Sinking fund Money periodically set aside into separate bank accounts for corporate and municipal bond issues in order to pay for the eventual repurchase or maturity of the bond.

Spread The purchase of one expiration month and the sale of a different expiration month, or the purchase of one type of futures contract and the sale of another type of contract. A spread is less risky than a pure one-sided speculative transaction.

Spread (asset-liability) management Controlling the relationship between rate-sensitive assets and rate-sensitive liabilities to obtain the desired risk-return tradeoff. The return objective is to obtain a return on assets that is greater than the cost of the liabilities. Risk occurs when the assets mature or are repriced at a different time than the liabilities.

Squeeze A situation in which there is an insufficient amount of the cash asset available to cover all of the probable futures deliveries, thereby causing prices to rise above their economic value. Squeezes create problems for market participants and for the allocation of that asset in the economy.

Static gap A gap where no new net changes of assets or liabilities occur over the period of the analysis. The static gap includes certain restrictive assumptions concerning the behavior of interest rates.

Static model Changes in the numerical inputs of the model are not allowed during the observation period.

Stochastic process A statistical term referring to a model that specifies the dynamic behavior of a given variable such as interest rates over time. For example, interest rate changes can be "random" or they may "revert to their mean value." Each process has a different implication for changes in the term structure over time.

Stock index fund A mutual fund that purchases stock in the same exact proportions as a given cash index—typically, the S&P 500 index.

Strip A series of futures with consecutive expirations.

Stronger basis The cash price increases more or falls less than the futures price (i.e., the difference between the cash and futures prices becomes more positive or less negative); in this case a short hedge generates positive returns while a long hedge generates negative returns.

Switching option The opportunity to change from a previous cheapest-to-deliver bond to the current cheapest bond, thereby increasing profits.

Synthetic fixed-rate loan Combining a short futures transaction with a variable-rate loan in order to create a synthetic instrument that acts similar to a fixed-rate loan.

Synthetic instrument Creating a new security by trading two or more other securities in an appropriate combination.

Synthetic security Generating a position by combining a cash instrument and a futures contract that replicates the characteristics of a different cash instrument. Such positions can provide higher returns than "equivalent" cash securities.

Systematic risk The variability associated with general market movements; also called undiversifiable risk.

Term structure The economic relationship between the term to maturity and the default-free interest rates.

Trader One who buys or sells an instrument; sometimes refers solely to a speculator, but in general it means anyone who executes a trade.

Twist in the yield curve A nonparallel change in the shape of the yield curve, in particular when the curve goes from upward sloping to downward sloping, or vice versa.

Underlying cash asset The specific asset that the buyer of the futures contract receives at delivery. The price of the futures contract is a function of this underlying cash asset.

Universal Life A life insurance policy where part of the premium is allocated to insurance and part to an investment, where the investment rate is fixed for a given term (e.g., one year) based on the current interest rate.

Unsystematic risk The variability associated with the unique characteristics of the individual asset; also called diversifiable risk.

Variable interest rate When the short-term interest rate changes over time, then it affects the costs/returns to the margin account.

Weaker basis The cash price increases less or falls more than the futures price (i.e., the difference between the cash and futures prices becomes less positive or more negative); in this case a short hedge generates negative returns while a long hedge generates positive returns.

Wild card option The right of the seller of the futures to announce delivery up to 8 P.M. on any business day during the delivery month, with the price based on the 2 P.M. futures close.

Yield curve The graphical depiction of the relationship between government bond yields (Y-axis) and time until maturity (X-axis).

Zero-coupon bond A bond that pays only an ending principal payment; it does not pay any intermediate cash flows (coupons). Zeros possess no uncertainty concerning the reinvestment rates of coupons encountered with regular bonds.

Credits

We gratefully acknowledge the use of the following material.

EXAMPLES, EXHIBITS, AND TABLES

Chapter 3 Exhibit 3-1, "Understanding the Delivery Process in Financial Futures," Copyright © Board of Trade of the City of Chicago. / Table 3-4, Zvi Bodie and Victor Rosansky, "Risk and Return in Commodity Futures," *Financial Analysis Journal*, Vol. 36, No. 3, May-June 1980, pp. 27–39.

Chapter 5 Example 5-3, *Business Week*, April 7, 1986, by special permission of Business Week. Copyright © 1986 by McGraw-Hill, Inc.

Chapter 7 Table 7-2, "Conversion Factor Tables," *Financial Instruments Guide*. Copyright © Board of Trade of the City of Chicago.

Chapter 8 Table 8-1, Anthony J. Vignola and Charles Dale, "The Efficiency of the Treasury Bill Futures Market: An Analysis of Alternative Specifications," *Journal of Financial Research*, Vol. 3, No. 2, 1980, pp. 169–188.

Chapter 9 Exhibit 9-4, "Inside T-Bill Futures," p. 12, Chicago Mercantile Exchange.

Chapter 10 Table 10-1, S.P. Hegde, "The Impact of Interest Rate Level and Volatility on the Performance of Interest Rate Hedges," *The Journal of Futures Markets*, Vol. 2, No. 4, Winter 1982. Reprinted by permission of John Wiley & Sons, Inc. / Table 10-2, Joanne Hill and Thomas Schneeweis, "Risk Reduction Potential of Financial Futures for Corporate Bond Positions," originally in *Interest Rate Futures: Concepts and Issues*, edited by Gay and Kolb, 1982. Reprinted with permission of the authors. / Table 10-3, Steven Figlewski, "Hedging with Stock Index Futures: Theory and Applications in a New Market," *Journal of Futures Markets*, Vol. 5, No. 2, Summer 1985, pp. 183–200. Reprinted by permission of John Wiley & Sons, Inc.

Chapter 11 Tables 11-3 and 11-4, Richard McEnally, "How to Neutralize Reinvestment Rate Risk," *The Journal of Portfolio Management*, Vol. 6, No. 3, Spring 1980, pp. 59–63. This copyrighted material is reprinted with permission of Institutional Investor, Inc. / Table 11-5, G.O. Bierwag, George Kaufman, and Alden Toevs, "Duration: Its Development and Use in Bond Portfolio Management," *Financial Analysis Journal*, Vol. 39, No. 4, July-August 1983, pp 15–35.

Chapter 12 Table 12-2, Robert Kolb and Raymond Chiang, "Duration, Immunization, and Hedging with Interest Rate Futures," *Journal of Financial Research*, Vol. 5, No. 2, Summer 1982, pp. 161–170. / Table 12-5, Laurie S. Goodman and N.R. Vijayaraghavan,

"Generalized Duration Hedging with Futures," *The Review of Futures Markets,* Vol. 6, No. 1, 1987, pp. 94–108. Copyright © Board of Trade of the City of Chicago.

Chapter 13 Example 13-1 and 13-2, "Concepts and Applications: Using Interest Rate Futures in Pension Fund Management," Chicago Board of Trade Pamphlet. Copyright © 1987 Board of Trade of the City of Chicago. / Table 13-1, "The Use of Futures in Tactical Asset Allocation" in *Stock Index Options and Futures,* September 17, 1987. Reprinted with permission of PaineWebber Capital Markets.

Chapter 14 Exhibit 14-1, "Inside T-Bill Futures," p. 13, Chicago Mercantile Exchange pamphlet. / Table 14-1, Terry S. Maness and A.J. Senchack, "Futures Hedging and the Reported Financial Position of Thrift Institutions," *The Review of Futures Markets,* Vol. 5, No. 2, 1986, pp. 142–159. Copyright © Board of Trade of the City of Chicago.

FIGURES

Chapter 3 Figure 3-3, Robert T. Daigler, "The S&P Index Futures: A Hedging Contract," *CME Financial Strategy Paper,* 1990, Chicago Mercantile Exchange. / Figure 3-5, Charles T. Howard, "Are T-Bill Futures Good Forecasters of Interest Rates?," *The Journal of Futures Markets,* Vol. 2, No. 4, Winter 1982, pp. 305–315. Reprinted by permission of John Wiley & Sons, Inc.

Chapter 5 Figures 5-2 and 5-3, "Dividend Payouts and the MMI," *Financial Futures Professional,* Vol. 14, No. 4, April 1990. Copyright © Board of Trade of the City of Chicago.

Chapter 7 Figure 7-2, Alex Kane and Alan J. Marcus, "The Quality Option in the Treasury Bond Futures Market: An Empirical Assessment," *The Journal of Futures Markets,* Vol. 6, No. 2, Summer 1986, pp. 231–248. Reprinted by permission of John Wiley & Sons, Inc. / Figure 7-6, Bruce G. Resnick and Elizabeth Hennigar, "The Relationship Between Futures and Cash Prices for U.S. Treasury Bonds," *The Review of Futures Markets,* Vol. 2, No. 3, 1983, pp. 282–299. Copyright © Board of Trade of the City of Chicago.

Chapter 8 Figure 8-1, Ira Kawaller and Timothy W. Koch, "Cash-and-Carry Trading and the Pricing of Treasury Bill Futures," *The Journal of Futures Markets,* Vol. 4, No. 2, Summer 1984, pp 115–124. Reprinted by permission of John Wiley & Sons, Inc.

Chapter 10 Figure 10-3, Robert C. Kuberek and Norman G. Peffey, "Hedging Corporate Debt with U.S. Treasury Bond Futures," *The Journal of Futures Markets,* Vol. 3, No. 4, Winter 1983, pp. 345–353. Reprinted with permission of John Wiley & sons, Inc. / Figure 10A-1, Charles D. Howard and Louis Antonio, "Treasury Bill Futures as a Hedging Tool: A Risk-Return Approach," *Journal of Financial Research,* Vol. IX, No. 1, Spring 1986, pp. 25–40.

Chapter 11 Figure 11-4, Richard McEnally, "How to Neutralize Reinvestment Rate Risk," *The Journal of Portfolio Management,* Vol. 6, No. 3, Spring 1980, pp 59–63. This copyrighted material is reprinted with permission of Institutional Investor, Inc.

Index

391

About the Publisher

PROBUS PUBLISHING COMPANY

Probus Publishing Company fills the informational needs of today's business professional by publishing authoritative, quality books on timely and relevant topics, including:

- Investing
- Futures/Options Trading
- Banking
- Finance
- Marketing and Sales
- Manufacturing and Project Management
- Personal Finance, Real Estate, Insurance and Estate Planning
- Entrepreneurship
- Management

Probus books are available at quantity discounts when purchased for business, educational or sales promotional use. For more information, please call the Director, Corporate/Institutional Sales at 1-800-PROBUS-1, or write:

Director, Corporate/Institutional Sales
Probus Publishing Company
1925 N. Clybourn Avenue
Chicago, Illinois 60614
FAX (312) 868-6250